D1264384

Iyer, Raghavan Narasimhan, ed.
    The glass curtain between Asia and
Europe; a symposium on the historical
encounters and the changing attitudes
of the peoples of the East and the
West, edited by Raghavan Iyer. With a
foreword by the Dalai Lama. London, New
York, Oxford University Press, 1965.
    xii, 356 p. 23 cm.

THE GLASS CURTAIN
BETWEEN ASIA
AND EUROPE

THE GLASS CURTAIN
BETWEEN ASIA
AND EUROPE

A symposium on the historical
encounters and the changing
attitudes of the peoples of
the East and the West

Edited by
RAGHAVAN IYER

With a foreword by
THE DALAI LAMA

LONDON
OXFORD UNIVERSITY PRESS
NEW YORK   TORONTO
1965

Oxford University Press, Amen House, London E.C.4

GLASGOW NEW YORK TORONTO MELBOURNE WELLINGTON
BOMBAY CALCUTTA MADRAS KARACHI LAHORE DACCA
CAPE TOWN SALISBURY NAIROBI IBADAN ACCRA
KUALA LUMPUR HONG KONG

Printed in Great Britain by
R. & R. Clark, Ltd
Edinburgh

94727

TO PICO

*and those of his generation
for whom
there will be no Curtain*

PREFACE

THE theme of this symposium is vast in scope but its aim is essentially modest. It attempts to provide a tentative framework for a frank and constructive appraisal by Asians and Europeans of the Glass Curtain that seems to separate them. A variety of viewpoints is presented here, and indeed no effort was made to ensure a uniformity of approach. Each contribution was prepared independently, after its author had seen only the transcript of the broadcast dialogue between Dr. Arnold Toynbee and myself, originally recorded in 1959. This transcript is appended to the symposium at the end of the book.

It is hoped that the volume, which does not seek to make any substantial addition to scholarship, will stimulate a wide range of readers. The number of footnotes has been kept down as far as possible, and a short bibliography has been included. A slight amount of overlapping and repetition is unavoidable in a symposium of this sort, but even in the few places where the same ideas or facts recur, the differences of emphasis and treatment may be of intrinsic interest. All the contributors have sought to be informative as well as to provoke further thought and discussion. What is set down in this book is part of the material for an inquiry that may be pursued in schools and universities and by those who recognize its practical importance.

Each contributor is responsible solely for the views expressed in his own essay, and any deficiencies in planning the entire volume must be ascribed to me alone. I wish to thank Dr. Arnold Toynbee and Mr. F. W. Deakin for their encouragement at an early stage, Dr. John Campbell for many useful suggestions, Sally Bourdillon for her generous secretarial assistance, and Nandini for her invaluable help. I am grateful to the Dalai Lama for his foreword, which he graciously consented to write when I met him in 1960.

RAGHAVAN IYER

FOREWORD

THE theme of this symposium is a laudable one—
to bring about understanding between the different so-called blocs in the world to-day. Anything
done to remove all these imaginary curtains,
whether iron, bamboo, or glass, should be welcomed and in my view, the future prosperity and
happiness of this world, as we know it, depends
upon such an understanding. Our redemption lies
in creating forces of tolerance, brotherhood, and
equality. I add my prayers to these efforts.

THE DALAI LAMA

September 18 1964
Swarg Ashram,
Dharmsala,
Kangra, Punjab.

CONTENTS

THE GLASS CURTAIN

Conditions are not constant; terms are not final.

What man knows is not to be compared with what he does not know.

If we look at the great from the standpoint of the small, we cannot reach its limit; and if we look at the small from the standpoint of the great, it eludes our sight.

If we know that east and west are convertible yet necessary terms, in relation to each other, then such (relative) functions may be determined.

If we know that Yao and Chieh each regarded himself as good and the other bad, then the (direction of) their interests becomes apparent.

CHUANG-TZU

I. THE GLASS CURTAIN
BETWEEN ASIA AND EUROPE

Raghavan Iyer

'The Glass Curtain'

They view us as one might the inhabitants of another planet through a
very powerful telescope. Everything is visible . . . but . . . the entire
image, clear and intelligible in detail, becomes incomprehensible in its
totality. . . . What we are confronted with here is not just honest misunderstanding, not just honest error, but a habit of mind, an induced
state, a condition.[1]

These compelling words of George Kennan stressed the utter lack
of comprehension, the failure in communication, signified by the
'Iron Curtain' between Eastern and Western Europe. Today fortunately there are chinks in this curtain. The rigid notion of irreconcilable hostility is receding in favour of an evolving concept of
co-existence. The Cold War was perhaps aggravated by the
attempt to elevate a political ideology to the status of a religion as
well as by the effort to enlist a religious faith in the service of a
secular cause. Some have suggested that the Cold War partly has
its roots, beyond the clash of current ideologies, in the cultural
barrier between Russia and Western Europe in the nineteenth century, if not much earlier in the historic divergence between Eastern
and Western Christendom. The emergence of the Iron Curtain may
be explained in a variety of ways, but its indefinite continuance is
now a matter of common concern.

Mr. Kennan's words are no less relevant to the traditional barrier—almost invisible yet seemingly impenetrable—between the
peoples of Asia and Europe. 'Asia' and 'Europe' are no doubt
essentially geographical names. They are at the most 'logical constructions', artificial concepts rather than concrete entities. This is

[1] G. F. Kennan, *Russia, the Atom and the West*, O.U.P., 1958, pp. 23–24.

even truer of the much vaguer, wholly relative, and overworked, terms 'East' and 'West', which are used to refer not just to areas of space but also to modes of thought and behaviour. It is, however, a fact that there are Asians and Europeans who cannot grasp reality apart from such categories that have persisted in the past and which in turn seem to be needed to the extent that there is no mutual understanding. Too many Asians and Europeans still see 'through a glass darkly', if they care to see each other at all. The psychological barrier seems real enough, but it is connected with a mixture of mythical and tangible differences wherein it is difficult to disentangle the myths from the facts. Repeated assertions are made about each other which, by their very nature, cannot be conclusively falsified, and indeed they often induce a set of defensive and even hostile reactions that confirm inherited prejudices. The actual experience of communication is still largely conditioned by what Asians and Europeans have come to expect from mutual encounter, as a result of a legacy of contacts that were superficial for centuries and rather painful for both in recent history.

Several Western writers have referred to the subtle barrier to mutual acceptance between Asians and Europeans. Over sixty years ago, Meredith Townsend regretted the presence of '*some invisible but impassable barrier*'.

The European familiar with the East always recognises this source of error in himself, and sometimes tries to overcome it, declaring with a sigh that the Eastern is always a sealed book, but he seldom recognises also that for the same reason the Asiatic despises him. . . . The Asiatic often watches the 'antics' of the European as we watch those of animals, with a sense of amusement which has no other explanation than that he does not understand.[1]

Similarly, in the twenties, an American historian wrote about '*a wall of exclusion*', the feeling of separateness, seclusion, and suspicion between Asians and Europeans.

Inhabitants of Eastern countries have called Europeans 'barbarians', 'infidels', and 'unclean wretches' and Westerners have returned the compliment by referring to Orientals as 'heathen', 'fanatics', and 'poor benighted Hindoos', while the Russians nicknamed the Japanese 'monkeys' before the Russo-Japanese War.[2]

---

[1] *Asia and Europe*, Constable, 1905, 3rd edition, pp. 390–1.
[2] N. D. Harris, *Europe and the East*, Allen & Unwin, pp. 8–9.

More recently, in 1960, F. D. Ommaney, after nearly seven years in the East, wondered what the barrier was that still stood between 'the moderately well-educated Westerner and the moderately well-educated Oriental. *It was always there, impalpable, never referred to, unnamed, invisible, but definite and impenetrable, or almost.*'[1]

All such statements convey, even if they exaggerate, an essential truth to which the experience of many testifies. For some people there may be no psychological barrier of any sort, while there may also be those who are merely unconscious of its existence. In any case, the real difficulty is that the smug denial of any serious obstacle to mutual understanding is met by the repeated insistence that there is nothing less than an 'eternal antithesis', an 'obstinate schism' between Asia and Europe. For example, Karl Jaspers, while warning us that this antithesis must not be 'metaphysically hypostatized' as it then becomes a terrifying spectre, can still regard it as a convenient 'cryptogram' which has at all times been an element in the make-up of Europe.[2] The London *Times* went even further in a recent editorial entitled 'Horace's Iron Curtain':

The division of humanity to east and west of the geographical axis persists through centuries as if by a law of nature. The meridian of cleavage oscillates, but is anchored to its poles. There is no such obstinate schism along the parallels of latitude . . . for a thousand years before Horace, and two thousand since, the irresoluble dichotomy persists.[3]

It is possible and indeed desirable to repudiate this dubious notion of an eternal schism without denying the presence of a subtle psychological barrier between many Asians and most Europeans. This barrier may itself be partly the result of the persisting belief in a basic dichotomy between Europe and Asia, an eternal East-West contrast. Asians may have borrowed this notion from Europeans but the barrier exists independently for both alike. It is only realistic to recognize that there has been some sort of Glass Curtain between Asia and Europe, a distorting sense of distance, if not actually of alienation, in the encounter between Asians and Europeans.

'The Glass Curtain' is a phrase with important implications—the frequent denial that there is any barrier at all; the fact that people

[1] *Eastern Windows*, Longmans, 1960, Readers Union edition, 1962, p. 32.
[2] *The Origin and Goal of World History*, Routledge & Kegan Paul, 1953, pp. 67–68.   [3] *The Times*, London, July 16, 1961.

B

find not only that their vision is hazy, coloured, and distorted, but also that they cannot sense and touch those beyond the curtain; and, further, that even if a few thinking men shatter the curtain with their analytical tools, it is rapidly replaced as words like 'Oriental' and 'Westerner' are periodically re-defined to suit changing prejudices. We are faced not merely with meagre knowledge or a mild suspicion of strangers but, what is worse, a seemingly invincible ignorance and a self-perpetuating sense of superiority reinforced by a basic failure in communication. Travel too often only confirms instead of removing the preconceptions with which Asians come to Europe or Europeans to Asia.[1] Alternatively, there are brown or yellow 'Europeans' and white 'Asians', as it were, who have lost their own roots in their effort to respond to those beyond the curtain.

In general, the inability to explain the unfamiliar in terms of the familiar results in attempts to explain away even the familiar (in thought and in conduct, art or music, politics and society) by reference to the mystique already imposed upon the 'inscrutable Orient' or the 'decadent West'. Propagandists and even scholars—whether 'Orientalists' or nationalists—give a new lease of life to stale clichés and pernicious myths such as 'Oriental despotism' or 'Western materialism', 'Oriental cunning' and 'European hypocrisy', 'Asiatic fatalism' and 'Western aggression', the meretricious 'glamour' of Asia and the 'vulgar' fascination of Europe. The supposed 'thought-barrier' between the East and the West may be the result of divergent conceptions of God, man, and nature as well as of the state, the individual, and society. It is certainly heightened by the rival claims and mutual misrepresentations of the dominant religions, although they all arose in Asia, and of competing political ideologies which originated in Europe. Furthermore, even universal values, beliefs, and tendencies are often made the basis of exclusive claims to uniqueness on both sides of the Glass Curtain, which in this is essentially different from the Iron Curtain. Altogether, the less people are rooted in their cultures and creeds, the more they need to make far-fetched claims and to denigrate the cultures and creeds of those they cannot intimidate. Egocentricity and ethnocentricity strengthen each other. The Glass Curtain does not exist perhaps for those fortunate few who have sufficient self-confidence

---

[1] See, for example, Alastair Cooke's 'A Letter from Asia', *The Listener*, September, 26 1963, and V. S. Pritchett's 'The Persian Road', ibid., July 11, 1963.

to approach with genuine humility beliefs and societies markedly different from their own, who can seize on the universal elements as well as what is distinctive in any culture or tradition.

The Glass Curtain may well prove to be more intransigent than the Iron Curtain. The transmission of ideas, goods, and influences was mainly from East to West in the ancient world and from West to East in the modern age; it was hardly at any time a balanced exchange on equitable terms of trade. Today the growing disparity in living standards could accentuate the tensions of the past. Also, Asian resentment of Europe's recent dominance is now matched by European frustration over its relative decline in status. To some extent the present barrier is really that between the traditional East and the modern West, a gap in time rather than in space, but it is increasingly difficult to keep alive the heritage of antiquity in contemporary Europe as well as in Asia. These may all be contributory factors that partly account for the Glass Curtain. But the psychological barrier is aggravated by the enormity and vagueness of terms like 'Asia' and 'Europe', the dubious notion of an eternal East-West conflict, the extravagant assumption of a basic dichotomy in modes of thought and ways of life, and the diffusion of persisting myths that are a tissue of lies and half-truths, delusions and aspersions.

'Asia' and 'Europe'

The origin of the terms 'Asia' and 'Europe' was already in the time of Herodotus unknown to the Greeks. These geographical names may have been derived from the Semitic-Babylonian verbs *aṣû*, 'to rise', and *erêbu*, 'to set', as applied to the sun. The Babylonian pair of terms, *Elamtu* (East) and *Amurrû* (West), answer to the Homeric expressions, πρὸς ἠῶ ἠέλιόντε and πρὸς ζόφον, to the later Greek names of countries, 'Ανατολή and 'Εσπερία, to the modern 'Orient' and 'Occident' (borrowed from the Latin). The explanation of such names, applied at first to the coasts of two continents facing one another on the east and the west, and afterwards to the lands lying behind each, lies in the position of the Aegean Archipelago. When, through the voyages of Greek vessels, the coasts of Pontus became known, these names 'Asia' and 'Europe' were applied to the northern and southern sides of the Black Sea, while the river Phasis in its remotest eastern corner was taken as the boundary. It was only after the extent of the Red Sea became known through the conquests of Alexander (thus revealing the boundary between Africa and Asia) that the boundary between Europe and Asia was moved from the easternmost to the northernmost corner of the Black Sea, from the Phasis to the Tanais (Don). Since then Asia and not Europe came to be see to be the most extensive continent.

Even if we regard 'Asia' and 'Europe' as geographical names rather than as cultural or political entities, it is not easy to fix a frontier that has shifted over a long course of history. There is no recognized division, geographical or racial. The region loosely known as the Near East in more recent times includes all the classical lands surrounding the eastern Mediterranean. The Semitic peoples are difficult to classify, Arabs as well as Jews. Further, what part of the great central land mass of the Old World should be included in 'Europe'? Should the eastern limit of northern Europe follow the traditional line of the Urals? The geographical dissection of Eurasia into a 'Russia-in-Europe' and a 'Russia-in-Asia' is no less controversial than the historical dissection of the Ottoman Empire into a 'Turkey-in-Europe' and a 'Turkey-in-Asia'.[1]

While it is difficult to demarcate the frontier between Asia and Europe, it is even more so to get agreement in viewing these terms as signifying cultural entities. Asia has a third of the earth's land surface and more than half the world's population. Its very size has led some Europeans to see it as 'the all-embracing matrix of the whole human race'—from which Europe emerged. And yet, it has seemed natural to Europeans (especially since the sixteenth century) to lump together four major civilizations—Arab, Iranian, Indian, and Sinic—under one head, to use 'Eastern' (or 'Oriental') and 'Asiatic' as generic labels, to regard Asia as more than a sumword for a variety of separate, though interacting, cultures to be met by sailing eastwards. Frequently, Asia is seen as a single unit with two great cultural spheres termed the 'Near East' and the 'Far East', tinersecting in India. Outside these spheres lie the vast steppes of Siberia, which rarely entered into Asian history.

Asians themselves have noted the difficulty of regarding Asia as an entity. Tagore, for example, wrote in 1929 that 'eastern civilization' is a negative term, that Asia never became a unified entity

[1] See 'Is Turkey Part of Europe?', *The Times*, December 1, 1964.

and therefore, unlike Europe, was unable to make a strong impact on the modern age. But this expression of regret was already a reflection of the new Asian self-consciousness aroused by Japan's victory over Russia in 1905. Even earlier, Kakasu Okakura had, unlike Tagore, stressed the cultural unity of Asia, 'the common thought-inheritance' of every Asiatic race, enabling them to produce all the great religions of the world. Not only was there no real barrier between the Chinese civilization with its 'communism of Confucius' and the Indian with its 'individualism of the Vedas', but all the Asiatic races were said to form a single mighty web.

Arab chivalry, Persian poetry, Chinese ethics, and Indian thought, all speak of a single ancient Asiatic peace, in which there grew up a common life, bearing in different regions different characteristic blossoms, but nowhere capable of a hard and fast dividing line.[1]

Similarly, others argued that a distinctly Asian *Weltanschauung* and *Lebensanschauung* were created when the stream of culture originating in India was combined with Chinese culture and swept over the east and south-east of Asia. Anesaki pointed to the 'concept of oneness' expressed in the Hindu term *advaita*, its Buddhist equivalent *ekatva*, and the Taoist *hsu-wu*. The Western scholar, von Glasenapp, also pointed to a metaphysical basis for the Pan-Asiatic idea.

Pan-Asianism has, however, foundered as an ideology if it ever was politically significant. No doubt, several delegates to the Asian Relations Conference in New Delhi in 1948 spoke of a new, dynamic spirit of renaissance in Asia as well as of the ancient way of peace and concord for which Asia rather than Europe stood. More recently, writers like Zengo Ohira have referred to an Asian mode of modernization and to the traditional values of philanthropy and brotherhood upheld in Asia. But Asia as an ideological concept has little political significance today, though it is undeniable that some sort of 'Asianism', as a reaction against the West, is an essential element in the Asian ambivalence towards the European impact. It would also be rash to deny in advance that significant differences in political thought and social development may appear in Asia as a result of the 'secularization' of Asian religions under the impact of Western political creeds. But even if Asia remains culturally distinct from Europe, phrases like 'Asian man' or

---

[1] Kakasu Okakura, *The Ideals of the East*, John Murray, 1903, p. 4.

'Asiatic society' are almost meaningless, whether used by Asians or Europeans.

While it is natural for modern Europeans to assume that Europe, if not Asia, is a cultural entity, it is no easier to get agreement about the geographical denotation and cultural connotation of Europe as a concept. We are repeatedly told that Europe is too rich to be contained in a single definition, that there is nothing more 'European' than doubts and disagreement on this matter, that Europe is the sole entity which brings together Asians in a common, if ambivalent, hostility. But even if we accept that Europe is an entity though elusive as a concept, when did Europe begin and where does it end? Is it so obvious that the differences between Swedes and Spaniards or Slavs and Scotsmen are less significant than those between Tatars and Tamils or Kurds and Koreans, that the contrasts between Judaism and Christianity, Papists and Nonconformists, Christians and European rationalists are less glaring than those between Hinduism and Buddhism, Mahayanists and Theravadins, orthodox Brahmins and neo-Confucianists? Such questions are hardly easy to answer for lack of precise and conclusive criteria. It is, however, undeniable that Europeans feel that the 'unity-in-diversity' of Europe has a historical and contemporary significance that is far more concrete than the 'unity-in-diversity' ascribed to Asia by Asians or Europeans.

Even if it is easier to see Europe than Asia as an entity in space, it is difficult to locate Europe as a concept in time. Emmanuel Berl has aptly observed:

People have argued that the Roman Empire was a first sketch of Europe, but it excluded Frankfurt, Copenhagen and Amsterdam. Spengler holds that Europe appears with the Holy Roman Empire of the German nation, but this excluded all Spain, all the Balkans, and the whole of Eastern Europe. The birth of Europe is no better known to us than its boundaries.[1]

The problem here is one of deciding how far back we can trace the continuity of Europe as a cultural entity. In classical antiquity, from Hippocrates to Strabo, Europe was viewed chiefly as the territory best favoured by climate. And yet, in extolling the Hellenic race in relation to Europeans, Aristotle depicted the latter as living in a cold climate, as 'full of spirit, but wanting in intelli-

[1] See *La Table Ronde*, January 1957.

gence and skill; and therefore they keep their freedom, but have no political organisation, and are incapable of ruling over others'.[1] It was only with the Crusades and a specifically territorial view of Christianity that 'Europe' became an emotive and ideological term.[2] It was first used as synonymous with Christendom by Urban II in 1095, but the emotive use of the term did not gain currency until the fourteenth and fifteenth centuries, until especially Pius II's reference to Europe as the 'interior of Christendom', Christians elsewhere being 'all tainted with error'. European self-consciousness really emerged only in the sixteenth century, when, for example, Camões in his *Lusiads* spoke of 'Proud Europe', 'Christian Europe' as 'more advanced and more renowned in its governance than the others' and of Portugal as the 'hostel of humanity'. Even in the seventeenth century, Samuel Purchas could contend that Europe is taught the way to scale Heaven 'not by Mathematicall principles, but by Divine veritie'. Thereafter, the concept of Europe became secular in content, connected with the wealth, power, and skill that lay behind European expansion, but the concept has even now not lost the last vestiges of its original religious flavour. The essential element in the concept for most Europeans is still the assumption thus expressed by Purchas: 'The Qualitie of Europe exceeds her Quantitie, in this the least, in that the best of the World'.

Whether we hold that the concept of Europe has its origin in Pius II's pronouncements or that Pierre Bayle's *Dictionnaire* is the 'cell' from which European culture has emerged, there is no doubt that Europe has been far more real to Europeans—and for much longer—than Asia has been for Asians. But the Pan-European ideology is hardly less recent than Pan-Asianism. Idealistic attempts to institutionalize the notion of Europe may go back to Sully, Penn, and Abbé de Saint-Pierre, but the ideology of Pan-Europe became important only after the First World War. In 1923 Count Coudenhove-Kalergi declared that 'between the Scylla of Russian military dictatorship and the Charybdis of American financial dictatorship lies but a narrow path to a better future'— Pan-Europa. Today, Pan-Europeanism has become more concrete through the emergence of a partial European *Zollverein*, whereas

---

[1] *Politics*, vii. 7; iii. 14.
[2] See Denys Hay, *Europe—the Emergence of an Idea*, Edinburgh University Press, 1957.

Pan-Asianism has, for better or worse, almost wholly evaporated at least for the present.

Altogether, the sheer magnitude and diversity and the shifting frontiers of Asia and Europe make these geographical terms, with their strong cultural and ideological connotations, difficult to define and clumsy to handle with any degree of precision and consistency. Even if we cannot dispense with a cultural standpoint and the need for historical concepts, we must safeguard against the danger of 'anthropomorphism' implicit in any organic view of civilizations. Further, cultural boundaries are always ill-defined and rarely coincide with geographical limits. It is also a common but dangerous error to identify the ecumenical and universal values of civilization as such with our own local and parochial structures. It is natural but deceptive to assign a privileged historical status to the experiences of any continent of the globe or any portion of mankind. It is again questionable whether there really is in fact the linear continuity that we impose on successive epochs and cultures, a cultural identity transcending the turning points in any civilization over a long period of time. In so far as we have to reckon with Asian and European self-consciousness as a psychological fact or a political force, we could regard 'Asia' and 'Europe' as categories of convenience without taking them to signify cultural entities.

The Notion of Perennial Conflict

Despite the enormity and vagueness of terms like 'Asia' and 'Europe', 'East' and 'West', there have been repeated attempts to dramatize the historical encounter between Asia and Europe in terms of an epic conflict, an eternal feud, 'a Homeric duel between the embattled East and West'. The theme of the cultural interaction and various confrontations between Asian and European peoples through the centuries is indeed fascinating and it has yet to receive full and fair treatment in scholarly works, let alone in popular textbooks. But the dubious notion of a ceaseless 'quarrel of the continents' dies hard and has been traced back to Herodotus, with more plausibility than accuracy. It is now fashionable to hold, like the ninth-century Arab writer Jahiz, that 'all sharp practices come from the Greeks'.

It is true that the virtual identification of Europe with Greece and of Asia with Persia goes back to Herodotus, and that he saw the conflict between Hellenes and Persians in the fifth century B.C. as the continuation of an older conflict between Hellenes and Phoenicians. Although he was willing in his *Euterpe* to acknowledge the many debts of the Greeks to the great civilization of the Egyptians, elsewhere he sharpened the contrast and dramatized the conflict between Hellenic freemen and the subjects of Persian despotism. He ascribed to the Persians the view that they had always regarded the Greeks as their enemies, who levied war against Asia before the Asiatics did upon Europe (i, 5, 6). He showed the Athenians claiming that though the power of the Medes was far greater than their own, they being ardent for liberty could not be persuaded to come to terms with the Persian monarch (viii, 143). But Herodotus freely conceded the bravery of the Persians and their exemplary respect for truth. In one place (iii, 115) he ridiculed the notion that any portion of mankind was one-eyed and distinct from the rest, and he also wondered (iv, 45) why three different names—derived from the names of women—had been given to the earth, 'which is but one'.

Professor Burns' recent work *Persia and the Greeks* helps us to see the Hellenocentric and Athenocentric attitudes of Herodotus in proper perspective. Whereas Persian society in the fifth century B.C. was socially aristocratic, politically feudal, and economically based on a food-producing peasantry, Greece had already become geared to trade as a way of life. If Homer's heroes had returned to earth at the time of the Marathon, they would have been more at ease with Darius's officers than with their own countrymen. The clue to the conflict between the Greeks and the Persians partly lay in family factions, the internal stresses and tensions in fifth-century Greece which already contained the seeds of its own decay. Although Athenians disapproved of tyrants and, further, did not wish to pay tribute to Persian masters, the Athenian noblemen also objected to democracy and had no qualms about despotic rule as a system so long as their own interests were served.

The modern European's rejection of other races and cultures and his frequent disdain for the Orient have been projected into the Greek past with a virulence the Hellene never felt. The Hellenic concept of *barbaroi* derived from an essentially linguistic and wholly negative criterion, though it was sometimes used pejoratively. Plato in his *Politicus* (262c–d) refers to the confusing popular notion that 'barbarians' are all people of one sort. If

Aristotle advised Alexander to show himself to Asiatics as a despotic master (δεσπότης), Eratosthenes could protest against this ethnic intolerance by pointing out that there were many undesirable sorts of Greeks and many civilized (ἀστεῖοι) kinds of 'barbarians'. The Greek thought more in terms of language and geography than of race, and continued to maintain a fruitful contact with Asia. Recent studies of Hellenistic culture—its fusion and diffusion—show that there never was an impervious wall between Greece and the East. Quite apart from the affinities between Greek and Indian systems of philosophy, medicine, and mathematics, the Asiatic Greeks— the Ionians being known by words like 'Yavan' in eastern languages from Hebrew to Sanskrit—acted as a leaven for the more sluggish mainland Greeks.

The European sense of an East-West polarity may go back to the Greeks and even earlier, but it is modern writers who have read into Herodotus the crude notion of an eternal epic conflict between Asia and Europe. In the late nineteenth century an Oxford classicist, George Swayne, could write that the Greek victories at Plataea and Mycale 'indicated for ever the superiority of Europeans over Asiatics', the latter being the 'first aggressors', and that the victory at Mycale was the 'beginning of the great retribution which has continued even to the present time'.[1] Similarly, in a textbook on world history published in 1910, Edgar Sanderson, a Cambridge man, wrote that the 'grand crisis in the history of the world' is the contest between freedom and despotism which was decided on the plain of Marathon. We are also told that the Chinaman is a pedant who could teach Europe nothing and that the Hindoo is a dreamer who has done nothing and 'achieved no foreign conquests', that Asia may be the land of 'births and beginnings' but it was on the soil of Europe 'that the great Aryan race was to carry forward humanity to political, religious, mental and social freedom'.[2] Herodotus was reinforced by Hegel in dishing out this sort of propagandist history focused upon an eternal conflict between the heroic, liberty-loving, creative, and dynamic West and the aggressive, despotic, stagnant, and unchanging East.

Once the dubious thesis of an epic conflict between Asia and Europe is pegged to a distorted view of the Greeks (based on a

---

[1] G. C. Swayne, *Herodotus*, Blackwood & Sons, 1870, pp. 5–6.
[2] E. Sanderson, *Outlines of the World's History*, Pt. 1, Blackie & Sons, 1910, pp. 3, 84.

hasty reading of Herodotus), it can be used to depict in dramatic terms the conflict between Rome and Carthage, the Crusades, Asian invasions of Europe, medieval (and subsequent) travellers' tales, modern European imperialism and 'the White Man's Burden', Asian nationalism and 'the Yellow Peril', the so-called 'Europeanization' of the East, 'the Cold War', the nightmare of 'Asiatic hordes', racial and economic warfare. But at every step, the thesis of East-West hostility is as plausible and as misleading as the initial reference to the Greeks, involving distortions in perspective and a tendentious selection of facts.

If the Romans seemed at times to share the Greek sense of an East-West polarity, it had even less relevance to them. Romans, like Athenians, had only rudimentary ideas of Asian geography and even less knowledge of the empires, arts, literature, and philosophies of the East, while Asians remained indifferent to Europe right until the Crusades though at times Asia Minor and Syria were as 'European' as 'Asiatic'. The Crusades may have fostered the feeling of inevitable hostility implicit in the concepts of Holy War and *Jehad* and in the notorious proclamation in the Song of Roland that 'pagans are wrong and Christians right'. But the Crusades left the opponents largely as they had begun, at least in that there was no sign of any European superiority; indeed the Christians had learnt much from those whose religion they hated and whose strength they feared. A continental antithesis as such was not evident in Byzantium, which straddled Asia and Europe. In the thirteenth century Roger Bacon credited some pagans with superiority 'in those virtues which conduce to human decency, social activity and intercourse'. The close of the Middle Ages saw the Byzantine Empire in the hands of the Turks, but soon after the fall of Constantinople in 1453 the Portuguese launched the European expansion eastwards. Here again, an obsession with military conquests and failures would overlook the subtle cultural interaction that went on. For example, the medieval renaissance of twelfth-century Europe was made possible by the stimulus of Arab culture and its transmission of Greek science and philosophy.

The modern age of European economic expansion and political domination brought with it an acutely messianic form of racial pride and religious smugness. Europe was seen as the natural 'overlord of the planet', with a divine mandate to colonize, civilize, and christianize the abject, decadent, and 'heathen' peoples of Asia. The ideology of European imperialism did not presuppose the notion of eternal hostility but it contained the seeds of inevitable conflict in its elevation of unequal status to the height of dogma. The doctrines of trusteeship, guardianship, utilitarianism, and evangelism, which went much further than the Hellenic concept of *epimeleia*, were supported by assertions about 'Oriental stagnation', 'Oriental despotism', 'Oriental backwardness', 'Oriental superstition and vice'.[1] The 'Peter Pan theory' of the East was also put forward, a theory compounded of two simple ideas—the East is unchanging and Orientals are at best like children. Asian nationalism threw up myths hardly less absurd, and it was equally militant and messianic in its rejection of cultural imperialism, in its humiliating search for a 'parity of esteem'.[2] In repudiating the monopolistic claims of European power, European Christianity, and European culture, Asians have been too apt to blame the intrusion of the West for their own social ills, too willing to idealize their own political systems, traditional religions, and cultures. Even the notion of an epic conflict between Asia and Europe has found echoes in some Asian writers.

Yet here again, an exclusive emphasis on the power conflict and the rival claims of European imperialism and Asian nationalism would have us ignore the profound and subtle cultural interaction that was the unintended result of the recent encounter between Europe and Asia. Europe transmitted the spirit of the European Renaissance, the Reformation, and the Enlightenment, and Asia has experienced its own renaissance, reformation, and revolution—a process that is hardly complete and the long-term effects of which cannot now be clearly foreseen. Even the complex cultural dialogue among Asians that began in the nineteenth century has yet to be fully studied.

The entire thesis of a perennial conflict between Asia and Europe derives its dubious force from a preoccupation with power and the ugly emotions of messianism, retaliation, and fear. Some have even tried to draw up a sinister balance-sheet of mutual

[1] For a fuller account see the author's 'Utilitarianism and All That', *South Asian Affairs*, Chatto & Windus, 1960, pp. 23–24.

[2] The extent of humiliation may be gauged from the words of Mao, the arch-messianist of Asia, in 1949: 'Our nation will never again be an insulted nation. We have stood up.' (See Doak Barnett, *Communist China and Asia*, Vintage Books, 1960, p. 67.)

aggression. For example, much has been made of the massive inroads of the Huns in the fourth and fifth centuries into Central and Southern Europe, the successive waves of Avars in the sixth century and their contact with the armies of Charlemagne, the assaults on Byzantium till the end of the seventh century, the subsequent Moslem invasions—of Arabs, Mongols, and Turks—from the eighth century onwards for a thousand years until the defeat of the Turks in their second siege of Vienna in 1681. Similarly, much could be made of Alexander's invasion of northern India and his abortive attempts to found an Eastern empire, the Roman mastery of a large portion of Asia for a long period, the short-lived kingdoms carved out by the Crusaders at the expense of the decadent Christian empire of the East, whose outposts in Asia Minor and Palestine they went to defend, and the modern Western dominance in the East.

The conception of a historic rivalry or hostility between Asia and Europe may have faint antecedents in earlier epochs, but it is really a modern invention. It is largely the product of imperialist or nationalist pride, of religious bigotry and racial prejudice, and of the nineteenth-century trend in German historicism which saw history as 'dynamic necessity' or some equally vacuous abstraction. To take a crude example, in the twenties the French Catholic nationalist Henri Massis propounded the notion of an intellectual and potentially political invasion of Europe by Asia. Charles Maurras had written in 1905 about the black and yellow 'mercenaries' of civilization, about the 'barbarian' who was arming, making progress, and who was threatening Europe. Massis now argued that the East was taking advantage of Europe's reduced resistance to 'deaden its will and destroy its last germs of unity'.[1] In a similar vein, the arch-racialist Lothrop Stoddard warned more concretely of the coming trade warfare, population pressure, and other forms of 'the Asiatic peril' and the 'colour conflict'. He contended that throughout history Asia was the positive, aggressive factor, 'Asia was the hammer and Europe the anvil on which our West was forged', though now and then the roles changed and Europe led. In the same volume we are told that Asia, in the guise of Bolshevism, 'with Semitic leadership and Chinese executioners', was planning an assault upon Western Europe.[2]

[1] Henri Massis, *The Defence of the West*, Faber & Gwyer, 1927, p. 6.
[2] Lothrop Stoddard, *The Rising Tide of Colour*, Chapman & Hall, 1925, p. xxi.

Equally silly pronouncements have been made by Asians. In 1905 a Burmese paper wrote:

The West has justified—perhaps with some reason—every aggression on weaker races by the doctrine of the Survival of the Fittest. . . . That doctrine applies equally well to any possible struggle between Aryan and Mongolian—whichever survives, should it ever come to a struggle between the two for world-mastery, will, on their own doctrine, be the one most fit to do so, and if the survivor is Mongolian, then is the Mongolian no 'peril' to humanity, but the better part of it.[1]

Again, in 1907, the Egyptian Yahya Siddyk wrote that Europe is already stricken with senility and may be obliged to yield its civilizing role to the Moslems, that history will repeat itself in the new era opening with the fourteenth century of the Hegira.[2] Shortly before the First World War a British-educated Afghan spoke of the coming struggle between Asia and Europe, a *Jehad* or 'Pan-Asia Holy War', a 'gigantic day of reckoning'.[3] In Japan Count Okuma talked of actually raising the East against the West, a military assault on the Balkans and Western Europe. Other Asians have thought in non-military terms of their future victory. While Vivekananda had lectured Indians about the 'spiritual conquest' of Europe, in China Ku Hung-Ming urged united action in throwing off 'Western barbarism' by persuasion and peaceful means, and the Japanese intellectual Kawakami referred to the time when Asia will have recovered in the matter of civilization 'a superiority that will throw Europe into the shade'.

The division of mankind into rival camps can no doubt be supported by a lot of vulgar myth-making in order to evoke sentiments of collective responsibility, resentment, and revenge. The absurdities inherent in the thesis of a perennial conflict between Asia and Europe are obvious, its dangers less readily seen, still less its roots in respectable conceptual errors. Crude images in the popular mind may be fostered by political or religious propagandists and by bad textbooks, but they are more bound up with the conceits of ethnocentric scholars than they would concede. Evidence can

---

[1] Quoted in *The American Reviews of Reviews*, February 1905, p. 219.

[2] Yahya Siddyk, *Le Réveil des peuples islamiques au quatorzième siècle de l'Hégire*, Cairo, 1907.

[3] Achmet Abdullah, 'Seen Through Mohammedan Spectacles', *Forum*, October 1914.

always be assembled to portray the so-called 'quarrel of the continents'. More generally, 'the mechanical mode of historical explanation' imports into history the principles of Newtonian science, assumes that human affairs move naturally in straight lines, imposes a supposed linear sequence over separate epochs, and explains movements in terms of impersonal 'forces' and objective 'laws'. This mechanical mode easily absorbs Darwinism, borrowing terms like evolution, growth, and decay, and thus an organic view of civilization is fitted into a mechanical model of historical events.

The pseudo-history of propagandists, addressed to the emotions, is perhaps the illegitimate and mis-shapen progeny of the pseudo-scientific history that is sometimes put forward with plausible rationality. It is no doubt bad history that often makes good propaganda, but all history can be perverted by the clever propagandist. Even distinguished historians find it difficult to discard the unitary view of civilization itself, to accept the irreducible plurality of civilizations, and to shed the immense optical illusion resulting from focusing entirely on the recent historical encounter of European and Asian peoples. It is also misleading to assume the direct descent of any contemporary civilization from remote ancestors as well as to reconstruct the history of any people through the distorting mirror of alien interpretations. To fit Asian history into Western models can be as confusing as the attempt of some Chinese writers to fit the modern European expansion into a Confucian or Marxist model. Parochial and nationalist historians, Asian or European, who wholly ignore the complex cultural interactions between civilizations, would do well to reflect on Paul Valéry's despairing cry:

History makes men dream dreams, it poisons whole peoples and lends them bogus pasts . . . it lures men into megalomania and persecution obsessions while rendering nations bitter, haughty, intolerable, futile.

Facile Contrasts and Persisting Myths

The notion of a perennial conflict between Asia and Europe is dangerously absurd but it is an uncommon aberration compared to the sweeping contrasts between Eastern and Western thought, values, societies, and even peoples that have frequently been made by many European and Asian writers. Glib generalizations have been repeatedly advanced and have gained a wide currency, subtly influencing even reputable scholars who would repudiate their crude and often contradictory formulations. These facile contrasts are sometimes needed as devices for criticizing the values and institutions found in Asia (or Europe) by idealizing those of Europe (or Asia), and more often are used for compensatory self-praise through a sly debunking of alien peoples. Even attempts at objective appraisal—such as those of Northrop or Abegg—have encouraged the belief in a basic dichotomy in mental processes between Asians and Europeans. The most extreme example is that of Haas, who argued that the consciousness of the Oriental is hope-lessly antagonistic to that of the Westerner, the former being self-centred, introvert, and subjective, the latter being expansive, extrovert, and objective. Much earlier, Maeterlinck contrasted the 'eastern lobe' in the human brain, secreting intuition, religion, the subconscious, with the 'western lobe', producing reason, science, consciousness. A similar contrast goes back to the *Theologica Germanica* and was attributed to Dionysius—the contrast between the 'eye of eternity' and the 'eye of time'—but it is only in recent times that this internal dichotomy in every man has been used to contrast 'Eastern man' with 'Western man'.

A few examples of facile contrasts, selected at random from European and Asian writers, would suffice here. Hegel contrasted the unreflective consciousness and subjective freedom of the 'static', 'despotic' Orient with the self-consciousness and objective freedom of dynamic, law-governed Europe. Weber sought to derive sociological implications from his contrast between Asia's part-mystical, part-aesthetic goal of self-discipline and the 'specifically Occidental significance of personality'. Western scholars and Christian apologists continue to produce variants of the sharp contrast between the mystical and the prophetic religious traditions, Indian and Israelite. Historians like Sansom and Romein have stressed the crucial economic basis of the contrast between Asian and European societies and cultures, while still avoiding a Marxian type of 'reductionism'.

Modern Asian writers have also been more or less complacent (or defensive) in their own sweeping contrasts between Asia and Europe, between Eastern and Western thought and culture. We have, for example, Liang Ch'i-ch'ao's contrast between Eastern wisdom and Western learning, Kitaro Nishida's distinction between the rule of the intellect in European culture and the stress on feeling in Eastern culture, Kitayama's opposition of 'space' and 'time' cultures, and Nagayo's emphasis on the difference between 'soul training' and 'mental culture'. Okakura held that Christian Europe never ascended above a human godhead to the Eastern vision of the universal in its 'eternal search for unity in variety'. The Lebanese Arab, Charles Ammoun, has contrasted the 'short-sighted' Occident with the 'long-sighted' Orient. Vivekananda pointed to the essential difference between the 'inward' and the 'outward' vision, between the predominance of the *Daivi* (divine) nature in Asian civilizations with their agricultural foundation and the ascendancy of the *Asuri* (non-divine) nature in the hilly and coastal civilizations of Europe with their basis in robbery and piracy.

All such vague generalities and sharp contrasts, suggesting a basic dichotomy between men or societies in Asia and Europe, obscure rather than illuminate undeniable differences in presuppositions and attitudes arising out of the Judaeo-Christian and Hindu-Buddhist traditions[1] or connected with divergent forms of social, economic, and political development. It has sometimes been suggested that Asians and Europeans can communicate more effectively only when they grasp the metaphysical presuppositions and value systems of each other—and the languages that help unlock such systems. But there is nothing to be gained from grandiose contrasts between Asia and Europe, for all such formulations impose a falsely monolithic model upon complex, diverse, and changing traditions and societies. Detailed studies of particular facets of different cultures or social systems may be of some value, but even here the same phenomena can be explained in markedly disparate ways. The sweeping contrasts repeatedly made by Asians or Europeans are hardly more enlightening than the pseudo-anthropological theory that Asians are descended from the chimpanzee and Europeans from the gorilla.

Quite apart from facile contrasts between Asia and Europe, there are certain myths that die hard, the most notorious being 'Oriental despotism' and 'Western materialism'. The former was first categorically formulated by Montesquieu, who knew little of

---

[1] For an instructive example of how such differences may be investigated, see Ninian Smart's 'Re-incarnation and Eastern attitudes', *The Listener*, August 9, 1962.

C

the history and political systems of Asia, whose conception of arbitrary power was self-contradictory, and whose eloquence made him prone to exaggerate. Burke took more pains to examine the constitution of Oriental governments and concluded that 'Asia is enlightened in that respect as well as Europe'. Yet James Mill elaborated the notion of 'Oriental despotism' to build up his monotonously black picture of Indian society and character, thus preserving in a secular form the earlier Evangelical indictment against an entire people. In 1908 Balfour blamed 'Oriental despotism' for 'Western decadence', the result of the Imperial system, which was 'perhaps too oriental for the occident'. Recently the notion of 'Oriental despotism' has been revived by Wittfogel with a mixture of circular reasoning and one-sided evidence, but despite the criticisms of specialists the notion has gained a new currency. A careful study of Asian systems of political thought and institutions will no doubt reveal significant differences from Western thought and tradition and perhaps a relative neglect of institutional safeguards against the abuse of power, but it will also show a basic concern with legitimacy and little to substantiate a monolithic model of despotism. In essence and origin, liberty is no more European than Asian, though it has assumed specific forms in European nation-states that are unique to them only in a tauto-logical sense. For better and for worse, the long and fierce struggle between Church and State that has moulded European political concepts has no parallel in Asian history.

The most extreme version of the equally absurd notion of 'Western materialism' was first put forward by Vivekananda in an essay on 'The East and the West'. He penned a ghastly portrait of Europeans—fierce like wild beasts, drenched in liquor, believing in matter only, addicted to the exploitation of others and self-aggrandizement through 'force, trick and treachery', having no faith in the life hereafter, and 'whose whole life is only in the senses and creature comforts'. Tagore too spoke of the 'one-sided materialism' of the West, but he also warned against mistrusting 'the religious force behind Europe's civilization'. Hu Shih went so far as to depict the West as more 'spiritual' than the 'truly materialistic civilization' of the East. And yet the notion of 'Western materialism' (as opposed to 'Eastern spirituality') dies hard even today. U Chan Htoon, a Burmese judge, recently asserted that since the dawn of history Asian life has developed on spiritual rather than on materialistic lines and that the spiritual light of Asia should be rekindled 'as a guiding beacon in the darkness of error afflicting mankind'.

All such myths as 'Oriental despotism' and 'Western materialism' are substitutes for analysis, molehills of truth magnified into mountains of exaggeration. There may be specific senses in which certain societies are more liberty-loving or more materialistic than others, and there may be special reasons for these differences over certain epochs. But social myths are dangerous when they seem to embody eternal truths, when we go as far as Balfour in asserting that 'the new crystals will always resemble the old ones'. Too often claims to uniqueness lead to suggestions of innate, irremovable, all-round superiority. Byron once remarked that there are beauties in Derbyshire which are no less than those of Switzerland. Asians and Europeans who boast about their Himalayan or Alpine glories deny to others their own Derbyshire, while resenting similar denials in other fields on the part of those who take pride in their own summits of achievement. Furthermore, the real difficulty with clichés about Asia and Europe is that their users often tend to explain the same phenomena by a simple change of epithet on opposite sides of the Glass Curtain. As early as 1913 Mallik gave several examples of this tendency in the use of terms like passivity and fortitude, sycophancy and civility, timidity and patience, bravery and terrorism, sedition and heroic resistance, tactics and atrocities, superstitious weakness and humanitarian sentiments.

So long as the same mental or physical attitude or attribute becomes an object of piaise or of blame according to the latitude or the longitude where it appears, cordial fellowship or even bare association [between East and West] cannot be expected.[1]

Past and Future

It has been shrewdly observed that the greatest problem of communication is the illusion that it has already been achieved. It is easy enough to show the confusion resulting from talking about vague and vast aggregates like East and West, Asia and Europe; from the notion of a historic conflict between continents; and from the facile contrasts and persisting myths suggesting a basic

[1] Manmath C. Mallik, *Orient and Occident*, T. Fisher Unwin, 1913, pp. 5–6.

dichotomy between Asian and European thought, culture, and society. But it is simple-minded to make the common intellectualist error of underrating or ignoring the enormous influence of the irrational and the absurd in human affairs. The psychological barrier, actual or apparent, felt by many Asians and Europeans is partly the result of mental habits that cannot be written off as mere vestiges of painful encounters in recent history. Even if such habits can be readily overcome, bridges are genuinely difficult to build and to cross where one culture is geographically remote from another culture and has been historically insulated from it for long periods. Asians and Europeans cannot afford to dispense with a due sense of the past in their present and future encounters. The ghosts of dead ideas still live with us, as Ibsen said, and we are influenced in unseen ways by inherited attitudes that we too readily repudiate. Those who are wholly alienated from past traditions are far from being godlike spectators of the contemporary scene. They may even be unhappy creatures who are very susceptible to new myths and who imagine their rootlessness to be a state of supreme freedom.

The reality of the Glass Curtain may be illustrated by a few examples, selected at random. It may now be laughable that Archbishop Montecorvino, after a stay of a few months in South India in the thirteenth century, reported to Rome that the people of India knew how to count only up to five and had no developed language. The tales of medieval and modern travellers about the exotic East may now be dismissed—sometimes unjustly—as the product of fleeting impressions and a luxuriant imagination. The garbled version of Hindu customs given by Abbé Dubois may today be no more than a historical curiosity. But contemporary images of the East are hardly free from traditional stereotypes—brutal Turks, sycophantic Arabs, evasive Indians, sly Mongol races. The Fu Manchu legend has kept alive the notion that the Chinese are a race of wily rogues with sparse, drooping moustaches. The mystique of the exotic East has by no means vanished. Some 'Orientalists' even today cannot resist the temptation of magnifying differences by reckless categorization.

The denigration or idealization of Asia goes on. It is not so long since Curzon wrote that the East is 'a journey the goal of which is always in sight but is never attained'. In the twenties Chesterton could write about the Asiatic 'demon', and in the thirties Marshall

Hall could win a court case in London against an Egyptian by declaring that an Oriental's word cannot be taken against a European's. In 1960 a retired diplomat wrote to *The Times* explaining the calling off of summit talks with the remark that 'the Russian tends to be oriental in his outlook and "face" to him is supremely important'. More recently, Mr. Koestler returned from his fleeting travels in India and Japan, undertaken 'in the mood of a pilgrim', only to record what he himself called 'a mixture of pedantic detail and sweeping generalizations'—a mixture that suited some appetites, though dubbed a poisonous potion by a few reviewers. Are such books to be dismissed as ephemeral and consequently negligible, or does a kind of Gresham's Law govern the fate of popular literature?

Literary examples of Asian misconceptions about Europeans are not so easy to find, but oral evidence is readily available to show how pervasive and persistent they are. There is no reason to believe that we have on either side of the Glass Curtain a monopoly or a greater preponderance of ignorance, prejudice, and pride. As early as the eighth century, an Arab judge could assert regarding Europeans:

. . . their temperaments have become cold and their humours rude, while their bodies have become large, their complexion light and their hair long. They lack withal sharpness of wit and penetration of intellect, while stupidity and folly prevail among them.

In the sixteenth century a Japanese record of the first Portuguese to reach Japan remarks:

They eat with their fingers instead of chopsticks. [The use of knives and forks was not yet common in Europe.] They show their feelings without any self-control. They cannot understand the meaning of written characters [i.e. Chinese script]. They spend their lives roaming about without any fixed abode and barter what they have for what they have not. They are, however, a harmless sort of people.

But such remarks are mild compared to Vivekananda's references to the European 'demon', no less disgraceful than Chesterton's talk about the 'great Asiatic demon'. If Gobineau could write about the great Asiatic marsh 'horribly fertile in monsters and in beings hostile to our species', a Chinese statesman of Sun-Yat-Sen's stature could dismiss the West as 'a shameless civilization, sweating with cunning and rotten with self-interested logic'. If Mr. Douglas Jerrold could recently assert that 'Western civilization has at its heart something which no other civilization has had—the knowledge of God's purposes for man in this world . . .', Asia is not lacking in messianists bearing, Atlas-like, the burden of the world's destiny. If Western missionaries vilified Eastern religions and societies by means of tactics ridiculed in Lowes Dickinson's *Letters of a Chinaman*, many examples of the vilification of European Christianity and culture by Asians are mentioned in Maurice Price's *Christian Missions and Oriental Civilizations*. Quite apart from deliberate or ignorant vilification, the Asian's distorted image of Europeans—sometimes amusing, sometimes insulting—is well illustrated in Hwuy-Ung's account of Europeans in *A Chinaman's Opinion of Us* translated by the Rev. J. A. Makepeace. Finally, a recent example may be given of the political significance of the Glass Curtain. In December 1961 an Indian judge wrote to *The Times* protesting against the 'European' view of India's military action in Goa. He contended that it was morally defensible in Asian eyes and concluded that 'Asia and the Nato powers are looking at this dispute from the opposite ends of the moral telescope'.

Even if we recognize the contemporary reality of the Glass Curtain, we cannot be dogmatic in deciding on its importance in the foreseeable future. Our forecasts will not merely depend upon our temperamental optimism or pessimism but also upon our answers to several large and difficult questions. Is it true, as writers like Guénon and Coomaraswamy have held, that there is no profound barrier between traditional cultures, but only between the traditional East and the modern West? Or was Lowes Dickinson right in thinking that the psychological barrier between East and West will disappear with the inevitable 'Westernization' of the East? Or will there be a distinctive Asian mode of modernization, or even a new Asian Renaissance? Are the ancient Asian cultures to be viewed as those of terminated, arrested civilizations, as Reincourt has argued? In regard to Europe, we could ask, like Heidegger, whether Europeans are late-comers or forerunners on the world stage. Are we, like Comte, to regard Europe as the *avant-garde* of humanity or must we, like Valéry, speak of the lost illusion of European culture? Have non-Europeans taken over European fertility, as del Corral contends? Is Europe today a burnt-out volcano, and is there a danger of Europe 'sinking back' into Asia, as Jaspers warns? Or should we, like Yeats, look forward to the begetting by Asia on Europe of a new spiritual era in the West?

Even more concretely, is the changed power balance between Asia and Europe the basis of a new understanding or a fresh and fierce conflict? Will the schism in world Communism between East and West become as ideologically significant as that which divided Christendom? Is the Soviet Union justified in accusing China of fostering a new racialism, a division between the white and the coloured races? Has the Kremlin now abandoned the faith of Zinoviev and Lenin that it 'shall conquer the West by way of the East'? What significance should we attach to Mao's statement that 'the east wind will prevail over the west wind'? Is the emotional legacy of a haphazard colonialism more potent than the liberating results of reluctant decolonization? In short, will the vertical division of mankind into blocs gradually lose significance in the face of the horizontal division into ranks, classes, and mental attitudes found among all peoples?

All such questions are easier asked than answered, and there are no decisive ways of resolving disagreement arising from differing presuppositions about the relative roles to be assigned to political and economic, cultural and ideological factors. But if Asians and Europeans are now to enter into a fruitful dialogue, they must take a fresh look at past historical encounters, the mutual attitudes of particular peoples in the recent period, their contrasting claims to uniqueness, and at the extent to which the spread of science or the reconciliation of religions could foster a new sense of moral solidarity in a world fragmented by inherited hostilities and new-fangled ideologies.

THE HISTORICAL CONTEXT

Good history cannot do as much service as money or science; but bad history can do almost as much harm as the most disastrous scientific discovery in the world. It will be the historians of Asia and Africa who will have the power to prejudice the next generations for or against us. If our claims are unrealistic, their claims are certain to be unrealistic too. If we can admit mistakes and even crimes where mistakes and crimes have been committed, there is some chance that they will admit, and will teach their posterity, that our connection with their countries has not been an unmitigated misfortune.

RICHARD PARES

II. THE HISTORICAL CONTEXT OF ENCOUNTERS BETWEEN ASIA AND EUROPE

as seen by an Asian

C. S. Venkatachar

I

The astounding ignorance of Europe on the part of Asians lasted for nearly two millenia. Until European mariners rudely awakened them from their slumbers, Asians were totally indifferent to the existence of Europe. In the expansionist periods of the Han and Tang imperial dynasties, the Chinese may have vaguely heard of Rome and brushed acquaintance with the legionaries on the Asiatic frontier of the Roman Empire. The Greeks have recorded the journeys of Indian philosophers to Greece. Buddhist traditions preserved in the Jatakas speak of the voyages of Indian merchants and philosophers to Alexandria. Such contacts were of a spasmodic character, forming no part of the historical memory of the Chinese and Indian civilizations. There were understandable reasons for this state of ignorance and indifference. The vast distance by land and sea prolonged the physical and mental isolation of Asia and of Europe. The agricultural civilizations of Asia, with their material abundance and self-sufficiency, had little urge to trade and exchange commodities other than a few articles of luxury. The curiosity of Asians towards the exterior world was limited to seeing the 'barbarians' on entry into their homeland; they showed the least desire to venture forth and see the outer world of the 'barbarians'.

By contrast, Europe's acquaintance with parts of Asia commences from the earliest times. Europe came to experience mixed emotions. The quest for silk from far-off Cathay and for the spices from the Indies kept alive a prying curiosity and a sustained interest in Asian lands. On the other hand, the attack by the Huns in the fifth century A.D., and by the Mongols in the thirteenth century, resulted in a revulsion towards Asia, rooted in the belief that the civilization of Europe represented by Rome was destroyed by an 'inferior' civilization from the depths of Asia, which was seen as the seat of permanent aggression against European civilization.

Earlier, the Greeks had clashed with the ancient Persians. In terms of historical geography, this was an inevitable clash between land and sea power. When Cyrus the Great raised an obscure Persic tribe to the hegemony of the Fertile Crescent, Persian land power overran the Greek settlements planted there by the expanding maritime power of Greece. In the eyes of modern Europe, this clash is seen as the beginning of conflict between the 'Oriental' and 'Occidental' spirits—the implications being that the 'Oriental spirit', represented by the Persians, was decadent and authoritarian and the 'Occidental', represented by the Hellenic Greeks, was liberty-loving, progressive, exalting the supremacy of the individual.

The European mariners who pioneered geographical science added confusion to the faulty legacy of the Greeks who had equated Hellenism with Europe and their enemy, the Persians, with Asia. These early mariners had no knowledge of the interior of the Asiatic continent, its peoples, and civilizations. They gained a lop-sided picture of the Continent which they viewed in terms of the 'Coasts'. Later, under Western imperialism, a fragmented picture of Asia became familiar under such geographical labels as the Middle East, Near East, South and South-east Asia, East Asia, Far East, Russian and Soviet Asia.

Asia is no more a single entity than Europe is. It is unclear as to why Europe developed a sharp antithesis between itself and Asia— an antithesis, by no means a passing prejudice or a fleeting fancy. It got embedded in the mind of Europe, breeding conflict which became more pronounced with Europe's assertion of its innate 'superiority' over non-European parts of the world. 'Asia', said a character in one of the stories of Kipling, 'is not going to be civilized after the methods of the West. There is too much Asia and she is too old.'

A corrective to the faulty legacies and perspectives of past history is to view the continent of Asia as a composite area of three main regions of Asian civilizations. The first of these is the area which includes India, China, the Indies, and the Islands of Japan—the home of ancient faiths and civilizations of more than a thousand million people. This may be called the Monsoon land. The second is the Great Steppe of the Eurasian land mass, the home of the nomads of history, who for 1,500 years lived in close contact with Asia and Europe. This we may call the Corridor. The third is that bridgehead between the Iranian upland and the Nile valley and North Africa—the home of Judaism, Islam, and early Christianity. This is the Fertile Crescent into which from the north erupted the Central Asian nomads and from the south, the Arabs; it confronted the Greco-Roman World and was involved in a struggle with Classical Europe and Western Christendom.

The differences between Asia and Europe stem from the profound influence of Asian physical geography and the prolonged and continuous interaction between the nomads and the settled agricultural societies of Asia. This subject of the inter-relation between the Steppe and the Sown awaits a closer study by historians. René Grousset attempted to deduce certain propositions for explaining the movements of the nomads and their repeated clashes with civilized peoples. He thought there was some pattern and even a cyclic rhythm in their movements, influenced possibly by climatic variations, economic causes, or ethnic superiority. The nomads moved on the extensive Corridor of grassland and steppe, extending from Manchuria to the Hungarian plains in a three-pronged direction—one across the southern way to Europe; another across the mountain barriers to India and China; the third over the Iranian uplands. The movements over these traffic areas of civilization lasted for 2,500 years, from the unrecorded time of the migration of the Aryan tribes to the first recording by Herodotus in the seventh century B.C. of the displacement of Scythic hordes towards Asia Minor and Persia, and extending into the early sixteenth century when a cultured Timurid, Babar, established Mogul rule in India.

Physical geography also conditioned that the Mongolian upland should be the reservoir of man-power for the nomadic hordes. Their homeland was extremely favourable for the development of cavalry, and this in turn gave them a military advantage. Though backward in material culture, the nomad was incredibly mobile, and consequently the mounted archer of the Steppe was easily able to run over the agricultural areas. As Grousset remarks, real invasion or conquest was only exception or accident, about one chance in a hundred, often disconcerting to the conquerors. The nomads were a stateless people with no political organization, and they were so deficient in the rudiments of civilization that it was a burden for them to presume to govern highly civilized peoples living in populous villages and cities.

In Asia the two most populous areas of civilization, China and India, acted as shock absorbers for nomadic incursions and resolutely faced the problem of assimilating the alien nomads into their societies. The Chinese showed a marvellous capacity for the ethnic absorption of the barbarians, which proceeded in a rhythmic cyclic fashion. The Indians set up a powerful social centrifuge which sorted out the aliens and assigned them a place in the social hierarchy of the caste system. Both faced the problem of upholding a stable society, rather a universal society within the framework of a universal state. The latter more often, as in the case of India, was weak, but society everywhere in Asia managed to survive without breaking away from Antiquity. The Asians have shown their capacity to survive by outliving the many cataclysms which threatened to overwhelm them.

The reason for this amazing vitality to survive lay in the peculiar viability of Asian societies. Their base was a highly developed, extremely close-knit, small social unit—the family in the old Chinese Confucian society, the caste group in India, and the *millat* in Islamic society. Over considerable periods of time these societies were on an escalator of progress, sometimes slipping away but always attempting to rise higher. They did not develop the attributes of a territorial nation-state of the Western type. They remained till the twentieth century areas of civilization with common memories of cultural unity or shared religious bonds.

The nomads enjoyed all to themselves the privilege of roaming and wandering over the vacancies of the land mass. They kept open the land routes in the Corridor and acted as carriers of ideas which they diffused and dispersed along the tracks of their movements. At other times, like the Mongols in the thirteenth century, they transplanted cultural forms from one region to another. Herein lies perhaps the chief explanation for the absence of hostility on the part of Asian societies to the impact of purely

Asian cultures. Nestorian Christianity travelled on land to China and by sea to the Malabar Coast of India. Mahayana Buddhism journeyed on the Silk Road across the Hindu Kush mountain range to China where it was welcomed. Along the same route travelled the religious ideas of Mazdaism and the cults of Iran. Various art forms were transported from the Kabul Valley through the Tarim basin to China. Outside the land routes Indian argonauts spread Indian civilization, alphabets, folk-lore, art, and architecture to South-east Asia in a peaceful manner. Nowhere were they imposed by force or aggression. The contact of peoples and races did not give rise, as in modern times, to a violent clash of cultures.

The experience of Europe was of a different order. The Roman empire cracked and dissolved under the weight of Teutonic invasions. The Huns did not destroy the Roman Empire. The European barbarians, an agriculturally settled people but inferior in civilization to the Romans who were disturbed by the Huns, claimed the heritage of Rome and became part of it. The toppling of the empire led to some far-reaching results: the idea of a nation-state took shape by stages, state power hardened and crystallized and the authority of the Church was institutionalized. The English geographer Mackinder has remarked that from the reaction of the Coastmen against this hammer-blow from the Heartland, there arose English and French nationalities, the sea power of Venice, and the supreme medieval institution of the Papacy.

We have some idea of the pounding as between the pestle and the mortar which went to the making of modern Europe. The pestle was the land-power from the Heartland.

Mackinder's Heartland in this phase of world history was the Asian Corridor. The expression 'land power' is somewhat misleading. The mobile hordes of nomads were not organized as a state. The political problem of encountering the organized power of a state was the contribution of the Greco-Roman world and of Western Christendom. Witness, for example, the conflict between Greece and Persia, Rome and Carthage, Rome and Persia, the Parthians and the Sassanids, Western Christendom and Islam. Unlike the Asians, the Europeans developed conceptions of political relations between states, principally of warring states. It is in the nomadic period of world history that we must look for some of the clues for the diverging historic destinies of Asia and Europe.

The Monsoon land and the Corridor remained outside the reach of Europe till the maritime age. Occasional glimpses of these were no doubt gleaned by the adventurous mariners of the Eastern Mediterranean and of Arabia in their voyages on the maritime route to peninsular India and to the China Sea, or by travellers like Marco Polo, John de Carpini, and William Rubruck. But Europe had no worthwhile contact of any kind with Asia outside the Fertile Crescent in which appears the so-called 'Eastern question', a live issue among Europeans since the days of conflict between the Greeks and the ancient Persians.

Alexander the Great became the first deified militarist and the first world conqueror in history to advance the political frontier of Europe into Asia. By his conquests, he established the political and cultural hegemony of Hellenism over non-Greek peoples. This was an experience unknown to Asia where cultural forms were voluntarily borrowed, exchanged, and shared in common but never imposed by superior political authority. Alexander innovated a number of other patterns. He originated colonial rule by planting colonies of Greeks in the Fertile Crescent and Hither Asia. By proclaiming the primacy and supremacy of Hellenic culture over the local indigenous cultures, the foundations were laid for political revolts when one people dominate another, politically, ethnically, culturally. Western aggression was stirring up local nationalism from the Nile to the Ganges. In faraway India, Chandragupta Maurya established a universal state in North India and undermined Hellenic influences, which in any case did not touch the hard core of Indian civilization, then located in the midlands of the north. Except for the Gandharan form of Buddha, widely dispersed by Mahayana Buddhism in the Central Asian empire of Kanishka, the history of India would in all essentials have been unaltered had the Greeks never existed. The reaction against Greek culture and Roman political power was carried out in Persia by the Parthians and their successors, the Sassanids, representing Persian nationalism. Semitic reaction was strongly represented by the Jewish theocracy.

Europe's sortie into Asia—the first political encounter between Europe and Asia backed by political and military power—advanced to the edge of the Pamirs and the Indus basin. Asia beyond the Fertile Crescent played no part in the uneven yet rhythmic process of Europe's retreat, at first initiated by the nationalism of the non-Greek societies of the Fertile Crescent, and subsequently carried forward as a conflict between Islam and Christianity. The task of pushing the Europeans out of the Fertile Crescent was undertaken by the Arabs and the Islamized Seljuk Turks. Says a European scholar:

With the fall of Antioch and Alexandria, the relations between Asia and Europe entered a new phase. Europe which had for so long imposed its will on the East was everywhere on the retreat. It was Asia's great revolt against the ideas of religion and the rule of Greece and Rome.[1]

The smouldering ethnic and cultural tension resulting from the imposition of Helleno-Romanism was transformed by Islam into a politico-religious conflict between a nascent Latin Christianity fighting for its survival and a triumphant Arabian Islam. Islam and Christianity, both tracing their roots to Semitic ideas of monotheism and divine authority, carried to the extreme the dogmas of religious exclusiveness. With such an attitude either one had to triumph over the other or both had to enter into a prolonged state of uneasy co-existence somewhat akin to the contemporary situation when democracy and communism are faced with a similar dilemma. Christianity was a revolutionary movement. It extinguished the pagan culture of Rome and 'judaized' the whole of Europe. In the sonorous words of Gibbon, it gradually insinuated itself in the minds of men, grew up in silence and obscurity, derived new vigour from opposition and finally erected the triumphant banner of the Cross on the ruins of the Capitol. Islam was carried forward with amazing speed by the furious drive and energy of the nomads of Arabia and Central Asia. Islamic power became a double-headed eagle, one facing the Atlantic and the other the Indus.

In the seventh century Islam reached the Corridor, and that was the turning point in the history of Central Asian nomads. The western half of the Corridor was Islamized and the eastern half fell under Chinese influence. Some historians think this to be a turning point in the history of Europe and Asia. Henceforth Western Christendom had to contend for seven long dreary centuries with the politics of Islam rather than with the resentment of Asians against Europe. The Crusades are from the European standpoint a very important chapter in this prolonged duel. They appear, in

[1] René Grousset, *A Sum of History*, English version by A. & H. Temple Patterson, p. 165.

D

the long-range view of the Asian world, as the failure of attempts by Western Christendom to subjugate Islam. This failure on land was turned into a triumphant achievement when European mariners launched out on the waterways of the world, thus initiating the encounter in depth between Europe and Asia.

II

In Antiquity there had been a sort of balanced relationship between the three main areas of civilizations of Europe and Asia— the Greco-Roman world, India, and China. Each radiated civilizing influences to its natural surroundings and adjacent areas. All the three independently developed one common quality, almost a virtue. They were supremely contemptuous of the world outside their own. The Chinese believed that their civilization was superior to that of any other country. As late as the eighteenth century, the Son of Heaven could write to the British envoy that even if the western barbarian was able to acquire the rudiments of Chinese civilization, 'You could not possibly transplant our manners and customs to your alien soil'. The Hindus stuck to notions of their own superiority; all aliens were dismissed as unclean *mlechhas*. The Greeks did not suffer from any modesty in proclaiming the supremacy of Greek thought and way of life; all non-Greeks were barbarians to them.

Round about A.D. 1500 the balance began to change. Asian societies were then undergoing some strange inexplicable experiences. There was a sudden decline in the mobility of the Asians, in particular the ominous cessation of maritime activity from the China seas to the Persian Gulf. On the eve of the maritime age the Chinese made one grand sortie into the Indian Ocean, only to close down their enterprise and forget the salt waters. After many centuries of intense maritime activity the Hindus withdrew from the ocean and left it to the Arabs to sail and trade from Arabia to the Indies. Everywhere in Asia there was abundant material for shipbuilding, intrepid and daring sailors, centuries of maritime tradition, memories of contact with other lands in the Indian Ocean and of exchange of commodities from Aden to Malacca. Yet on the sea routes as well as in the Corridor life was suddenly silenced.

Intriguing, too, is the reason for the somnolence of Asian societies. Perhaps they had had enough of the Tatar hurricane, its depredations, and devastations. In the tenth century Alberuni had noted of the Hindus that if they travel and live with other people, they would soon change their mind. Hindu society became extremely static in confrontation with Islam. The smaller societies of South-east Asia ceased to be activated by cultural radiations from China and India; they too withdrew into the shell of their parochial national societies while retaining the cultural legacies of their great neighbours. China decided to live in utter indifference to the changing and expanding external world; she congealed her life and society under largely unmodified Confucian codes.

At the other end in Europe, nation-states emerged with their conception of a defined community of people speaking one language, following one law and (till Protestantism arose) one form of religion, inhabiting one continuous territory under one unified government, invariably a centralized monarchy which controlled at least defence.[1] The physical power of the state was strengthened by the technical superiority acquired through the invention of artillery. Hereafter, Power and Glory were pursued not by a ruthless individual but by and on behalf of an entity which organized collective efforts and sacrifices to achieve its ambitions. The European state system was accompanied by the principle of Balance of Power, which had no place in the relation between the Asian Steppe and the Sown. It did not apply to the political relations between the various Asian societies. It certainly was out of place in the Roman Empire where there was the voice of one authority, Imperial Rome. The new states of Western Europe, competing for power, were confronted with the problem of living as neighbours and settling their ambitions and rivalries without resorting to war. It is the projection of European quarrels into the non-European parts of the world which initiated disturbance in the hitherto static East-West relations. The projection followed the swift orientations of the routes and direction of the traffic in the maritime age.

In the Corridor the flank of the nomads was turned by the Cossacks stealthily penetrating into the forests of Siberia. This is the significance of the ride of Yermack, the Cossack, across Siberia to Vladivostock—an event which took place only thirty-five years after Vasco da Gama had entered the Indian Ocean and barely a dozen years or so after Magellan had circumnavigated the world.

---

[1] *Encyclopaedia Britannica*, 1929, 'Europe'.

By turning the flank of Islam, European mariners weakened Islamic power in the Fertile Crescent and the Corridor. The maritime power of Venice and the Central European Hapsburgs held in check the pressure of the Turks. The five competing nation-states, all having oceanic interests on the West European coastland, launched out vigorously on the waterways of the world; they roamed over the oceans of the world without any opposition. In the opening phase of their momentous career, neither economic nor military nor political power was decisively against Asia and in favour of Europe. A proper sense of history enables us to grasp the stupendous changes in the conditions of mankind which began round about 1750. It is then, economists point out, there began along with industrialization the explosive process of European economic development. Until then average real incomes had scarcely risen, from one century to another.

The Portuguese did not aspire to be a land-power; they went in for a commercial empire, in pursuit of which they annexed a few strategic footholds such as Ormuz, Socotra, Goa, Malacca, etc. While European mariners were able to move on the seas without any hindrance, the Moguls and the Manchus were free to establish land empires. Babar established Mogul rule in India, twenty-five years after Vasco da Gama had landed in Calicut. At the zenith of Mogul power the English merchants were suppliants for the favour of the Mogul Viceroys and on a few occasions of the Emperor himself. European merchants on the China coast lived in foreign *Hongs*, where they were given the privilege of participating in Chinese beneficence. The Japanese took a close look at the guns of the Portuguese ship intruding into Japan, suffered the presence of the Dutch for a time, only to throw them out and then closed the door to all foreigners for two centuries till they heard the rude knock of the American Perry. Thus the Dutch in Indonesia became the pioneers of colonial rule since they were able to over-run the Indonesians in their widely dispersed islands.

Nor did the divergences between Asian religions and European Christianity confer any innate superiority over the latter. Christianity, originally an Asian faith, was moulded by the mind of Europe and is undoubtedly the main axis of Europe's history—of decisive influence in the shaping of Europe, politically and spiritually. At least as significant were the Asian faiths to their adherents. When an English writer says that 'Asians have not the same sentiment of independence and freedom as Europeans; individuals are thought of as members of a family, state or religion rather than as entities with a destiny and rights of their own; this leads to autocracy in politics, fatalism in religion and conservatism in both'[1]—he is importing a prejudice much later diffused in Europe to explain away its self-assumed superiority over the non-European world with that typical self-sufficiency which sees non-European peoples as objects of benign curiosity.

A similar reproach attaches to many other so-called fundamental causes of divergence often postulated by Europeans. For example, there is the presumption that Helleno-Roman culture has a residuary superiority over all others, not owing to its Western origin but because of its very distinctive qualities of mind and spirit. The West alone has developed ideas of political liberty! Again, it is the Western mind which has shaped the world, finds its assurances within the world and not outside it. The West is endowed with peculiar facilities and has special dispensations for shaping the entire world. These and many other such assertions sounded well when Hegel said that 'the world is now explored and circumnavigated and for Europeans it is a whole sphere. Such of it as they have failed to dominate is either not worth dominating or destined never to be dominated.'[2] Now that the universal sway of Europe has been shattered, Europeans are bewildered, wondering and questioning how it all happened and what went wrong.

As non-participants in the historic processes of the maritime age, Asians may not attempt to explain the divergence in development in relation to actual experiences, but tentatively three considerations may be suggested. The first of these is the difference in attitude towards change in general, whether in the political, social, or economic sphere. It is more convenient to retain the word 'change' in preference to 'progress' which, it is sometimes argued, is a concept alien to 'oriental' civilization and which came from the Jews, with their insistence on the purposefulness of history, into the mainstream of Christianity. Now it cannot be seriously argued that the societies of India and China had failed to change, even slowly and imperceptibly, out of their original matrix. Had they not done so, they would not have survived. It is, however, the capacity to break through that is the ultimate test of survival. Since petrification

---

[1] Sir Charles Eliot, Asia, History, *Encyclopaedia Britannica*, 1911.
[2] Hegel, *Vorlesungen über die Philosophie der Weltgeschichte*, Leipzig, 1944, p. 202.

had long set in in their ageing civilizations, greater efforts were needed in Asia to achieve a breakthrough, not excluding those jumps and spurts of violent activity which go by the name of revolutions in European society. Asian societies mistakenly found virtue in a rigid fixity in their ancient institutions. Their intellectual elites were hidebound in their traditionalism; they missed the opportunity to take measure of the forces at work in a world of fast-moving changes. Their social structure was hierarchical, non-competitive; it excluded fluidity and mobility. There was no class within it which would show deep dissatisfaction with ancestral ways and introduce changes and innovations. There was no element which could jolt society from inside. China, for example, had the necessary elements to break through from the ancient type of agricultural society. She had ample capital, a strong central government over long intervals, an inquiring and rational mind, a respectable output of science and technology in the pre-scientific age of the world. Why China did not change remains a puzzle. Somewhere she lacked the restless mind or even the inquisitive prying mind of the Japanese, whose Rangakusha scholars and the so-called 'Western Group' of Takashima and Noboru played a significant part in the modernization of Japan.

The West, as Karl Jaspers says, did not coagulate the universal into 'a dogmatic fixity of definitive institutions and notions. In no sense did the West become stabilized.'[1] There is always a perpetual sense of disquiet in the West, continued dissatisfaction, inability to be content with any sort of fulfilment. In the innermost mind of the European are set up many battle-fronts, which manifest themselves in concrete historical tensions. Europe started its new career with the clarity of opposites, the polarity of spiritual conflicts. From wars of religion Europe shifted to wars of ideas and ideologies. Western Europe, in particular, renewed itself by profound changes.

Furthermore, the mere desire for change is not enough. There must be levers within society to bring about the desired changes. The instrument for effecting the changes in Europe was furnished by the new social groups. The opening of sea-borne commerce provided vast opportunities to the merchants and the bankers. Secularized governments sought the help of officials to run organized administrations and secular intellectual elites, from which came the political thinkers and scientists who gave a power-

---

[1] *The Origin and Goal of History*, Routledge & Kegan Paul, 1953, p. 64.

ful stimulus to independent thinking and the growth of new ideas. Nothing like these groups was to be found in the traditional societies of Asia till the West began to assault and pull them down.

Thirdly, the ageing Asian societies were most vulnerable not in a political sense—the Mogul or Manchu power was strong enough for two centuries to throw out European intruders—but to the impact of the new economic power which came with the revolutionary system of transportation for conveying men and merchandise. The older land routes lay in the empty spaces of Asia and North Africa. Ideas, culture-forms, religions, and war bands traversed over them but there was little movement of merchandise in bulk. Transportation over water showed its definite superiority over land routes in every respect. The revolutionary changes in transportation could be better understood when we look to the transition from the period of the sailing ships to the era of power-driven ships, which were linked with railroads for the transport of bulk cargoes over land and water. The year 1878 marks a change in relation to the influence of transport not only on European economies but also in altering the balance of relations between different parts of the world. The decisive weight behind the economic power launched by the West from China to Peru was the revolution in transport. Its economic impact toppled over the bases of Asian societies on which their secular stability had rested from time immemorial.

India furnishes the classic example of the economic and social consequences of the European impact; with modifications here and there, it illustrates the general pattern for Asia. The traditional balance between agriculture and the village industries, already growing insecure, was destroyed. This balance had been sufficient to maintain the civilized life of Asian societies on a subsistence level in a static form for many centuries, viable enough to withstand internal political changes. Reincourt has shrewdly pointed out that 'quite unwittingly the British struck the Achilles' heel of the Indian Civilization and brought the Indian giant down to its knees'.[1] In support he quotes what an official of the East India Company said before a committee of Parliament in 1840:

India is as much a manufacturing country as an agriculturist; and he who seeks to reduce her to the position of an agricultural country seeks to lower her in the scale of civilization.

[1] *The Soul of India*, Jonathan Cape, pp. 208-9.

Western economic forces dealt a knockout blow, under the weight of which Asian societies reeled but luckily were not destroyed. This ultimately set the task for Asians, the task of transforming their traditional societies if they are to survive in the modern world. Except for Japan, no Asian society showed for long any awareness of this problem and the cultural adaptation required came slowly, if at all. The economic collision was something new in the experience of Asians, very different in character from the intrusion of the nomads or the impact of those harbingers of cultural and religious ideas from other far-off Asian lands.

III

We have noted that the period of European dominance from A.D. 1500 to 1750 was not of much consequence either to Asia or to Europe. If by accident of history the Europeans of this period had withdrawn from their settlements on the Asian coastlands they, would have left a few relics of historical curiosity, of antiquarian interest. The effective period of encounter must be reckoned as from 1750 to 1950, if it is to be seen in its proper perspective. This is necessary because, of late, there has been a noticeable tendency to dramatize the entire period of 450 years by imagining that Vasco da Gama and his followers suddenly wheeled out the course of history on to a new track and that this adventure came to an end precisely in 1950. The suggestion of such a neat ending to the da Gaman period is only an emotional reaction to the termination of a worldwide experience and the passing away with dramatic suddenness of that which was once great.

The da Gaman period, however, has a single theme of historic continuity. European dominance opened with a quarrel; it ended in a grand quarrel among the Europeans: that is the framework of the period of dominance. With the end of the medieval period the unity of Western Christendom broke up. The emerging nation states quarrelled among themselves in their competition for power on the oceans of the world. The Pope threw the apple of discord by dividing the world between Portugal and Spain; this intensified the quarrel over the possession of non-European territories. European expansionism overseas did not resolve or mitigate the quarrel in Europe itself; the exercise of international power by England in the nineteenth century moderated the quarrel over the mastery of Europe—first attempted by Napoleon from the West, then taken up by Germany in the twentieth century from Central Europe and now handed over to Soviet Russia in Eastern Europe. The two bloody European Civil Wars in this century have torn a ghastly rent in the seamless garment of the spirit of Europe, now divided politically and ideologically into East and West. The bewildered Asians, who had witnessed the Europeans coming as quarrelsome mariners, saw them depart, weakened but still quarrelling westerners. The continuing quarrel over the unresolved problem of a divided Europe is now dubbed the Cold War.

We must also put in perspective the unfinished business of the encounter of the last two centuries. We must adjust the time shutter, focus on selected regions of encounter and get a sharp picture of the response of the assaulted societies to the radiating effects of the intrusive, alien civilization of Europe. Japan alone was able to control her destiny. China was battered, humiliated, and, short of occupation of the whole country, subjected to colonial domination. With the nominal exception of Afghanistan, Tibet, and Thailand, India with all other countries in Asia came under colonial rule. The stage was thus set for an explosive encounter, the consequences of which no one understood, foresaw, much less cared for. In India, this modern encounter came under very different auspices and under vastly different circumstances from the encounters in Antiquity. In the past, the encounters with the West had occurred at the periphery of Indian civilization. The modern attack was from within, on the strongholds of Indian society, and was delivered on a vast front and in depth.

Europe completely usurped the political sovereignty of the colonized peoples by taking the place of the indigenous rulers. When finally the West abdicated, the ex-colonial peoples were left with the cruel choice of adopting Western forms of democracy and capitalism, or opting for Communism which was competing for their mind and allegiance as a new messianic faith, or of clinging to some form of neo-traditional authoritarianism. The economies of India and other colonial countries were at the time of independence still in a nineteenth-century state. As Barbara Ward has aptly pointed out,[1] Britain's impact on the Indian economy illustrates in the clearest and most sustained way the general rule that, outside the Atlantic area, Western colonialism and Western investment

---

[1] *India and the West*, Hamish Hamilton, 1961, p. 118.

launched but did not complete the process of 'economic modernization'. In politics as in economics, the encounter ended as a sad,
unfinished business. The resentment against the West stems
from it.

The political and economic history of the two centuries of
colonial overlordship with its sombre and dark patches of high-
handed chicanery, racialism, exclusion of indigenous peoples from
the seat of authority and power, economic exploitation—all these
tempered now and then, as in India, by homeopathic doses of
liberalism—haunts and will continue to haunt for years the minds
of men in Asia. A dying old order, a new one yet to emerge, im-
perfect and unfinished 'modernization', a voluminous charge
sheet against the West for its misdemeanours—encompassed in an
all-round frustration—may at first sight appear to be the sum total
of the encounter. Was it so ill-fated as to leave behind permanent
psychological barriers between Europe and Asia? We are too close
to the period just ended to give any categorical answer. There are
a few, hitherto neglected, aspects of the encounter, which may
suggest the trend for the future if not furnish an answer.

The memories of colonialism, at present dominant in the minds
of the ex-colonial peoples, will in course of time fade out. Already,
as in India, an assessment is being made of the heritage taken over
from the colonial period. European civilization would have remained parochial had not the maritime age carried it far beyond
the small area of European coastland and extended it to the
Americas and the Indian Ocean basin. India, the mainstay of the
far-flung British empire, incongruously became an outpost for the
interplay of ideas of the East and the West. In opting for Marxism,
the Chinese mind has found in the philosophic tradition of European thought a new connecting thread, a new orthodoxy to replace
the bankrupt Confucian civilization with a 'modernistic' way of
life. Marxism reached China by devious routes on land as Buddhism did in ancient times. It may be a Western heterodoxy but it
is definitely not an Eastern ideology or faith. Lenin once claimed
that Marxism is the legitimate inheritor of the best that humanity
created in the nineteenth century in the form of German philosophy, English political economy, and French socialism.

We must also note the consequence of the spiritual impact of the
West on Asia. It is pleasing to record that religious issues do not
divide Europe and Asia. The spiritual assault on the traditional

Asian societies by the Christian missions must be reckoned a failure. The Italian Jesuit, Robert de Nobili, failed in his attempts to convert the Brahmins of Madura in the stronghold of Hinduism in the South but the failure was amply compensated by his acquisition of Tamil and Telugu lore. By the middle of the eighteenth century the elaborate structure built up by the Jesuits in China from the days of Matteo Ricci was wrecked beyond repair. So complete was the failure of Christianity in China that a Western student was able to assess that by the middle of the twentieth century, barely one per cent of Chinese population was converted, most of it made up of 'rice Christians'. Right through the centuries, the wonderful tolerance and eclecticism of Asian faiths have enabled Asians to perceive the wide divergence between the professions of Christianity and its practice with all its political implications. It was a Mongol Khan, a nomad professing none of the great Asian religions, who expressed with great clarity the attitude of the Asian mind to Christianity, when he told the Franciscan friar, William Rubruck:

We Moals, we believe there is but one God. . . . Even as God has given several fingers to the hand, so has he given man several ways. God has made us know the Holy Scriptures, and your Christians do not observe them. You do not see in them that one should blame another, do you? . . . God has given you a Testament and you do not follow it; to us, he has given soothsayers, and we do what they tell us and we live peacefully.[1]

The failure of Christianity to subvert the traditional Asian faiths has left no rancour in the minds of Asians. The old cliché 'the East is spiritual, the West materialistic' holds no deep meaning. It was a convenient phrase for regaining self-respect and mustering strength to get even with the West. Christianity has exercised a subtle influence on the reformist movements within Hinduism and other Asian religions. For example, in India there is a generous appreciation of Christian ethics and the Christian ethos. Again, modern India is not contemptuous of devotion to material interests, nor does she now charge the West with having a low standard of values.

We must also note the result of the intellectual impact of the West which had dynamic, unanticipated, startling consequences in

[1] *Contemporaries of Marco Polo*, edited by Manuel Komroff, Jonathan Cape, 1928, pp. 179–80.

Asian societies. This now appears to be the central theme of the continuing encounter of the minds of East and West. The intellectual impact began when the curiosity of the servants of the East India Company led them to probe into the unknown and long-forgotten past of Indian civilization. The pioneering works of William Jones, 'Hindu' Stewart, Prinsep, Fergusson Cunningham —to mention a few outstanding names—revealed the great and rich legacy of India's past. Not only in India but all over Asia European historians, philologists, anthropologists, and archaeologists unravelled the long-forgotten past of Asian cultures by incessant digging, exploring, researching in the midst of trackless sands and humid jungles. Western scientists and scholars added new dimensions to past history and the great traffic in civilization in Asia. Their labours reawakened the dormant and garbled memories of the Asian past and began to light up the minds of the Asian peoples. These discoveries gripped their imagination and activated their thinking. The era of awakening began, and with it a reassessment of the baffling elements of the past and the present. A new pride and self-respect sprang up. Asian societies started, in the context of their own national traditions, on the memorable journey of uniting the memory of their past with the knowledge, thought, and ideas of the modern West. This process of cultural renewal and interaction is the key to the regeneration of Asian societies and their road to further development.

The West had unwittingly provided the key to the unlocking of the Eastern mind. Where were the instruments of change and how arose the leadership needed to innovate the change? Largely unnoticed, the forces of encounter furnished the answer. Under colonial rule, the local societies partially disintegrated and the traditional groups of elites—the Moslem mullah, the Brahmin priest, the Buddhist monk, the Chinese mandarin—were replaced by the intelligentsia drawn from a new middle class of Western-educated, secularistic elites, who assumed the leadership of a nationalist, modernist, revolutionary movement, opting for radical political and social reform and manipulating the politics of mass opinion and mass revolt. The intelligentsia is the most vital social group in all emerging Asian societies and it controls the levers of change and of government, be it democratic, communist, or some sort of military autocracy.

The immense output of scholarship in the studies of the past and of the contemporary history and civilization of Asia did not contribute to a better understanding in Europe of the mind of Asia. The West failed to bring about an effective interchange or a fruitful integration of ideas, let alone a new synthesis. No significant two-way traffic of ideas developed. Europe showed some interest in Asian languages, philology, comparative religions, and philosophies. The French were enthusiastic Sinologues; the Germans misappropriated some notions of Indian metaphysics to formulate their awe-inspiring philosophy of history. The British, supreme pragmatists wedded to a *laissez-faire* philosophy, preferred to 'rule the waves' and run a Traders' Empire. Generally, the interest of a European in the art and culture of the East was quite hubristic. He viewed them as the frozen elements of the past of a people who had entered upon a state of decadence.

It was taken as almost axiomatic that the 'unchanging East' was incapable of changing; at times it was grudgingly conceded that some changes over long decades may occur under European tutelage. Obsessed with their superior military power and their own achievements in science and technology, the Europeans were largely content to hold the ring and administer their vast possessions. They became static in their thinking at a time when Asians were renewing themselves in mind and spirit. The European rulers developed the mechanical mind of the controllers of society. The people whom they administered were often seen as no more than obstacles to the smooth functioning of the system. The rulers for the most part remained aloof from the common people and their regimes came to resemble the floating isle of Laputa (in *Gulliver's Travels*), which contained many admirable things but remained suspended far above the ordinary world.

With little or no contact of minds between Asians and Europeans, their intellectual separation was complete; they merely developed distorted images of themselves and in relation to each other. For most Europeans, Asia remained an unreal world, sometimes a romantic conception, more often a great distortion, popularly an exotic myth; there arose many fashions in European images of Asian lands. The revolting Asians did not hesitate to turn against Europeans their own ideas and institutions, which were sometimes even perverted to serve the ends of nationalism. Asians refused to recognize or see any heroic image of Europe. Instead, they shaped in their minds a species of villainous images of the West. Europeans for their part detested with passion all those Asians who threatened Europe's precarious superiority by turning its weapons against itself.

IV

Between Europe and the non-Communistic parts of Asia there is no iron or bamboo curtain. There are, however, quite obstinate types of psychological barriers, largely the product of the colonial period. The barriers in a concrete form are represented by the images developed both by Europeans and by Asians in the course of the historic association between Asia and Europe in the modern world. These images are numerous—some persistent, a lot more ephemeral, a few notorious and now debunked by scholars, others have lost their excitement with the passing away of colonial rule, a few continue to rankle and irritate. Imperialist myopia, pride, and prejudice warped the European mind and projected a series of distorted images of Asian societies—of a 'fatalistic' peasantry, a 'rootless' intelligentsia, 'debilitating' religions, cultural 'stagnation' and 'fragmentation'. On the other hand, Asian nationalism too has created its own myths. The minds of many Asian intellectuals are still dominated by the tormenting question of their national status in the modern world. Asian elites will not get over their present uneasiness of mind until they are creative and not reproductive of Western thought and until they can create true images of their own authentic cultures. Internal stresses—rather than external political and economic pressures—are at present causing Asian intellectuals to be ambivalent, confused, dissatisfied with themselves, critical of the world outside.

The plain truth is that Asian societies in transition are still under the dominance of the cultural hegemony of the West and of its scientific knowledge and technology. Hurried attempts are under way to find Western solutions to the problems of Asian development; prefabricated Western political and economic structures, divorced from their roots, are being transplanted. A few may be assimilated; many others will have to undergo transformation over long periods before they become indigenous. In place of the old political imbalance between Asia and Europe it is now apparent there is a cultural imbalance. Self-sustaining intellectual independence and social transformation are intertwined problems.

They assist each other in achieving the desired end and when the changes are completed Asian images of Europe, shaped in the days of the unfinished business of encounter, will have faded away. By then Europe, chastened by the new experience of living together on terms of equality with Asian peoples, will have cast away those horrid old imperialist images, become more receptive to the best in Asian cultures, and found a healthy balanced relation in a few universal ideas which may be the new links between the Western and Eastern peoples of the globe.

Will Europe retain with the loss of political power—which in any event was short-lived, ephemeral, exotically romantic—its power to influence the minds of Asians by sharing with them the best in its own traditions? If by good fortune or accident of history the Indian bridgehead were to survive, there is a possibility that some important 'western' values which Indians prize as their own may radiate outward into the non-communistic, non-European world. Civil liberties, individual initiative, the art of compromise born out of a sceptical temper, a concern for limits, a few fundamental attributes of a modern, democratic way of life—such as a free press, an independent judiciary, the rule of law—these are precious to all those in Asia and Europe who see the merits of a truly free and open society.

There are many imponderables in the modern encounter of minds between Europe and Asia which began under strange and unpropitious circumstances in the maritime age of world history. Certainly the encounter will continue—for how long we cannot tell—in our present world, now united forcibly by science and technology and made interdependent, however much Europeans and Asians alike may struggle to be exclusive, isolationist, and aggressively nationalistic.

III. THE HISTORICAL CONTEXT OF ENCOUNTERS BETWEEN ASIA AND EUROPE

as seen by a European

Geoffrey Hudson

The European image of Asia was first formed by the Greeks; geographically it represented not the modern geographer's division of continents at the Urals, but the contrast between the western and eastern sides of the Aegean Sea. To the north of the Black Sea there was no significant difference in the fifth century B.C. between the tribal peoples of Asia and Europe, except that desert conditions existed east of the Volga enforcing a greater degree of nomadism than on the Dnieper or the Danube. But in the Aegean there was a confrontation of the vast Persian empire, extending from the coast of Anatolia eastward to the Indus and southward to Upper Egypt, and the numerous small Greek city states of European Greece and the Aegean islands. The contrast was one not only of size but of political institutions; the Persian empire was governed by an autocratic monarch residing in Susa or Persepolis in southern Iran and administered by a bureaucracy of permanent officials with 'satraps' appointed from the centre as governors of provinces, while the Greek cities were republics, with their government carried on by citizen assemblies and councils and elected magistrates.

It was natural that the Greek mind should be deeply impressed by the antithesis between the Hellenic republican *Kleinstaaterei* and the immense dominion of the Achaemenid dynasty, the more so because of the dramatic clash between the two ways of life produced by the attempt of Xerxes to conquer Greece. The story is told in the pages of Herodotus, who celebrates the successful resistance offered by the European Greeks—the Greek cities on the Asian side of the Aegean having fallen under Persian rule—but there is no disdain for Persian power in his narrative, and indeed the Greeks regarded this mighty political structure with respect, and even with awe, in spite of their refusal to submit to its domination. We have no equivalent records of what the Persians thought of the Greeks during this period, but we can be sure that Persian satraps considered that the little Greek states with their frequent wars and internal revolutions would be better off under the orderly imperial administration of the *Pax Persica*. They had a right to be proud of it, for its creation had been a marvellous administrative achievement; it had taken over the smaller, though already massive, state organizations of Babylon and Egypt, and united a larger area under a single government than any state before it.

In the perspective of world history the political trend represented by Achaemenid Persia was far more normal than that which gave rise to the institutions of ancient Athens and Sparta, Syracuse and Rome. Indeed the Greek city-republic may be regarded as a mutation in political evolution, establishing itself as a type only because of very exceptional conditions. The normal course of political development, corresponding to the spread of intensive agriculture and the growth of towns, was from tribe to kingdom and from kingdom to the amalgamation of kingdoms in a large-scale monarchical empire. This kind of development took place in the Nile valley and in the Fertile Crescent of western Asia, in India and China, and in a completely separate environment, in Mexico and Peru; it took place also in Europe, but restricted and modified in various ways by Greco-Roman republican traditions.

The geographical and economic base of the typical large-scale monarchical state was a large plain or continuous area of cultivated land providing revenue to support a corps of professional soldiers and officials through whom the royal power was maintained and extended. The foundations of such a society in an age before mechanized industry and transport can only be agrarian and the ruling class one of landlords, civil and military officials, and priests; merchants may be numerous and wealthy, but their social and political position will be secondary and they will be regarded by the government primarily as objects of taxation. Only if a city devoted to commerce is an independent state and a republic can a mercantile class adapt its laws and policies to their needs. The city-

E

republic is thus essential as a political form for the rise of a capitalist economy, and in fact it was in the independent or semi-independent cities of late medieval Europe that modern capitalism was born. But although some kind of city-state or municipal autonomy is a necessary political condition for the successful development of a capitalist economic system, the city-state does not necessarily produce it, and the ancient Greek city did not do so on any significant scale. Lack of space forbids consideration here of the historical question why it was in medieval Florence, Genoa, and Venice rather than in ancient Athens, Corinth, and Rhodes that a system of genuine capitalist enterprises was engendered. It is sufficient to point out the fact that the considerable commercial activity of ancient Greece and Italy ended in stagnation and decline, whereas the late medieval revival of trade led on through an increasing economic growth towards the industrial revolution of modern Europe.

The encounter between Europe and Asia of which Herodotus wrote was succeeded by another a century and a half later, in which the European and not the Asian was the invader. Xerxes had failed to conquer Greece, but Alexander the Great overran the Persian empire from end to end and stopped his eastward march only when his troops mutinied in the Punjab. This was no longer, however, a victory of the Greek city-states; Macedon, although Greek, was a mainland kingdom, and Alexander's generals, who inherited his conquests, adopted the manners and methods of the Persian autocracy. 'Hellenistic' rule continued in what had been the Mediterranean littoral provinces of the Persian empire—Anatolia, Syria, Palestine, and Egypt, and the whole region was afterwards incorporated in the Roman Empire; there was extensive Greek settlement, but except in Anatolia the bulk of the population remained non-Greek in language and culture. The influence of Greek civilization was more pervasive in Italy and Western Europe, and in the Roman ascendancy the republican principle reasserted itself, for Rome subdued all the lands around the Mediterranean while still remaining a city-state. But Rome failed to consolidate her empire on this basis; the republic gave way to the autocratic rule of the emperors, who created a vast imperial bureaucracy on models derived from Egypt and Persia through the Hellenistic kingdoms. By the time of Constantine the state system of the Roman Empire bore a far greater resemblance to that of Xerxes than to the institutions of Periclean Athens or Cicero's Rome. The empire had indeed been 'orientalized', and this was because the city-republic, with all its vigour of political life, was not a form fitted to provide a central government for a territory extending from the Atlantic to the Euphrates.

With Constantine the Roman Europe was 'orientalized' in another way also; it accepted a religion spreading from Palestine and derived from the religious traditions of Semitic Asia. Christianity was an Asian faith, quite alien in its origins to Greece and Rome, although the Gospels were written in Greek and their teaching was carried to all parts of the Roman Empire. Finally Christianity became the state religion of the empire and was propagated also beyond the boundaries of the empire in northern Europe. But in the seventh century it was confronted with a formidable rival derived from the same Hebraic origin; Islam, spreading from Arabia with the power of Arab armies, cut off Syria, Egypt, and North Africa from the Roman Empire and won over Persia, which under the Arsacid and Sassanid dynasties had been since the time of Julius Caesar the most important independent neighbour of the Roman world. From Persia the ascendancy of Islam later extended north of the Caucasus and up the Volga, so that the domain of the religion of Muhammad came to enclose that of Christianity to the south and east. As a result of the territorial expansion of the two rival religions, the division between them came to coincide roughly with that between Europe and Asia. Christian communities survived in Asia—the Greeks of Anatolia, the Maronites of Syria, the Georgians and Armenians—and the Moslem Turks established themselves in the Balkans from the fourteenth century onwards, but broadly speaking Christianity became the religion of Europe while Islam prevailed in western Asia.

Christendom and Islam were sharply divided; each claimed to have the only true divine revelation and was identified with a number of secular governments which made religious and political conflicts frequently coincide; the Moslem *jehad* was answered by the Christian zeal of the Crusades and of the reconquest of Spain. The division was also one of language and cultural tradition, for Christendom used Greek and Latin as its main ecclesiastical languages, while Arabic was the sacred tongue of Islam. But with all their differences of belief and hostile confrontation the Christians and Moslems of the Middle Ages belonged to one world; they had far more in common with each other in their inheritance of ideas and outlook on life than either had with ancient or modern Europe. They had more in common with each other also than they had with Hindus, Buddhists, or Confucian Chinese; if emphasis is laid on the common element of Hebraic monotheism in Christianity and Islam, then the significant division is not between Asia and Europe, but between the ex-Hebraic religious domain and the cultural regions to the east of it—a frontier which stood somewhere near the Khyber Pass in the tenth century but shifted eastwards to Bengal with the Moslem conquest of northern India.

What caused Christendom, or rather Europe, to diverge increasingly from the world of Islam and later to classify it along with India and China as 'Oriental' or 'Asiatic' was not Christian theology or the spirit of the Crusades, but the dynamic development of a new economic system in Western Europe towards the end of the Middle Ages, particularly in northern Italy and the Low Countries. As already mentioned, modern capitalism originated in the city-republics of late medieval Europe. The vigour of these urban units was in striking contrast to the failure of medieval Europe to produce any large centrally governed state to replace the Roman Empire. Although the ideal of a universal monarchy corresponding to a universal Church persisted through the Middle Ages, there was no restoration of imperial unity. The attempts of Charlemagne and the Ottos to revive it ended in failure; Italy completely disintegrated and Germany was broken up. At the end of the fifteenth century there was no Christian European state which could compare in territorial extent with the Ottoman Empire. The *Kleinstaaterei* of late medieval Europe was not, however, a symptom of economic backwardness nor was it a consequence of the tribal particularism of the Teutonic invaders of the Roman Empire; on the contrary, it flourished most in the areas of highest economic development, and in Italy the independent cities partitioned the area which had been ruled as a unit by the Lombard kings.

The economic activity of these cities ushered in a new epoch of world history, but there was no sharp break, nor was it immediately apparent that Europe was drawing ahead of Asia in the production of wealth and in military and naval power. Around the year 1400 it was Asia that was encroaching on Europe rather than the opposite; the Ottoman Turks had overrun the Balkans in the fourteenth century and in 1453 they captured Constantinople and made it their capital. Russia had emancipated herself from the Tatar yoke, but the Tatars still held Astrakhan, Kazan, and the Crimea. Even on the sea Asia was formidable, for the Ottomans created a powerful navy in the eastern Mediterranean and later on took Cyprus and Crete from the Venetians. Asia at that time probably had more than three times the population of Europe, for not only did it have a far larger total area of cultivated land, but the wet rice agriculture of India, China, and South-east Asia supported a greater density of population in an essentially agrarian economy. The volume of commerce was as great, or greater, in Persia, India, and China, and the material standards of living in their cities at least as high as in Europe. Even in technology and in the natural sciences associated with it—the field in which Europe was soon to achieve a decisive superiority—there were no marked differences of attainment at the beginning of the fifteenth century. Nor was there any European consciousness of superiority in material civilization over the peoples of Asia. Marco Polo and other European travellers who journeyed through Asia in the period of the great Mongol Empire show no such sense of elevation; they were deeply impressed by the power and wealth of the principal Asian countries, and especially by China. As Christians they believed in the exclusive truth of their own religion, but in the secular sphere they were not aware of having any advantage over 'unbelievers'.

There was nevertheless an impetus of technological development, linked with the rise of commercial capitalism in Western Europe, which was to put the European ahead, first of all in navigation and sea-power and the transport required for the expansion of long-distance maritime trade. It was the kingdoms of Portugal and Spain and not the Italian or Flemish cities which promoted the voyaging round Africa to India and the Far East—and incidentally explored the Americas—but behind their policies there was the money of Florence and Antwerp and the seamanship of the Genoese, who were the creators of the Portuguese navy. A sign of the times was the production of the portolan charts—maps for seamen superior to any that had been made before. Along with the new arts of navigation, which early in the sixteenth century brought about the first circumnavigation of the globe, went the development of the new power of naval gunnery. With their well-armed ships the Portuguese not only reached India and Indonesia by oceanic voyages but drove the Arab merchants out of the lucrative spice trade which they had formerly controlled and which had transmitted pepper, cinnamon, cloves, and nutmegs to Europe by way of the Red Sea and Egypt.

The naval supremacy established by the Portuguese in the Indian Ocean in the opening years of the sixteenth century passed from them to other European nations, but it was never seriously challenged by an Asian power until a Japanese fleet passed through the Straits of Malacca in 1942. This failure to counter the ascendancy of European sea-power maintained at such a vast distance from the European homelands was symptomatic of the agrarian-mindedness of the principal Asian states and of the indifference of their royal courts and governing classes to the interests of maritime trade. The European ascendancy on the sea was based on a combination of good shipbuilding, seamanship, navigational science, artillery fire-power, commercial enterprise, and adequate financial backing for the maintenance of all this capability; to have driven the Europeans from their coasts the Asian kingdoms would have had to promote the same kind of development. But their social and political institutions as well as their prevailing ideological outlook were against it. Their resources were spent on their armies in which feudal cavalry were the predominant element; navies were secondary and usually neglected elements in the power of the state. The merchants had little or no political power to engage the policies of the royal courts on their behalf; the rulers found it as profitable to derive revenue from customs duties on foreign traders in their ports as from taxing the profits of the commerce of their own subjects. Moreover, with the consolidation of the great religions of Asia on scholastic lines, the social status of the mercantile class tended to become more and more depressed. During the first millennium A.D. there had been far-ranging Indian commercial enterprise, but in later centuries the doctrine that travellers incurred ritual pollution by crossing the sea was a disincentive to voyaging; Islam had no such teaching, but the intense conservatism of the Moslem clergy from the fourteenth century onwards was adverse to any social change. In China Confucian theory ranked the merchant lower than not only the scholar-official but also the peasant and the artisan. In Europe it was a long time before the bourgeoisie found an ideology which adequately justified its activities, but by the end of the Middle Ages, the burghers were already too powerful to care much what the theologians thought of them; it was in societies where they lacked self-governing political institutions that unfavourable religious and social theories were effective in reducing the self-esteem and self-reliance of the merchant class.

As yet it was only on the sea that the Europeans prevailed; on land the Ottoman, Persian, Mogul, and Chinese armies were still too formidable to be challenged by the very small numbers of soldiers which the European maritime powers could bring round Africa to the southern and eastern coasts of Asia. On Asia's western front—although Turkish sea-power in the Mediterranean declined during the sixteenth century—the Ottoman Empire continued to be feared as a military power; its troops overran Hungary early in the sixteenth century and laid siege to Vienna as late as 1668. The Portuguese Empire in Asia in the sixteenth century consisted of scattered outposts on the mainland littoral or offshore islands—Goa in India, Ormuz off the coast of Persia, Malacca in the Malay peninsula, and Macao in China. The first three had been taken by force; Macao was given by China in consideration of Portuguese services in suppressing piracy, but as Portugal's capacity to do this was due to her naval efficiency, this was also an indirect outcome of her sea-power. It was not until the middle of the eighteenth century that, as a result of the evolution of firearms and disciplined infantry tactics in Europe, European land forces began to have a superiority over Asian armies comparable to that which European warships had had in Asian seas since 1500. But at a much earlier date some would-be empire builders had dreamed of major territorial conquests in Asia. In 1585 a Spanish official in the Philippines, which by this time had been brought under Spanish rule, estimated that China, or at least the maritime provinces, could be conquered by an army of 5,000 Spaniards; in the following year the Governor, not quite so optimistic, reported that it would need 10,000 or 12,000 men from Spain and an equal number of Filipino and Japanese mercenaries. But the troops required were never forthcoming, and China remained undisturbed by European arms—except for some skirmishing with the Russians in the remote borderlands of Siberia—until the second quarter of the nineteenth century.

With the arrival of the Dutch and English in Indian and Far Eastern waters the drive of the new capitalist economy behind

European sea-power became more clearly apparent, for Asia was now confronted with chartered trading companies which had their own armed forces and territorial jurisdiction. Groups of merchants behaving as organized political powers with the attributes of governments were a new phenomenon in Asia, and the bewilderment caused by these mysterious collective authorities among Asian peoples was manifest in the attempt to personify them as 'John Company'—a name applied to both the Dutch and the English East India Companies. The Dutch East India Company gradually extended its rule over Indonesia, while the English becames upreme in India in the period of political confusion there following the disintegration of the Mogul Empire.

By the end of the eighteenth century it was obvious that Europe had in general an advantage over Asia both in economic efficiency and in naval and military power. This superiority increased greatly during the nineteenth century. Some Asian countries fell under European rule and became 'colonies' of European nations, though without substantial ethnic settlement from Europe except in Siberia; others remained independent, but became so weak militarily and so bound economically by Western financial power that they were reduced to a 'semi-colonial' status.

The increasing ascendancy of the West produced changes of outlook among both Europeans and Asians. Europeans tended to assume attitudes towards Asians which varied from condescending patronage to arrogant contempt. The sense of superior power and efficiency was reinforced among the more highly educated classes in Europe by an interpretation of history which showed Europeans from ancient times as inherently superior to 'Orientals' and 'Asiatics'. Literary education was in the Greek and Latin classics or in the literature of modern European languages; history was European history with the histories of Asian peoples as unimportant sideroads which were destined to become dead ends with the prevalence of Western civilization throughout the world. Criticism by canons of judgement narrowly framed in accordance with European achievements found the philosophy, literature, and art of Asian countries to be of relatively little value. It was indeed natural for Europeans to be preoccupied with their own civilization, and they were no more so than traditionally educated Persians, Hindus, or Chinese, but since they had become so predominant in wealth and power, their estimate of themselves con-

ditioned their whole approach to Asian peoples, whether in diplomacy, colonial administration, religious missions, or philanthropic
activities.

In thus emphasizing the sense of all-round and inherent
superiority—sometimes combined with a belief in the 'white race'
as a superior breed of mankind—we should not, however, forget
the minority of Europeans in the East at all periods who developed
a strong respect or admiration for Eastern peoples and their cultures either from living among them or from studies as Oriental
scholars. The scholarly studies began with the Jesuits and developed greatly in the nineteenth century, both in European and
American universities and among 'amateurs'. They were of great
significance because they brought to bear on the literature,
history, and institutions of Eastern countries the methods of
scientific criticism and analysis first developed for European
studies, and thus served later on to assist Asian scholars in the
knowledge and understanding of their own past. But the Western
contribution to Oriental scholarship in the nineteenth century,
important as it was in itself, should not be over-estimated as a
factor in shaping the normal European attitude towards the
Orient. In the first place, many 'Orientalists' were far from sympathetic towards their own subjects; although they became
eminently learned in their fields of study, they retained strong
prejudices, whether of religious or secular origin, against Eastern
modes of thought and feeling, and their adverse judgements could
be quoted as justification for the unlearned responses of ordinary
Western residents or travellers. Further, even those Orientalists
who had a deep and sympathetic understanding of Asian civilizations could have little influence on general education in their own
countries; they were academic specialists with only infinitesimal
numbers of pupils, whereas the minds of the vast majority of
educated people were formed by European classical and historical
studies in which the East had no place except for occasional armed
encounters in which the West normally had the better of it.

In the early part of the eighteenth century, there was a temporary cult of *chinoiserie* in Europe which was nourished on the
one hand by imports of Chinese porcelain, textiles, and lacquer
goods through maritime trade with China, and on the other by a
considerable knowledge of Chinese institutions and ideas transmitted by the Jesuits, who were the first European 'sinologues'. In

European art the fashion for Chinese decorative art was a major factor in the evolution of the rococo style; in political philosophy Confucianism as a secular religion without divine revelation or priestcraft made a strong appeal to European advocates of an anti-clerical *despotisme éclairé* as the ideal method of government. But this admiration for China soon waned and disappeared with the French Revolution; the rococo style was superseded by revived classicism or neo-Gothic, while dissidence from medieval traditions in Europe took the form of democratic liberalism and no longer craved for an enlightened monarch.

In the nineteenth century there was again a cultural attraction of the East for certain European intellectuals, but it was far less influential than the *chinoiserie* of the eighteenth and was of a very different kind. Whereas the pioneers of the Enlightenment in Europe saw in China a model of a well-ordered secular and humanist civilization to be set against Christian Europe, no part of Asia could any longer make such an appeal in the nineteenth century, and it was the mystical and pantheistic elements in Asian traditional cultures which exerted an influence on minds dissatisfied with Christian orthodoxy but even more hostile to the increasing vogue of scientific materialism in the Western world. In this context it was India rather than China that attracted attention, and in China it was no longer Confucianism but Taoism that aroused interest—an interest which has persisted to the present day as manifest in the extraordinary number of translations of the *Tao tê ching* which have appeared in various European languages. Yet all this concern with Eastern religions during the nineteenth century—often mixed with a less reputable taste for supposed occult marvels and magic—was marginal and unrepresentative. The most that it achieved was to contribute to the science of comparative religion and to encourage among some people in the West the idea that all religions were different paths leading to the same goal.

Christian religious missions played a considerable part in relations between the West and Asia during the nineteenth century. The religious factor was different from what it had been in the Middle Ages or even in the sixteenth century; Crusades were out of date and the Christian churches no longer had the dominant position in European society and cultural life that they had once enjoyed. On the other hand, there was a revival of Christian missionary activity early in the nineteenth century and the superior power of European states enabled it to take advantage in various ways of a secular protection. In India, where the early penetration of the East India Company was inspired by commercial or strategic motives unmixed with thoughts of religious conversion, the English Evangelical Revival was reflected in a considerable support by some of the Company's servants for Christian religious propaganda from about 1820 onwards. In so far as this was closely linked with an increased sense of responsibility for the welfare of the people who were now under British rule, it had its beneficial aspect even in a purely secular context; but the belief which became widespread among both Hindus and Moslems that it was British policy to convert them to Christianity by any available means was a major factor in bringing about the Indian Mutiny of 1857, and this experience caused the British Raj in India to be thereafter scrupulously careful in avoiding religious discrimination. Such impartiality was never the rule with the French in Indo-China, where the French colonial empire owed its foundation to intervention on behalf of persecuted Catholic missions, and the religious cleavages accentuated by a pro-Catholic colonial administration continued after the end of French rule in persecutions of Catholics by Communists and of Buddhists by Catholics. In China, where a government which had claimed the right to suppress religious propaganda subversive of the established order was compelled by the superior power of Western states to tolerate Christian missions, not only the missionaries but also their Chinese converts came to be under the protection of foreign governments, so that there were cases of Chinese who became converts because of the legal advantage they obtained in dealings with their own officials.

It was an inevitable consequence of such support from Western secular power that Asian nationalist movements were often hostile to the Christian religion. The influence of the missions was nevertheless far-reaching and not to be estimated by the number of their formal converts; apart from their religious preaching, they founded hospitals, schools, and even universities, which became centres for the diffusion of Western science and political and social ideas. The missionaries were frequently men and women of the highest character and dedication to their task, who rendered great services to the countries in which they sought to propagate their faith. But their attitude towards traditional Asian cultures was often highly prejudiced and intolerant, and in order to raise funds for their work in their own homelands they tended to emphasize the darkest features of the non-Christian Asian scene, thereby confirming the ordinary European in his conviction that he enjoyed a decisive moral as well as material superiority over Oriental peoples.

The Asian responses to the ascendancy of the West were of two kinds. On the one hand, the adherents of traditional civilizations resisted Western influence, but could not keep it out because their lack of power denied them the very means of doing so; even when they had not become subjects of Western colonial governments, they had to admit Western traders, travellers, and missionaries within their borders. Since they could not challenge Western power except by social and cultural changes which they were unwilling to contemplate, they had only the choice between futile gestures of opposition like the Boxer rising in China or compromises with the West, which caused them to be regarded as collaborators by ardent nationalists. On the other hand, the nationalists, who sought to end colonial or semi-colonial subjection by acquiring the science, technology, and political organization of the West, got themselves into the paradoxical position of denouncing the West as the invader and oppressor of their countries while at the same time adopting Western ways of life and repudiating the whole past heritage of their own cultures.

The iconoclasm of revolutionaries in any society who seek to change ancient ways is rendered much more destructive if the impulse to transformation does not come spontaneously from within the society, but is derived from outside it, and this is particularly unsuitable for a patriotic movement, since a patriotism without pride in the national past can hardly be emotionally satisfying. Hence the varied attempts of revolutionary movements in Asia in recent times to come to terms with the Asian past and to reconcile 'westernization' with an independence that is not only political and economic, but also spiritual and cultural. In the process of these adjustments it has been difficult for Asians to accept a historical image of European civilization that is not distorted by continuing resentments and feelings of injury and wounded self-esteem. The collapse of the Western empires during the last two decades and the achievement of 'decolonization' almost everywhere has not automatically brought to an end the antagonisms arising out of the relations imposed in the era of European ascend-ancy, especially as Asia in general has been left with acute problems of over-population and standards of economic productivity and consumption so much lower than those of the West.

For a new understanding between Asia and Europe, there is need of a mutual comprehension in terms not only of current political and economic issues but also of past history. The feelings of superiority engendered in the West and of resentment created in the East in the two centuries of Western ascendancy between 1750 and 1950 can only be resolved in a sense of common humanity and world inheritance, through a concept of genuinely inclusive world-history which will both inform the specialized studies of historians and also be diffused through education in all countries. There will still be plenty of room for controversies on particular issues within such a framework, but the framework is essential, for until there is general acceptance of the principle that a civilized man ought to have a comprehensive idea of the whole past history of mankind, and not merely of his own country or even continent, there will continue to be a 'glass curtain' between Europe and Asia.

CHANGING ATTITUDES

It is worse than futile for the Oriental to pose within the cloak of Eastern dignity, to trade upon a past reputation, while at the same time greedily assimilating the very Western weaknesses he affects to despise and condemn. Let him hold fast to what is best . . . in the history of his people and . . . while retaining his self-respect, the more surely win the respect of his Western neighbours. Equally, the Western should abandon an attitude as stupidly inconsistent as that which demands from his Oriental neighbour conformity to his own ideals of propriety, while denying him every facility and encouragement.

The only lesson to be learnt is that East and West are no more than names. Human beings are the same everywhere. He who wants to will conduct himself with decency. There is no people for whom the moral life is a special mission. Everything depends on the individual himself.

If we look into the future, is it not a heritage that we have to leave to posterity, that all the different races commingle and produce a civilization that perhaps the world has not yet seen? There are difficulties and mis-understandings, but I do believe . . . 'we shall know each other better when the mists have rolled away'.

MAHATMA GANDHI

IV. THE GREEKS AND
THE WEST

John Campbell and Philip Sherrard

One of the difficulties in discussing Greek attitudes in the context of this symposium lies in establishing the identity of the Greeks themselves. As a national political entity Greece has only existed for slightly over a century. Prior to that there has been no Greek state, politically speaking, unless one makes exception for the degree of political coherence conferred by the Macedonians on the ancient Greek city-state world during the relatively brief period which followed on the conquest of Greek territories by Philip II of Macedon. Thus it cannot simply be their participation in a political entity that defines the existence of the Greeks. Nor do they represent a distinct racial entity. Indeed, the Greeks are perhaps the most mixed of European peoples (the admixture including, it must be remembered, peoples of non-European stock); and one of the most remarkable facts of Greek history has been the capacity of the Greek *milieu* to absorb, and to preserve its identity through, an almost uninterrupted series of invasions, racial, political, and cultural.

This last fact may indeed give one a clue to the historical identity of the Greeks—an identity which, we have said, is by no means limited to a political, racial, or *a fortiori*, territorial boundary. Except for the strictly modern period (though even here the exception is not unqualified), the existence of the Greeks has depended more on the sharing of a certain *milieu*, almost a state of mind, than on anything else. To say this may appear merely to beg the question: for if this is the case, then what defines the *milieu*?

Here the first thing to be said is that this *milieu* is not a static affair—not the consequence of an ideology established in some supposedly 'Golden Age' (generally identified where Greece is

F

concerned with the classical age) and continually preserved despite the many apparent changes and contradictions of history. The myth of the 'eternal Greece', of '*le miracle grec*', is one of the more inept and persistent inventions of the classical-minded European. Rather one must regard this *milieu* as in itself something that undergoes transformations; that is enriched by the addition of certain elements, impoverished by the loss of others; that has its times of fruition and times of dearth. But changes occur not through a complete break with the existing form of a certain period, but through the development of some of the possibilities latent in that form and the exclusion of others. And one of the ways in which the changing historical form of this *milieu* may be indicated is precisely through the attempt to grasp how its characteristics are reflected in the changing attitudes of its participants (the Greeks) to their western and eastern neighbours; for these attitudes will in their turn reflect what at any particular time constitutes the dominant ideas or values that define the *milieu* itself.

Where ancient Greece is concerned, the familiar distinction is that between Greeks and barbarians. At first this does not appear to have had any political or national significance. Thucydides notes that in the Homeric poems allusion is made to Danaans, Argives, Achaeans, while the words 'Greek' and 'Greeks' are merely topographical denominations defining a group of people in the district of Thessaly. On the other hand, the word *barbarophonoi* does occur in Homer. Thus, in so far as the barbarians are distinguished at all it is in virtue of their non-Greek language: 'barbarian' has originally only a linguistic connotation and indicates those who do not speak the Greek language; and indeed the consciousness of possessing a common Greek language has been one of the most important factors defining the Greek *milieu* from the time of Homer down to the present day.

The attribution of a political or national significance to what was primarily a linguistic distinction was greatly encouraged by, if not directly the result of, the emergence to the East and West of the ancient Greek city-state world of new and challenging power blocs. The confused, amorphous, disorganized barbarian (non-Greek-speaking) world began to take political (and non-Greek) shape in the form of two nations. In the East, Cyrus, Cambyses, and Darius absorbed and organized the Near Eastern world, including

Egypt, into the Persian Empire; while in the West, Carthage, a city of sailors and merchants, grew into the commercial rival of the Greek city-states in Italy, with particular reference to Sicily. To the formation of these national 'imperial' threats Greece opposed a world of city-states living in a habitual state of egotism and discord. Until now there had been, we have noted, no explicit Greek consciousness of forming a people spiritually and culturally distinct from other peoples living to the East or West: indeed, it must be remembered here that, as in the Byzantine world through Orthodox Christianity, so in the ancient world through Orphism, the teachings of Pythagoras and other pre-Socratics, Greece was linked spiritually and culturally to the East; and it may be added in passing that the attempt to turn away from, or to deny, this eastern heritage has always implied for Greece a cheapening and coarsening of spiritual and cultural values.

Greek imperialism, or colonization, had been the result of the action of individual city-states, not a collective enterprise. The geographical conformation of Greece, its poverty, its lack of rivers and hinterland, while they fostered the growth of local autonomous communities, made the organization of any united political or imperial structure difficult. Greek civilization in the ancient period was the product of a variety of local human communities established in an equally great variety of geographical settings: politically speaking, there were Aetolians, Achaeans, Arcadians, Spartans, Argives, Athenians; but not Greeks. Now, however, in response to pressures from East and West a true Greek consciousness began to develop, although it must be remembered that this was still due to a sense of sharing common cultural and linguistic values rather than to a sense of a common nationality; and that it in no way inhibited the internecine political rivalries of the city-states.

Thus by the end of the classical period the distinction between Greek and barbarian had become, in the Greek mind, far more than a matter of language; it was now felt to be based upon the participation of the city-states in a common framework of superior cultural values which the barbarian world did not share. Already Herodotus, in spite of his interest in and admiration for Persia, Egypt, and Greece's other eastern neighbours, can remark that the Hellenic race has been distinguished since ancient times from the barbarians by its superior cleverness and its freedom from childish folly. And later: 'When could the barbarian race ever be friend to the Hellenes?' asks one of Euripides' characters; and the answer is: 'It never could be'. Or again, also spoken by one of Euripides' characters: 'It is right for Hellenes to rule barbarians, not for barbarians to rule Hellenes'. More generally, Plato could write: 'The Hellenic people are one family, related among themselves, but foreign to and unlike the barbarians'. Hellenism, a *milieu* of common cultural values, had been born. Its development made the Macedonians' task of destroying the city-states and their secular institutions and of creating a political unity based on a pan-hellenic consciousness of common cultural standards a practical proposition; while it was the sense of the superiority of these standards over those of the barbarian world that provided the ideological justification of the imperial conquests of Alexander the Great—conquests which issued in the spread of Hellenism and its values over the entire Middle East.

Hellenism, product originally of local Greek city-states, has now become an international cultural currency, to be acquired (cf. Isocrates) by means of an 'Athenian' education. But in the process of becoming international not only has it lost its local Greek roots; it has also lost its particular Greek religious attachments (the number and variety of gods and cults in the Hellenistic world are beyond reckoning). It might indeed be said that Hellenism has itself become a religion—or rather has become the so-called cultured person's substitute for religion. This means that it cuts across not only political and racial, but also religious, boundaries. It means in addition that from now on one has to make a distinction between 'Greek' and 'Hellenic', the first indicating a people, or peoples, dwelling within a certain territorial area and normally speaking the Greek language, the second indicating an international cultural tradition. From this point of view, one can be a Greek without being 'Hellenic', and one can be a 'Hellene' without being Greek. After their conquest of the Hellenistic world the Romans became 'hellenized'. They did not become Greeks. The Greeks on the other hand, or rather those that occupied the geographical area of continental Greece, ceased, after the Roman conquest and particularly after the subsequent Slav invasions, to be 'Hellenic'. In a sense, they were indeed barbarians—i.e. outside the orbit of the cultural tradition of Hellenism, until their assimilation to the Byzantine world between the ninth and eleventh centuries.

In considering the Byzantine Greeks this last distinction is important. The Empire, particularly after the time of the Emperor Heraclius in the seventh century, may have come to possess an increasingly strong element of Greek culture, but it was not Hellenic. It is true that by maintaining the study of the ancient Greek language and literature it preserved Hellenism through the medieval period, as it retained the Hellenistic distinction between Hellene and barbarian. But Byzantium, as a Christian Empire, was an enemy of Hellenism, and throughout its history regarded the philosophical, religious, and moral conceptions of antiquity with hostility—a hostility symbolized by Justinian's closing of the School at Athens. For the Byzantines, Hellenism is paganism and polytheism; and even Scholarios, Patriarch of Constantinople at the end of the Byzantine period, refused to allow himself to be called a 'Hellene'. The Byzantines' sense of their difference from, and superiority to, their western and eastern neighbours did not primarily derive from the fact that they were the bearers of the cultural tradition of Hellenism, or that they used the Greek language, or that they were the racial descendants of the ancient Greeks.[1] It derived rather from the fact that the Byzantines regarded themselves as God's chosen people, and their Empire as the quasi-divine instrument through which was to be fulfilled His threefold promise to Abraham. This gave the Byzantines a position in the universal scheme of things so elect and exclusive that one Archbishop of Thessalonika found it necessary to remind his congregation that God had made the barbarians as well as themselves, and heard their prayers no less. This sense of their position, combined with the fact that they were in addition the bearers of the cultural tradition of the ancient world, in its turn determined the attitude of the Byzantines to their eastern and western neighbours: in so far as these did not accept the religious principles of Orthodox Catholic Christianity they were either heretical or schismatic; in so far as they lacked culture, they were barbarians. The Moslems, the traditional eastern enemies of Byzantium, were heretical, a fact

[1] Although the Arab conquests in the seventh century, by depriving the Empire of Egypt, Syria, and North Africa, increased the territorial significance of Greek lands and their population in the Empire, it must be remembered that, in addition to the Armenian migrations, some forcible, into northern Greece in the sixth and seventh centuries, the Slavs in the same centuries largely overran the whole remaining area of continental Greece, so that only in a few areas in the eastern Peloponnesus and central Greece did the Greek population remain.

which did not prevent the Byzantines from allowing them free worship at their own mosque in Constantinople, or one of the Patriarchs of Constantinople from addressing the Caliph of Baghdad as equal in majesty to his own Emperor; although it did commit them, as defenders and propagators of the idea of a Christian Empire, to the waging of a kind of ceaseless sacred war against them. As for the West, the whole of this, particularly after the official religious schism of the eleventh century and the subsequent appearance of the Crusaders in Byzantine territories, was generally regarded as one gigantic apostasy from Christ and genuine culture. The Franks (the collective name for Westerners) were primitive, crude, bellicose, predatory—in a word, barbaric—and were not to be compared in intelligence or refinement with either the Byzantines or the Moslems.

This hostility to the Latins was aggravated when, towards the end of the Byzantine period, a movement, aristocratic and literary rather than popular in character, developed among a section of the Byzantine intelligentsia to form a national Greek state within the geographical area of the ancient Greek world. This movement, crystallizing round the figure of Gemistos Plethon and based on Mistra, in the heart of the Peloponnesus, itself had implications of a curious nature. For the Christian Byzantines, it will be recalled, Hellenism was paganism and polytheism. At the same time, the Byzantine idea of a Christian Empire was supranational, not national, in character. When therefore the intellectual leaders of the movement to found an independent national Greek state in southern Greece sought, in order to provide the ideological basis for such a state, to resuscitate the philosophical and political conceptions of antique Hellenism, they were 'anti-Byzantine' and 'anti-Christian' in two vital respects: the revival of Hellenism involved the revival of polytheism, and the proposal to form a national Greek state ran counter to the claims of a universal status which were implicit in the Byzantine idea of a Christian Empire. Thus, before the end of the Byzantine period, and before the Turks had overrun the Greek mainland, the idea of building a national Greek state was proposed in terms that implied a 'split in consciousness' the full effects of which were not to be seen until some four hundred years later, when the national state of modern Greece in fact came into being. For the intellectual leaders of the movement saw as its necessary ideological complement the revival of a non-Christian, anti-Byzantine Hellenism; yet the bulk of the Greek people themselves, un-hellenized and unaffected by the intellectual theories of the Hellenists, remained loyal to its Byzantine and Orthodox Christian heritage. If at the beginning of the fifteenth century this latent dichotomy could remain more or less concealed, this was because both intellectual 'nationalists' and the Greek people were united in their anti-Latin sentiments: for the people regarded the Latins as the perverters of the true faith who sought to impose themselves in the Orthodox Christian world, while the Hellenists had to conquer the actual territory of their proposed new state not from the Turks but from the Latins. In fact, the subsequent Turkish conquest of continental Greece put an end to any immediate possibilities there may have been for the founding of a Greek state, and removed the prospect of continued Latin domination.

Indeed, in one sense, the fall of Constantinople in 1453 and the subsequent Turkish occupation of continental Greece was a profound relief for the Greek Orthodox world, since it represented salvation from the Latins and from the temptation to buy their assistance against the Turks at the price of a union of the churches on Latin terms. The religious antipathy between the Greek East and the Latin West was a very real one. For the orthodox, Christianity meant a 'way' to perfection, and the possibility of a form of 'deification' through a type of spiritual knowledge, or 'gnosis', accessible to initiated Christians through the cultivation of the heart rather than of the mind. Latin Christianity on the other hand came to be more rational in form, and to attach greater importance to the logical working of the human mind in the pursuit of divine knowledge. And these two expressions of the Christian revelation in the two halves of Christendom were differently refracted through the accidents of history and cultural tradition. No doubt the sharpness of doctrinal controversy and conviction over such questions as the 'filioque' were supported by considerations of purely political rivalry between the Papacy and the Empire. Similarly the events of the fourth crusade and the Byzantine experience of Latin intolerance and condescension in the years which followed had their effect. Yet the importance of the different modes of religious thought and feeling in East and West must be kept always in mind. Doctrine was the concern not only of the theologians but the entire Christian community of the Empire which was God's Kingdom on earth. If man was not in the right relation to God all else was surely in vain. It was as much the strength and bitterness of this aversion to the Latins as the relative leniency of the actual conditions of their participation in the Ottoman Empire that determined Greek political behaviour in the succeeding centuries of subjugation.

The rapidity with which the Ottoman Empire advanced its European frontier posed the problem of how these infidel populations were to be assimilated. The absence of the necessary machinery for detailed civil administration on the one hand, and on the other, the prohibition in Islamic sacred law against the forcible conversion of 'People of the Book', Jews and Christians, who submitted themselves without resistance, contributed to the growth of forms of local self-government in which the regular provision of fiscal supplies was balanced against the right of the Christians to manage their own affairs and practise their religion. This principle also operated at the imperial level of administration; but since the Ottoman State, like the Byzantine Empire to which it succeeded, was a theocratic structure, it could recognize its subject non-Moslem peoples only as religious communities. In particular, the Sultan recognized as the Head of the Community of Orthodox Christians the Greek Patriarch of Constantinople who became responsible for the civil as well as the ecclesiastical administration of all the Orthodox Ottoman subjects of whatever ethnic origin. In effect the Patriarch, succeeding to the offices of both the Byzantine Emperor and the Patriarch, came to preside over a state within a state which, after the victories of the Sultan over Serbs, Bulgars, and Latins, was in a limited sense a reconstitution of Byzantium: an Ecumenical community transcending ethnic differences and using the Greek language as its common cultural medium. And it followed, not inconsistently, that the hierarchy of the Church should preach to its flock that the Sultan who 'protected' the Orthodox community did so by the foresight and grace of God.

Nevertheless the situation of the Orthodox had its disadvantages. Christians were forbidden to carry arms or marry Moslem women; they were forced to wear distinctive clothing and they could not object to marriages between Moslem men and Christian women. Such marks of social inferiority and exclusion were particularly galling to the Greeks with their remarkably developed sense of self-esteem. The peculiar way in which the Orthodox Christians were simultaneously included in, and excluded from, the ruling institutions is well illustrated by the Devshirme system through which selected Christian children were trained for positions in the Sultan's army and slave household. During the fifteenth and sixteenth centuries, indeed, almost all the senior offices in the Sultan's service, including the Grand Viziership, were filled by ex-Christian convert slaves.[1] The institution, while it flourished, related in an incomplete but striking fashion the two most considerable groups in the Empire and it affirmed the fundamental principle that the criteria of membership in these groups, and of eligibility for office, were religious and not ethnic.

Yet what particularly impressed the Greek Orthodox Christians in the first two centuries of Turkish sovereignty, encouraging a degree of social assimilation and discouraging them from rebellion, was the morale and bearing of the Turks themselves and their prestige in the eyes of Western Europeans. Power and pride excited the admiration and envy of the Greeks who in dress and manners attempted to emulate the Turks as closely as they dared. In the many conversions of Orthodox Christians to Islam considerations of prestige as well as policy were present. Men persuaded themselves that since Moslems sung the psalms of David and recognized Christ, the distance between the faiths was not so great; while at the same time to ease their consciences and assist their salvation many remained crypto-Christians, a form of insurance to which the Church in its necessity showed some tolerance. Through the eighteenth century, then, the Greek-speaking population of the Empire remained essentially an Eastern people, not indeed merely because of their experiences under the Turks, but through the continuity of the cultural and religious tradition of Byzantium, whose Empire, like that of the Ottomans, had its centre in Asia Minor and not in European Greece. That the full continuity of this tradition was in fact preserved was a consequence of the Ottoman conquest; and that this conquest also preserved the territorial limits and the religious institutions of the Byzantine Empire was to tempt the Greeks for five hundred years with the possibility of its imminent resurrection.

---

[1] There is no doubt that in general this child-tribute was deeply resented, yet there is evidence that Christian parents sometimes went to considerable lengths to ensure that a child was selected for this privileged slavery; and that the slaves, if they reached positions of influence, preserved a certain sympathy for the Orthodox community.

The fall of Constantinople was critical in another respect, for with the collapse of Byzantine institutions of higher learning Greek intellectuals migrated to Europe, bringing with them their often profound knowledge of ancient Greek authors. In particular, they gave a new bias to the teachings of Aristotle. The effect of Aristotelianism had already been curiously different in the two halves of Christendom. In the East where its emphasis on logical form offered no threat to the spirit of Orthodox doctrine, it had been absorbed without difficulty into Christian thought; but in the West, precisely because of those rational tendencies in Latin theology which we remarked earlier, the impact of annotated Arabic texts of Aristotle in the twelfth century had been so considerable that it had forced the scholastics to changes which represented almost an inversion of the traditional 'Augustinian' theology. But the teaching of the new Aristotelianism, mainly by Greek *émigrés* at the University of Padua, fell little short of being purely naturalistic. It was the development of this teaching that led to an increasing emphasis on the empirical study of natural phenomena, and in the eighteenth and nineteenth centuries, by a direct line of descent, to notions of progress and evolution.

This rationalistic Western learning, itself, in part, the product of the impact of classical Greek philosophy on Western medieval thought, gradually began to penetrate the Greek East, still secure in its Byzantine traditions, during the seventeenth century. It came, particularly in the beginning, from Padua where an increasing number of young Greeks came to study the new learning; and through Crete and the Ionian islands which were still under Venetian control. But a second centre for its dissemination existed, where it might have been least expected, in the Academy of the Patriarchate at Constantinople. For, in their struggle to resist the encroachments of Turks and Latins and to strengthen the hold of the Greek element and the Greek language on the leadership of the Orthodox community, some members of the hierarchy and the Greek Phanariote families which provided the high officials of the Patriarch's civil administration, had come to believe that their task was not only to preserve the Christian faith but also to revive a Hellenism with roots in classical and Hellenistic Greece. A Patriarch like Cyril Loukaris (1572–1638), ignoring the traditional incompatibility of Hellenism and Christianity, could embrace, without concern and for reasons mainly opportunist, a new and rational form of Hellenism—reimported from the West—whose destructive power was only understood after the damage had been done.

In the closing decades of the seventeenth century the Ottoman armies ceased to be invincible and by the end of the eighteenth the whole imperial structure was in visible decay. The Greeks, gradually discovering after 'the second renaissance' the sentimental interest of enlightened Europeans in the fate of the enslaved descendants of the ancients, and noting also, even in the case of the Hapsburgs, a new and comforting tone of religious tolerance, or indifference, which accompanied the growth of rational humanism in the West, began to speculate how they might use the new ascendancy of Europe to rid themselves of the Turks and reassume their Byzantine inheritance. Two methods, however, were proposed, each corresponding to a different conception of the Greek *milieu* and to a different kind of political entity which it was proposed to substitute for the Ottoman Empire, and whose inherent incompatibility was to lead to that 'split in consciousness' already foreshadowed at Mistra before the fall of Byzantium.

As the capacity of the Ottoman Empire to impose a military solution in its differences with Europe had decreased, the corresponding need for negotiators with linguistic and diplomatic abilities led during the eighteenth century to the appointment of Greek Phanariotes to offices of great influence in the state, in particular to the 'thrones' of the princedoms of Moldavia and Wallachia, and to the position of Dragoman of the Porte. Indeed so great became the new prestige of the Phanariotes that they began to believe that with patience it would be possible to infiltrate the ruling institutions of the Empire to such a degree that imperceptibly there would emerge an 'Ottoman Empire of the Greeks' with political institutions analogous to those of the Hapsburg Empire, dominated by a Greek administration but containing the other Christian ethnic groups within the organization of the Ecumenical church. This conception, which had the merit of coinciding approximately with the popular belief in the resurrection of Byzantium expressed in demotic songs and legends, may be described as the Eastern solution of the Greek problem.

The protagonists of the purely Western solution of the problem were the class of Greek merchant bourgeoisie which by the end of the eighteenth century had representatives in many European commercial centres. These men by the nature of their work were peculiarly exposed to the influence of Western urban values of human progress and commercial profit. They discovered also the extraordinary veneration in which their classical 'ancestors' were now held and a corresponding attitude, which varied between sympathy and contempt, for their own 'degenerate' condition. Both pride and, as they believed, profit urged them to a radical solution, the model for which lay conveniently at hand in the revolutionary nation state. This political conception as it had developed in the writings of Rousseau and in the practical events of the French revolution was something fundamentally different from the universal Ecumenical state in which Greek tradition and experience had been enclosed for more than a thousand years. No longer was the state a community of persons professing in common a certain form of relationship to God; it now included only those people who by the particularist criteria of language and tradition might be described as sharing in the same homogeneous national spirit. In the event, the outbreak of the revolutionary war in 1821 prejudged which of these political forms Modern Greece would assume. And, ironically, the narrow limits of the midget state which the protecting powers Russia, France, and England established in 1830, although they were the outcome of conflicting policies and interests, happened also to reflect what Europeans then considered to be homogeneously 'Greek' and what, moreover, their classical education had taught them ought to be Greek.

More Greeks, however, continued to live outside the new Greece than in it. External debt, the greedy expectations of faction leaders, and politically organized brigandage, to name only three of the ills that attacked the state, encouraged its leaders to cultivate the one political aim which all its citizens held in common, the redemption of the Greeks still living under Ottoman sovereignty. The 'Great Idea', as this policy came to be known, was clearly inspired by the popular belief in a resurrection of a Christian empire. But it pursued these ends through the forms of Western nationalism and the nation state. The consequences of the injection of these political concepts into the *milieu* of a universal Ecumenical State were predictable. After more than a thousand years of administration under the Byzantine and Ottoman Empires many areas of the Balkans and of Asia Minor had become an inextricable patchwork of village communities of different ethnic origins, languages, and religions. In the circumstances the creation of a homogeneous Greek-speaking nation within defined frontiers, and including all the unredeemed Greeks of the Ottoman Empire, could only be achieved by the forced assimilation of many who were not Greeks or by a vast exchange of populations. Yet although the contradictions in the premises of the 'Great Idea' were sufficiently obvious (and became ever clearer with the development of Serb and Bulgar nationalisms), this notion was to dominate the thought and politics of Greece for a hundred years.

In adopting the Western political form of the nation state Greeks had had to discover what were the traditions representing the principle of their common nationality through which the general will of the nation might be expressed. In the years immediately before the revolution Korais, the intellectual leader of the Greek diaspora in the West, following the lead given by the German romantic philologists such as Herder and Fichte, had taught that what distinguished a nation is not its religion or indeed geographical factors, but the possession of a common language and literature inherited through the centuries. Therefore because an undoubted continuity may be traced between classical Greek and the modern language, the modern Greeks are necessarily the linguistic, and by implication true racial, descendants of the ancients in whose culture and philosophy, consequently, the ideals of the modern Greek nation must be rediscovered. For the classicism of Periclean Athens, although preserved into the Roman and Hellenistic periods, had been submerged in the dark ages of Christian Byzantium. Fortunately through the timely enlightenment of Europe which had itself been achieved through the study of classical texts, it was now possible for Europe in its turn to enlighten Greece and set her again on her right and destined path. In effect the task which Korais undertook, and which was soon to become the principal end of the educational system of the new state, was the conversion of the Greek-speaking Christian population of an Eastern empire into humanist Hellenes who might however continue to profess the Christian religion for its moral utility. Moreover, the argument proceeds, since the inspiration of European civilization lies precisely in that classicism of which their ancestors were the creators, modern Greeks need feel neither inferior nor grateful to the Europeans from whom in fact they only take back what is rightfully their own. It is then only one short step to the claim that they are a chosen people exemplifying ideal types of humanity.

There is a corollary to this theorem. Although the Greeks had regarded themselves as part of 'the East', whether in Byzantium as the Eastern half of Christendom, or under the Turks as being contained within an Eastern empire, in this new conception of their place in the world they did not feel themselves assimilated to 'Europe' or the 'West', precisely because the 'elect' position of Greece depended on the claim that European civilization was in fact derivative from Greek culture (in which the ancient and the modern were now happily confused); and therefore, to maintain this position, it was argued that Greek culture must be distinct from and superior to European civilization.

It is these notions that do much to account for the strength and fascination of the 'Great Idea' during the nineteenth century. It was able to concentrate the support not only of the Orthodox Greek people, for whom it signified the restoration of the Christian Empire, but also of the new Western educated bourgeoisie within Greece who substituted for its Christian content an ideological Hellenism whose political counterpart demanded the redemption of other Greeks still in captivity in barbarian (i.e. Turkish) lands. It was the fusion, or confusion, in the consciousness of the Greeks of their double 'election', both by choice of God and by virtue of their own genius as Hellenes, that explains the fatal and continuous attraction of what must appear to be this extraordinary 'Idea'. The Greeks, it came to be believed, were infallible and only in this light could the facts of their history be properly interpreted. By the same arguments Greeks were superior to other peoples so that no restriction in their future role in the world could be reasonably tolerated, whether politically in the aspirations of a bankrupt nation of a million people to succeed to the dominion of the Ottoman Empire, or culturally in its self-imposed mission of redeeming the 'barbaric' East. The general effect of these beliefs was to create a complete divorce between the ideals which Greeks pursued and the reality they lived.

The establishment of a Western nation state in Greece had, also, other consequences. It introduced institutions of centralized administration, and after 1843 of representative government based on a wide franchise, into a society of corporate village com-

munities the majority of which lived within the limits of closed
economies of subsistence agriculture or pastoralism. Under the
Ottoman dispensation such communities very often enjoyed privileges of self-government and were corporately responsible under
their elected leaders for the collection and payment of their taxes.
Each village, a commonwealth of Christian families, actually and
symbolically divided and defended from the natural or non-
Christian world by the chapels and icon-stands on its boundaries,
represented a microcosm of the Christian 'Ecumene'. Within the
limitations set by the divisive influences of the Greek peasant's
agonistic social values of honour, pride, and self-assertion, but
contained within corporate forms and responsibilities, it participated however imperfectly in the ideals of a community of
Orthodox brotherhood, a static image of life concerned particularly
with the sacred obligations of family life.

From the earliest days of the new state the government, in the
name of the novel concept of progress, adopted a policy calculated
to destroy the effectiveness and even the identity of these communities. For it was impossible to improve the deplorably primitive
agriculture, the government argued, if the agents of enlightened
administration could not legislate within these closed circles of
ignorance and conservatism. But also progress and the very existence of the regime itself depended on security which in principle
was threatened by the existence of local communities to which men
felt stronger loyalties than to the state. For these reasons the
government replaced the village as the unit of local administration
by the commune, an entirely artificial local grouping administered
by a mayor, an appointee of the central government.

Since the village community had been deprived of the means to
protect its people from the oppressions of the agents of the state
(whose positions were a reward for political support and as such
might not continue beyond the life of the government), influential
individuals in a village discovered patrons with political influence
in the local towns who, in exchange for their vote and the votes of
their kinsmen and friends, protected their affairs and the affairs of
those associated with them through the patron's own 'friendship'
with administrators, deputies, and army officers. This indeed was
the simple structural principle on which political life in the Greek
state was to be organized for a hundred years. It has important
consequences. Patronage emphasizes that some receive but many

do not. It destroys the moral force and justification which representative institutions may possess in other circumstances. And it was connected in the mind of the peasant with a distinction he quickly learned to make between 'kratos', the state with its administrative machinery which threatens and takes away but returns nothing, and the 'ethnos', the community of Orthodox Hellenism to which his devotion is due.

It now became the general ambition to escape from this dependence, either directly through migration to the growing towns, or vicariously by the education of children for the public service or the legal profession. For it was more preferable to exploit than to be exploited and human destiny was worthy of something better than the animal conditions of village life, no longer regarded as reflecting or participating in any higher reality. Those who left the countryside for the towns took with them their values of pride and self-assertion, which now unchecked by any corporate ideal, or the scrutiny of village opinion, encouraged the growth of a vicious individualism that accepted few moral obligations outside the family and judged the honour of a man in terms of political influence or material ostentation with little reference to the morality of his conduct.

Individualism, the shifting alliances of patrons and clients to advance or protect selfish interests, the dissolution of corporate loyalties and static ideals of communal and religious life, bred a sense of corruption and fragmentation in Greek political life which could only be redeemed by the united devotion of Greeks, and their sacrifice of selfish interests, to the ideals of the 'Great Idea'. Only in unselfishly worshipping themselves through the tenets of this unreasonable conception could they efface reality. Thus the complementary relationship between the 'Great Idea' and the growth of individualism, however catastrophic the impact of these ideals on the values and institutions of Greek society, had a certain functional value.

When, at length, the 'Great Idea' was destroyed in the military defeat of the Greco-Turkish war (1921-2) and in the massive exchange of population which followed, it seemed that modern Hellenism had been emptied of all content and purpose. Between the two world wars political life became a prolonged and bitter inquiry into the origins of the catastrophe and the identity of the guilty, a debate which contributed to the political schism between monarchists and liberals. A measure of agreement existed only in the universal condemnation of Western treachery, and in an increasing criticism of Western institutions of parliamentary democracy which had promoted faction and corruption in the nation. And indeed it was true that these evils could no longer be transcended in a common concern for the ideal values of the 'Great Idea'.

The humiliations of the incessant political interference which Greece had endured for ninety years at the hands of her Western 'protectors' in the illusory hope that these powers would recognize, at length, the justice of her claims, had been largely in vain. The memory of these indignities, the simple shame of failure, and the belief that the apathy of the English and the apostasy of the French (who had supported the Turks) were responsible for the destruction of the sacred Idea, produced at last a perceptible reaction against Western liberalism and democracy that was to find, in time, political expression in the dictatorship of Metaxas (1936–41) and the subsequent attempts of the Communist party to seize the state at the end of the German occupation. Metaxas struggled to revive the life of the villages, to create new corporate loyalties in the towns through the youth movement and to preach the need for self-discipline and an inward search for national values to replace vacuous imitations of Western culture. And communism through the efficiency and austerity of its administration under the occupation had a positive appeal, at first, for many who had remained unsatisfied in a political system based on patronage. Some, too, may have been moved by a secular version of the old Ecumenical brotherhood of the Orthodox. But neither of these reactionary movements from the left or from the right commanded the consent of the majority; and after the suppression of the communist sedition Greece renewed her dependence on the West to achieve a new and insipid ideal of industrial development and material affluence.

The conclusion might seem to be that after three thousand years the Greek *milieu* has achieved a political identity, but has done this only through a surrender to the West in terms which imply a denial of that Eastern heritage that has in both the pre-Christian and the Christian past inspired its major spiritual and cultural achievements. It is true that there have been many individuals prepared to speak against the contamination of Greek life by Western values: Ion Dragoumis, for instance, the political theorist, warning the Greeks to return to their Eastern way of life and thought if

G

they do not wish to lose their identity; or the poet Sikelianos more fundamentally attacking materialism and seeing in the Greek demotic tradition the survival of a more complete and mystical way of life that can be traced back to sources in 'venerable' Asia; or the writer Papadiamantis who sees the only hope for Greece in a revival of the Orthodox Christian tradition. And it is true that potentially, at least, Greece is in a position, through a revival of the Orthodox tradition, to re-establish contact with its spiritual and cultural (and non-Western) roots. But for the moment the worship of Western materialist culture, and reliance on its techniques, still dominate the political and social scene; and it is difficult to envisage any radical change except in the context of a revolution in values which affects Europe and the West as a whole.

V. THE RUSSIANS IN RELATION
TO ASIA AND EUROPE

S. V. Utechin

The Geographical Background

Wherever you draw the imaginary line on the Eurasian continent dividing Europe from Asia, it will cut across present-day Russia.[1] This was not always so, and a glance at the territorial development of Russia is necessary to put the evolution of Russian attitudes towards Europe and Asia into the right geographical perspective.

From the ninth century, when the Russian intellectual tradition began, until the middle of the sixteenth century, Russian ethnic territory remained almost unchanged. Throughout this period it included the basin of the Western Bug and the upper parts of the Neman and Western Dvina in the west and the area between the upper Volga and the Oka in the east; the upper Dniester and middle Dnieper in the south and the lake district in the north. The main changes were a gradual contraction in the south-west, where Bessarabia was lost, and in the west, where the Russian population west of the Bug was progressively Polonized, together with expansion in the north and north-east towards the Arctic Ocean and the Ural Mountains, where with the advance of Russian colonization the indigenous Finnish tribes were gradually being assimilated. The conquest of the Tatar khanates of Kazan', Astrakhan', and Siberia in the second half of the sixteenth century opened the way to Russian colonization of the middle and lower Volga, the Urals, and the whole of Northern Asia, so that the Pacific coast was

---

[1] For a survey of where this line has been placed at different periods by European geographers, see W. H. Parker, 'Europe: How Far', *Geographical Journal*, vol. cxxvi, pp. 278–97.

reached by the middle of the seventeenth century. The sixteenth and seventeenth centuries also witnessed the growth of autonomous communities of Cossacks in the south—on the lower Dnieper, the Don, and the lower Volga. During the eighteenth and nineteenth centuries, the northern shores of the Black Sea, previously belonging to Turkey and its vassal the Crimean Khanate and almost uninhabited, were colonized by the Russians, as were the steppe areas of Northern Caucasus, and, at the opposite end of the Empire, the Maritime area on the Pacific, ceded by China in 1858–60. The annexation of Transcaucasia and of Central Asia took place during the nineteenth century, but Russian settlement there was at first insignificant; it increased during the twentieth century, but Russians are still in a minority in these areas. They also form sizeable minorities, since the 1940s, in the former Baltic states of Estonia, Latvia, and Lithuania, and have completely replaced the German inhabitants of the northern half of former East Prussia, and the Japanese in southern Sakhalin and the Kurile Islands, annexed in 1945. The main area of Russian colonization during this century, however, has been the Kazakh steppe between Western Siberia and Central Asia which, as a result of several waves of migration (most recently during the Virgin Land Campaign of the mid-1950s), has become overwhelmingly Russian. On the other hand, separate national consciousness has developed during the nineteenth and twentieth centuries among the Ukrainians and to a lesser extent the Belorussians, and it is arguable how far they still consider themselves Russians.

This gradual expansion of the area of Russian settlement has been accompanied by corresponding changes in the idea of the 'Russian land' in the minds of the people. This idea of the 'Russian land', of the ethnic Russian territory, rather than of the state boundaries at any particular moment in history, has influenced Russian attitudes to Europe and Asia and to Russia's own ambivalent relations with them.

A survey of Russian attitudes to Europe and Asia can conveniently be divided in accordance with the main chronological phases of Russian intellectual history in general. These are (1) the period before the Mongol conquest, from the ninth century to 1240; (2) the Mongol suzerainty, 1240–1480; (3) the late Muscovite period, 1480–1700; (4) the Petrine Empire, 1700–1830; (5) the search for identity, 1830–1920; (6) the Soviet period.

Before the Mongol Conquest (9th century–1240)

Very little is known about Russian intellectual attitudes before the establishment of Christianity as the state religion in 988. The main external contacts were with Scandinavia, whence came the dynasty which by the middle of the tenth century established itself over all the East Slav tribes; with the Khazar Khanate (Turkic-speaking and partly Jewish by religion) on the northern shores of the Caspian, to whom some of the East Slav tribes had previously paid tribute; and with the nomadic, also Turkic-speaking, Pechenegs who harassed the southern areas bordering on the steppe. But already then the country which had the greatest attraction was Byzantium, relations with which, both in war and peace, were felt to be the most important.

Russian chronicles have preserved a legend according to which the Kievan Prince Vladimir, having decided to cast off paganism, was not at first sure what religion to embrace. Four possibilities were seriously considered—Christianity in its Western (Roman) and Eastern (Greek) forms, Islam and Judaism. The choice fell on Eastern Christianity, and this fact, more than any other, determined the Russians' own ideas on their position in relation to Europe and Asia. Russia became, and remained for five hundred years, culturally a satellite of Byzantium. A considerable part (at first the overwhelming majority) of books copied and read in Russia were translations of Byzantine writers. Under the influence of this literature, 'the West' came to mean for Russians the Roman Empire and the Roman Church. The Roman Empire, a direct predecessor of Byzantium, was considered one of the main roots of political and cultural tradition relevant to Russia's own development. On the other hand, the contemporary Roman Church was viewed with suspicion, especially after the final break in 1054. 'The East' came to mean the countries that had once been conquered by Alexander the Great, most of which had since become Muslim: it was thus exotic and romantic, but also hostile and dangerous. But whereas the Islamic danger was vicarious, there was another threat from the East nearer home, the Cumans, who, coming from the territory of present-day Kazakhstan, replaced the Pechenegs as a constant menace in the south. And thus in the popular mind Asia began to be identified with the hostile, nomadic steppe.

Between the schismatic West and the infidel East, there was a zone of the true faith, running from the Holy Land through Byzantium and the Balkan Slavs to Russia. Thus from the very beginning of its intellectual history, Russia found itself in an intermediate position between 'East' and 'West', Asia and Europe. The ties with the West were closer (including dynastic marriages with various West European houses) and it was better known at least in the neighbouring countries of Sweden, Poland, and Hungary; the linguistic affinity with the Western Slavs, especially Poles and Czechs, also played a role. But the Orthodox world, headed by Byzantium, was the only one where the medieval Russian felt spiritually and culturally at home. Historically a synthesis of Occident and Orient, this Orthodox world was now, for the Russians, an antithesis of both.

The Mongol Suzerainty (1240–1480)

The Mongol conquest in 1237–40 radically changed the political situation. Until then an independent state fairly high up in the ideal hierarchy of states headed by the Byzantine Empire, Russia suddenly became a vassal of the Great Khan of far-away Karakorum, and not even a direct vassal, for it was incorporated into the Kypchak (Cuman) realm—commonly known in Russia and Western Europe as the Golden Horde. The nomadic steppe became the master of the Russian land itself. Yet the Mongols, or Tatars as they came to be known in Russia (they were in fact mostly Cumans and the small Mongol leadership was soon Turkicized), remained essentially an external force. After the initial period of conquest and destruction, physical contact was rather rare. At first there were Mongol tax-collectors in the main towns with troops at their disposal, but soon the khans decided to shift this duty of collecting tribute on to the Russian princes. The princes themselves sometimes had to travel to the Horde or even to Karakorum to settle disputes among themselves or with Mongol officials, or to be confirmed in their office. In the initial period the Mongols demanded the participation of Russian troops in their military campaigns, but this practice soon ceased. The main form of physical contact Russians were likely to have with the Tatars throughout their suzerainty were intermittent raids undertaken both to collect booty (including prisoners to be sold in the slave markets in Central Asia or the Near East) and to keep the Russians, so far as possible, in a state of fear. During the time of their more or less direct domination, the Mongols introduced certain administrative practices which remained after their withdrawal, notably population counts for the purposes of taxation, and a system of overland mail routes. The political supremacy of the Tatars could hardly fail to affect the social attitudes and habits of the upper strata of the Russian population. The whole tone of Russian life became harsher, punishments more severe, the treatment of women (especially of the upper classes) worse. There were distinct 'Oriental' (Central Asian) influences upon clothes. Beyond all this, there was scarcely any intellectual contact. The Mongol-Tatar conquerors were pagans; during the time of their domination in Russia they succumbed to the influence of the great Islamic centres in Central Asia and embraced Islam, but they did not interfere with the religion of their Russian subjects, and even exempted the Russian Church from taxation. The Tatar domination was always considered in Russia a yoke, a temporary phenomenon which would end when God had mercy upon His people and when the Russians themselves were strong enough to shake it off. After the first victory of Russian forces led by the Grand Prince of Moscow, Dmitry Donskoy, over the Tatars in 1380, the dependence on the Tatars became more and more nominal, though even after the Golden Horde had split into several khanates the Russians continued to pay tribute to one of them until 1480.

The conditions just described did not prevail in the whole of the Russian land during the period from the thirteenth to the fifteenth century. Some border territories in the west were never conquered by the Mongols but fell to the neighbouring Grand Duchy of Lithuania, which was soon able to extend its frontiers far into Russia so that by the middle of the fourteenth century almost the whole west and south-west of the country, including its old capital of Kiev, were in Lithuania, while the extreme south-western principality of Galicia had fallen to Poland. Free from the Mongol domination, these western Russian lands were progressively drawn closer to the political and cultural life of Western Europe, especially after the Grand Dukes of Lithuania became also the Kings of Poland (in 1389). The Grand Duchy was overwhelmingly Russian ethnically and culturally, and the Orthodox Church strongly resisted Roman Catholic influences until the fusion of Lithuania with Poland in 1569. Soon afterwards (in 1596), a union of the Orthodox Church in the Polish Common-wealth with Rome was effected, and this ecclesiastic connection gave to a part of the Russian population in the West a distinctly 'Western' outlook.

Yet another course of development had been taken by Novgorod and its dependent territories in the north-west and extreme north. Novgorod had not been conquered by the Mongols, and their overlordship there had been little more than nominal throughout. An old trading centre with its commercial contacts mostly in northern and western Europe, Novgorod developed into a republic similar to the trading city-republics of Germany and Northern Italy. Without becoming a member of the Hanseatic League, Novgorod was associated with it rather in the same manner as London was. But its relations with Western Europe were not only commercial, for Novgorod had to defend itself against two powerful enemies—Sweden and the Teutonic Knights. Novgorod checked the advance of both of them, but the fact that they attacked Russia at the very time when it was being devastated by the Mongols, and soon after the sacking of Constantinople by the Crusaders, contributed to the bitterness of Novgorod's feeling against Roman Catholics. Not until the late fifteenth century did a certain Cathloic influence become noticeable in Novgorod.

The Late Muscovite Period (1480–1700)

While the period of the Tatar yoke was a time when different parts of the Russian land were exposed to different influences which were pulling them in opposite directions, the late Muscovite period was characterized by a confluence of these influences which resulted in a new cultural blend. But before we describe this process we must consider another tendency which was essentially hostile to both the 'Western' and the 'Eastern' influences. This was an attempt at asserting Russian self-sufficiency through an appeal to its Byzantine heritage. The conquest of Constantinople by the Turks in 1453 was seen in Russia as God's punishment for the wavering of the Greeks in matters of faith. In the eyes of the Muscovite ideologists, the role of the Byzantine Emperor, both as the political head of the Christian world and as the defender of the Orthodox faith, fell on the Grand Princes of Muscovy, who were more and more often styled Tsar, that is, Emperor. The monk Philotheus gave this ideology the form of an elaborate doctrine of Moscow as the Third Rome; according to him, 'two Romes have fallen while the third is standing and there will be no fourth'. This revival of Byzantinism was reinforced by the fact that Ivan III, the Moscow Grand Prince who stopped the payment of tribute to the Tatars in 1480, had earlier married the niece of the last Byzantine Emperor and had adopted much of the outward panoply of the Byzantine Court. The theory of Russian self-sufficiency proved to be a powerful ideological weapon against both the 'Eastern' and the 'Western' influences which had made themselves felt in the previous period.

Yet in a more real sense than as heirs of the Byzantine emperors, the Muscovite Tsars were the heirs of the khans of the Golden Horde whom they succeeded as sovereigns and many of whose administrative practices they continued. Hardly less important than the administrative traditions was the great influx of Tatar nobles into the Muscovite state service and thus into the Russian nobility during the fifteenth and sixteenth centuries. Although they soon became Christian, and Russian by language, the general social and cultural outlook of the upper strata of Russian society was greatly affected. The conquest of the Tatar khanates of Kazan', Astrakhan', and Siberia in the second half of the sixteenth century, the annexation of the rest of Siberia during the seventeenth century, and the migration of the Kalmyks into the Russian-held territory on the lower Volga brought the Russians into contact with many Asian peoples, including Buddhists. Trade and diplomatic relations were established (more often than not through the Tatars) with most of Russia's Asiatic neighbours from Turkey through the Caucasus, Persia, Afghanistan, and Central Asia to China. The Cossack communities which formed an almost continuous chain of Russian outposts along the southern frontiers assumed many of the ways of the Asian nomads and semi-nomads against whom they were protecting the frontiers.

The 'Western' influences were even stronger. They were of two kinds. One, and the more important, was the result of the gradual incorporation into the Muscovite state of the western Russian territories which had previously either been independent (Novgorod) or had been in the Polish-Lithuanian Commonwealth. Deeply involved in the commercial and political life of Western

Europe, the Novgorodians, Belorussians, and Ukrainians were anxious to infuse Muscovy, which they considered intellectually and culturally backward, with the ideas that they themselves had either acquired from the West or had developed as the result of their encounter with the West. The Belorussians and Ukrainians introduced into Muscovy a strong Polish cultural element. But more important was the fact that the Orthodox Belorussians and Ukrainians in Poland and Lithuania had been directly confronted with Roman Catholicism and exposed to the impact of the Re-formation and Counter-Reformation. As a result western Russian scholars were far more sophisticated than the rather simple and conservative Muscovites; their impact on the life of the Church, on education and literature, especially in the seventeenth century, was great and gave these spheres of Russian life a somewhat 'Western' character.

The other 'Western' influences were from further afield. Mus-covy's relations with her western neighbours, Poland, the Livonian Order, and Sweden, were not happy and there were long wars against them during the sixteenth and seventeenth centuries. The chief reasons were the Russian desire to gain access to the Baltic Sea and the Muscovite policy of 'gathering the Russian lands', the latter in direct competition with Poland which had inherited the same claim from the Grand Duchy of Lithuania. With other West European countries (especially the German Empire, Venice, England, and the Netherlands) the relations were much better, and there was considerable commercial and diplomatic activity. For the first time since the Kievan period, Russia reappeared as a member of the concert of European powers in the seventeenth century when Muscovy was a signatory of the Treaty of Westphalia in 1648. The artistic and technical superiority of the West was apparent to the Russians, and this found striking expression in the invitation to Italian architects to build much of the new Kremlin in the fifteenth century, in a continual influx of artisans and tech-nicians of various kinds from Germany and Holland, and finally in the formation of the first Western-type military units in the seventeenth century.

The Petrine Empire (1700–1830)

Thus the wholesale 'Westernization' of Russia during the eighteenth and early nineteenth centuries was not entirely unprepared or unexpected. What was new was the determination of Peter the Great and his successors to 'westernize' the country at all costs and as rapidly as possible, disregarding conservative sentiments and wounded national pride and crushing any opposition. Within a few decades, first the army and navy, then the administrative apparatus, the mining and manufacturing industries, the dress and the style of life of the nobility, and finally the educational system, were thoroughly 'westernized', so that by the time of the French Revolution and the Napoleonic wars Russia seemed to be, and in many respects undoubtedly was, a completely European country—as any reader of Tolstoy's *War and Peace* immediately becomes aware. This deliberate break with the Muscovite past was symbolized by the new Imperial capital on the shores of the Baltic and underlined by the influx into the higher ranks of the Imperial administration of German aristocrats from the Baltic provinces annexed by Peter the Great. The nobility responded to 'Westernization' remarkably quickly and on the whole easily, acquiring at first, together with the ideas of the Enlightenment, a peculiarly French outlook, which, however, was tempered by the 1820s by the influences of German universities and English literature. Russian educated society took on a more balanced 'European' character. Political, literary, and scholarly developments in France, Germany, and England were closely followed and in one way or another reflected, with Russians generally regarding themselves as pupils and junior cousins.

The Search for Identity (1830–1920)

As long as rationalism and the spirit of the Enlightenment prevailed, any doubts about the wisdom of wholesale 'Westernization' could be dismissed as mere obscurantism, but the situation changed with the rise of the Romantic movement which, like the Enlightenment before it, Russia experienced simultaneously with Western Europe. The upsurge of the new movement was connected in Russia with an intellectual shock from which the country has barely recovered even now. This was the famous first *Philosophical Letter* by Chaadayev, published in 1836. Turning for inspiration from abstract reason to the historical past, Chaadayev, to his utter dismay, found nothing in Russian history that seemed at all meaningful, no thread of continuity, no guiding principles, nothing but chaotic perturbations and missed opportunities. All this contrasted sharply in his mind with the clear principles of Western Europe and their progressive realization there. The only solution was to abandon any pretence that there was anything of independent value in the Russian past or present, and to identify Russia in future completely with the West. There was a good chance of success in this, for the very absence of any indigenous values should make the identification easier; once it was complete, Russia might even produce something great, and the opportunity should not be missed.

Few people shared Chaadayev's extreme position, but the problems raised by him dominated much of the thinking on Russia's place in the world throughout the nineteenth and early twentieth centuries. Three basic standpoints crystallized during the 1830s and 1840s. The first is often referred to as the theory of Official Nationality. It was formulated by the Minister of Education, Count Uvarov, in 1832, and remained the official philosophy of the Imperial Government. According to this view, Russia had its main spiritual and political roots in the pre-Petrine period; these were Orthodoxy, autocracy, and nationality, the latter being understood as the intrinsically Russian character of the state. This reversal to the Muscovite ideology was, however, combined with an acceptance of Peter the Great's work and of the continued need for further borrowing from the West, though as time went on the stress on the roots increased while allowance for Western innovations diminished.

The second, far more original, position was that of the Slavophiles, evolved as a direct response to Chaadayev's challenge. Worked out by Khomyakov and Kireevskii, the Slavophile theory conceived of Russia as being different from both the West and the East in a new and peculiar sense. There are two principles which, according to Khomyakov, have shaped and continue to shape the history of mankind—principles which he calls Iranian and Kushite. The former is one of light, freedom, and organic creativity, the latter of darkness, necessity, and mechanical construction. The Iranian principle finds its expression in religious and political systems based on spirituality, love, mutual consent, and co-operation; the Kushite in those based on sensuality, law, compulsion, and struggle. The two principles, and the antagonism between them, are universal, but they are scarcely ever seen in

94727

history in their pure forms, historical phenomena usually reflecting various combinations of the two. The most perfect historical embodiments of the Iranian principle are Christianity in its Eastern Orthodox form and the social life of the Slavs. Both the Orthodox Church and the Slav village community are based upon *sobornost'* ('conciliarism'), the idea of organic community, which combines most aspects of the Iranian principle. There are valuable manifestations of the Iranian principle outside the Orthodox-Slav world—Brahminism in India, English common law (especially the jury system), certain aspects of Protestantism—but on the whole both the East and the West are the domains of Kushism: Islam, 'Shivaism', and even Buddhism (which Khomyakov saw as a mere negation of the 'sensuality' exemplified in 'Shivaism') on the one hand, and Roman Catholicism and modern constitutionalism, both rooted in the legalism of ancient Rome, on the other. This Slavophile doctrine strongly influenced subsequent Russian thought, especially through its juxtaposition of the formalism and fragmentation of the Western mind and life and the organicism and wholeness of the Slavs.

The opponents of the Slavophiles were known as Westernists. There were conservatives, liberals, and radicals of various shades among them, each trend identifying itself by reference to its West European counterpart. This identification with West European movements and Western thought rather than any positive programme of 'Westernization' was a distinctive feature of the trend. As time went on the liberal and the socialist tendencies gained ground in the Westernist camp, while the conservatives fell back more and more on the theory of Official Nationality described earlier, which in its turn progressively shifted its stress to the Muscovite roots and away from the Petrine innovations.

Two more sets of ideas relevant to Russia's position *vis-à-vis* the West that were current in the second half of the nineteenth century and the beginning of the twentieth deserve attention. One was Leont'ev's Byzantinism born out of his aesthetic and moral aversion to the vulgarity of the current idols of both the Westernists and the Slavophiles—the conformism of the Western bourgeoisie and the egalitarianism preached by the Socialists, on the one hand, and the brutishness of the Russian peasant mass on the other. As against these, Leont'ev stressed the beautiful spirituality of Byzantine Orthodoxy. The other trend, one that was Western in its origins but came to fruition in Russia at the time when it was at its lowest ebb in the West, was Babouvism. Introduced into Russia around 1860, this theory concerning the establishment of communism by a determined minority triumphed under the name of Leninism sixty years later, in 1917–20.

Preoccupied as they were with Russia's position in relation to Western Europe, the Russians of the nineteenth and early twentieth centuries had little interest in Asia. The official views on Asia were in general those of a European great power with colonial possessions and engaged in rivalry with other great powers for influence in Asia. Among the people at large, 'Asiatic' was a term of abuse, although there was never a feeling of racial superiority on the part of the Russian colonists in Asia and intermarriage was not infrequent where religious difference did not prevent it. The intelligentsia was in the habit of calling 'Asiatic' those features of Russian life, both public and private, which contrasted with their idea of progressive European conditions. Many, including the first Russian Marxist, Plekhanov, described the Russian political system as 'Oriental despotism'. An extreme anti-Asian position was taken by the most outstanding Russian philosopher of the time, Vladimir Solov'ëv, who advocated the re-unification of the Roman Catholic and the Orthodox Churches as an essential precondition for a regeneration of Europe, and who warned against the 'yellow peril' of China.

The pro-Asian tendencies were few and weak, but one finds among their protagonists two great names—the scientist Mendeleev and the poet Blok. Mendeleev, whose main concern was the development of Russia's productive forces and economy and who was apprehensive about the industrially stronger Western countries, saw in China a natural partner for Russia with complementary resources and capacities. While Mendeleev's 'pro-Asianism' was based upon stable and rational conviction, Blok's was mystical and emotional. In his poem 'The Scythians', written in 1918, he asserted that Russians were 'Scythians, Asiatics with slanted and greedy eyes', a sentiment that was later built upon by the Eurasian school.

The Soviet Period (1920–   )

The imposition of an official ideology after the Communist victory in the Civil War greatly reduced the range of ideas that could be expressed in public. There was and is no room in the official Marxist-Leninist doctrine for any but socio-economic criteria for determining a country's place among others. According to the official view Russia, as the country most advanced on the road to Communism, occupies a higher place than any other; other countries with Communist governments, both in Europe and in Asia, are officially regarded as being in the process of building Socialism, and thus above the rest of mankind. The attitude to the countries comprising this rest is no less utilitarian and functional; they are divided into highly developed capitalist, usually termed 'imperialist', countries, to which Japan belongs just as much as Western Europe or the United States, and colonial or semi-colonial countries, again indiscriminately Asian, African, or Latin American. Both categories are regarded by the Communists with mixed feelings. The capitalist countries are on the one hand meant to be ripe for a Socialist revolution and transition into the category of Socialist states, but on the other hand so long as they are ruled by 'bourgeois' governments they are regarded as a constant threat to the existence of Communist regimes everywhere. The colonial and semi-colonial countries, being anti-imperialist, are potential allies of the Communists on the principle that 'my enemy's enemy is my friend'. But, being for the most part at a pre-capitalist, or at any rate pre-imperialist, stage of economic and social development, they are supposed to be unable to develop independently towards Socialism. This latter view has been somewhat modified during the later 1950s. It is now contended that the mere existence of the 'Socialist camp' makes it possible for those under-developed countries which, having gained independence, adopt a hostile attitude to the 'Imperialist camp', to enter the path of Socialism. In principle all this also applies irrespective of the country's geographical position or cultural complexion, but since in fact most newly independent countries are in Asia or Africa there is an appearance of greater cordiality in Soviet writings towards the East in contrast to their hostility to the West.

It would be naïve, however, to imagine that the imposition of an official ideology could suddenly cut short the interest in, and speculation about, Russia's place in relation to her neighbours in cultural rather than political or economic terms. And in fact one of the most interesting theories of this kind was produced in the 1920s. The leaders of this new, so-called 'Eurasian' school of thought were scholars living as *émigrés* in Western Europe, in Sofia, Prague, and Paris. But there is no doubt that they gave theoretical expression to sentiments shared by a section of the intelligentsia in Russia itself. Starting from the criticism of the Western Romano-Germanic civilization in the manner of the Slavophiles, and attributing, as they had done, great importance to Orthodox Christianity in Russian life, the Eurasians rejected the identification of Russia either with the Slav family or with Byzantine civilization. They proceeded instead to trace features in the Russian mental and cultural make-up which linked Russia with certain Asian—Iranian and especially Turkic—peoples. The area inhabited by Russians and Central Asian Turks, roughly coinciding with the inter-war frontiers of the Soviet Union, was seen by them as the home of a peculiar Eurasian culture, neither 'properly' European nor 'properly' Asian, the latter term being reserved for the peoples of Eastern and Southern Asia. The ideal realization of the potentialities of this Eurasian culture they saw in the fifteenth-seventeenth century Muscovy, and they condemned without any reservations the subsequent 'Westernization' as imposing an alien veneer on an organic indigenous culture. From this vantage point, the revolution of 1917 and the Communist regime which seemed to have swept away this alien veneer were regarded by the Eurasians as a re-assertion of the true Eurasian nature of Russia. In the 1930s a part of the movement went further and found in the Soviet social and political system a renaissance of that social unity and autocracy which they believed had existed in Muscovy.

The latest phase in the development of Russian attitudes to Europe and Asia, and to Russia's own position in relation to them, dates from the mid-1950s. It is the product of three separate factors: the general liberalization of the intellectual atmosphere in the country after Stalin's death in 1953, the apparent official Communist cordiality towards the new Asian and African states, and the persistent use in the foreign press of the term 'East' in relation to Russia and the countries of the Communist bloc. The search for independent intellectual orientation, whether through the study of the pre-Communist Russian past or of contemporary life abroad, leads many to stress the essentially European character of present-day Russian culture and to seek inspiration in Western Europe and especially in the United States, from whom it is felt that Russia could still learn much, particularly in the intellectual and political spheres. This new 'Europeanism' contrasts sharply with the attitude of the same people towards the Chinese, an attitude composed of incomprehension, contempt, and fear, not unlike that which the Russians often meet with in the West.

As this brief survey shows, the Russians have throughout their history had to deal with the problem of their relations to their Eastern and Western neighbours and have often asserted their own identity in terms of these relations. The search for Russia's identity in relation to Europe and Asia was at its most intense during the nineteenth century and the first three decades of the twentieth, the periods often referred to as respectively the golden and the silver ages of Russian culture. The interminable debate during these years produced such a variety of theoretical constructions and emotional complexes that it would seem that all the possible approaches have been explored and exhausted. Most of these theories contained some elements of truth, and the three main doctrines—the Westernist, the Slavophile, and the Eurasian —have greatly contributed to an understanding of the Russian mental make-up and history. Shorn of their extremes in the process of the debate, they are more and more becoming component parts of the common national consciousness. In this light, the latest Europeanism must be seen not as a new and separate school of thought but rather as a mood, perhaps as one of the milder forms of intellectual opposition to the official view of the world propagated by the ruling party. At the same time, this mood once again demonstrates the basic fact of Russia's intermediate position between East and West, adopting as it does towards the Chinese the very attitude which is so much resented when manifested by Western Europeans towards Russians. Logic, alas, rarely plays a prominent part in shaping popular feeling.

H

VI. CHINESE ATTITUDES
TO THE WEST

Evan Luard

Points of the compass are by definition relative concepts. This relativity affects not only the terms employed, which can without difficulty be transposed. It conditions the categories implicit in the model. Cultural, social, and historical phenomena can rarely be accurately assimilated to simple geographical classifications. But the world-image is inevitably largely created out of the most easily apprehended relationships. And geographical classifications may thus condition the way in which all other phenomena are apprehended.

Persistent attempts by Europeans to generalize about 'the East' as a uniform entity are one aspect of this supremacy of the geographical category. But converse attitudes are equally affected. The confident bisection of the Eurasian land-mass somewhere between the Black Sea and the White is not necessarily self-evident to non-European cultures. To China the West comprehends Persia, India, Central Asia, and the Himalayas as much as Europe. The 'Western peoples', for most of her history, meant the war-like marauders of the steppes that periodically ravaged her borders. And the conceptions of 'East' and 'West' as characteristic entities, and of 'continents' that are distinct geographical units, have been somewhat sketchily assimilated into Chinese thinking, under the impact of the West, only within the last century.

The literal meaning of the word China in the Chinese language is 'the central nation'. Throughout ancient times, and until only a few decades ago, China herself was regarded as the centre of the universe. It was surrounded by 'outer peoples', barbarians, who did not share those blessings conferred on the Chinese Empire through the special relationship existing between the heavenly powers and its own Emperor, the Son of Heaven. Just as Greeks and Romans drew maps in which the Mediterranean was represented as the central point, depicted with tolerable accuracy, while the outer parts sank into increasing vagueness and fantasy, culminating finally in *terra incognita*, where dwelt dragons, dwarfs, and other mythical creatures; so the Chinese, though drawing few maps, equally saw the areas beyond their own borders as obscure and mysterious regions, occupied by ferocious, red-haired barbarians to the west, and by the strange inhabitants of the Land of the Root of the Sun in the east. 'Under-Heaven' comprehended the Chinese Empire alone. It was its most common name.

China had no means of adjusting this ethnocentric world image, as the many others who had once shared it had done, with the correcting lenses of alternative images. Here the effect of the geographical environment in which China found herself was crucial. On three sides she was surrounded by natural barriers. To the east, the open sea; to the south, high mountains; to the west, vast deserts. On the fourth side, in the north-west, she had some contacts, but only with totally uncivilized peoples. And there she herself provided a man-made barrier, the longest fortification on earth, to preserve the Heavenly Kingdom inviolate against the incursions of the warlike tribes beyond.

So enclosed, she was able to evolve the distinctive features of her elegant civilization, in almost total isolation from the disturbing contact of other cultures. Though once she enjoyed a neolithic culture similar, even in its details, to that which emerged elsewhere, the civilization which she developed on this basis was, for long, immune from outside influence. She received, especially during the expansion of the Han Empire to the west during the last two centuries B.C., momentary glimpses of Central Asia, India, Persia, Greek Bactria, and so, indirectly, of the Roman Empire. A mission sought Rome though it never seems to have got beyond Babylonia. The silk trade brought regular commercial exchanges of some Chinese and European products. But such fleeting contacts were not sufficient to bring even accurate information, let alone any consistent cultural exchanges. Culturally, ideologically, militarily, China became almost totally self-sufficient.

The image of the area to her west that emerged, therefore, was a largely undifferentiated one. Among a few, at certain moments, there was a vague awareness that there existed centres of culture and wealth, as well as of nomads and marauders, towards her west. But no ordinary Chinese, and few educated, can have been conscious of this fact. Until about A.D. 1500, the main techno- logical borrowings that took place were by the West from the East, rather than vice versa. Silk, paper, printing, gun-powder, the compass, the harness, and other Chinese inventions were adopted in Europe. In China the main cultural import, that of Buddhism, was not from Europe, but from another part of Asia. And this too was transformed on arrival in China. Thus even the near west was almost unknown: there never took place such a flow of cultural influences from India to China as that which took place to the Mediterranean world in the centuries succeeding Alexander's conquests.

The form in which China's image of the West was finally appre- hended was thus conditioned by the divergent process of develop- ment that took place in each. The forms of social organization and habits of thought that emerged in China were very different from any that developed in Europe. In the political field, the authority of the ancient priest-king developed in time into a form of im- perial autocracy, subject to few restraints other than the traditions of the state. Executive power was gradually vested in a highly educated elite, applying the paternalist principles of Confucian doctrine. While the good of the people was upheld, as in most other parts of the world, as the supreme end of government, and the techniques of government evolved to a fine art, the belief that the people should exercise any direct voice in determining that process was never propounded. Social codes and family morality rather than legal enforcement played the dominant part in governing conduct.

To this tradition, the political principles which Europe brought with it were totally alien. In the West too priest-king had evolved first into divine Emperor, later into divinely ordained monarch. But that order had been increasingly overlaid by other influences. The rise of a flourishing commercial class, and so of a centre of literacy independent of the regime, introduced a factor that China never knew. The merchant republics of the Mediterranean world, and the merchant cities of Medieval Europe, established traditions of popular control of public affairs that were totally foreign to China. Because absolutism had in Europe, unlike in China, become increasingly divorced from moral principles, the ultimate basis of the state was eventually acknowledged as force alone; and thus required to be subjected to popular control. In China, theoretically governed by moral purposes, demanding eventually their own retribution through the inexorable workings of the heavenly mandate, the need for such a sanction of consent appeared less obvious.

There was an equally fundamental gulf in religious concepts. The earliest and the strongest of the traditions in China, the veneration of ancestors and the offering of ceremonial sacrifices for their welfare, had never played so dominant a part in the religious life of other civilizations. The more evolved spiritual and philosophical concepts which emerged from the sixth and fifth centuries B.C. equally, although paralleled by a similar growth in other parts of the world, bore little affinity to those which developed elsewhere. The Chinese never manifested a need, either for the intense metaphysical speculation and mystical religious exercise which was exhibited at its highest in India; nor for the personal support of, and communion with, an anthropomorphic deity, that received its most characteristic expression in the West. The two characteristically Chinese religions, Confucianism and Taoism, are singularly lacking in metaphysical pronouncements. They offer no role comparable to that played by the deity elsewhere. Confucianism, conceived in an age of political and social confusion, was, like most of the rival schools of that day, primarily a political and social code, which sought to define correct relationships within the state and to lay down the forms of conduct, among rulers and ruled alike, that would best preserve the stability and harmony of the social order. Taoism, emerging equally in those disordered times, prescribed detachment from society, repudiating social obligations, law, morality, love, and intellect alike, and demanding total absorption in the underlying rhythm of nature.

To those brought up in this tradition, the concepts of the West, when they finally became known, appeared almost incomprehensible. For the image of a personal god provided a new and disconcerting element. Moral exhortation, which for Chinese was largely secular, in the West they found closely linked with belief in the deity, moral prescriptions attributed to his command, and moral values, such as love, pity, forgiveness, and righteousness, closely associated with his personality. The search for eternal life, which the Chinese pursued by means of magical rites and the pronouncement of Taoist texts, in the West they found closely linked with the personality of the saviour-god who might procure it. Once again the gap between the two systems of thought was so wide that the effort of adjustment, once contact occurred, must inevitably be a slow one.

Most important of all, intellectual development was totally divergent. The Chinese mind was basically pragmatic, realistic, and empirical. It was supremely capable of procuring the means of attaining those practical objectives that appeared to it worth while. But it was not, like the European mind, concerned to understand the basic processes underlying the workings of the world in which it found itself. Being by nature essentially artistic, it found appeal primarily in the specific, the concrete, and the colourful. The facluty for abstract generalization was largely lacking. As a result, the Chinese never started to undertake the slow but progressively more effective observation, recording, and classification of natural phenomena that was undertaken fitfully from Greek times, methodically from the seventeenth century, in Europe. While many vitally important practical inventions were made, and while the general level of technology was, until medieval times, certainly higher than in the West, the Chinese never even began to procure the underlying theoretical framework for measuring energy and mass on a systematic basis; for analysing matter into its component elements; for classifying plant and animal; or for systematizing the study of behaviour and society. Chinese civilization produced poetry of a refinement, painting of a subtlety, porcelain of a delicacy, that the West had never dreamt of. But Chinese thought remained discursive, and for long was fatally conditioned by the intellectual framework of the state ideology.

The mental adjustment that would have been required, therefore, by the sudden confrontation with this new world revealed from Europe, by the totally different image of the universe this brought, and the totally new productive techniques and way of life it made available, would have been profound enough in any case. Because the form in which Western knowledge was first fully revealed to China was in the cruisers and cannon by which the Western invaders battered their way into that cloistered Empire, the adjustment was, inevitably, an especially painful one.

The bridge to be gulfed was still enormous.

From the early Christian era spasmodic glimpses of a distant world in the West became more persistent. Missions from Byzantium were received. Arab traders regularly sailed to Chinese ports. Jewish merchants founded a substantial colony in Canton. Yet none of these made sufficient impact to evoke a consistent image of the West.

From about 1250 this began to be less the case. Two of the last three Chinese dynasties were themselves foreign. The Mongols not only transformed, at least temporarily, many of the basic institutions of the Empire. They brought alien officials, craftsmen, dancers, and others from all parts of their widespread territories; Persians, Arabs, Central Asians, and Europeans; Catholics, Nestorians, Buddhists, and Muslims, to the service of their Court. So while Europe learnt, through William de Rubruck and the Polo brothers, something of Cathay, China too got to know something of a few Western lands and their crafts. The Mings, though a native dynasty, showed briefly a greater interest in the Western world than any of their predecessors, undertaking a number of naval expeditions in the Indian Ocean, and penetrating momentarily to the Persian Gulf, Africa, South India, and Indonesia. They allowed the Portuguese to establish themselves in Macao for trading purposes. They received Jesuit and other Catholic missionaries in Peking. And they even allowed these to make some Chinese converts, including the last Empress of the dynasty.

The last dynasty, the Manchus, at first showed still greater regard for the Jesuits, from whom they acquired knowledge of astronomy, surveying, mathematics, Western medicine, and painting. While the orthodox Confucian scholars showed some hostility to the introduction of alien ideas, the attitude of the Court and high officials was one mainly of curiosity. Ku Yen-wu, the scholar and philosopher (1613–82), recognized that 'there are some Chinese customs which are inferior to those of foreign countries'.[1] But he declared that the main purpose of China should be to 'use Chinese institutions to transform the barbarians'.[2] Wang Fu-chih (1619–1692) believed that different traditions produced unbridgeable differences between the peoples of different regions, and that it was therefore essential for China to preserve herself from the

---

[1] Ku Yen-wu, *Jih-chih-lu chi-shih*, 10. 5. The English text of this, and some of the other Chinese writings quoted may be found in Teng and Fairbank, *China's Response to the West*, Harvard, 1954.
[2] Ku Yen-wu, *T'ing-lin wen-chi*, 6. 17.

barbarians.[1] But the interest was primarily in the techniques and the knowledge which the strangers brought with them; not of the lands from which they came. Curiosity remained closely conditioned by the needs and traditions of the Chinese Empire.

From the eighteenth century, this mood began to change. Increasingly the attitude became one of impatient irritation. At this time the Chinese Empire had reached a position of power which it has never attained at any other time before or since. But while Chinese power was being extended to the West, the Westerners too were expanding to the East. They began increasingly to impinge on the Celestial Empire. A mood of growing suspicion developed. The dealings of some Western seamen and merchants convinced the Chinese that they were dealing still with barbarian peoples. The teachings of the missionaries began increasingly to be regarded as a danger to the state and its ideology. As a result, a policy of insulation began. In the south, the foreign merchants were subjected to rigid and humiliating restrictions. In the north, the Catholic missionaries were expelled. Emigration of Chinese was forbidden. Permanent envoys from the West were refused. And visiting missions were constrained to adopt the form of obeisance traditionally prescribed for tributary states. 'The virtue and prestige of the Celestial Dynasty having spread far and wide, the kings of the myriad nations come by land and sea with all sorts of precious things', the Emperor Ch'ien Lung wrote to King George III; but 'there were well-established regulations governing tributary envoys from the outer states to Peking . . . limiting their going and coming'.[2]

In the nineteenth century, the mood towards the European again began to be transformed. For while, in earlier days, the West had been known only through the dealings of individuals, by now the Chinese Empire was brought into contact more and more with the European powers themselves. These made increasing demands. To the European powers, brought up in a flourishing commercial tradition, and enjoying unrestricted trade elsewhere, the permission to trade appeared a self-evident right that no civilized people could withhold. To the Chinese it was a generous concession, strictly subject to the Emperor's discretion. Equally, to

[1] Wang Fu-chih, *Shih kuang-chuan*, 3. 5.
[2] This occurs in the famous imperial edict of Ch'ien Lung to George III of 1793.

the European, accustomed to the prescribed code of diplomatic intercourse among sovereign states, the privilege of access to the sovereign through accreditation at his court seemed a right not to be refused. To the Chinese, who had no concept of sovereignty, and who had received at their court only tribute-bearers from defeated neighbours, embassies to the Empire could be required only for the purpose of conveying allegiance from foreign monarchs.

When, therefore, the Europeans proceeded ultimately to win for themselves, by force of arms, the privileges they had been persistently denied, such a proceeding represented a blow to traditional concepts and values, from which they were never able to recover.

The way the intervening curtain was torn aside crucially conditioned the view through the window which was thereby afforded. For long afterwards the glass was distorted by the inevitable refractions that resentment created. The privileges that Europe acquired for itself were those that she had been accustomed to enjoy in other parts of the world: trading rights, extraterritoriality, rights for missionaries, customs' concessions, diplomatic representation; later spheres of influence; and, finally, leases, bases, and settlements. But they were equally those most likely to arouse a growing sense of resentment and hostility against the West, in China as in other parts of the world made subject to Western domination.

China, for long surrounded by the mysterious regions of *terra incognita*, suddenly found the mythical dragons depicted there deposited on her doorstep. In time those dragons pressed more and more closely down on her. The Western European powers increasingly controlled her eastern coast. Russia advanced on her to the north-west. Japan drew closer to the north-east. The Celestial Empire suddenly found itself face to face with streamlined modern nations, less cultured perhaps, but undoubtedly infinitely more powerful, than she was herself. And she found herself obliged, willy-nilly, to take increasing account of the culture, the concepts, and the material civilization that had been brought to her doorstep.

The reaction of the Chinese official class to this confrontation was conditioned by the deeply rooted traditions of the national ideology. Because China had little previous experience of culture contact, the process of adaptation was inevitably a slow one. While China had always been easily able to absorb foreign racial stock, she had never before needed to absorb foreign cultural traditions. Thus while Japan, whose entire cultural equipment was largely borrowed in the first place, was able quickly to react to the Western powers by beating them, within less than forty years, with their own weapons, China, whose civilization was entirely home-made, was wholly without the mental resources to indulge in such a rapid transformation. There some, for more than fifty years, preserved the hope that all the essential elements of the ancient Chinese system could be preserved, and the influence of the Europeans so far as possible minimized. The superiority of Chinese civilization was usually assumed. Differences only concerned the extent to which it might be necessary to make temporary concessions. On the one hand, the villagers of Sau Yuan-li declared, in a 'Placard of the patriotic people of Kwang-tung', that the English 'had formed the habits and developed the nature of wolves'; and that 'if we do not exterminate you English barbarians, we will not be human beings'. On the other hand, the Manchu noble Ch'i-ying, in a memorial to the emperor, more cautiously observed that 'the methods by which to conciliate the barbarians and get them under control . . . could not but adapt themselves to the times'; and that while 'certainly we have to curb them by sincerity, it has been even more necessary to control them by skilful methods'.[1]

The benefits that might be won through use of the techniques the West had devised began to be recognized. At first these were regarded mainly as implements for use against the West itself; a form of imitative magic to exorcise the foreign devils. Wei Yuan, the compiler of the first geography of the West, declared: 'We must learn the superior skills of the barbarians in order to control them'.[2] The first Chinese Ambassador in London recommended that his countrymen should 'investigate carefully the entire history [of the foreigners] and itemize the actual causes of their becoming rich and strong . . .'.[3] Feng Kuei-fen, the scholar and teacher, wrote: 'What we have to learn from the barbarians is only one thing:

[1] Ch'i-ying, *I-wu shih-mo*, 73.
[2] Wei Yuan, *Hai-kuo t'u chih*, 1844.
[3] Kuo Sung-tao, *Yang-chi shu-wu wen-chi*, 11. 3.

solid ships and effective guns'.[1] It was therefore, as before, mainly the gadgets and gimmicks of the West that attracted Chinese attention. Just as, in the seventeenth century, they had shown interest mainly in the European clocks, telescopes, and binoculars, rather than in the scientific principles that had produced them; so, in the nineteenth century, they sought at first to copy the secrets of military and industrial success without the political and social infrastructure that had made them possible.

From about the eighties, there was a movement towards a more fundamental reform of the traditional Chinese system. Translations of many important Western political and social thinkers began to be undertaken. The reforms that were advocated at home were inevitably largely moulded by the new influences received from the West. And attitudes to Western concepts were themselves partly influenced by attitudes towards indigenous institutions.

By this time, therefore, Chinese writers and reformers were prepared to go a good deal further than before in borrowing from the new culture with which they had been confronted. The writer Chang Chih-tung demanded: 'Chinese learning for the structure: Western knowledge for the practical use'. Kang Yu-wei, and other leaders of the reform movement at the close of the century, recommended political institutions and methods strongly influenced by Western political ideas. Finally, Sun Yat-sen, brought up as a Christian in a Christian school, and personally acquainted with Western societies, reflected more clearly than any before the impact of Western political thought. His 'three people's principles' of nationalism, democracy, and people's livelihood were formulated during his stay in Europe, and under the impact of European ideas. While, like his predecessors, intensely hostile to Western political domination in China, he was ready to welcome Western political principles:

It is necessary . . . to change the national polity and the people's livelihood. And though there are a myriad ways and means to achieve this goal, the essential spirit that runs through them all is freedom, equality and fraternity.[2]

The adoption of Western concepts and institutions did not in itself serve to modify the Chinese image of the lands from which

---

[1] Feng Kuei-fen, *Chiao-pin-lu k'ang-i*, 2. 40–44.
[2] Sun Yat-sen, *Chung-san ch'uan-shu*, manifesto.

they were borrowed. This was especially true of the mass of the population. A slightly clearer picture of the Western world began to emerge. One or two simple geographies, based on Western sources, began to appear during the forties and fifties.[1] But the picture these painted was still a crude one. While by the end of the century the books which had appeared in English alone that were concerned with aspects of Chinese history and institutions could be numbered in hundreds, the number of corresponding Chinese works on the West could probably have been counted on the fingers. For the man in the street foreigners remained 'big noses', 'ocean men', or even 'foreign devils'. The peasants detested the strange railways that foreigners had brought, belching smoke among the valleys and angering the spirits of the localities. The court distrusted, with some reason, the designs of the foreign powers against China. The scholars resented, with less, the invasion of influences that might undermine the Confucian faith. Even the intellectuals were far from unqualified admirers of the Western customs and constitutions. And the culmination of these underlying resentments was the bloody Boxer Rising, in which court and countryside turned against European and Europeanized Chinese alike.

In the field of religion adjustment was especially reluctant. Here the concepts that Europe brought were so alien that they never took deep root. Chinese Christians numbered at their peak something like two or three million. This was itself a minute proportion of the total population. And for many their faith was little more than nominal. For the most part the response of the Chinese to the Christian religion was sceptical; sometimes bitterly hostile. From the start there were conceptual conflicts. The Jesuit missionaries had great difficulty in finding adequate translations for many of the important ideas of the Christian faith, including the name of the deity himself. And until the present day Protestant and Catholics have continued to make use of different appellations for their God, a source of not unnatural perplexity to many Chinese. Thus Christianity was never able to attract more than a tiny segment of the Chinese people, and then often for reasons that were not exclusively religious.

Many concepts, original sin, redemption and atonement, the

[1] The best known were those of Wu-yuan, published in 1844, and that of Hsu Chi-yu of 1850.

Holy Trinity, the ritual of Holy Communion, these and others were so alien to Chinese traditions that they were not intelligible to most Chinese minds. Since the churches were mainly reluctant to permit any modification of belief or practice to conform with Chinese culture and tradition, Western religion continued to appear largely incomprehensible to most Chinese. Certain rites were identified with black magic. Even until the twenties of the twentieth century missionaries were sometimes, partly for this reason, the object of mob-violence. And in the long run, the long and honourable tradition of missionary activity in China may be regarded as significant, rather for the knowledge of China it brought to the West than for the instruction it provided in the opposite direction.

During the twentieth century, the incoherent sense of hostility towards the foreigner began to take the form of a more explicit desire to expel the Westerner from the position he had extorted in China. There emerged the ambition to raise China once more to the status of a great power. 'China is the China of the Chinese', declared a manifesto issued by Sun Yat-sen in 1905. 'The government of China should be in the hands of the Chinese.' The immediate aim remained to transform Chinese society. But after the revolution of 1911, and even more after the betrayal of Chinese interests at Versailles, the main object of hostility became the Westerner himself.

The dominant attitude towards the West was thus conditioned by the political relationship of China to the West. In his desire, once the country had been unified, to evict the European powers altogether, Sun Yat-sen was representative of his entire generation. In seeking, in the early twenties, the support of the Soviet Union to assist him in this task, he was displaying no ideological predilection. But he served in so doing to identify Russia and its new political faith with the East against the West, with Asia against Europe. 'In the Russian Revolution', he declared, the Russians 'had insisted on the rule of right and denounced the rule of might' and so 'had joined with the Orient and parted company with the West'. The annexation of Russia for the East was one that even those ideologically more committed could never entirely stomach. But the identification of the West with 'might', firmly embattled against the forces of 'right', was one that was, inevitably, widely shared by intellectuals of the time; not least by many of those most impregnated with Western ideologies.

There was indeed a paradox about the situation. For thirty years, from the twenties onwards, China was plunged in an internal struggle that was fought out almost entirely in terms of political theories and slogans borrowed from the West. For while the old Chinese traditions were now universally disregarded, no new one had yet emerged to take their place. Thus the Nationalists, turning against their allies in the Communist party, acted in the name of democracy, parliamentarianism, freedom, and many other catchwords of the West Europeans. The Chinese Communists, in their turn, pronounced adherence to the dogmas of proletarian struggle, class war, the inevitable decay of capitalism, and all the other slogans propounded in the eastern half of Europe. Yet in essence that contest was a power struggle between factions that were equally authoritarian, equally nationalistic, and, in the final resort, equally antipathetic to much that the West represented.

An opposite paradox took place on the social plane. For though overtly hostility to the West was almost everywhere proclaimed, China none the less became more and more dominated by Western concepts, traditions, and manners. This applied to Nationalists and Communists alike. Nationalists wore Western clothes, built Western-style houses, were educated in Western-run schools, danced Western-style dances in Western-style night clubs, even devised Western forms for their Chinese names. Communists adopted the Western calendar, sought to replace Chinese characters with the Western alphabet, analysed in Western political categories, and established Western-style institutions that, at first at least, were almost indistinguishable from their counterparts in the Soviet Union. Western thought, Western art, and Western science became everywhere the norm among the intellectual class.

This cultural submission was eventually partly compensated by greater political independence. Even between the wars China recovered some of the concessions and privileges formerly wrested from her. During the Second World War the rest were signed away. China took part in summit conferences on equal terms with the U.S. and Britain. After it, she was made one of the five permanent members of the new peace-keeping organization then established. China was able to deal with the West on equal terms once more.

In consequence of these developments the Chinese image of the West began to be adjusted. It was no longer seen primarily in terms of an alien culture. For that culture was no longer wholly alien. It was no longer seen in terms of political domination. For that domination had already been relinquished. The West came now increasingly to be analysed in terms of its relation to the ideological struggle in China. For this mirrored that being undertaken in the world as a whole. As elsewhere, the ideological factions which struggled for supremacy in China identified themselves with those outside powers that proclaimed similar or comparable ideologies. The West thus altogether ceased to be a homogeneous entity. In the eyes of Chinese, Europe was bisected, polarized between the respective allies of the two dominant forces in China.

When, therefore, one of the two factions disputing the country emerged finally totally victorious, and imposed its own image on the entire country, this inevitably determined the form in which the West, in its dual form, was to be represented among the coming generation.

Here once more, there was a paradox. For though China was now linked with parts of Europe by a nominal allegiance to a single political ideology, the distance that still separated her from these was barely less crucial than that which divided her from other regions of the West. And it was inevitable that, as time progressed and China became increasingly independent, that distance should become more and more apparent.

During the last fifteen years, therefore, Chinese attitudes towards the West have been conditioned by the national political posture. East and West have acquired new significance, only marginally related to geographical situation. 'The West' has become a technical term, denoting Western Europe, the U.S., their allies, and all their capitalist works. And the glass curtain dividing China from the outside world has become thus deeply tinted with the lines of ideological prejudice.

The prevailing orthodoxy, though itself derived from Europe, was in many ways well adapted to provide the political philosophy, appropriate to Chinese conditions, which, since the decline of Confucianism, China had lacked. Being a philosophy of history, whose approach was essentially dynamic, it was able to furnish a more satisfying ideological support for a society in violent transition than the more static formulations of Western European political thought. Being received in China only in its Leninist form, that is as adapted to the era of imperialism, it could provide an intellectual framework both for the nationalistic and anti-colonial sentiment cherished by most Chinese; and for the more general anti-Western feeling which the ruling powers wished to promote. It contained the justification for the authoritarian bureaucracy that China had always known, and which many perhaps still regarded as well suited to her condition. It provided, in its materialist and positivist approach, a form of dogma well suited to the naturally non-religious temperament of the Chinese, and a new ethic for the fervent and puritanical mood which had now possessed many in the country. It afforded, in the conception of the dialectic, the alternation of thesis and antithesis, providing the driving power behind historical progress, an echo of the ancient conception of Yin and Yang, the interaction between dark and light, the motive force behind the mysterious rhythm of the universe. And it could furnish for the first time the image of a millennium in the future, as well as in the past, in which the mighty would be cast down from their seat, the faithful justified, and the chosen people of Communism become a light to lighten the gentiles towards the golden age to come.

Thus the conventional world image began once more to bear some traces of the ancient exclusiveness of the Chinese Empire. The former picture of a solitary oasis of civilization, surrounded by a horde of benighted barbarians, was perhaps still to be discerned in the new concept of a coalition of progressive forces of the world, the 'socialist camp', surrounded by the powers of darkness, that is of reactionary imperialism, the 'capitalist bloc' without. Such concepts had the benefit of allying ideological conviction with national aspiration. For it was a basic article of the faith that, through those processes of history, today the 'East wind prevailed over the West wind'.

None can tell with certainty how far public pronouncements mirrored private judgements. The brief, but intensive, Chinese exploration of the thought and institutions of Europe during the previous fifty years of this century, was undertaken perhaps as much through curiosity as through any deep personal affection or conviction. Many doubted their relevance to China's situation.

Others resisted on traditional or nationalist grounds. The majority remained ignorant.

Yet, for some at least, that contact must have left a deeper impression. Scientists and scholars who had experience of the tradition of free inquiry in Western academic institutions must have retained of this a memory that could still exert its impact when the tradition was publicly repudiated. Students and travellers who knew at first hand of the working of the societies of Western lands must preserve an image to offset the more imaginative picture propounded to the succeeding generation. Those who had experienced or learnt of the working of democratic institutions in Europe and America and of the political theories on which these were based, cannot have blotted the memory of them totally from their minds.

But to inhabitants of the Far East, the Communist bloc was itself largely a Western coalition. China had perhaps never wholeheartedly identified herself with that grouping. She never became a member of the Warsaw Pact or Comecon. And in the course of time China's growing power, the growing differences of ideological mood between herself and her less militant allies, above all, perhaps, the difference in their stage of economic development, increased the gap between Asian and European Communists. By the beginning of the sixties, the Soviet Union's hegemony within the Communist bloc was being openly challenged and its leaders publicly denounced. The belief that the East Wind would prevail over the West was perhaps applied, by some, within the Communist bloc, as well as without it.

Even in the Mid-West, Asia, and the Middle East, a temporary phase of conciliation soon gave way to intransigent and doctrinaire intolerance. Thus today, apart from one or two small and insignificant allies in both East and West, China is almost alone in the world. To some extent she might claim such isolation had been imposed from without. But China's existing attitude cannot be explained wholly on this basis. Had her basic instincts towards other lands been more co-operative, she could certainly have retained fruitful friendships elsewhere. Had she inherited a tradition of intercourse and common action, such as many other nations of the world enjoyed, she might have played a more malleable and constructive role, both among her ideological and continental partners. Perhaps because of her background, she has felt an instinctive distaste for binding herself to formal group-loyalties.

I

She is understandably reluctant to accept any position of sub-ordination. Even collaboration she finds difficult.

China's attitudes to the West, Communist and non-Communist, today are therefore the product of complex factors. Ideological prejudices are only one among these. Traditional ethnocentricity is another. Consciousness of growing Chinese power is a more important one. Perhaps most crucial of all is the righteousness bred of revolutionary fervour, and the messianic world-image that this engenders. The identification of national with moral purposes is part of a consistent strain of revivalist emotion that dates back to the 'self-strengthening' movement of the last century. This was perhaps a natural response to the simultaneous humiliation of national pride and the destruction of an ancient value system. So, the resentments built up by a century of wrongs, added to the self-confidence and self-sufficiency inherited from millennia of un-disputed cultural and military supremacy, have superimposed the passions of nationalism on the fervour of ideology. And national self-assertion is expressed, as elsewhere, in a crusading zeal to annex the world, not for the nation, but for native political gods.

The Western world, therefore, non-Communist and Communist alike, is at present viewed in largely religious terms. 'The West', in the conventional sense, become the heathen, the godless still to be converted. The Soviet Union, and other modern revisionists, become heretics, lapsed from a former state of grace. Such, at least, are the attitudes that receive public expression. Perhaps they truly represent the world-view of China's leaders. How far they are shared by the Chinese man in the street must be a matter of con-jecture only. Allowed no personal vision of the world without, and injected through every channel of communication with the approved two-dimensional image of the world, he is probably at the very least, by mere force of repetition, profoundly influenced by such a view-point. What certainly he shares with his leaders is a passionate desire to see his country justified in the eyes of the world. The attempt to elevate the political writings of the present leader to the status of a holy book, the evolution of characteristically Chinese forms of institution within the Communist state, the attempt to present their own system as the model for developing areas in every part of the world, the image of China as leader of a world-wide revolutionary movement: all these are the contemporary manifestations of the evangelistic mood of the country.

When the first fervour of revolution has been exhausted, the ambition to rebuild the country's greatness satisfied, and the resentments inherited from the past worked out, these attitudes may begin to fade. The overwhelming weight of Chinese numbers may, even then, perpetuate the ambition to play a dominating role in world affairs. But such an ambition, among a country that may number from a quarter to a third of the population of the world, would be difficult to challenge. As their external circumstances improve, however, it may be that the natural kindliness, good humour, and intelligence of the Chinese people will come to play a larger role in conditioning attitudes to the outside world. The ancient ideals of courtliness and formality may be applied to the relations of diplomatic intercourse. Within the more integrated international polity then being evolved, China may be ready to play a role that is more cautious, conciliatory, and co-operative than that of today.

How far, in these conditions, the Chinese continue to retain a distinctive image of the West will depend on how far other parts of the earth are ready to take steps to minimize, on the economic as much as the political plane, the new differences then dividing the continents. China may increasingly seek to make herself the dominant champion of the less-developed against the wealthy. Only if class-barriers, based on the differing status of these, can be avoided may resentments be allayed.

So the isolation that has long coloured Chinese attitudes may be overcome. In such a world, distinctions based on the compass-points alone may become less meaningful. China may no longer see need to adopt any system of categories distinguishing between East and West. New forms of relationship, and new categories to comprehend them, more appropriate to the international community then emerging, may be evolved in East and West alike.

VII. JAPANESE ATTITUDES
TO THE WEST

Richard Storry

The Japanese word for 'foreigner' is *Gaijin*. This means, literally, 'an outsider'; and it has certain connotations. For example, it can carry overtones very complimentary to the foreigner—implying that he is not only the possessor of superior technological competence but also the envied inheritor of a logically constructed system of beliefs, religious and philosophical, that has spread irresistibly across the globe. On the other hand, *Gaijin* can be taken to mean a man who is at best naïvely uncultivated and, at worst, a capricious vulgarian. *Gaijin da kara!* ('It's because he's a foreigner')—this is a phrase still heard in Japan. It means: 'he knows no better' (seeing that he is, after all, a benighted *Gaijin*). In this context the *Gaijin* is indeed an *outsider*, in the old-fashioned pejorative sense of this now somewhat outmoded English word.

It is noteworthy that as a rule the Japanese do not refer to Asian foreigners—Koreans, Chinese, Indians, Pakistanis, and Arabs—as *Gaijin*, although this is the formal, official designation of all non-Japanese. In daily conversation the Japanese describe an Asian in terms of his specific nationality. *Gaijin*, then, means in common parlance a white man, a 'Westerner'. He was originally known as an *Ijin*—literally 'a strange person'. When this term was first widely used, in the sixteenth century, it had a neutral flavour. But in time it acquired distinctly insulting connotations—particularly during the eighteen-fifties, when Japan was subjected to intrusion by the West after more than two centuries of self-imposed isolation. The fact was that *Ijin* could be written in two different sets of ideographs—one being rude, the other inoffensive. Another term for the white man, now archaic (like *Ijin*), was *Gaiban*, 'outer barbarian'; and the Portuguese merchants and priests in sixteenth-century Japan were usually known as *Nam-banjin* ('southern barbarians'). Yet the sense in which this term was used was, as often as not, friendly and affectionate rather than abusive.

This varied nomenclature reflects the ambivalent attitude of the Japanese to the West, to what is implied in the phrase 'the Western World'. It is an attitude compounded, historically, of attachment and dislike, of admiration and fear. But it has never been remotely associated with any tinge of complacent indifference. And the basic element has been curiosity.

It is apparent that the first Europeans—Portuguese castaways in 1542—were welcomed with open arms. Other Portuguese, traders and missionaries, were received in friendly fashion as the years went by. For this there were practical reasons. The foreigners brought into Japan a weapon not seen there before—namely, the arquebus, or smooth-bore musket. This was Japan's introduction to firearms; and the new weapons were soon copied with success by Japanese smiths. Furthermore, the Portuguese brought the benefits of foreign trade; and there was rivalry between the feudatories of South-western Japan to attract this commerce to their own harbours.

It is less easy to account for the initial success of the Catholic missionaries. One reason no doubt was the high personal calibre of the Jesuit fathers who formed the spearhead of European missionary endeavour in those years. Personal example always impresses the Japanese. The Jesuits took pains to adapt themselves to Japanese ways of life; and they mastered the Japanese language to such effect that they were able to conduct telling debates with the Buddhist priesthood. It has been pointed out, too, that a possible clue to the appeal of Christian doctrine to the Japanese was the resemblance between the ecstatic states of mind reached by Japanese Christians and those enjoyed by devotees of the Pure Land and Lotus sects.[1]

It is perhaps significant that in those parts of Japan where the Jodo (Pure Land) sect was most firmly established there were few converts to Christianity.[2]

Yet, as another authority has put it, in reviewing the influence of Christianity we can say that 'the Japanese people have never

[1] G. B. Sansom, *The Western World and Japan*, The Cresset Press, London, 1950, p. 139.   [2] Ibid., p. 140.

shown easy susceptibility to its exclusive monotheism or to its doctrine of original sin'.[1]

Nevertheless, it was certainly political as much as religious considerations that led to the suppression of Christianity in Japan during the seventeenth century. Indeed in the context of Japanese history it is often unreal to draw a sharp distinction between the religious and the political. A basic and recurring civic concept in Japan—carried forward well into the twentieth century—was 'the unity of government and religion'. The success of the Catholic missionaries—there were some 300,000 converts by 1600—suggested that Christianity, like Buddhism in the sixth century, was going to take root. And in fact it might have done so, if Japan had relapsed during the seventeenth century into the condition of endemic civil war that had prevailed a hundred years earlier. But precisely because the Tokugawa Shogunate was determined to preserve the hegemony won and consolidated by Ieyasu, it was obsessively afraid of an armed challenge to its authority from a combination of dissatisfied territorial lords. Among the latter those of the South-west were potentially the most dangerous; and it was in this region that Christianity had made the most headway. Now Christianity was identified with the Catholic Church—the Japanese at that time did not regard Dutch or English Protestants as Christians—and the Catholic Church became identified with the Pope and with the King of Spain, the conqueror of the Philippines. Eventually the Shogunate decreed and enforced the total expulsion of the Iberians, the suppression of Christianity, and the closing of the country to all 'strange persons', save the Dutch, who were confined to the tiny trading settlement of Deshima at Nagasaki. Here they were virtually isolated from general contact with the local population. Welcome to the West had turned full-circle to almost complete rejection within rather less than a hundred years.

The 'Christian century' in Japan foreshadowed, in some degree, what was to happen during the 'Marxist decade' (1920–30). In both periods the authorities, basing their policy on 'the unity of government and religion', labelled an alien faith blasphemous as well as politically subversive—the adjectives being nearly synonymous—and in both periods a hard core of converts defied all efforts to induce apostasy.

[1] M. Anesaki, 'Religions in Japan', *Western Influences in Modern Japan*, by Inazo Nitobe and others, University of Chicago Press, 1931, p. 112.

The Japanese are whole-hoggers. They rarely do things by halves. Thus, when an English vessel dropped anchor off Nagasaki in 1673 it was turned away on the grounds that Charles II was married to Catherine of Braganza. Even the most tenuous contacts with Portugal were utterly forbidden. It was the same with Catholic Christianity. The slightest reference to this religion in a foreign book was sufficient to ensure its destruction.

For two centuries only the Dutch, cooped up at Deshima, formed a link with the civilization of the West. Once a year the principal Dutch merchant and a few of his assistants journeyed under close supervision to the Shogun's capital, bearing, in the manner of suppliant vassals, presents and a report on happenings in Europe. In this way a trickle of scientific knowledge reached government officials at the capital and in Nagasaki. Often surprisingly little attention was paid to such knowledge. For example, in 1717 the leading Dutch merchant, on his annual visit to the Shogun, was invited to translate the title of a book on zoology presented by one of his predecessors in 1663.[1] Nevertheless, a few inquisitive Japanese made some study of European affairs through a laborious investigation of the few books and maps that the Dutch were allowed to hand over to the Japanese. The situation here became a little easier in 1720, when it was decreed that books which did not actually expound Christianity might circulate in Japan.

Among those few Japanese who became, in the eyes of their compatriots, experts on Western learning (*Rangaku*—'Dutch studies'—as it was called) there were some who adopted the attitude of total acceptance. This was important in the intellectual history of Japan because admiration of European models implied derogation of China's high standing as the fount of all wisdom and culture. One of the most interesting of these specialists in Western learning, Toshiaki Honda, wrote about Europe—at the end of the eighteenth century—in terms of the highest praise. Referring to the cities of London, Paris, and Amsterdam, he declared:

In these three capitals live people virtually without peer in the world, who are the handsomest of men. . . . Their prosperity is probably due to the excellence of their political system and the great number of years of experience that they have had. This is not an isolated instance,

[1] Donald Keene, *The Japanese Discovery of Europe*, Routledge & Kegan Paul, 1952, p. 15.

and the excellence of their whole society cannot be conjectured from Japanese and Chinese equivalents.[1]

But side by side with a modest but important development of interest in Western studies there occurred, in the late eighteenth and early nineteenth centuries, a revival of an ethnocentric concern with Shinto traditions. This was both destructive of China's cultural prestige and hostile to Western learning. Thus, when Japan was forced to come to terms with the United States, Great Britain, and other powers in the middle of the nineteenth century, her attitude was extraordinarily confused. Admiration struggled with fear; and curiosity often fought against a physical repulsion. For the Europeans, thanks to their diet of meat and butter, carried an odour unpleasant to the fish-eating Japanese. In a literal sense Yokohama and other centres of foreign commerce were invaded by *Yoshu*, 'the smell of the West'.

Many officials believed, with some justification, that unregulated intrusion by the West must mean profound disturbance to the entire social order. The phrase 'wicked commoners and sly foreign barbarians' appears very often in missives addressed to the Shogunate by those members of the oligarchy who objected to the treaties signed with Perry and other foreign representatives. The very presence of Westerners, it was feared, would help slacken the links that had held intact the hierarchical structure of the Tokugawa state. An early example of this particular phobia can be seen from a police report on conditions at Uraga, the fishing village where Commodore Perry's sailors landed in 1853.

Foreigners are by nature well versed in winning over ignorant people; and if they take advantage of the prevalent dissatisfaction of the people and grant them ample favours, it will lead to the most disastrous consequences.[2]

But Europeans would disturb not only the class structure of Japanese society. They would destroy the accepted relationship between the sexes. Thus one contemporary Japanese complaint was that foreigners paid far too much deference to women (failing thereby to distinguish between *yin* and *yang*). This particular Japanese objection (expressed by Totsuan Ohashi) maintained that in the matter of respect to women the Westerners resembled

---

[1] Donald Keene, *The Japanese Discovery of Europe*, Routledge & Kegan Paul, 1952, pp. 208–9.

[2] The writer is indebted, for this quotation, to Professor Masao Maruyama.

animals more than human beings, for animals pay much more attention to mothers than to fathers. Another Japanese, Seishisai Aizawa, wrote:

The Westerners are like beasts. They have a system of monogamy which forbids them to keep concubines, even though the wife may be childless and the family line in danger of dying out.[1]

It is misleading, however, to suppose that there was some neat division between hide-bound conservatives and open-minded 'progressives' in this matter of the Japanese response to nineteenth-century Europe. People changed sides. Violent xenophobes would be converted to a belief in the necessity of forming close friendship with the West. Admirers of the West sometimes became ardent nationalists once they came into contact with Europeans.

Eventually, after more than ten years of confusion and spasmodic bloodshed, Japan embarked upon wholesale modernization—in other words, Westernization; the motive being the efficient enhancement of national power. The slogan of the day was: 'A Rich Country and a Strong Army'; and within a surprisingly short time almost the entire apparatus of Western civilization had its counterpart or its enthusiastic advocates in Japan. Some Japanese in high office went so far as to urge intermarriage with Europeans on a large scale, in order to improve the Japanese racial stock. Others advocated the abolition of Chinese and Japanese ideographs in favour of the alphabet. Beef-eating—hitherto an unorthodox practice to say the least—was officially encouraged on the grounds that it was a symbol of advanced civilization and beneficial to the national physique.

Nevertheless the government's policy on 'Westernization' was in fact selective. The aim from the first was to borrow and adapt from Europe and North America only such material objects, techniques, institutions, and ideas as would serve to make Japan more powerful without undermining the structure of certain traditional beliefs—Shinto, Confucian, and Buddhist—that the oligarchy regarded as basic to the *Kokutai* ('the national policy'), to what we might describe as the 'Japanism' of Japan. As the famous 'Charter Oath', of the Emperor Meiji in 1868, declared: 'Knowledge shall be sought for all over the world, and thereby the foundations of Imperial rule shall be strengthened'.

[1] Carmen Blacker, *Ohashi Totsuan*, Transactions of the Asiatic Society of Japan, Third Series, vol. vii, 1959, pp. 155-6.

It was, of course, the institutions and ideas of the West, rather than Western technology, that attracted the most critical scrutiny. The most famous popularizer of things Western, Yukichi Fukuzawa, revealed in his autobiography that when he went to America in 1860 nothing surprised him in the scientific, technological field. He had already read about such things in books at home. But he was 'completely lost with social matters (parliamentary government, banking, hospitals, etc)'.[1]

So it was only with reluctance that Christianity was tolerated. Popular representation in a national parliament, even on a much restricted suffrage, was resisted for many years. It was finally conceded in 1889 in the form of a Russian-type constitution handed down *de haut en bas* by the Emperor Meiji. Popular government, however, was anathema; and the minority of intellectuals that supported it lived in peril of arrest and persecution.

The same risk attended the propagation of such ideas as birth-control, equality of the sexes, pacifism, anarchism, and every shade of Marxism. For in 1890 a document was promulgated by the Emperor that quickly acquired the sanctity of holy writ. This was the celebrated Rescript on Education. It was distributed to every school in the land, to be brought out on days of national celebration and read aloud by the headmaster or college principal to a respectful assembly of pupils. For the next fifty-five years the Rescript was the venerated statement *ex cathedra* of Japan's fundamental ethical code; and its prestige in the eyes of the masses, if not in the minds of a sophisticated or radical minority, can hardly be exaggerated. The Rescript adjured the young people of Japan to observe the Confucian obligations of filial piety, obedience, and benevolence, in their various relationships and to offer themselves 'courageously to the State' should need arise. It also included the following significant passage:

The Way here set forth is indeed the teaching bequeathed by Our Imperial Ancestors, to be observed alike by Their Descendants and the subjects, infallible for all ages and true in all places.

There was no specific or even implied admonition in the Rescript against 'dangerous foreign ideas'. But it is known that the Emperor was disturbed by the educational conditions he had observed on

---

[1] Quoted by M. Takeyama in his 'The Secularization of Feudal Japan', *Japan Quarterly*, vol. vi, no. 1, January–March 1959.

various tours of inspection. He was worried, it appears, by the stress laid on scientific and technical education and by the failure, as he saw it, to give adequate teaching in Japanese studies, in Confucianism and moral subjects in general. A visit in 1886 to Tokyo Imperial University seems to have caused the Emperor Meiji particular concern. At this period he was much influenced by a Court official, Eifu Motoda, an elderly Confucian scholar who had long felt outraged by the tide of Western influence flooding into Japan. In fact Motoda regarded Western learning as a menace to the very foundations of Japanese life. An extract from one of his essays will demonstrate not only his own views but also those of many implacable conservatives in Japan at that time.

A leading aim of the Restoration was the destruction of harmful habits. With the excellent view of making the expanse of knowledge world-wide, we temporarily took the strong points of the West, and this daily brought results. But an evil from this current [of Westernization] is the placing of humaneness, righteousness, loyalty, and filial piety in a secondary position.[1]

Motoda played a major part in drafting the Rescript; and it seems almost certain that he desired the inclusion of some words critical of the West. However, others concerned opposed this. As one consultant put it: 'No intimation of Chinese learning or Western ways should be expressed'.[2] Thus in its final form the Rescript on Education made no mention of the West. But, as we have seen, it was a powerful assertion of Japanese nationalist feeling. To this extent, then, it could not fail to act as a barrier to the uncritical acceptance of ideas from abroad.

The Rescript was promulgated in the year after the grant of the Meiji Constitution, and indeed it may be looked upon as an insurance policy taken out by the oligarchy against the risks that must be incurred in later years from a liberal interpretation of the Constitution. Moreover, the Rescript made its appearance at a moment in history when the Japanese were still smarting from their disappointment at failing to persuade England and other powers to revise the 'unequal treaties' concluded with Japan some thirty years earlier. In the 1880s great efforts had been made by the authorities to impress upon the Western world the high degree of civilization and enlightenment attained by Japan. To this end

[1] W. W. Smith, *Confucianism in Modern Japan*, Hokuseido Press, 1959, p. 71.
[2] Ibid., p. 85 (letter from Kowashi Inoue to Aritomo Yamagata).

the criminal and civil legal codes had been thoroughly revised. At the same time the government encouraged rather more superficial measures to demonstrate to Europeans and Americans that Tokyo could hold its own with the other great capital cities of the world. For example, the ladies of the Court put on the bustle in place of the *kimono*, and learned the niceties of European cookery, dress-making, and music. An English architect was commissioned to design a special building in which government officials could give Western dances and dinners. Yet all this endeavour failed to achieve its end. By the close of the eighties treaty revision had foundered. Not unnaturally a reaction set in. The Rescript on Education was part of it.

Of great significance, however, is the fact that the Rescript symbolizes an attitude towards the West that was to prevail, with varying intensity, until the late summer of 1945. The attitude was an old one, adopted by most anti-Westernizers in the middle years of the nineteenth century. It can be summed up in the Japanese phrase—*Toyo dotoku, Seiyo geijutsu*, which means: 'Eastern ethics and Western science'. A rather more blunt way of putting this would be: 'Take their machines but not their morals: respect their ingenuity but not their ideals'.

It is true that this attitude often reflected no more than a quiet pride in Japan's cultural heritage. Until the thirties claims for the superiority of 'the Japanese spirit' *vis-à-vis* 'Western materialism' were not emphasized, as a rule, in an overt, aggressive manner. But with the growing intervention, after 1931, by military men in state affairs a strident nationalism began to infect the whole of society. There was no blanket denigration of the West—and indeed Japan allied herself with the two main fascist powers of the West—but militarist propaganda tended to arrange the nations of the world in a hierarchy, with Japan at its apex; and according to this view European fascism, as well as Western democracy or the Christian religion, were both alien and inferior to *Toyo dotoku* ('Eastern ethics'), of which the highest expression was to be found in *Yamato damashii* ('the Japanese spirit').

This attitude, particularly marked among the fighting services, led of course to appalling results. For when Japan faced deadlock with the United States in the autumn of 1941 the vital factor of America's overwhelming power was undervalued, if not actually dismissed out of hand, as being in the last resort solely 'material' and therefore no match for the resources of Japan backed by *Yamato damashii*. So Japan entered unnecessarily a war which she had no chance of winning. However, rapid and spectacular victories in the early days naturally tended to confirm the belief in Japan's invincible 'spiritual' superiority; so much so, that this faith was not wholly shaken by the successive defeats of the last eighteen months of the struggle. To the very end Japan's army commanders appeared to be convinced that final victory could be attained. Indeed this conviction increased with the imminence of an enemy landing on the Japanese homeland. The atomic bombs provided the ultimate demonstration of 'Western science'; and the corresponding demonstration of 'Eastern ethics', in Japanese eyes, was the Emperor's broadcast Rescript announcing the surrender.

There followed the third and greatest intrusion by the West. All attempts by the oligarchy to be selective, to pick and choose, were brushed aside by the Occupation authorities. In any case the mass of the Japanese people were in no mood to resist the flood-tide of the West. But acceptance of the manifold reforms inspired by the Occupation was not merely passive. At the popular level it soon became enthusiastic; and during the honeymoon period of the Occupation—until about the middle of 1948—it could be claimed that the Americans, like the sixteenth-century Portuguese, were greeted by the Japanese with open arms.

Thanks to the very nature of the Occupation it was primarily in terms of the United States, and of Americans, that the Japanese pictured the post-war Western world. Today too the Westerner in Japan is often called 'the man from over there' (*achira no hito*); 'over there' meaning across the Pacific. At first the object of un-discriminating approval, the image of the 'man from over there', began to change from about the fourth or fifth year of the Occupa-tion, from 1949 or 1950. In other words, his failings as well as his virtues appeared in sharper focus. His image never became wholly tarnished; but it lost the almost charismatic quality that it once possessed. For this there were all kinds of reasons. As life in the ruined cities returned to some semblance of normality, and as the privations of the immediate post-war years were left behind, the Japanese had the stamina and, as it were, the time to take the measure of their conquerors. The main programme of reforms, affecting most sides of life, had been carried through by 1949; and the excitement, as well as the shock, of a bloodless social revolution had waned. The standard of living had improved sufficiently to make the Japanese the more conscious of the privileges—in terms of housing, travel facilities, food supplies, and general amenities—enjoyed by the thousands of Americans in their midst. The occupation in fact was beginning to be a bore.

Besides, the Cold War drove the Americans to shift the emphasis of their Occupation policy from reform to reconstruction. They came, so it seemed, to attach less importance to the prevention of a Right-Wing revival than to placing restraints on Left-Wing agitation. When the Cold War burst into flames in Korea the Japanese were disturbed by the foretaste of rearmament implicit in the creation, on promptings from MacArthur, of an embryo defence force, the so-called National Police Reserve. Many Japanese, it is true, were gratified by this turn of events; and of course the Korean War gave a remarkable fillip to the national economy, providing thereby the foundations of the prosperity that obtains today. But the great majority of the Japanese have been deeply pacifist since the Surrender. Rearmament—the outcome of unremitting American pressure—is unpopular. So the Americans are often regarded as possibly dangerous allies—an illusion which the Bikini Bomb accident of 1954 did nothing to dispel.

The somewhat ambiguous image, in Japanese eyes, during the nineteen-fifties, of the 'man from over there' is well illustrated by an analysis made of three popular Japanese films in which Americans played important roles. The films were made between 1952 and 1956. A study of their content showed that among favourable traits attributed to Americans were benevolence, individualism, pragmatism, efficiency, sociability, and common sense. The unfavourable traits included ignorance, carelessness, commercialism, rudeness, sensuality, and 'superficial sweetness'.[1]

These comments can hardly be dismissed as totally unrealistic. At any rate they do not seem to be coloured by ethnocentric, nationalist bias. It would be rash to claim that the concept of the superiority of 'Eastern ethics' has entirely vanished—part of the appeal exercised by Communist China rests on a belief that the Peking Government possesses an inherently 'Eastern' morality[2]—

[1] K. Adachi, 'The Image of America in Contemporary Japanese Fiction' in *Japanese Popular Culture*, edited by Hidetoshi Kato, Tuttle, 1959, p. 58.

[2] For example, the young novelist, Kenzaburo Oe, on his return from a visit to China in 1960, declared: 'Chairman Mao Tse-tung impressed me as an

but it is rare in present-day Japan to come across suggestions that the traditional culture is unequalled and ineffable. For between 1945 and 1952 the Western world—overwhelmingly in its North American guise—pierced Japanese society and Japanese ideas to their very roots.

The Western tide, to be sure, receded in the nineteen-fifties. But if xenophobia ever returns it will surely lack the strongly irrational character that it possessed before 1945. The fact is that, for better or worse, the Japanese are now the most Westernized race in Asia. One is speaking here in terms of political and social institutions, and—in the case of young people—of psychological outlook.

If history is anything to go by, the Japanese response to the Western world—between the middle of the nineteenth century and the middle of the twentieth—will be seen from the vantage-ground of later years as the early and uncomfortable phase of a prolonged process of digestion. The dyspeptic stage indeed is over. What we are beginning to witness is a characteristically Japanese synthesis of the native and the alien. A thousand years ago Japanese art and culture burst into full flower from a soil that for some five centuries or more had been fertilized from China and Korea. Foreign importations are first swallowed whole, are then imitated and adapted, and are finally transmuted into something distinctly Japanese.

The procedure at times is necessarily painful and humiliating. The reaction to the outer world indeed can be illustrated by analogy from a typical domestic and personal situation. Nearly every country lad in Japan dreams of seeking his fortune in a big city, preferably Tokyo. For Tokyo represents what is modern and exciting. It also represents escape from family obligations, from routine, from the weight of custom and tradition. But of course if the dream is realized, adjustment to the disturbing novelties of city life is rarely smooth. At the individual level, the Japanese reaction to the West follows much the same course. Most Japanese adults with any enterprise or imagination dream of paying a visit to Europe or the United States; and this dream too is compounded of fantasies of discovery and escape. The West, glamorous and

Oriental philosopher and political leader who fills one with a sense of humane, spiritual uplift. . . . The inspiration I received during our meeting with Mao was strong enough to restore Oriental pride and spirit in me—a young man who has studied French literature at the university.' *Bungei Shunju*, October 1960.

inscrutable, will surely offer new products, new techniques, new ideas, to be studied and brought home for use and improvement in office, workshop, and school. But the West will also be a temporary haven from the stresses and strains of Japanese social life, from all the intangible but wearisome ties that still bind a man not only to his family and all its ramifications, but also to his professional associates and friends.

Residence in the West usually creates either a much enhanced sense of nationality, with a correspondingly strong aversion from the alien society in which the Japanese finds himself, or a deep emotional identification with the foreign country in which he is living. Even after returning home many Japanese remain, in some degree, spiritual expatriates.

Certain commentators, Japanese as well as foreign, claim that in their attitude to the West the Japanese have displayed signs of a deep-seated complex. Perhaps the instances of love and hate cited in this essay support this view. If this theory has any validity—and one cannot be at all dogmatic here—a possible contributory cause of diffidence, namely the generally short physical stature of the Japanese race, is now rapidly fading. An authority on social welfare in Japan has reported on the changes in physique of young people brought about by the more balanced diet during the past thirteen or fourteen years.

From babies to university students, the postwar improvement in Japanese physique has been quite remarkable. The national average height of the junior school students of today is as high as that of the adults of the Meiji Period (1868–1912), and it has become quite common for junior high school boys to be bigger than their fathers. The Ministry of Welfare estimates that people will continue to become gradually taller and that in another forty years they will be as tall as Europeans.[1]

This passage has been quoted because, apart from its intrinsic interest, it reveals in its first and last sentences a certain attitude to the West. 'The postwar improvement in Japanese physique has been quite remarkable . . . in another forty years they will be as tall as Europeans.' There is a significant equation here: 'as tall as Europeans' equals improvement in physique. This does not suggest that the Japanese have been happy about being shorter in stature than Europeans and Americans. And this brings us to a

[1] Hiroshi Takeuchi, 'Taller and Broader', *Japan Quarterly*, vol. ix, no. 1, January–March 1962.

consideration of physical factors often neglected and yet basic to
the concept of the Glass Curtain.

How does the Japanese see the typical *hakujin*, 'the white man'?
Does he regard him, in terms of physical appearance, as being
closer to an ape or to an angel?

Traditional paintings of the sixteenth and seventeenth centuries,
and woodblock prints of the mid-nineteenth century, give us some
idea of those physical features of Europeans that attracted most
attention in Japan. They are the colour of the eyes (hazel or blue)
and of the hair (blond), the long, angular nose, the large feet, and
the tall stature. The hair and eyes, one feels, produced an almost
diabolical impression; and you are made aware of the fact that the
large, ungainly body is out of scale with the dimensions of Japanese
social living. Those long legs will not adjust themselves, save in the
most awkward fashion, to *seiza* (the formal sitting posture on the
tatami of the traditional room): indeed they are unfitted for anything except a chair or settee. The head is struck many a painful
blow by the lintels of Japanese doorways. European arms and
hands are made for the opening and closing of doors in direct,
uncompromising fashion; they are unused to the more delicate,
catlike motion of sliding open paper screens and wooden shutters.[1]

But of course such disharmonies become less apparent as
Japanese habits of life continue to grow closer to those of the West.
Moreover, as the Japanese have to a large extent changed their
daily diet since the war, it is now rare to hear a foreigner described
as *bata-kusai* ('smelling of butter').

Certain *mores* typical of the Westerner remain conspicuous in
the Japanese setting. The European, for example, employs laughter
almost exclusively in the context of jocularity and good humour—
a limitation that strikes the average Japanese as strange. Again, the
European in his discourse is inclined to be frank and explicit to a
degree commonly unacceptable outside the ranks of the pre-war
officer corps. The European, it is evident, has no knowledge of
haragei (literally, 'stomach technique'), or the art of saying one
thing and yet conveying, unmistakably another.

Yet in this respect too the gap is narrowing. For the young

[1] This—symbolic of much—was first pointed out to the writer by the potter,
Bernard Leach, who remarked: 'In the West we grasp the doorknob firmly and
open or close the door in a movement from the elbow. The Japanese slide their
doors from the wrist.'

K

people of Japan—those born during and after the Pacific War—are strangers to their elders precisely because, thanks to post-war education and post-war ideas, they are often mentally closer to their contemporaries in Europe and the United States than to their own parents. But geographical distance and the homogeneity of the Japanese race will continue to preserve some kind of gap or, shall we say, glass barrier between Japan and the West. The Japanese themselves would hardly wish it were otherwise.

VIII. INDIAN ATTITUDES
TO EUROPE

A. H. Somjee

I

The varied and changing attitudes of Indians to Europe had their sources, broadly speaking, in contacts with Europeans in India, in the gradual awareness of the thought and culture which these Europeans represented, in the increasing number of visits of Indians to Europe, and in the facilities provided by European languages (particularly English), together with other means of communication, for getting to know more about Europeans. Whilst a few exceptional individuals transcended the limitations imposed by their own epoch and viewed the European encounter from an Asian or even a universal standpoint, a large number of Indians, as one would expect, entirely succumbed to the historical conditioning of their attitudes.

Of the earliest encounters between Indians and Europeans, and particularly of what the former thought of the latter, not much is known. There are only a few stray comments in the Indian epics and literary and philosophical writings. Indians are notorious for their lack of desire to record their observations, their reactions to novel situations and encounters with outsiders. With a few exceptions, it is only after the beginning of the nineteenth century that we get some authentic glimpses of what they thought of Europeans. What we know about Indian attitudes to Europe before that period largely rests on the testimony of European travellers and on inferences drawn from the infrequent comments that are recorded.

The earliest contacts of Indians with Europeans were perhaps those in the trade centres of the countries of the Middle East. Although very few Indians reached these markets owing to the middlemanship of the Arab traders, their casual contacts with

Europeans must have excited some interest. But of the mutual accounts that emerged from the meetings of traders in distant lands those of European traders about the Indians were perhaps more exciting and must have appealed to a larger audience. India was then the major exporting country and there was a great demand for her ivory, rice, cinnamon, ginger, pepper, beryl-stone, and muslin in the countries of the Mediterranean. These exotic commodities must have been as full of interest to Europeans in India at the time as were radio sets, aeroplanes, and sputniks to Indians in the twentieth century. The essential difference, however, was a touch of mystery about the former. European interest in India was aroused at a time when belief in the mysteriousness of things was not so uncommon as it is today. Added to this was the typical Indian idiom of magnification and a preference for the unknown. The net result of it all was that from the earliest meetings of Indians with Europeans, India easily lent itself to a great deal of myth-making at the hands of Europeans. So very persistent in Europe has been the Indian reputation for mystery and unfathomability that even contemporary Indians feel that Europeans do not take anything else in India very seriously. A television programme on modern India for a European audience may all too often begin with a symbolic snake arousing all the mysterious associations of Kipling's *Jungle Book*.

Before Alexander's invasion, Indians did not have any reason to take Europeans and their civilization very seriously. Nor indeed did the Greek invasion bring about any lasting change in the Indian attitude. Like their Greek counterparts Indians were ignorant of the literature and civilization of alien peoples.[1] Between India and Greece lay the barriers of nature, of language, and of temperament. Indians and Greeks alike were smug and exclusive. Alexander's invasion was the first opportunity for a direct and significant contact between India and Europe.[2] On their own soil Indians saw people who were different in colour, dress, and language from their own. The military prowess of the Greeks evoked some admiration among Indians but no effective dialogue could take place between the two for the simple reason that the Greek soldiers could not properly represent the views of Greek

---

[1] H. G. Rawlinson, *Intercourse between India and the Western world*, Cambridge University Press, 1916, p. 158.
[2] G. N. Banerjee, *Hellenism in Ancient India*, Calcutta, 1920, p. 3.

thinkers. From whatever little is known about the Indo-Greek contact it appears that Indians were not willing to concede much to the conquerors. Their philosophers, who are supposed to have entered into some sort of a dialogue with the Greeks, adopted a rigid and supercilious attitude. They gave the impression that they were more concerned with the problems of life and the nature of the universe than with the habits and customs of alien peoples. Indians did not regard the Greeks as their intellectual or moral superiors. What impressed them most was their military skill and to some extent their plastic arts and coinage. But they proved to be far too smug to borrow much from the Greeks.[1]

During the Roman period the affluence of the Romans as well as the safety of trade routes gave rise to an unprecedented demand for luxury goods from the East. Fine muslins, pearls and other precious stones, cosmetics, drugs, spices, and pepper were in great demand. The Romans paid gold coins in return. So large was the import bill that it was considered to be a serious drain on Roman finance. Mommsen estimated the value of trade with India, China, and Arabia as nearly £1,100,000, half of which went to India. Indians being largely at the producing end of the Roman imports, which passed through a number of hands, did not have first-hand contact with the people who finally consumed what they produced. Whatever Indians knew about the Romans must have been largely confined to trading circles and a few rulers who benefited by such trade. Not much is known about their attitudes to the Romans apart from their desire to continue trade and ensure the inflow of beautifully struck Roman coins.

In spite of the Greek conquest of North-western India and the prolonged importation of Indian goods by the Romans, Europeans did not become a part of the vital experience of Indians in the classical period. Neither their presence in the country nor the continuous flow of their much-coveted gold coins shook the Indians from their complacency. While the extent of Indian familiarity with the different schools of Greek thought or the Roman system of laws remains largely a matter of guesswork, one is forced to conclude that the first round of contact with Europeans neither excited any appreciable degree of curiosity in Indians nor was able to become a basis of comparison of European and Indian culture.

The attitude of Indians to aliens in general and Europeans in

[1] Ibid., p. 26.

particular was reflected in the changing use of the term *yavana* during this period. Originally used to denote the Ionians, the term *yavana* became quite handy for referring to aliens, including Bactrians, Persians, Huns, and Moslems. In the later period it was used as a synonym for the derisory term *mlechchas*.[1] From some stray comments in ancient Indian literature we find that the term was used to denote not only aliens but all oppressors as well. The great Indian grammarian, Panini, used it in order to pay a partial compliment to the military prowess of the Greeks in India—he called them 'viciously valiant *yavanas*'. Then there are a few references to the term *yavana* in the Indian epic, the Mahabharata. In one place high tribute is paid to the knowledgeability of the Greeks, the 'all-knowing *yavanas*'. But the epic also contains a prophecy that when the *yavanas*, meaning here alien oppressors, would rule India, it would be a period of *Kaliyuga* or the rule by unrighteous people in a dark age. In course of time, the contact with alien invaders led Indians to make the inevitable distinction between 'we' and 'they', civilized and barbarians, righteous and unrighteous, and to look on strangers with some suspicion, fear, and contempt.

Christianity came to India long before the Europeans. The Church of Malabar in South India, for instance, claims its apostolic origin from St. Thomas and has been in existence since A.D. 182. The early non-European Christianity did not lean on the strength of conquering nations and was therefore free from political over-tones. Gradually it came to be accepted as one of the many religions of the Indian sub-continent. The Christianity which came with the Portuguese, the Dutch, the Danes, the French, and the British was, however, a different matter. Initially it was used by them in order to justify their expeditions and to boost the morale of mariners undertaking voyages fraught with immense risks. The prospect of 'christianizing' millions of dark and distant 'heathen' was honourable enough, apart from the gains in trade and the loot on the high seas. Most Indians viewed Christianity, even when it established European schools and hospitals, mainly as an instrument in the hands of conquering and ruling powers rather than as a universal creed. The claim advanced by Christian missionaries to a monopoly of truth, in a country which had far more sophisticated approaches to the very problem of truth, could

[1] G. N. Banerjee, *Hellenism in Ancient India*, p. 229.

not be taken seriously by thinking Indians. The intolerance and even racial arrogance of European missionaries in the name of religion was quite alien to the Indian spirit. With nearly four hundred years of support from conquering and ruling powers, European Christianity could not attract more than one per cent of Indians to its side.[1] Of these a great many accepted it chiefly in order to escape the social and economic disadvantages imposed on them by a decadent Hinduism. Among the rest, conversion achieved unintended results—the search for cultural roots and the fight for political rights.

European Christianity, by the time it arrived in India, was more or less a finished product and had assimilated innumerable traits of the people among whom it had initially flourished. It was therefore not in a position to embody or even respect the cultural and intellectual traditions of Indians. This seems to be the basic reason for its limited appeal. Even those who came under its influence invariably found themselves out of the main stream of Indian life. Religion alone was not responsible for this alienation, but it did inculcate a pseudo-European outlook on life as exemplified by British rulers and soldiers away from home. The missionary venture came at a time when thinking Indians were making bold attempts to understand and even adopt what they thought was the best in European culture. Consequently, even to this day the difference in the outlook of the Indians who are 'Europeanized' through religion on the one hand, and education and understanding on the other, continues to be seen.

By the time Europeans reached India by the sea route, towards the end of the fifteenth century, a great change had occurred in the attitude of Indians to aliens as such. Having lived through a period of bitter internal feuds and ruthless conquests by alien Muslims for nearly four hundred years, Indians had withdrawn completely into the confines of a protective social system. Apart from occasional attempts at rebellion, they had allowed a free hand to Muslims in matters of government and had concentrated all their energies on the social and ritual aspects of their life. Withdrawal from politics and obsessive interest in ritual conformity made them innocuous to the Muslim rulers and helped them to remain the preservers of their own culture, with the consequent disadvantages of stagnation and timidity. Those Indians

[1] Amaury de Riencourt, *The Soul of India*, Jonathan Cape, p. 194.

who emerged from their protective shell in the nineteenth and twentieth centuries gave continuity to the cultural life of India which, unlike modern Greece or Egypt, did not register a complete break with the past.

Preoccupation with social and ritual life coupled with a conscious attempt to stifle curiosity concerning those who came and went, so as to remain within the bounds of safety, enabled Indians to view the activities of European traders, plunderers, and conquerors with a touch of resignation. The accounts of fifteenth-century travellers such as Nicolo Conti, Athanasius, Nikitin, and Stefano are remarkable in that respect. Nowhere do they mention any significant reaction to their presence in India or Indian curiosity regarding them and their countries.[1] Indians even in the fifteenth century were not interested in reprimanding a rogue Portuguese captain, who, when in need of money, collected a number of dogs and threatened to drown them if he was not given a large sum of money.[2]

Europeans had been in India in various capacities since the fifteenth century, but not till the beginning of the nineteenth century did Indians start taking interest in their way of life, religion, system of thought, literature, and technology. Some interest in their religion was no doubt shown by Akbar and the Brahmins of Madura, in their clocks by the courtiers of the Moghuls, and in their capacity for drink by Jahangir. But by its very nature this interest was superficial. Nor did the contact of Indians with Europeans in the subsequent period go very deep. The Portuguese, who had come as crusaders and conquerors, with some psychological and technological advantages on their side, tried to create an atmosphere of artificial equality by marrying Indian women. This, however, was vitiated by their desire to dominate Indians politically. The British, however, under the influence of Calvinistic Protestantism, laid great stress in the beginning on the legitimacy of profitable trade, and later on, on their historic mandate for conquest and colonization.

As traders the British were forced to meet Indians socially and not much colour prejudice was noticeable on their part. For the purposes of business and comfort in a distant country they even superficially tried to Indianize themselves. Their Indianization,

---

[1] See *India in the Fifteenth Century*, The Hakluyt Society.
[2] Oaten, *Travellers in India*, Kegan Paul, 1908, p. 90.

however, was a mere matter of clothes, food, and entertainment. They started putting on *banians*, eating highly spiced food, smoking *hookas*, and watching *nautch*. With all these superficial attempts to meet Indians half-way they remained very much British at heart.[1] With the gradual influx of the military element among them there started the talk about the racial inferiority of Indians. Added to that was the recruitment of people in the civil service who knew nothing about India and would have nothing to do with Indians. The need to despise the Indians was supplied by the growing number of British missionaries who just could not make any sense out of the countless castes, rituals, and gods and goddesses of the 'heathen'. Soon a stage was reached when someone expressed the ridiculous sentiment, 'how nice India would be if it wasn't for the Indians'.[2]

The eighteenth century in India was the era of oppression, plunder, and disintegration on a large scale for Indians, whereas for the British it was a period of decisive trial of diplomatic skill, heroism, and administrative consolidation. As a nation the British were exerting themselves to their utmost and as a people perhaps they were at their best. Their discipline, intellectual confidence, and rallying round the British cause made a tremendous impression on very many Indians at a time when their own mutual dealings were not always above board. Indians missed these qualities in themselves and were in a mood to praise them wherever they could find them. So deep was the impression created by these qualities that for a long time they glossed over the racial arrogance, bureaucratic callousness, and cruelty of word and attitude of the British. Even to this day the British are remembered in India, among other things, for the qualities that they displayed in the earlier years of their rule.

II

What impressed Indians most as they emerged from a prolonged period of hibernation was what the Age of Enlightenment had achieved in Europe. They were struck by the idea of secular progress and the rational approach to the consideration of social problems. The ideas of the Encyclopaedists considerably influenced Henry Derozio, a Eurasian poet, and Raja Ram Mohan Roy,

---

[1] T. G. P. Spear, *The Nabobs*, Oxford University Press, 1932, p. 22.
[2] Ibid., p. 142.

an erudite religious thinker and social reformer. In the early nineteenth century, Derozio, in a critical spirit typical of thinkers of the French Enlightenment, started questioning the premises and assumptions of Hindu religious beliefs. Surrounded by ardent young disciples in Calcutta, Derozio became a symbol of the growing popularity of European intellectual traditions in India.

As Indians turned their attention from Europeans in India to Europe itself, the achievements of France appeared to them to be at least as impressive as those of Britain. France has remained a source of inspiration to radical intellectuals all over the world, and the young Indians who were questioning a few aspects of their own cultural life were influenced by the attitudes and example of French thinkers. This phase, however, did not last for long. Soon they identified Europe largely with Britain and continued to do so till the end of the Second World War. Even the considerable German interest in Indian literature and philosophy in the second half of the nineteenth century, and the giving of political asylum to Indian terrorists, did not alter the situation. Indians had far too much to learn and to digest from what a dynamic Britain had to offer.

This short-lived transitional period of shift in the attention of Indians from Europe to Britain is reflected in the writings of Raja Ram Mohan Roy. He started off with an encyclopaedic background. He knew several European and Oriental languages. He studied Greek and Hebrew in order to have a better understanding of Christianity. After reading the New Testament he wanted to take into account its ethical teaching and to set aside the doctrinal element. His rejection of the divinity of Christ brought him into conflict with the orthodox Christian bigots in India. He protested against the malicious attacks of missionaries against Hinduism. In a manner typical of the Encyclopaedists he asked them to depend more on the intellectual validity of their arguments rather than on their consciousness of political power. The increasing denunciation of everything Indian at the hands of missionaries and the semi-enlightened among the British made him rush to the defence of his own culture. Only so far as the introduction of 'useful mechanical arts' was concerned, he maintained, were Indians indebted; but with respect to science, literature, and religion they were placed under no such obligation.

Such a reaction was typical of an educated Indian of this period.

The more he came in contact with European thought and literature, the more he understood the greatness of his own culture. He, no doubt, felt the need to pump new life into age-old culture but the arrogance of the self-styled representatives of European culture made him come out with an exaggerated defence of his own. For a long time, therefore, the contact with European culture stirred the desire not only to revive Indian culture but also to emphasize its uniqueness. In doing so, the need for a balanced perspective was quite often overlooked by many Indians.

The attitudes of Dayananda Saraswati, the Indian religious reformer, represent a reaction against the growing 'Europeanization' of educated Indians. He maintained that it was useless for Indians to imitate the Europeans in their thought and appearance. On the other hand, what was worth imitating was what he called 'the virtues of the Europeans'. These included the education of boys and girls, supervision of their company, freedom to choose one's mate, decision after thorough discussion in representative assemblies, willingness to make sacrifices for one's country, dutifulness and obedience, helping one's own country in trade and commerce, and so on. It is interesting to note that nowhere does he recognize the real significance of modern European thought. He merely praised instead the disciplined character of the Europeans, particularly the British. So far as ideas were concerned he preferred to emphasize the indigenous sources. In his attitude to Europe Dayananda, in fact, represented the growing sensitivity of Indian nationalists.

While Dayananda preferred to ignore European culture and ideas, Swami Vivekananda, the religious and social reformer, wanted to spread the understanding of Indian culture in the West by emphasizing the excesses of European materialism and the need to balance it with Indian spirituality. He was the first Indian to go to Europe and America chiefly to lecture on the basic soundness of Indian culture. Unlike Dayananda, he acknowledged the greatness of Europe in the field of science and technology but pointed out that this was not enough. What Europe needed, according to him, was some kind of 'adjustment' on the spiritual plane which it neglected. 'Adjustments' became necessary in every civilization. He felt that Western civilization suffered from an excessive emphasis on material comforts; consequently, it reduced men to some sort of 'money-making machines'. Indians, on the other hand, had neglected the material base of their existence and in that respect they had something to learn from Europeans. His own emphasis, however, was heavily in favour of an 'adjustment' dominated by the spiritual side. By his speeches and writings Vivekananda tried to stem the tide of 'Westernization' of educated Indians. He wanted to restore their confidence in their own past, which they were slowly beginning to scorn. In order to ram home his point he frequently made a comparison of Western materialism with Eastern spirituality, pointing out the greatness of the latter.

The work started by Vivekananda, of putting Western civilization in proper perspective for Indians and emphasizing their own spiritual resources in the face of the overwhelming technological superiority of the West, was carried to its logical conclusion by Tagore and Gandhi. Like him, they pointed out that the materialistic bias of European civilization was not an unmixed blessing and that it invariably gave rise to grave problems.

Rabindranath Tagore came of age at a time when Indians were experiencing the rapid dissolution of the traditional structure of beliefs and customs. Different Indians were reacting to it differently. Some went out of their way to embrace all that was European, while others tried to ignore the changes that were taking place in their environment. Still there was the third section—and the entire Tagore family belonged to it—which took the introduction of European culture and ideas as a great challenge.[1] The social and cultural *milieu* with which he was familiar was fast disappearing and he himself was in danger of becoming culturally rootless. As a poet he could merely have voiced his own predicament but he preferred not to do so. Instead he revitalized the cultural soil of his own time so as to be able to strike roots in it. His criticism of European civilization was directed against its materialism, which made it go in search of colonies, and its emphasis on organized political power, which made a mockery of its professed individual freedom. Together, he thought, they had done a great deal of harm to the European as well as to the non-European world.

The cultural conceit of the British rulers and their frequent attempts to run down 'Orientals' had made Tagore extremely Asia-conscious. In his various addresses to the people of Asia he sought to stress that although they were common sufferers at the

[1] See the author's paper on 'The Political Philosophy of Rabindranath Tagore', *The Indian Journal of Political Science*, June 1961.

hands of European nations they could show their superiority by keeping to the path of righteousness and non-violence. Nor did he want them to belittle European greatness. The West had, no doubt, ruined the economic life of the countries of Asia by flooding them with consumer goods, tourists, machine-guns, and such superfluities, but it had also done some good. Among other things, it had brought the force of its living mind to bear upon their lives and had thereby stimulated their thinking. Tagore's last work, *Crisis in Civilization*, written in 1941, reflected his feeling of despair. Europe, he maintained, had been moving towards such a crisis for centuries and at last it had come. Its civilization had produced contemporary science and technology which were remarkable feats of human intellect; but it had hardly deserved them. It used them for the purposes of destruction more than for anything else. For its moral crisis Europe had only itself to blame.

Rejection of current Western norms and reliance on the ancient moral and religious traditions of India, as initiated by Vivekananda, reached its high-water mark in Mahatma Gandhi's attitude to Europe. Himself a product of the religious humanism of the East as well as the West, Gandhi very forcefully pointed out the weaknesses of European civilization and its unsuitability to Indian conditions. His alternative to it came close to the ideals of Kropotkin, Tolstoy, and Thoreau, which he thought had once been exemplified in the idyllic life of rural India. Although Gandhi had personally known and experienced some of the worst features of European civilization, his rejection of it was remarkably free from anger and acrimony. As a student he had known the evils of industrialism in post-Dickensian Britain; as a social and political worker he had experienced the worst features of racialism in South Africa; as the leader of the Indian masses he had studied the inhuman aspects of repressive colonialism; as an unrelenting ascetic he was concerned about the ceaseless multiplication of wants in modern society; as a deeply reflective person he was troubled by the alarmingly destructive capacity of modern warfare. All these excesses, he maintained, sprang from modern Western civilization as it stands today, and consequently it needs some serious rethinking and rectification.

As early as 1909, when Gandhi was hardly forty years of age, his attitude to European civilization had crystallized. His subsequent experiences confirmed what he came to believe at this stage. He felt that although modern civilization had produced innumerable labour-saving devices, rapid means of communication, and a lot of push buttons in place of painful human labour, it also gave rise to unpleasant conditions of work and unknown diseases. Further, it introduced endless rush, tension, and complexity in the everyday life of modern man. Behind this criticism lay Gandhi's judgement in *Hind Swaraj* that 'the civilization India has evolved is not to be beaten in the world', and that there was something essentially sound in a civilization which had withstood the severe trials and tribulations of its history. A lot of newfangled notions coming from the West had done some harm but fortunately they had not penetrated deeply into the Indian way of life. Gandhi, nevertheless, made a significant distinction between Europeans and their civilization. He was conscious of the harm which their own civilization had done to them. He could not bring himself to hate the British in India. Repeatedly he maintained that he had no quarrel with them but only with their present-day industrial civilization.

Mahatma Gandhi's extreme rejection of Western civilization baffled many Indians. He sometimes went so far as to declare that India's civilization to be true to itself had to unlearn much of what it had adopted in the last fifty years. The imported superstructure of modern Western civilization may have to go; and the so-called upper classes have to learn consciously, deliberately, and religiously the simple peasant life, with its secret of true happiness. This view was neither understood nor digested even by Gandhi's close associates such as Nehru. Many of Gandhi's fundamental concepts were obscured by the need to fight foreign rule by restoring the confidence of Indians in their own civilization. After Indian independence Gandhi's attitudes either came to be questioned or ignored, and the person who most radically departed from them was Nehru himself.

Unlike Vivekananda, Tagore, and Gandhi, Jawaharlal Nehru was highly 'Europeanized' as a result of his upbringing and education. As opposed to their partial or total rejection of the modern West and their idealization of traditional Indian culture, he had self-consciously to go in search of his Indian roots. His reading of world history merely confirmed his intense concern with the problems of societies which had stagnated for centuries and then aspired to catch up with technologically developed countries.

His restless and meliorist outlook, which bore the unmistakable marks of an unresolved conflict between tradition and modernity, was in fact more representative of the mind of educated Indians today than they realized.

Nehru felt that the real significance of the West for India lay in its dynamism, which he missed in his own society; what he found unacceptable was its comparative neglect of certain universal principles.

The very thing India lacked, the modern West possessed and possessed to excess. It had the dynamic outlook. It was engrossed in the changing world, caring little for ultimate principles, the unchanging, the universal. It paid little attention to duties and obligations and emphasized rights. It was active, aggressive, acquisitive, seeking power and domination, living in the present and ignoring the future consequences of its actions.[1]

Despite the fact that the aggressive West colonized, exploited, and even thwarted the development of, countries like India, Nehru was in no mood to write off its greatness. On the contrary, it was in the light of its economic and social development that he was in a position to perceive the relative material backwardness of his own society. Secularism, industrialism, planned development, economic and social equality, the welfare state, democratic socialism, and co-operative enterprise—these all had a profound influence on Nehru's outlook, and ever since Indian independence he tried to introduce them into Indian life.

Nehru's recognition of the achievements of Europe in areas other than those acknowledged by his predecessors, and his conscious attempt to borrow a great deal from it for the social and economic reconstruction of India, had far-reaching effects on a generation of Indians who were fed on the notion of European shortcomings and Indian greatness. Once again the confidence of Indians in themselves, which was laboriously built up by leaders from Raja Ram Mohan onwards, was shaken. This time they did not even have a blameless Indian civilization to fall back upon. What was therefore very much evident in Nehru's India was the need to catch up with the developed countries and a feeling of second-rateness on the part of the intellectuals, as an inevitable consequence of large-scale borrowing. The latter painfully reflected

[1] Jawaharlal Nehru, *The Discovery of India*, Meridian Books, 1956, p. 519.

itself in the spurious eclecticism, the hesitation, and the paralysis of the literary and artistic life of contemporary Indians.

Nehru had made a determined bid to see traditional India through her period of transition. For him the achievements of the West were now a part of the heritage of mankind. There was therefore no shame involved in sharing it. This heritage, he believed, would help in the release of tremendous energy in the emerging countries. For him the decline of the political supremacy of Europe was a fact and he looked forward to a stage when the differences between countries would be cultural rather than technological. In the meantime his own faith in the possibility of catching up with Western and Eastern Europe made him come out with bold experiments in all walks of Indian life.

III

Quite apart from the attitudes of leading Indian thinkers, the views and reactions of the bulk of the semi-Westernized Indian middle class are no less significant. As opposed to the conscious attitudes of Indian thinkers, with their considerable understanding of Indian culture, the attitudes to Europe of this semi-Westernized class is largely a product of their education, professional interests and contacts, and imported entertainment. Some of them are partly or totally unaware of the views of recent Indian thinkers about Europe and its civilization. The professional segment within this class confines its interests to people and institutions in various callings and acquires a superficial understanding of what Europe stands for. The rest remains largely at the receiving end of popular literature, movies, music, dancing, fashions, etc., as distributed and popularized by efficient international agencies. The latter segment is made up of the undiscriminating cosmopolitans who are now to be found in every society, developed or under-developed.

In this imitative class one finds much admiration for Europe's well-established educational institutions and academic life in general. It misses them in India. It looks forward, even at the cost of great hardships and sacrifices, to sending its children to Europe for education and training, and the young visitors remain sentimentally attached to foreign countries for years to come. This class is appreciative of the type of social freedom enjoyed by the average European which it misses in its own country owing to innumerable social divisions and barriers. It reserves its highest praise for some of the political ideals and institutions developed by European countries such as Britain, Switzerland, and Sweden. In recent years this class has shown the depth of its interest in Europe by resisting the attempts of anglophobes and ultra-nationalists to remove the English language which serves as a vital link with Europe.

All this, however, merely states one side of its attitudes to Europe. There is also another side which deserves to be mentioned. For a long time what had impressed Indians most was Europe's technological supremacy. This has now passed out of its hands. Europe's second-rateness in the field of science and technology together with its most unacceptable features to the Indian— materialism, dissolution of family life, sexual promiscuity—have made it an object of frequent criticism. Added to that is its colonial record, racialism, religious bigotry, and utter lack of interest in other civilizations including the Indian. All these have come in for criticism and scorn at the hands of the semi-Westernized middle class.

To conclude, Indian attitudes to Europe have not merely changed from time to time, but the change is much more rapid than it has ever been in the past. Important events which occur from day to day, such as the Immigration Bill in Britain, OAS terrorism in Algeria, the voting of European countries in the United Nations and the like, significantly influence the attitudes of Indians to Europe. The change in contemporary attitudes is some-times so very rapid and radical that it defies any attempt at systematic analysis, let alone a firm appraisal.

L

IX. MODERN ARAB ATTITUDES
TO THE WEST

John Parker

In attempting to give a brief survey of the main influences which modern European civilization has exerted upon the Arab peoples, and of their varying reactions to these influences, it is necessary to begin by limiting the scope of the subject. Here the period to be considered will be that of the direct contact between Western Europe and the Arab world in modern times, which means the decades from Napoleon's occupation of Egypt in 1798–1801 down to the present day. This period falls into three obvious divisions.

In the first three-quarters of the nineteenth century the scientific and technological achievements of some Western European societies, their powers of organization and co-operation, and the spirit of unfettered intellectual curiosity which seemed to flourish in them together made a profound impression upon the limited but important section of the Arabic-speaking world to which these things were revealed. Many were left with a disturbing awareness that the Islamic community to which they belonged had somehow failed to keep abreast of the general movement of history, and it was largely this feeling which motivated the first attempts to produce schemes of reform and national regeneration, aiming, ultimately, at 'catching up' with the West. There followed the period of European political domination, foreshadowed by the French invasion of Algeria in 1830, beginning in earnest with their seizure of Tunis in 1881 and the British occupation of Egypt a year later, and, after the Italian conquest of Libya and the French protectorate established over Morocco in 1912, culminating in the mandate system imposed by the allies on the eastern Arab lands at the end of the First World War, a system which lasted, with a few changes of form rather than of substance, until after the end of the Second. Thirdly, there is the period of 'the decline of the West in the Middle East'.[1] Perhaps most attention should be given to this last phase, since it was then that European military and political predominance came up against articulate and aggressive Arabism; it is in the last ten years or so that the two sides of the relationship have been seen in the sharpest distinction. But contemporary attitudes towards the nations of the West, their institutions and their ideologies, can only usefully be discussed in the light of the cumulative experience with which these 160 years of contact have endowed the Arabs.

In the broadest terms: the admiration for European energy, effectiveness, inventiveness, and 'progress', the desire to acquire these qualities and to share in the benefits deriving from them came in time to be mingled with exasperation and disillusionment, bringing about resistance to European imperial power and varyingly hostile reactions against the culture that seemed to be tainted by it. Finally, after political liberation, come new attempts to formulate and re-appraise those aspects of 'modern Western civilization' (if so dangerously vague a term may be used) that still seem valuable in the light of what, after a century and a half of chequered experience, are found to be the special needs of Arab societies in a world that, for all its revolutionary changes and shifts of power, is still being riven by ideologies and transformed by technological developments that were 'Western' in origin. Thus the all but universal repudiation of European rule, control, and exploitation has not led to any general rejection of European standards and 'Western culture', but it has often been accompanied by feelings of being rejected, underrated, or misled by these and a consequent determination to be more critical and selective in future. Behind contemporary efforts to build up a truly independent, cohesive, and modern Arab society there lies a crowded epoch of shifting intellectual and emotional response to the idea and the realities of 'the West'; astonishment, admiration, mistrust, critical analysis, disenchantment, some hatred, and a good deal of bewilderment.

It has been, throughout, an unequal confrontation of two very different kinds of society, with widely dissimilar backgrounds. For

---

[1] The title of two articles by A. H. Hourani (*International Affairs*, January–April 1953) which give an illuminating assessment of the forces and factors that have shaped this period of Arab-Western relations.

the Arabs there were, as the central facts of their historical consciousness, Islam and its early glories, and their own predominant share in these. But for many centuries almost all the Arab and Arabized peoples had been under non-Arab rulers, and although the fact that most of these had accepted Islam (and often used Arabic as the language of culture and official business) mitigated and to some extent disguised the fact of subjugation, Ottoman rule in particular had acted as a barrier against the penetration of new intellectual currents from outside the Islamic world. When Napoleon in the Near East demonstrated something of the power, enterprise, and organized effort of which a vigorous modern nation-state was capable, he and his lieutenants were performing to an audience which had not, for centuries, played any part in European affairs.

Despite their very considerable share in preserving and transmitting the ancient cultural heritage of the West, the Arabs had been excluded, by geography and the Ottoman Empire, from any direct participation in modern European history, and from any but the most restricted knowledge of the ideas and forces that had come to shape its course since the Renaissance. There were a few exceptions: religious missions in the Lebanon, Palestine, and Iraq, traders in Aleppo and Alexandria and occasional travellers nearly everywhere outside the Arabian deserts had brought some knowledge of European ways and ideas, mainly to the Levant and to Christian Arabs. A few of these had travelled to the West and been educated there, some later contributing to the early progress of Oriental studies, but they tended to be cut off from their fellow-Arabs in the Empire by reason of belonging to a religious minority. In contrast to the Turk, a familiar figure in the thought, literature, art, and diplomacy of Europe for more than two centuries, the Arab was a remote and mysterious being, most often visualized, perhaps, in terms of the *Arabian Nights* or popular accounts of the crusades.

This limited knowledge of the Arabs and their past continued for a long time after contacts began. The French in Egypt had made enthusiastic efforts to bridge the gap of ignorance; but this splendid beginning was inevitably not sustained after the end of their brief occupation and only in recent times have European governments begun to take energetic measures to support and extend Oriental studies. The fact that the historical background of the Arabs was so indissolubly linked with their religion complicated the task of understanding, since there was, on the European side, particularly little comprehension of Islam as a faith, but rather the inherited attitudes deriving from centuries of misunderstanding and misrepresentation.[1] On the Arab side, however, it was undoubtedly of the greatest importance that by the time Western influences began to penetrate the Muslim world European civilization had lost most of its earlier Christian colouring and in many of its aspects had become consciously and even aggressively non-doctrinal. As Bernard Lewis has emphasized,[2] it was precisely this secular quality that made nineteenth-century European ideas and practices so readily assimilable in the Ottoman Empire. But it also meant that from the start 'pro-Western' Arabs got, and doubtless for the most part still tend to get, an incomplete and unbalanced idea of the European tradition as a whole.[3] Whether, as some have suggested, it also meant that European civilization only began to influence the Arabs when it was already past its best is too large a question to be broached here.[4]

When, therefore, after 1798 parts of the Arab world were brought into increasingly close contact with some aspects of modern European civilization the encounter was a meeting of strangers. This was shown in the excitement and sense of novelty felt on both sides, illustrated, for instance, in the travellers' tales of the Egyptian Rifāʿ Rāfiʿ al-Tahtāwī and the Syrian Ahmed

[1] Norman Daniel, *Islam and the West*, Edinburgh University Press, 1960.

[2] Bernard Lewis, *The Emergence of Modern Turkey*, Oxford University Press, 1961, pp. 53–54.

[3] The almost universal Muslim lack of interest in Christianity, its ideas, and its historical development, and the reasons for this indifference have often been commented upon. Summarizing, in a book written nearly twenty years ago, what in the way of European culture had been assimilated by Westernized Arabs, Albert Hourani noted that '. . . Christianity, European philosophy, music and art, the whole culture of Russia and central Europe and the literature of the ancient world are still very imperfectly known' (*Syria and Lebanon, a political essay*, Oxford University Press, 1946, p. 75). The very impressive flow of low-priced translations and popular expository works from the U.A.R. and Beirut, as well as Cairo Radio's 'second programme' (modelled on the BBC's Third) have probably done a lot to change the position in recent years; but it still seems to be true, in the words of Wilfred Cantwell Smith, 'not merely that Muslims do not at all understand the faith of Christians, but that in general they do not even know that they do not understand' (*Islam in Modern History*, Princeton University Press, 1957, p. 108).

[4] 'It was a tragedy for both sides that the Western domination of the Middle East came at a time when the West was in full economic flowering but also in full spiritual decline.' Hourani, 'Decline of the West in the Middle East', p. 32; cf. the concluding paragraph of the second article.

Faris Shidyāq,[1] as in the writings of Kinglake, Burton, and Lane. The most obvious contrast seemed to lie in the scientific and technological superiority of Europeans, their powers of political organization, their conscious and purposeful moulding of life and society exemplified in the Napoleonic reforms and innovations and in the tremendous adjustments of 'the Age of Reform' in Britain. The efforts of Muhammad Ali and his successors to emulate this activity in Egypt brought lasting economic benefits and gave the country a long lead over other Arabic-speaking lands. Despite the resistance which their Westernizing policy aroused,[2] most of the Albanian-Turkish rulers of Egypt sought in every way possible to acquire the fruits of European progress, and little attempt was made to count the cost either in financial or political terms until it was too late. 'Egypt is no longer in Africa—it has become part of Europe', said Khedive Ismail (1863–79), and the opening of the Suez Canal in 1869 meant that this would be so in ways that he did not intend.

Elsewhere a knowledge of European ideas and institutions was carried by various means, in Algeria by military conquest and French settlement, in Syria by the short Egyptian occupation (under Muhammad Ali's son Ibrahim) in the 1830s and by the work of European and American missions, by the political intervention of the European powers in 1860 and also, at second hand, as a result of the unrest and the reform movements among the non-Arab communities in the Ottoman Empire, and among the Turks themselves. For, just as was the case with the other national groups, many Arabs were beginning to grow restless under a political system which, though generally tolerable and by no means wholly alien in spirit, had lost much of its earlier flexibility and efficiency. The short career of the first Ottoman parliament (1876–1878) and the reaction under Sultan Abdul Hamid were to some Arabs both a demonstration of the scope and attractiveness of Western political institutions and a lesson that if they wished to enjoy the benefits of these they would have to rely on self-help. 'Westernism' thus seemed to provide a means of escape from an Ottomanism that was growing more and more irksome.

The earliest movements to kindle and express national feeling

[1] Extracts from Arabic writers illustrating these reactions are given in Arnold Hottinger, *Die Araber*, Zürich, 1960, pp. 161 ff.
[2] There was a temporary reaction under Abbas I, 1849–54.

among the Arabs owed much to European examples, and it was
natural for their leaders to hope for a measure of support from the
great powers as the Ottoman Empire more and more visibly
declined. Britain, which during the nineteenth century had done
so much to encourage the national aspirations of Greeks, South
Americans, Belgians, Hungarians, Italians, and others would
surely look with a benevolent eye on reviving Arabdom; on the
other hand, the thwarted nationalists of Egypt might, after 1882,
hope for backing from the Government of France, which for more
than twenty years let slip few opportunities to make the position
of the British occupiers as embarrassing as possible. In fact such
hopes turned out in the end to be delusory.

Although in the decades before the First World War Arab
political exiles, journalists, and others found refuge in Britain and
France, and held their first Pan-Arab conference in Paris in 1913,[1]
they never managed to attract anything like the generous enthusiasm and interest that had earlier been given to Garibaldi,
Mazzini, and Kossuth. Partly, of course, this was because the Arab
movements in those years were far less developed and incompar-
ably less articulate than had been the European ones; their cause
was quite unfamiliar and they lacked the attractive element of
romantic heroism (although Wilfrid Scawen Blunt did his best
for Ahmed Orabi the Egyptian, as did the French writer Juliette
Adam for the later nationalist leader Mustafa Kamil). On a
governmental level there were sound reasons of policy to justify a
cautious and somewhat sceptical approach; for the British, apart
from their increasingly direct interest in the Near East, there was
the fear lest any widespread Arab movement might have Islamic
repercussions somehow unsettling to the Muslims in India, and
the French, with Tunisia and Algeria to think of, could never give
their support too whole-heartedly to the nationalist movement in
Egypt. Thus such hopes as the nascent Arab and Egyptian movements had of effective European help had fairly petered out by the
time that Turkey's participation in the First World War, with the
probability it entailed of fundamental changes in the whole
political structure of the Near East, revived these hopes in new
and vivid forms.

Of the subsequent disillusion it is not necessary to say much
here. By 1920 all the Arab-speaking provinces of the Ottoman

[1] George Antonius, *The Arab Awakening*, London, 1938, pp. 114–16.

Empire (as well as Morocco, which had lain outside its borders) had fallen under British, French, or Italian control except for the inland regions of Arabia. The Arabs, it rapidly became clear, had escaped from one form of domination only to come under another, more obvious, more anomalous, perhaps more irksome and certainly more alien, which divided them off from each other by the erection of arbitrary political and economic barriers. Two factors increased the bitterness and sense of disappointment: in Syria, Palestine, and Iraq there was the complex and often-told story of the British undertakings to various Arab leaders during the war, and the subsequent breaking or evasion of these pledges;[1] secondly, European control was most visible and direct just where it would be most resented, in the areas 'that cannot be said to be purely Arab'[2] but which were in a few years to become most forcefully and articulately so—coastal Syria and Palestine, and, it may be added, Egypt, where in spite of the ending of the British protectorate and the granting of independence in 1922 British military power and ultimate political control were to remain for another generation. These areas were the most 'advanced' in Western terms, and so, it might have been supposed, to be the most favoured when the great reapportionment of the Arab lands took place. But the considerations governing this reapportionment were strategic, with the two allies suspiciously watching each other's moves; the war-time and post-war diplomacy that decided the details was an unedifying combination of clumsiness, ignorance, cynicism, and selfishness[3] and the resultant settlement, which re-drew the map of the Arab world between the two wars, was both an overwhelming demonstration of Western power and, to a whole generation of educated Arabs, a convincing proof that the European nations whose achievements and culture they and their fathers had so warmly admired had no intention of treating them as equal fellow-men but saw in them only means or obstacles to the attainment of their own purposes.

Perhaps 1919 is the really decisive date in considering Arab

[1] Antonius, op. cit., chapters 8, 9, 13, 14.
[2] In the famous phrase of Sir Henry McMahon's letter to the Sharīf Hussein, October 24, 1915, Antonius, p. 169.
[3] The ignorance of British policy-makers about the probable effects of their policies on both Arab and Jewish opinion is most strikingly revealed in the detailed narrative of Leonard Stein, *The Balfour Declaration*, London, 1960—a book in which the part played in inter-allied diplomacy by the other three qualities mentioned is also amply illustrated.

attitudes towards the European powers, the year in which it became clear that neither Egypt nor the areas just freed from Turkish control were to be allowed to work out their future according to their own ideas and aspirations, which by now were both more clearly formulated and far more ardently upheld. Few were taken in by the formal independence granted to Egypt in 1922, to Iraq ten years later, and promised to other areas when they would be ready, in the estimation of Britain and France, to stand on their own feet; the realities of great-power influence were always in the background, and sometimes in the foreground as well, helping to spread a mood of deluded cynicism[1] not only about Anglo-French policies and purposes, but about political motives and activities of all kinds. In the mandated and formerly protected countries the realities of power were often so very different from the façade that a belief in the hidden hand, the sinister power behind the throne, the stooge and the opportunist gradually became second nature to many who came to maturity in those years. The sense of disillusionment grew especially strong in Egypt in the later 1930s, and a number of writers gave it expression in books which stated plainly their conviction that the morale of the Muslim world had been undermined by Western penetration;[2] and more than one veteran nationalist leader came to believe that in helping Europeans to break up the Ottoman Empire the Arabs had backed the wrong horse.

After the end of the Second World War it became increasingly clear that the relationship was once more undergoing a decisive change. But despite the swift ending of Italian rule in Libya and of French control in the Levant states, the general pattern of European withdrawal from pre-war positions has been that of a grudging and reluctant evacuation, exacerbated at many stages by sharp local crises, since Britain and France by now tended to see in political Arabism (which had become a wholly articulate if by no means wholly effective force) something directed specifically against themselves and their interests. For the Arabs the fact that

---

[1] It must seem strange to many students of the Middle Eastern press and wireless that there is no way of translating this word into Arabic except by cumbersome and imprecise periphrases. Conceivably the attitude of mind it denotes was originally a 'Western' import—though this seems unlikely—but there can be no doubt that it has by now become completely Arabized.

[2] Nadav Safran, *Egypt in search of Political Community*, Harvard University Press, 1961, pp. 209–31.

in departing European imperialism had left the wholly alien state of Israel planted in the heart of their lands robbed the withdrawal of almost all the goodwill which it might otherwise have earned; it was, besides, too hesitant and unwilling, too hedged about with conditions and reservations to catch the imagination. There were no splendid gestures of renunciation; it was made abundantly clear that the British and French governments did not trust the Arab states whose creation they had originally sponsored to co-operate in upholding Western interests; and this hesitation inevitably increased suspicions about the real nature of those interests.

It is, then, much too soon for the hatreds, suspicions, the disillusion, and the certain sense of alienation from 'the West' as this term used to be understood, to have cleared away. But if this widespread feeling of political and cultural disenchantment is allowed for, can one try to determine what is left of the original enthusiasms, what elements in the life, thought, and practice of modern European societies are still thought to be worthy of emulation? Even among Arabs of Western education many widely differing answers would be given to this question, and all an outsider can hope to do is to select for discussion what seem to be a few representative trends.

The idea of 'Europe' has, in the first place, become much more complex and elusive (not only for Arabs) since the Second World War and the fundamental political changes that have taken place on the continent since then. Particularly in the course of the last seven or eight years very many Arabs have been brought into contact with a far wider range of Europeans than previously, many of them quite free from any imperialist stigma. Not only is there a greater variety of European nationalities and ideologies represented in the Middle East today, but also of professions and social backgrounds. Any idea that 'modern European' culture is or can be a single entity, or that one must needs become 'Europeanized' by following any one set of rules has surely to be abandoned—it was, after all, something of an illusion from the beginning—and in its place there is the more complicated but perhaps more comforting picture of a number of groups in audible disagreement about many of the most fundamental questions of life, religion, politics, and economics, all of them to a greater or less degree being anxious to stand well in Arab estimation. In the Arab world as elsewhere among the 'uncommitted' nations the business of cultural salesmanship has become highly developed, with the rival blocs competing in a buyer's market. On a superficial level this all gives an opening for malicious humour at the expense of former imperial masters; more importantly, these ideological divisions make it much easier for the Arab countries to obtain and accept the economic and technical assistance they still need so badly.

Thus 'Europe' is not really a significant entity in Arab minds today, and the West, in books and newspapers, is usually distinguished from the Soviet not the Muslim East. The older categories have for most purposes been replaced by a new terminology, a threefold division of nations into the camps of Imperialism, Communism, and 'Non-alignment'.[1] It is not surprising that imperialism almost always has a Western reference—it is generally used in the press and in popular rhetoric to give the picture of a kind of international club, by turns sinister and ineffective, of which Britain and France are the founder-members. The United States, since the Palestine disaster and the more recent growth of journalistic interest in Latin America and the Far East, is regarded as the treasurer and moving spirit, and other states go in and out from time to time as their policies may or may not seem to be in conflict with the aims of Arab nationalism. Obviously this word has by now been robbed of any precise connotation (and, one feels, of much of its original emotional force) by inveterate overuse; but the wide extensions of which it is capable (e.g. Western education can be represented as 'cultural imperialism' designed to cut off Arabs from their roots in their own past) serve as a constant reminder that their experience of European domination has left a great many Arabs genuinely suspicious of all Western political motives. The belief that Britain, France, and the U.S.A., having apparently done so much to hinder the achievement of unity in the past are irrevocably committed to opposing it by all possible means in the present and future is undoubtedly very widespread, and the many setbacks and disappointments which have attended the quest for this unity are generally attributed, in part at least, to their machinations. Thus the feeling of a common Arabness, which has undoubtedly grown much stronger and more widespread in recent years, is still mingled with a sense of being underrated,

[1] The Arab equivalent of this phrase has been given wide currency by the speeches of President Gamāl Abdul Nāsir.

rejected, and somehow 'divided' by the West.[1] The familiar ghosts of 'Western Imperialism', however often and frivolously they are summoned up, will not lack for an audience until some solution of the Palestine problem, acceptable to the Arabs, has been achieved; the issue is still so much a living one, and the memory and the myth keep alive a sense of having been, at Western hands, the victims of an unparalleled historical injustice.

Unique as their own experience of imperialism is claimed to have been, it can provide a sentimental link with other former victims, and since the Bandung conference of 1955 the feeling of common Arabness has at times been supplemented by the awareness—sporadic, and of varying intensity, but occasionally arising to a genuine and reassuring conviction—of being part of a larger, world-wide entity, 'Afro-Asia', 'the uncommitted world', etc., which, vague and inchoate as it still is, can seem to represent something real and reassuring to Arabs trying to redefine their position in a changing world.

Apart from the sins of 'Imperialism' other factors have worked to lower the prestige of 'modern Western civilization' in the minds of educated Arabs today. The two world wars, with the appalling savagery that accompanied them, have made it easy enough for some to cultivate a certain sense of detached moral superiority; faced with the well-published scientific horrors of the annihilation camps and the atomic raids Arabs can feel with justification that their own culture, however 'backward' in some ways, need not suffer too much by comparison. The astonishing prevalence of Western race and colour discrimination, especially in the Anglo-Saxon countries, tends to strengthen this conviction, since Arabs can see themselves (and are increasingly encouraged to do so) as having been the victims of just this kind of double standard—Europeans first, natives second—in Palestine.[2]

---

[1] Flattery and assurances of goodwill (assiduous but often very naïve and unskilful) from the Eastern bloc have not done much to assuage or compensate for this general feeling of injury.

[2] In view of this it is not surprising that (if the writer's experience is at all typical) characteristically 'Western' anti-semitic attitudes and myths should be spreading rapidly among certain sections of the Arab intelligentsia. In discussion and argument one may nowadays be asked with depressing frequency if one knows how many Jews control the New York money market, or the London press, or if one has read the works of Mr. Douglas Reed. (A Palestinian refugee in Libya pressed *Somewhere South of Suez* upon the writer with the assurance that it was strictly prohibited in Britain.) It was surprising to see a shelf-full of the *Protocols of the Elders of Zion* in the Information Department in Cairo in

Among the new regimes there can be noticed a genuine dis-
approval of what are felt to be the excessively material values of
the West. In zealously Islamic circles this is of course nothing
new; but the fabulous oil-wealth acquired, mostly from Western
sources, by the rulers of some Arab states, and the reputed corruption and stagnation of their governments have sharpened it and
given it a wider currency. Although most Arabs who have sampled
the comforts and freedoms of European and American society
retain a lasting appreciation of them, the decline of the slavishly
imitative 'Levantine' type as a leading element in many Arab
countries has been accompanied by a general feeling against any
too obvious display of this appreciation.

In one particular respect the attitudes towards the political institutions and traditions of Europe prevalent among educated
Arabs have undergone a notable change in the past ten years or so.
In the period of early theoretical nationalism before 1914, it was
almost universally assumed that the reformed Muslim and Arab
societies which it was hoped to set up were to be liberal democracies, in sharp contrast to the Turkish despotism from which
they would have broken away. 'Liberalism was expressed in terms
of nationalism, nationalism in terms of democracy.'[1] The special
problems arising from the Islamic past, the religious and cultural
traditions of the Arab peoples, were not overlooked, but in general
it was held that Western political experience was relevant, and
even that the Islamic past, properly understood, provided pre-
cedents for democratic institutions. Today democracy remains a
word pronounced almost everywhere with fervour and respect,
but in many of the newly independent Arab countries it has taken
on specially defined meanings. The argument is frequently heard
(and not only from officials of non-Parliamentary regimes, who
may of course have very interested reasons for resorting to it) that
the Arab background, and in particular the fact of recent political and economic subjection to Western imperialism makes it

1959; the intelligent and amiable young official in whose office they were
attributed their presence to a personal foible of his immediate superior. Too
much should not, perhaps, be made of such incidents. But it does seem curious, in
retrospect, that it never occurred to the many prominent gentiles who advocated
Zionism as the only means of eradicating anti-semitism from European society
that a result might be to spread this revolting infection amongst people who had
hitherto been remarkably free from it.
[1] John Marlowe, *Arab Nationalism and British Imperialism*, London, 1961,
p. 13.

impossible to introduce democracy on liberal Western lines yet; vital social and political reforms must come first. Whereas in 1914 one of the most influential of the Egyptian 'Westernizers' and nationalist thinkers was maintaining the view that Socialism would only strengthen the existing tendency of the people to acquiesce in strong paternal government. Material development also was second in importance to liberty. The reclamation of the land, the building of canals, the adoption of European technology were all important and beneficial, but if they were only to be attained at the expense of liberty they should be rejected[1]—in progressive Arab circles today a large majority would probably reverse these priorities, whilst at the same time denying that there is any final conflict between them, since economic development is the ultimate guarantee of real political liberty and social progress. British officials in the past often believed that their work was preparing the Arabs for future self-government on a liberal British pattern; but an important part of the contemporary reassessment of European institutions is the often-stated conviction that it was precisely those decades of Western tutelage that have unfitted Arab societies for the immediate adoption of some of these institutions. The protected and mandated areas, the argument runs, achieved independence in name only, and so the bases of a really effective social unity must be firmly laid before luxuries such as opposition parties, a free press and radio, *habeas corpus*, etc., can be afforded.

There is undoubtedly a great deal of plausibility in this doctrine; and in any case Arabs are not unaware that in Western Europe itself it is now generally realized that a genuine working democratic system is a far more complex and elusive thing, and far harder to institute *de novo*, than was apparent to Liberal enthusiasts a century ago. In considering the changed attitudes of Arabs and others towards 'modern Western civilization' it ought never to be forgotten how drastically the modern West's image of itself has altered, and how much earlier complacency and self-satisfaction have been lost.

The scientific and technological superiority of Western man is at least not so daunting as it once was; his achievements, it is clear, can be imitated, equalled, and ultimately bettered. Some Egyptian

---

[1] Ahmed Lutfi al Sayyid, quoted by Jamal Muhammad Ahmed, *The Intellectual Origins of Egyptian Nationalism*, Oxford University Press, 1960, p. 109.

writers were remarkably quick to see the implications of Japan's demonstration of this fact nearly sixty years ago; no Arab country has the resources to become another Japan, but the call to industrialize, to become independent of 'economic imperialism' of all kinds, is one of the most assertive and popular themes in modern Arab nationalism. In part this is a consequence of the widespread conviction that European imperialism always deliberately retarded the industrial development of its dependencies, treating them as convenient primary producers. Thus the factory and the five-year plan become symbols of real independence, pledges of ultimate success in the race to 'catch up'.

How long it will take to 'catch up' in this sense—how soon Arabs can cease to feel that they are merely receivers, unable to make any contribution of their own to the headlong and exciting progress of modern technology, is a question that is certainly pondered by some of them[1] but to which, obviously, no definite answer can be given. Quite apart from the material factors there are other formidable obstacles to be overcome; the attitudes of mind fostered by an educational tradition that has for centuries been purely literary in outlook and excessively narrow and tradition-bound in content and method are still a most serious handicap. Although Western schools and colleges have been active in parts of the Arab world for over a century, in many places the theory and practice of education are only beginning to be adapted to the requirements of modern life. Despite the widespread zest for the up-to-date and the mechanically ingenious the Arab mind still tends to be unadventurous, charmed by the reassuring power of elegantly expressed orthodoxy and the accepted idea. This is, of course, a more formidable barrier to the assimilation of unfamiliar intellectual concepts than to the mastery of new technical skills. Too often it becomes clear that a restricting and stereotyped literary education has produced the habit of over-simplifying complex problems and situations, of seeing human character in terms of sharply opposed categories and history as the unending conflict of heroes and villains.

There is also the especially noticeable tendency to ascribe an

---

[1] In 1960 an exceedingly intelligent and highly educated Egyptian university professor expressed to the writer his disappointment that after eight years the revolution in his country had still contributed nothing to the general benefit and advancement of mankind, and agreed only with reluctance that this was, in the circumstances, far too short a period for such results to be expected.

inordinate and sometimes stultifying symbolical importance to things whose essence is—to Western minds at least—purely utilitarian. So much emphasis can be laid on the mere fact of having at last achieved one's own government, factory, airline, hospital, etc., that the subsequent problem of efficient maintenance tends to be underrated. This is, however, a somewhat rash and tentative generalization, and there are indications that the Arabs who have been longest exposed to European contacts can refute it. The very high degree of efficiency with which Egypt has managed the Suez Canal since nationalization is surely a clear case in point, and the High Dam, overloaded as it has become with symbolical meaning, may turn out to be another. But in places where the experience of Western ideas and methods is of more recent date illustrations of this weakness for overestimating the practical efficacy of symbolical associations can still be found with disconcerting frequency.[1]

Some fifty years ago Ahmed Lutfi el Sayyid, one of the leaders of liberal nationalism in Egypt, wrote:

The dominant civilization of today is European, and the only possible foundation for our progress . . . is the transmission of the principles of that civilization.[2]

He was expressing a view which had by then become something of a commonplace among liberal thinkers in Egypt, although there were still many who would have disputed it. The intervening period has shown how difficult and at times hazardous such deliberate cultural borrowing can be for people with so strongly-marked and warmly-cherished a tradition of their own, and one that is in many ways so sharply contrasted with that of Western Europe. Whether, after these 160 years since their first confrontation, educated Arabs see 'modern Western civilization' in a truer light than they did is hardly a profitable question to discuss, the idea of Europe and the concept of civilization itself having altered considerably in the meantime; all that can usefully be said is that their experience of it has by now been a long and varied one. As a result of this experience their inherited ways of life and habits of

---

[1] See H. A. R. Gibb, 'Islam in the Modern World' in *The Arab Middle East and Muslim Africa*, ed. by Tibor Kerekes, London, 1961, pp. 12–25, for some extremely relevant and suggestive remarks on this topic. Gibb sees 'the primacy of the symbol' as 'running through all aspects and regions of Arab life' and 'the element of objectivation' ('the assignment of positive and self-validating values to actions, institutions, etc., in themselves') as one of the most prominent characteristics of modern Islamic societies. [2] J. M. Ahmed, op. cit., p. 97.

thought have been greatly affected; they have learned to be deeply dissatisfied with their position in the modern world, have found many new ways of expressing and analysing their discontent, and have acquired at least some of the tools with which they may eventually succeed in carrying out their revolution.

M

X. MODERN TURKISH ATTITUDES TO EUROPE

Geoffrey Lewis

In 1957, the Turkish Linguistic Society published a new edition of its *Guide to Spelling*. The following quotation is from a review of this work in the Society's journal:

After this explanation we may arrive at these conclusions: (1) Our alphabet belongs within the phonetic-alphabetic system of writing used by the civilized nations. (2) The classification of the phonemes is like the Westerners' classification of their own phonemes. But this is not a classification ever to be made by neglecting the essences and attributes of our own phonemes.[1]

In these words the malaise of contemporary Turkey is touchingly revealed: we *are* Western; we are just like real Westerners, but we must never forget we are different.

To understand the origins of this malaise, it is necessary to go back into history, although it is not our purpose here to attempt a detailed chronological account of Turkish attitudes towards the West. Indeed, for most of the six hundred years of the Ottoman period it is impossible to speak of 'Turkish attitudes' in isolation from Islamic attitudes.

A thousand years ago, the Turks who had wandered into the Arab empire in Western Asia accepted the religion of the Arabs. Four centuries passed and the Turks under the Ottoman dynasty founded a greater empire, the greatest and most long-lived of all the Islamic empires. Within this empire the Turks submerged their identity; the very name 'Turk' meant peasant, yokel. Europeans might speak of the 'Turkish Empire'; for the Turks it was the High State, the Guarded Dominions, the Abode of the Faith. True, Turkish was the language of the administration, but the language of religion was Arabic, and Persian the language of

[1] *Türk Dili*, vol. vii, no. 73, October 1957, p. 9.

literary culture. Further, though the highest positions in the
religious hierarchy were open to Turks, from the fourteenth to the
seventeenth centuries Turks were denied high administrative
office.[1] The senior administrators, the Palace officials and the
Janissaries, the main military arm of the state, were recruited in
boyhood by press-gangs from the Christian subject-peoples.[2]
Once converted to Islam and having learned Turkish, these recruits
found that there was no bar, save inefficiency, to their advancement; how could there be, when all their superiors except the
Sultan himself had been born Christians and non-Turks? Nor was
the Sultan, whose slaves they were, in any position to look down
on them as not being born of the dominant race, if by some strange
prescience this modern concept had crossed his mind. For it was
exceptional for the sultans to marry Turkish women; of the thirty-
six members of the House of Osman who reigned from 1281 to
1922, only five are known to have had Turkish mothers, and it has
been calculated that the proportion of Turkish blood in the veins
of the last Sultan was one part in over sixteen thousand.[3]

So the rulers of the Empire never thought of themselves as
Turks; they were Ottomans and Muslims. The *raison d'être* of
their Empire was the enlargement of the territories of the Faith;
in principle it was in a state of constant warfare with Christian
Europe. Those who obdurately refused to accept Muhammad as a
later and greater prophet than Jesus were the objects not only of
hostility but also of contempt. For so long as the military power
of the Ottoman Empire was irresistible, this contempt could be
justified. Even when the tide had turned, when the Ottoman
armies had been forced to abandon the siege of Vienna in 1683, the
Ottomans continued to regard themselves as possessing a God-
given superiority over the 'abject infidel', a perfectly understandable attitude which was the simple corollary to the *Paien unt tort e
crestiens unt dreit* of the *Song of Roland.*

Though clever with their hands in making useful devices like guns,
clocks, and printing presses, the Europeans were still benighted and

---

[1] This, the received doctrine on the subject, has been shaken, though not
demolished, by Norman Itzkowitz in a paper entitled 'Eighteenth Century
Ottoman Realities', *Studia Islamica*, fasc. xvi, 1962, pp. 73–94.
[2] G. L. Lewis, *Turkey*, London, 1957, pp. 25–28; V. L. Ménage, article on
Devshirme in new *Encyclopaedia of Islam.*
[3] A. D. Alderson, *Structure of the Ottoman Dynasty*, Oxford University Press,
1956, pp. 83, 91–92.

barbarous infidels, whose history, philosophy, science, and literature, if indeed they existed at all, could hold nothing of value for the people of the universal Islamic Empire.[1]

But though Ottoman pride might survive the realization that the benighted infidel could beat the Ottoman armies in the field, it could not long survive the shock of discovering that the universal Islamic Empire did not command the allegiance of all its Muslim subjects. The Turks were the only people of the Empire with no national consciousness. The Greeks founded their *Philiké Hetairia* in 1814, and by 1830 there was an independent Greece to serve as an example of what could be done. In the second half of the century the Armenians and Bulgars began working for independence; but so too did the Arabs, and this was the hardest blow of all.

The name 'Young Turks' was applied by European writers to the organization founded in 1865 which called itself 'Young Ottomans'. It is significant that all its founders belonged to the Army Medical School, being men who, by virtue of both aspects of their professional training, were in the closest touch with the West. The Turks within this organization were certainly aware of their Turkish identity, if only by a process of elimination—they were the only people not fighting for their independence. But they did not choose to draw attention to their Turkishness, as they needed the support of the non-Turks to achieve their goal of constitutional government and, after 1876, the overthrow of the despotism of Abdul Hamid. Turkish nationalism as a political creed made its public appearance after the achievement of the latter aim, in 1908, when the Party of Union and Progress came to power.

There was no unanimity about the course the Empire should thenceforth follow. Inside and outside the Party, various incompatible creeds vied for supremacy, often within the same individual skulls. All the Turks wished to hold the Empire together; in this respect they may all be termed Ottomanists. Some wished, or professed to wish, to see all the peoples of the Empire living as equal partners united under the Ottoman sultanate, in what we should nowadays call a multiracial commonwealth. Others, seeing the impracticality of hoping that the non-Turks would for long maintain their allegiance to the dynasty which had in recent years—indeed,

[1] Bernard Lewis, *The Emergence of Modern Turkey*, Oxford University Press, 1961, p. 52.

in recent centuries—brought little happiness to its subjects, were thinking in terms of a modernized Empire under Turkish control. All saw that the dilapidated structure needed to be strengthened. Some thought the answer was to adopt Western civilization. Others believed that their ancestral civilization was adequate in itself; what was needed was not to ape the West but to bring about an Islamic renaissance, with all the Muslims of the world united under the Sultan-Caliph. Between the two parties were those who held (like their ancestors of seven and eight generations before) that it was possible to take over the outward forms, the technical advances, while maintaining their loyalty to Islamic ethics and law.

It is not easy for men to concede that their ancestral values are inadequate and to abandon them for an alien system. Hence the violence of the protests made by the traditionalists against the doctrines of the westernizers. Dervish Vahdeti, one of the leaders of the Muhammadan Unity Party, founded in 1909, declaring that the Young Turks had inaugurated 'an era of devils', said:

Let us take care that a handful of dishonourable scoundrels from Europe do not impose on us the morals of the Europeans. For example, let us not countenance the appearance in our land of things inconsistent with Islam, such as the gradual unveiling of our women, or, on the plea that Muslims are free men, the opening of taverns and brothels.[1]

The Balkan Wars, which cost the Empire its European provinces, put an end to Ottomanism. The First World War did the same for Panislamism, when the Arabs joined forces with the infidel against the Sultan-Caliph. The Turks were on their own.

There is no need to retell the story of how Mustafa Kemal, the most successful war-time general of the Ottoman armies, set himself at the head of his people and drove them on towards his goal, which was to make the new-born Turkey into a modern Western state, with no interference from Islam. His reverence for Western civilization fell little short of idolatry; indeed, he did not usually bother to specify *Western* civilization: for him, the alternative was not Eastern civilization but darkness and barbarism.

Resistance to the flood-tide of civilization is vain; she is quite merciless to those who ignore or disobey her. Civilization pierces the mountains,

---

[1] T. Z. Tunaya, *Türkiyenin Siyasî Hayatında Batılılaşma Hareketleri*, Istanbul, 1960, p. 86. There had in fact been taverns in Istanbul since the sixteenth century if not before.

soars in the skies, sees and illuminates and studies all things, from the invisible atoms to the stars. Nations which try to function with medieval minds, with primitive superstitions, in the presence of her might and her sublime majesty, are doomed to annihilation or, at best, to servitude or ignominy.[1]

The articulate Turks were behind him; the inarticulate majority, as ever, did as they were told. They discarded their fezzes, they accepted that one wife was as many as a civilized man ought to have (very few men had been able to afford more than one anyway), they stopped using, or not using, the Arabic alphabet and began to use, or not to use, the new Latin letters.

In order to effect all this, and more, without utterly demoralizing the Turks, Mustafa Kemal had to persuade them that the Western civilization they were entering was not an alien organism; that their own ancestors had played their part in its creation. It would have been a simple task to point out the contribution Islam had made, e.g. in the transmission of classical learning to Europe in the 'Dark Ages'. But it was no part of his purpose that the Turks should continue to identify themselves with Islam. Instead, the young Turk was taught at school that all the great civilizations of antiquity had been created or at least enriched by Turks. The pristine glories of the Turks had then been contaminated by the alien creed of Islam, which had gained a stranglehold on the Ottoman state. But however good such doctrines might be for popular morale, they never really satisfied thinking people. Even if you accepted that Alexander the Great and Julius Caesar were, in a Pickwickian sense, Turks, that was no consolation for your having to turn to the despised infidel for instruction in all the arts of living. Thus, with the best of intentions, a deadly blow was struck at Turkish self-respect. Some people took refuge in extreme nationalism, maintaining that the Turks were a master-race, the decline in whose fortunes since the sixteenth century was due to the machinations of the non-Turks in their midst. Among the exponents of this view there were—and are—the Panturanians, who are willing to admit the Finns and Hungarians to parity with the Turks, on the basis of the obsolescent theory of a Ural-Altaic family of languages including Finnish, Hungarian, and Turkish. The Panturanians do not extend similar recognition to Basques

---

[1] From a speech delivered at Inebolu in August 1925. *Atatürk'ün Söylev ve Demeçleri*, Ankara, 1952, vol. ii, p. 214.

and Red Indians, possibly not realizing that these people too speak agglutinating languages.

Leaving aside such eccentricities, Turkish nationalism, as inculcated in all schoolchildren, is of a remarkable intensity. It is the one subject on which it is impossible for a Turk to make or see a joke. The Turkish penal code recognizes a crime for which it would be hard to find a parallel in any other Western legal system: *Türklüğü tahkir*, insult to Turkdom or Turk-disparagement.

So the Turks were equipped with a national consciousness and were led into the Western world. Now that the traditional Turco-Islamic culture was to be abandoned, the training-schools for Muslim clerics attracted fewer and fewer students. Between 1933 and 1949 there was no higher religious education at all.[1] The result is that the religious masses, deprived of their natural leaders, have too often in recent years been the prey of the ignorant and fanatical, so that a well-intentioned young Imam who starts a football team and a one-man programme of adult education in his village is a subject for astonishment and headlines in the newspapers.

The old Turco-Islamic code demanded that children should behave quietly and respectfully in the presence of their elders. So too did the old European code, but the young Turk can hardly be expected to know or care about that. In August 1962 a large gang of Turkish teenagers demonstrated how Westernized they were by dressing in black leather jackets and rioting in an Istanbul cinema.

Mustafa Kemal told the Turks that their traditional culture was bankrupt. Had he lived longer, he might well have completed the process of Westernization, or at least carried it to the point where its own impetus would have done the rest. But he died in 1938, at the age of 57, and since then the Kemalists have virtually deified him. In allusion to his chosen surname of Atatürk, Father-Turk, he is commonly referred to as Ata, the Father, and the third-person pronoun when it relates to him is spelt with a capital letter. A writer in an Istanbul newspaper, apostrophizing the young lieutenant who was the sole casualty of the *coup d'état* of May 1960 and who was buried in the shadow of Atatürk's mausoleum, used these words: 'Sleep well, great dead, in the arms of the Father. Embrace your martyred brothers of the Universities and sleep well,

---

[1] It was announced in August 1962 that only 5,000 of the country's 60,000 Muslim men of religion could read and write.

in the Father's tranquil bosom.' Language like this denatures the great man to the status of a symbol; it deprives him of his humanity and frees the young Turk from the responsibility of striving to emulate him. Worse, it makes it impossible for any leader to emerge and say that perhaps Kemal went too far and too fast. What this amounts to is that Mustafa Kemal pushed the Turks into Western civilization and locked the door behind them. His followers have thrown away the key.

Adnan Menderes, Prime Minister from 1950 to 1960, who had a remarkably keen insight into the mind of the Turkish peasant, encouraged the revival of Turkish Islam, including some reactionary and obscurantist manifestations of it. In so doing he acted unconstitutionally and this was among the reasons for his downfall and death. But even at the height of his popularity he never tried to amend Atatürk's Constitution, thinking it safer to pay lip-service to it. One episode during his trial casts light on the immense prestige of Atatürk. The newspaper headlines proclaimed one day: 'Menderes, in his defence, does not shrink from maligning the Father'. From the text below, it emerged that what he had said was that it was unfair to blame him for not creating a flourishing democracy during his ten years as Prime Minister, as even Atatürk had seen the failure of two attempts in his lifetime to set up a parliamentary opposition. To foreigners who read this, it seemed that the writers of the headlines were guilty of deliberate distortion. But they were not. To the Kemalist way of thinking, it was a studied insult to Atatürk to use his name in the same sentence as the word 'failure'.

So, for better or worse, Turkey is committed to Westernization. There is a well-known make of refrigerator with shelves in its door, and this feature is described by the trade-name 'Shelvador'. Some time ago, one of these refrigerators was displayed in a Turkish shop-window, with a big placard bearing the legend *Şelvador'u var!*—It has the Shelvador! These words, which conveyed absolutely nothing to the Turkish passer-by, epitomize the way in which Western civilization has been pushed down Turkish throats, in one huge indigestible lump. Part of the lump is democracy. Menderes's party was called the Democrat Party, or, to give it its Turkish title, *Demokrat Parti*. What did this convey to the average citizen? One Turkish secondary-school boy wrote in a recent essay that *parti* meant 'government'. And *Demokrat*? The peasants pronounced this word *demirkırat*, meaning 'iron-break-horse', which does not convey very much but perhaps more than *Demokrat*.

The 1960 *coup d'état* had as its avowed object the overthrow of the undemocratic government of the Democrat Party. The army officers who brought it about, unlike the colonels and generals in several other countries, resisted the temptation to maintain themselves in power. In October 1961 they held free elections to choose a new civilian government, which did nothing for eight months except raise its own salaries and wrangle about an amnesty for the imprisoned members of the former regime. The result has been disillusion and despair. The prevailing impression among thinking Turks seems to be that there is some innate defect in their chromosomes militating against their making a success of democracy. They will not consider the centuries it has taken for democracy to establish itself in other lands, nor will they accept that temperament and tradition cannot be changed overnight.

Particularly resistant to change is the bureaucracy, with its roots going back to the days when Istanbul was 'East Rome which is Constantinople'. If some fairy godmother were willing to alter one thing in Turkey, she could hardly do better than repeal the law prohibiting disrespect to officials. The press is free in Turkey, but, because of this pernicious law, criticism of official conduct can be couched only in general terms: you may say the Civil Service is hidebound or wanting in humanity, but you cannot say Mr. So-and-so is a pompous ass.[1] Within these limits criticism is plentiful and pointed: for example, the recent announcement that one of the ministries in Ankara had bought a computer was accompanied in one newspaper by a cartoon showing officials of the ministry feeding questions into the machine and receiving the typical official reply, 'Go away and come back tomorrow!'

Too many Turks will now tell you that the one hope for the future is to import a board of foreigners to run the country. The more responsible papers frequently point out, when describing some newly revealed piece of inefficiency or chicanery, 'This sort of thing could never happen in England'—or America, or France, or whatever Western country the leader-writer has visited most recently. In March 1962 it was deemed necessary to pass a new

---

[1] By the summer of 1963, however, one or two courageous journalists had taken to making detailed personal attacks on members of the government.

law, punishing with up to two years' imprisonment anyone who says that democracy cannot be made to work in Turkey.

There can be no going back. Turkey belongs to the West. Turkish bookstalls are full of translations of Western works of fiction and non-fiction. Every Turkish student's dream is to finish his studies in France or Germany or England or America. Apart from a handful of extreme pietists, no Turks feel any special kinship with their Muslim co-religionists of other lands. It was as progressive Westerners, not as Muslims, that the Turks added their voice to the appeals for Algerian independence.

Turkey is now part of Europe, as a glance at the British *Post Office Guide* or British European Airways' time-tables will show. She is a member, and a loyal member, of the Council of Europe and indeed of the North Atlantic Treaty Organization, although, as the late Lord Reading once said, Turkey is not a country on whose shores the waves of the Atlantic conspicuously wash. Nevertheless, in Taksim Square in Istanbul, which is in Europe geographically as well as politically, there stands a signpost pointing the way to Europe. It was erected by no Turkish authority but by the Shell Company of Turkey, yet it has not been torn down by an offended populace. Humbly they accept it.

The glass curtain is very real. It is a vast shop-window in which are displayed all the riches of the West: democracy, a national health service, prosperity, *habeas corpus*, mass education, comfort, and self-respect. And the Turk, dignified, hardworking, patient, bewildered, heedless of Asia behind him, stands wistfully pressing his nose up against the glass.

XI. ASIA AS SEEN BY THE
FRENCH ENLIGHTENMENT

Robert Shackleton

The imaginative cartographers of the sixteenth century used to take pleasure in drawing a map of Europe in which a few changes of detail and a little tendentious shading gave the continent the form of a woman. Often her head, wearing a royal crown, was the Iberian peninsula, while Sicily was the orb in her hand. This was not simply a mapmaker's fancy. It corresponded to a concept of the unity of Europe and its primacy: *prima pars terrae* is the legend the map sometimes bears. Asia also was personified by some cartographers of that age, being shown in the form of a horse, ill-defined but ungainly, and of course being the servant of man. Such primitive notions were shaken by the reflection that Asia had been the cradle of the three great monotheistic religions and must therefore have a unique degree of intellectual excellence, albeit to be explained by the conjunctions of the stars or the heat of the sun which inflamed the imagination of men. The elimination, by the serious accounts of travellers, of the fantastic elements in men's views of the East, was only very slowly effected. It was as late as 1637 that a supplement to a very popular travel book, the *Relazioni universali* of Giovanni Botero, gave horrifying pictures of men whose bodies tailed off into a single leg with a huge foot, which on hot days was used to afford shelter to the prone body, of men with the heads of dogs, of men with elephants' trunks at the ends of which grew ears. These habitants of often not very remote lands were described on the venerable authority of the *Natural History* of Pliny.

The desire to be seriously informed about the East developed in France as the end of the seventeenth century approached, encouraged by the reception of envoys from Siam at Louis XIV's court. The narratives of travellers enjoyed a great vogue, and often their intrinsic worth merited it. Chardin and Tavernier, French protestants of whom the first, settling in London, became Sir John Chardin, F.R.S., and a prominent figure in English society, wrote accounts of travels in Asia which it is still a delight to read. These works, especially Chardin's in the much enlarged edition of 1711, were rich sources of information, not simply about the accidents of travel, dramatic as those sometimes were, but also about the institutions, thought, and religion of Eastern peoples.

In *belles-lettres* the East had already been accepted as a recognized setting for seventeenth-century tragedy. When a Racine character declared, '*Nourri dans le sérail, j'en connais les détours*', he evoked associations to which the French were accustomed. The East was for them a region of mystery and fatalism and cruelty, where monarchs were unscrupulous and lovers were bold. This vogue exploited by a Genoese writer, Gian-Paolo Marana, in a work which, originally written in Italian and having the title *L'Esploratore turco*, was presented to Louis XIV in manuscript in 1683. It was translated into French and then into English, and was so greatly expanded that the English edition of 1741, which claims to be the 23rd edition of volume I, is entitled *The Eight Volumes of Letters writ by a Turkish Spy*. What is significant above all about the work of Marana and his continuators is that the Eastern background serves mainly as an enabling device by means of which free criticism of French ideas and institutions, political and religious alike, can be expressed indirectly, being put into the mouth of an infidel and a Turk.

The travel accounts of Chardin and Tavernier and the literary ventriloquism of Marana represent and indeed shape the two major forms of interest in the East shown in the literature of the French Enlightenment: interest in the East for its own sake, and interest in the East as affording a device for comparison and thus favouring both free-thought itself and the literary expression of free-thought.

This philosophically useful interest in the East is illustrated by Fontenelle in his *De l'origine des fables* (published in 1724), one of the first studies in comparative religion, where the author, nominally and explicitly concerned with Eastern mythology, expressed ideas of an advanced character about the polygenesis of fables, which need only a small analogical jump on the reader's part to be applied to Western religion. So Pierre Bayle, immersed in controversy about the origin of evil, uses ancient Persia and the doctrines of the Manicheans as the occasion for expressing the heretical theory of the two principles of good and of evil, whose dialectical efficacy against the orthodox he made clear in the articles *Manichéens, Marcionites,* and *Pauliciens* of his widely read *Dictionnaire historique et critique* (1697, first edition).

But it is Montesquieu in his *Lettres persanes* (1721) who carries the technique of literary utilization of the East to the point of near perfection. Now he uses genuine information about the East as a basis of comparison in his attack on prejudice, now the Moslem spokesman is simply a vehicle for the safer expression of his own ideas. The Pope is described as the Mufti of the Christians; the administration of the Grand Turk is described as the form of government closest to Louis XIV's own heart. Elements of deism and elements of materialism emerge in a work which, perhaps more than any other, inaugurated the French Enlightenment. Montesquieu relied for his information on Chardin and Tavernier; Marana's *Turkish Spy,* with other works, was his literary model. He perfected a genre of which the eighteenth century was to show many exponents. *Lettres chinoises, Lettres turques, Lettres juives* abound. Goldsmith publishes his *Citizen of the World,* on the same model, in England, Cadalso his *Cartas marruecas* in Spain.

What is notable about the East as known in France in both fact and fiction in the early eighteenth century is that it is almost always a question of the Moslem East, of Turkey and Persia in particular. The life of Mahomet fascinated the public. Moslem polygamy lent itself to literary treatment very readily in an age of *sensibilité*. Often evoked were details of the Koranic notion of heaven, peopled with fair maidens with black eyes and white skin, who had the secret of eternal youth and whose virginity was each day restored. Not for nothing had the *Thousand and One Nights* been translated in French. When Voltaire sought to attack religious fanaticism in a tragedy which he wished to present, acceptably, to the Pope, it is on the life of Mahomet that it is based. When he wished to revive the Othello theme, to portray a virtuous pagan, to evoke the tragic situation of a girl from a Christian family brought up in another faith, Orosmane was his hero, Zaïre (the letter Z being a traditional initial in tales of the East) was his heroine, and the setting, inevitably, was in the Turkish Empire.

The output of travel books in the first decades of the century was appreciable without being overwhelming; but the majority deal with no regions farther east than Persia. Thévenot's travels in the Levant, the publication of which started in 1664, were reprinted in 1727. The accounts of the travels of Cornelius de Bruin appeared in French in 1700, 1714, 1718, and 1725. Tournefort's *Relation d'un voyage du Levant* was published in 1717. Chardin was reprinted in 1711, 1723, and 1735, while the travels in the Near East of Laurent d'Arvieux appeared posthumously in 1717, 1718, and 1735. But all this, even with the massive *Histoire générale des voyages* of which the Abbé Prévost initiated the publication in 1746, represents an output of travellers' tales about the Moslem East which, in new material, was by no means enormous. The increase in documentation available to the eighteenth century was not proportionate to the increase in interest. The increase in documentation concerned another area.

This is illustrated by a simple test. The *Grand Dictionnaire historique* of Moreri was the eighteenth century's standard work of reference, even after the publication of the *Encyclopédie*, for matters historical and geographical. The sixth edition of Moreri, published in 1696, devoted no more than two of its folio pages to China and to India, and less than one to Japan. The last edition which appeared in 1759 does not devote much more space to Japan or to India, but in the case of China the article is expanded to twelve pages and gives a thoroughly documented account of its history, religion, philosophy, and economic resources.

The interest in China thus attested is significant. The problem of Asia for many eighteenth-century thinkers became increasingly identified with the problem of China, much more than with India or Japan or even the Moslem East. *Philosophes* and ecclesiastics alike were engrossed, and traditional alignments and hostilities were often upset. Discussion of China contributed appreciably to the development of the Enlightenment in France, and it is paradoxical that most of the information and some of the interpretation of it came to France in the writings of Jesuits, who achieved a historic if unintended role in promoting the growth of deism, materialism, atheism, and the spirit of toleration.

The effective founder of the Jesuit mission in China was the Italian Matteo Ricci, who entered China in 1581. What position was a Christian missionary to adopt in relation to the highly organized and sophisticated civilization of China, and especially to its complicated and tenaciously observed ritualism? Ricci initially adopted the dress and rank of a Buddhist bonze, but later, in order to strengthen his position in Chinese society, assumed the habit of a Western literate. He was respectful of Chinese rites, in particular when they related to the ancestor cult, and described them as certainly not idolatrous, and perhaps not even superstitious, though he admitted that it would be better, when the Chinese were converted, to divert the expenditure to the provision of alms for the poor.[1] When other non-Jesuit missionaries first went to China, they were shocked at the extent to which the Jesuits had made concessions to existing Chinese rites, and a bitter controversy ensued, in which one of the charges, that the missionaries had eliminated the crucifixion from their preaching of the gospel, was made by Pascal in the fifth *Lettre provinciale* (1656), and of which the end came only with the Constitution *Ex quo*, unfavourable to the Jesuits, issued by Benedict XIV in 1742.

Documentation about China came in the first place from letters written to their European colleagues by Jesuit missionaries in China. These were published along with letters from other mission fields, in a large collection, started in 1706, entitled *Lettres édifiantes et curieuses*, on which any eighteenth-century person, however anti-clerical, who was interested in China had to draw. But other sources were available too. Eusèbe Renaudot, a friend of Boileau, a scholar and an academician, published towards the end of his long life a translation of two *Anciennes Relations des Indes et de la Chine* (1719) by two Moslem travellers of the ninth century, and added some essays of his own, one of which, *Éclaircissements sur les sciences des Chinois*, is particularly interesting and was much used. His standpoint is orthodox Christian, unwilling to compromise, and seeking to counter the idealized picture of the Chinese given by the Dutch scholar Isaac Vossius, and in the *Historiae Sinicae decas prima* of Martino Martini, S.J., published in 1658.

A few Chinese were from time to time received in Paris, and were interrogated about their country. One of these, Arcadio Hoange (1679–1716), who, coming to France around 1710, was given an appointment in the Bibliothèque du Roi, became well known among the learned. He knew Desmolets, a scholarly Oratorian, Fréret, the most erudite of all the *philosophes*,

[1] *Fonti Ricciane*, Rome, 1942, vol. i, p. 118.

Fourmont who became his heir, and Montesquieu, some of whose notes on conversations with Hoange remain.[1] It was through Hoange's activity that Fourmont and Fréret learned Chinese. Later in the century two young Chinese came to France to educate themselves, and were for a time supported by a pension given them by Louis XV. After making astonishingly rapid progress in physics and chemistry under the instruction of two members of the Académie des Sciences, they mastered some practical disciplines, and in due course returned to China. They sent now to Paris a series of papers on historical, literary, and scientific subjects concerning China, and these formed the nucleus of a vast and comprehensive collection of *Mémoires concernant l'histoire, les sciences, les arts, des Chinois* (1776–1814, 16 vols. 4to) edited by Jesuits, which supplemented, but did not replace, the invaluable *Description de la Chine* of Père du Halde (1735, 4 vols. 4to).

Intercourse with returned missionaries was incessant, as was indeed correspondence with missionaries still in China. Montesquieu reports his encounter in Italy with Mattia Ripa, who was promoting the establishment in Naples of a college for the Chinese. Two of the most learned of the Jesuits were Parrenin and Prémare. The first, who died at Pekin in 1741, learnt Manchu as well as Chinese, and engaged in celebrated controversy with the distinguished scientist Dortous de Mairan about Chinese origins. Prémare, who died at Macao in 1736, published a critique of Renaudot, writings of Chinese language and religion, and a translation of a Chinese tragedy which inspired Voltaire's play *L'Orphelin de la Chine*. He was a correspondent of the Chevalier Andrew Michael Ramsay, who was connected with almost every philosophical grouping in the first half of the eighteenth century. Particularly noteworthy was Jean-François Fouquet, who returned from his Chinese mission to establish himself, with a titular bishopric, in Rome. A visit to Fouquet was almost a necessity for any philosophically minded Frenchman on the Grand Tour. His papers, which still exist,[2] show that he had an interest in natural religion, in Bayle, and in Manicheism, which is striking in a Jesuit and a bishop.

---

[1] These are found in his notebook *Geographica*; see *Œuvres complètes*, ed. A. Masson, Paris (Nagel), vol. ii, 1953.

[2] Vatican Library, MSS. Borg. lat. 565–7.

Why was enlightened French opinion so concerned with China and what lessons did it draw? Certainly it was the problem of rites which first presented China to the French in a sensational light. Voltaire devoted to them the whole of the last chapter of *Le Siècle de Louis XIV* (1751), while Montesquieu discussed them at length in *L'Esprit des lois*, arguing that Chinese legislators used them to link together religion, laws, customs, and manners, so that in the rites became articulate the *esprit général* of the nation, with which all policies of governments must harmonize.[1] The attitude of the Jesuits to the rites raised interesting problems. If Christian missionaries in China were to respect some elements of existing religious usage, did not this concession of principle strike at the whole basis of missionary activity? Did it not involve a derogation from the uniqueness of the Christian revelation? The material for such arguments was welcome to most of the *philosophes*. It was doubly welcome when it came to them from their enemies the Jesuits, and when the compromises accepted by missionaries themselves could be alleged as arguments against missionary activity.

In order to justify their concessions, the Jesuits had insisted that the ethical views of the Chinese in general, and of Confucius in particular, were excellent, and were not based on any pagan religion. And since they were, obviously, not based on the Christian religion, the Jesuits were in the position of having admitted that a purely lay morality could exist and could be of value. This had been the contention already of the precursors of the *philosophes*, notably of La Mothe Le Vayer in his *De la vertu des païens* and above all of Bayle, and the view expressed by the Jesuits now gave an enormous debating advantage to the *philosophes*, for even those of their number who denied the premise welcomed the implicit conclusion. The premise—of the moral worth of the Chinese— was indeed often denied, though not by Voltaire or Diderot. It was denied at an early date by the orthodox Renaudot; it was denied later by a traveller who enjoyed great repute in France, Admiral Anson, who from his own experience condemned the Jesuits for over-favourable accounts and told how the Chinese, when selling chickens by weight, made them, at the eventual cost of their lives, swallow stones to increase their value.[2] Montesquieu,

---

[1] *L'Esprit des lois*, bk. xix, ch. 19.
[2] G. Anson, *A Voyage round the World*, London, 1748, pp. 524–5.

N

who read Anson with delight, pointed out that deceit was legitimate in China.[1]

What were the religious views of the Chinese? For some, they approximated to the views of Spinoza, or rather to the image of Spinoza which was generally accepted in the eighteenth century and which made him an atheist. Thus Malebranche, wishing to express his own Christian views in dialogue form, chooses a Chinese thinker as interlocutor, and writes his *Entretiens d'un philosophe chrétien et d'un philosophe chinois* (1708). If the Chinese were atheists, however, there arose an important connection with early eighteenth-century thought. Bayle, in his *Pensées diverses sur la comète* of 1683, had argued in words which became famous that atheism was no impediment to the existence of a viable society. Many (and in due course even some of the less extreme of the *philosophes*, such as Montesquieu) protested and maintained that a society of atheists could not exist. But here was China, giving a practical demonstration of the truth of Bayle's view. And Bayle had gone on to institute a comparison, which became not less famous, between atheists and idolaters. But the Chinese, with their ritual devotion to images, were, according to some witnesses, idolatrous. A race which was simultaneously atheistic and idolatrous presented therefore an unimagined problem to the *philosophes* and to their opponents. Bayle himself had pointed out, citing Arnauld, that the literate of China were atheists by belief and idolaters by dissimulation and hypocrisy.[2] Voltaire, declaring that those who assert the atheism of the Chinese were the same persons as those who vehemently denied Bayle's claim that a society of atheists could exist, shows his usual sympathy for the Chinese when he attributes to them a religion simple, honest, and free from superstition.[3] It is rare to find objective discussion of religious belief.

Atheists or not, the Chinese had offered to the Western world, in opening their frontiers to missionaries, a needed lesson in religious toleration and open-mindedness. But before the arrival of the missionaries, there had been (Voltaire points out) no religious quarrels in the country. The Jesuits had cited miraculous crosses seen near the horizon as signs of divine approval of their mission. But it could be said, again with Voltaire, that if God had

---

[1] *L'Esprit des lois*, bk. xix, ch. 20.
[2] *Dictionnaire historique et critique*, s.v. Maldonat, rem. L.
[3] *Œuvres complètes*, ed. L. Moland, Paris, 1878, vol. xi, p. 57.

wished the Chinese to be converted, he would have placed crosses not in the air, but in the hearts of the Chinese.[1] And a Chinese emperor himself, according to the article *Chinois (philosophie des)* in the *Encyclopédie*, put the old question of invincible ignorance: if a knowledge of Jesus Christ is necessary for salvation, and if God wishes to save men, how can he have left the Chinese so long in ignorance? This is a question, adds Diderot, which is debated every day on the benches of the Sorbonne. When the Emperor Yung-Chin, virtuous, capable, and enlightened, expelled the missionaries in 1724, he became the rival almost of Julian the Apostate in the esteem of some of the *philosophes*.

The civilization of China was clearly of great antiquity, and discussion of exactly how old it was could involve serious and potentially dangerous problems: the authenticity of Biblical chronology, the flood, the family of Noah, the monogenesis of mankind. Following suggestions made in the previous century by Kircher and Huet, Mairan, in a public letter to Parrenin, advanced the suggestion that the Chinese were descended from an Egyptian colony which migrated fifteen or sixteen centuries before Christ. Mairan, who was a close friend of Fontenelle and Montesquieu and can fairly be regarded as one of the *philosophes*, appears to have had no special motive in proposing this theory, and his discussion is based on serious evidence, notably on the apparent similarity between Egyptian hieroglyphics and Chinese ideograms. Parrenin replied to him, both privately and in the pages of the *Lettres édifiantes*, and his rejection of the theory appeared decisive —more so at least than the attempt made by an English divine, Samuel Shuckford, to effect a reconciliation by claiming that the ark came to rest on the frontiers of China, that the Chinese were descended from children born to Noah after the flood, and that Noah and Fohi, the first recorded king of China, were one and the same person.[2]

But in the 1750s the controversy was reopened by John Needham, an English catholic priest who was a scientist and an antiquarian. He declared that a bust of Isis, kept at Turin, bore Egyptian characters very close in appearance to Chinese. The learned François de Guignes read to the Académie des Inscriptions

---

[1] *Siècle de Louis XIV (Œuvres complètes*, ed. L. Moland, vol. xv, p. 84).
[2] *The Sacred and Profane History of the World connected*, London, 1731–7 (second edition), vol. i, p. 102.

in 1758 a paper, published the next year, in which he sought to prove, once again on the basis of hieroglyphics, the theory of Egyptian origin, and remarks in support that all the dangerous consequences of Chinese history disappear if the Egyptian theory is accepted.

It was, of course, these dangerous consequences, much more than the theory itself, which interested such men as Diderot and Voltaire. In the *Encyclopédie* article on the philosophy of the Chinese, Diderot says that the Chinese and Mosaic chronologies are incompatible, and that he is disinclined to prefer the Chinese since it was framed by the same people who asserted that the mother of Fohi was made pregnant by a rainbow. In the same volume, published in 1753, came the article *Chronologie sacrée*, in which Diderot first declares that the Biblical chronology is the true one, and then proceeds obliquely to unsay this, finally claiming that only small-mindedness or lack of reading can lead one to reject the Chinese system. Voltaire, in *La Philosophie de l'histoire* (1765), later prefaced to the *Essai sur les mœurs*, is more direct: the Chinese records are reliable, being based on sound astronomy; their empire certainly existed four thousand years ago, and probably long before that; they knew no primitive catastrophes such as fire or floods; they were living as an organized community when the French were still wandering in the forest of the Ardennes.

The political system of the Chinese was bound to win the approval of the *philosophes* at least in relation to the social and political recognition given to men of letters. Even Renaudot had admitted that in China philosophers were kings, though he insisted that the Chinese had not greatly profited thereby. The first volume of the great collection of *Mémoires* on China (1776) had as its frontispiece a portrait of the Emperor Kien-Long with the inscription:

> Occupé sans relâche à tous les soins divers
> D'un gouvernement qu'on admire,
> Le plus grand potentat qui soit dans l'univers
> Est le meilleur lettré qui soit dans son empire.

And when Voltaire maintains that whereas in other countries the function of the laws is to punish crime, in China they reward virtue, he is in part thinking of literary excellence. But Rousseau, in natural dissent, seeking in his *Discours sur les sciences et les arts* of 1750, to deplore civilization, cites China to prove his thesis: no country honours the sciences more, no country is more vicious.

The study of Chinese politics encouraged developments in French political theory in the eighteenth century. The Sultan of Turkey was traditionally the prototype of the despotic prince; and Montesquieu's theory of despotism, in spite of occasional guarded references to dangers in store for European powers, is essentially based on Moslem exemplars. Montesquieu was determined, however, to make up his mind about China. He examines the country in search of his three principles of government—virtue, honour, and fear. Considering the brigandage of the mandarins and the dictum which, distorting it, he attributes to the Jesuit Du Halde, that 'c'est le bâton qui gouverne la Chine', he decides that virtue and honour are not the motive forces in the Chinese state, that the missionaries have been deluded, that fear is omnipresent, and that China is a despotic state.

Montesquieu had his disciples in his view of despotism. They were numerous and influential, and perhaps the most interesting was Nicolas-Antoine Boulanger who in his *Recherches sur l'origine du despotisme oriental* (1761) advanced curious and new theories on the growth of religious sentiment. But dissent was not slow to express itself. Anquetil-Duperron in his *Législation orientale* attacked Montesquieu's view in relation to Turkey, Persia, and India.[1] In relation to China the attack was made, in two articles entitled *Despotisme de la Chine*,[2] by François Quesnay, who combined expertise in philosophy and economics with the profession of medicine, and who was once described as the Confucius of Europe. He produced a new definition of despotism, designed to fit the Chinese form of government, more in accordance, perhaps, with the etymology of the term, but in flat contradiction to Montesquieu. He defines despot as a '*maître ou seigneur*' and proceeds immediately to insist that the term can be applied as legitimately to a sovereign whose power is regulated by laws as to an arbitrary usurper. In reply to the foreseen objection that one should describe the first of these as a monarch, not as a despot, he replies that it is necessary to differentiate between an absolute prince and one whose power is constitutionally limited or shared with others. The Emperor of China observes wise and irrevocable

---

[1] See F. Venturi, 'Despotismo orientale', *Rivista storica italiana*, 1960.
[2] *Ephémérides du citoyen*, Paris, 1767, vols. iii and iv.

laws; and Quesnay goes on to enumerate the fundamental laws of the Chinese Empire. At this point the strength of the agrument is enfeebled, and the reader wonders if some pages have dropped from the edition he is using. The fundamental laws are divided into two groups: natural laws, which when listed prove to relate only to belief in God, ritual, and the subordination of ranks; and the sacred books, which deal purely with religion. The validity of this system is not at present in question (Montesquieu, one imagines, could make a vigorous riposte); but its historical importance is great. For although the term is not used (and the term, as Franco Venturi points out, is used by subsequent historians and not by eighteenth-century political theorists), this is what came to be known as enlightened despotism, and it is, with Quesnay, a consideration of China which gave birth to the concept.

It may be said in conclusion that Asia, as seen by the French Enlightenment, means primarily the Near East and China. Other areas are discussed. When India is mentioned, except in Raynal's monumental history, it is usually to discuss either widow-burning or, more frequently, metempsychosis, which fascinates both Voltaire and Montesquieu. The latter produces of it an ingenious climatic explanation, that the doctrine was invented in hot climates to protect the few cattle that can live there, by its claim that human souls have passed into their bodies.[1] The article *Indiens* (*philosophie des*) of the *Encyclopédie*, unsigned and probably by Diderot, is interesting in its stress on the difference between the esoteric doctrine of the Buddhists, which is in conformity with right reason, and their exoteric doctrine which is equivalent to Spinozism. In relation to Japan, Montesquieu stresses the severity of the penal code, saying that there despotism has made an effort and has become more cruel than itself, and produces a few generalized comments on the national character of the Japanese,[2] while Diderot in the *Encyclopédie*, immediately after alluding to the false miracles in Japanese Buddhism, says that in many respects it resembles Christianity, and characteristically adds the ironical comment that God has permitted this similarity in order to make adherence to the Christian faith more meritorious.[3]

Essentially, however, the history of French attitudes to Asia in the eighteenth century is a move from a great preoccupation with

---

[1] *L'Esprit des lois*, bk. xxiv, ch. 24.   [2] Ibid., bk. vi, ch. 13.
[3] Article, *Japonais* (*philosophie des*).

Moslem Asia to great concern with China. In the case of Islam there was a strong literary vogue which was seldom wholly separated from philosophical attitudes. But it largely preceded them, and in important measure led to them. The interest in China was from the start much more a philosophical interest. The cult of *chinoiserie* in decoration existed already in the seventeenth century, but the eighteenth century's interest in China had no great aesthetic content. That vast country, becoming known through an agency which most of the *philosophes* regarded as tainted, had an enormous relevance to the ideas already circulating in eighteenth-century France. Islam had its relevance too, initially of a different kind. The enthusiasm of the *philosophes*, as distinct from a few dedicated scholars like Parrenin, for the study both of Islam and of China was not a disinterested devotion to knowledge. It was based on that relevance and on the utility, in philosophic debate, of ideas and attitudes and information of oriental origin.

But it is often, perhaps usually, such interested motives which cause knowledge to grow.

XII. THE EAST AND
GERMAN ROMANTICISM

Ronald Taylor

In 1789 the remarkable Sir William Jones—jurist, Oriental scholar and founder of the Bengal Asiatic Society—published an English translation of *Sakuntala*, a play by the fourth-century Indian dramatist Kalidasa. The work caught the imagination of European writers, among them the author and traveller Johann Georg Forster, who at once set to work on a German version of Jones's translation, adding his own commentary on the philosophy and mythology which underlies the drama. Forster's work appeared in 1791, and in May of that year he sent a copy to Johann Friedrich Herder.

For Herder, who had long devoted himself with characteristic fervour to the dissemination of foreign literatures, this was a moment of triumph. Over twenty years earlier, in his essay *Über den Ursprung der Sprache*, he had pointed to the East as the original source of language and claimed Oriental alphabets as the prototypes of those in the West; in his *Auch eine Philosophie der Geschichte zur Bildung der Menschheit* of 1774 his zeal had led him to an even more embracing expression of his convictions: 'Behold the East— the cradle of the human race, of human emotions, of all religion!'[1] But all that Herder knew of the East at that time was derived from travel-books and essays. Later Forster drew his attention to Charles Wilkins's translations of the Hindu *Bhagavadgita* (1785) and *Hito-padesa* (1787); and now, a few years later, came the full vindication of his faith—an authentic work of Sanskrit literature accessible in his mother tongue, a work which revealed with unmistakable im-

---

[1] *Sämtliche Werke*, ed. B. Suphan, Berlin, 1877 ff., vol. v, p. 562.

mediacy those noble human qualities which he had proclaimed as expressive of Indian civilization:

Where Sakuntala dwelt with her once lost scion,
Where Dushyanta welcomed her back from the realm of the Gods—
O Holy Land, I salute thee, thou Source of all Music,
Thou voice of the Heart—O raise me aloft to thy spheres![1]

It was this temper of reverence, this commitment to an idealization, which set the tone for the German Romantics' view of the East—and when they talked of the East, their thoughts were almost invariably of India. Here was a world of new treasures, a world not buried in the past but accessible and, above all, relevant, to the present. Cultural history had been seen in terms of simple linear evolution: from the Orient via the civilizations of the Old Testament to Greece, Rome, and modern Europe, each absorbing and transmuting the inherited values of its predecessor. Now came a direct confrontation with the oldest of Aryan cultures, and with it the discovery that characteristic European literary genres such as drama and religious epic, gnomic poetry and fable, had already flourished in classical Sanskrit literature.

The realization of this fact of literary and cultural history, however, striking as it was, would hardly of itself have stimulated the Indophile emotions expressed by so many German poets and thinkers in the last decades of the eighteenth century and in the early nineteenth. Nor was there anything historically new in the claim that India was the fountain-head of wisdom. Its effect was made possible by the desire—a desire itself the product of differing and sometimes conflicting casts of mind—for a rallying-point towards which men's minds could be turned and from which new inspiration for dealing with human affairs could be drawn. At this time, as at others in the history of their country, many German intellectuals were looking to the outside world for a sense of direction, and were thus peculiarly susceptible to the attractions of a doctrine, be it metaphysical, political, or aesthetic, which seemed to promise a fulfilment of their needs. Indeed, the Germans were disposed to idealize the stimuli which they received, magnifying those qualities which they felt most pertinent to their situation and ignoring what appeared to lie outside this pertinence.

Thus thinkers such as Herder and his spiritual mentor Johann

[1] Ed. cit., vol. xxix, p. 665.

Georg Hamann remained essentially 'Western' in their dealings with the East. Herder looked above all for ethical values which could be employed to his own didactic purpose, and even before coming upon Wilkins's and Jones's translations, he extolled the moral excellencies which travelogues had attributed to Indian civilization:

The Hindus are the gentlest race on earth. They dislike causing pain; they respect all living creatures, drawing their sustenance from milk, rice, fruit and health-giving herbs—the pure, undefiled food which Nature offers.[1]

It was not surprising that Herder, in this Rousseauesque frame of mind, should turn a blind eye to the aggressive exploits of the Mahratta cavalry, the cult of military bravery and personal glory among the Rajputs, and the set caste-structure which was principally responsible for sustaining the qualities he so enthusiastically greeted.

The nebulous ideal of human progress which Herder called *Humanität* gained stature from the discovered relevance to it— even if a less complete relevance than Herder believed—of values from the Indian world. 'Humanity', which was later to be reinterpreted in the context of the philosophy of German Romanticism, was a dynamic, if unprecise, evocative concept of the latent perfectibility of man, a quasi-religious persuasion that the hope of immortality contains the seed of the supreme ethical and cultural achievements of the human race. 'The highest form of "Humanity" is religion', he declared.[2] And as the attainment of 'Humanity' challenged man at his most profoundly human, so religion was one of man's imperative, most elemental needs, a religion to be made manifest through the facts of human experience and in the language of human life; Nature was ruled by a Universal Spirit, and all knowledge existed within a harmonious framework, a Providential Plan.

In Kalidasa's drama *Shakuntala* Herder found the imminent, all-embracing spirit—the presence which Friedrich Schlegel was to call the *Allheit*—in whose shadow he believed his ideal could be nurtured. 'I doubt', he wrote in his preface to the second edition of Forster's translation of the play, 'whether one could imagine any more refined, more sublime conceits in the whole of our

---

[1] *Ideen zur Philosophie der Geschichte der Menschheit* vi, 3, ed. cit., vol. xiii, p. 222.   [2] *Ideen* . . . iv, 6, ed. cit., vol. xiii, p. 161.

universe than this regal dignity, this sense of nature, this love—
India's divine possessions.'[1] But there is a *caveat*: this is not a book
to be read 'in the European spirit, that is to say, with a fleeting
curiosity, just for the sake of finding out how it ends; but in the
Indian spirit—attentively, in tranquillity, and in deep meditation[2].'
One will see in *Shakuntala*, not sententious idealizations of desirable
qualities, not elaborate allegorizations of the human condition, but
the portrayal of real human virtue in real human circumstances, a
microcosm of authentic experience.

Even more significant for Herder, in *Shakuntala* the Gods are
directly involved in human events, not figures standing above and
aloof from the world. Mythology is woven into the fabric of man's
affairs; the real and the supernatural unite in a single, multi-
dimensional context within which the story of the drama is played
out. Divine revelation, the source of all knowledge, thus penetrates
the very core of human existence, and in the society which is sustained by this faith there prevail those values of which man stands
in the greatest need.

So we return to Herder's starting-point, the contemporary
situation from which the trail of his moral argument has proceeded.
The nobility of Hindu culture puts to shame those European
colonizers, missionaries, and would-be educators who, through
their misunderstanding of the forms of the Hindu religion and their
lack of sympathy for the manifestations of Hindu civilization,
betray a false pride and an unforgivable condescension: 'Christians,
you have a great deal to atone for, a great deal to make good'.[3]

Of the artistic qualities of *Shakuntala*, the *Bhagavadgita* and
other works of Sanskrit, Persian, and Arabic literature with which
he became familiar in English or German translations, Herder has,
not surprisingly, little to say. As his attitudes hardened, and notwithstanding his claims to the contrary, his didactic purposes made
him largely indifferent to the aesthetic values of art, and he drew
the moralist's line between ethical good and sensuous beauty. In
his rhymeless adaptations of William Jones's translations from the
Persian, for example, a language in whose poetry rhyme plays an
integral part, his lack of regard for purely poetic values left
a fundamental aspect of the original untouched and uncom-
municated. It is wholly in character that he should prefer the

[1] Ed. cit., vol. xxiv, p. 578.   [2] Ed. cit., vol. xvi, p. 88.
[3] Ed. cit., vol. xxiii, p. 505.

moralizing of Sadi to the hedonism of Hafiz: 'We are almost satiated with Hafiz' odes; Sadi has proved more edifying'.[1]

In his stimulation of interest in the East, as in many others of his spheres of activity and influence, Herder's true spiritual inheritors were the philosophers and poets of the German Romantic movement. To be sure, others were also to feel the attraction of the Orient. In his hymn *At the Source of the Danube*, Hölderlin invokes a shadowy image of Mother Asia, whose mighty patriarchs and prophets were

> The first who understood
> How to speak alone
> To God.

Wilhelm von Humboldt devoted three essays to the *Bhagavadgita*, declaring it 'the most beautiful, perhaps even the only truly philosophical poem to be found in all the literatures known to us'.[2] Goethe, too, who in his early career had owed much to Herder, received *Shakuntala* with great enthusiasm, and subsequently professed a scholarly interest in the embryonic academic discipline of Indology, even making attempts to write in Devanagari characters (they can still be seen in the Goethe-Archiv at Weimar). But Goethe's was not the mind to surrender its supremely 'European' quality to the attractions of the East, and close as the religion of Hinduism came in some respects to the pantheism of his own beliefs, he rejected Indian mythology as an unnatural and unhealthy world peopled by creatures half-human, half-beast, the utter antithesis of those ideals, both in human and divine shape, which were embodied in the noble myths of Greece. 'That modicum of serenity for whose existence the Greeks . . . may be said to be responsible, will be completely obscured by these dark and dismal fantasies of Indian and Egyptian provenance.'[3] The only traces of Indian themes in his work are the two poems *Gott und die Bajadere* and *Der Paria*—neither of them taken directly from Sanskrit literature but from a travel-book—and the 'Vorspiel auf dem Theater' in *Faust*, which is usually held to be modelled on the prologue to *Shakuntala*. Later his encounter with Josef Hammer-Purgstall's German translation of the odes of the fourteenth-

[1] Ed. cit., vol. xxiv, p. 356.
[2] *Gesammelte Schriften*, ed. A. Leitzmann, vol. v, 1906, p. 59.
[3] Letter to J. H. Meyer, August 25, 1819.

century Persian poet Hafiz was to lead to *Der West-östliche Divan*, but here again he shows himself, in letter and in spirit, in form, attitude, and manner, to be a poet of the West.

To Friedrich and August Wilhelm Schlegel, however, as to Novalis, Tieck, Schleiermacher, Görres, and the other early Romantics, Herder's revelations took on a prophetic quality, and his enthusiasms assumed the power of commands. Vagueness, lack of personal knowledge, an uncritical *Schwärmerei* for things Oriental conditioned the first thoughts of the young Romantics as they looked towards the East for the divine revelation of the Golden Age in which Herder had taught them to believe. The aura which surrounded the Indian world became one of the symbols by which they expressed their visions of life and their yearnings for happiness, a symbol to serve the ideals of Love and Art. 'Under the spell of music', wrote Novalis, 'the spirit, stirred by vague desires, is set free; everything appears familiar to it in the happiness so redolent of its native clime, and for these fleeting moments it lives in its Indian motherland.'[1] But it was not the current moral values of the 'Indian motherland' which moved him, not the Hindu's dedication to the conquest of the objective world and its illusoriness, but the perfection of the illusion, the transcendence of its purely temporal manifestations, the creation of a new world of the spirit.

The Romantic philosophy of passivity, the cult of aimlessness in life, found what appeared to be an echo in the religion of India, in the mode of existence of her people, in her art. Here was an ideal, it seemed, of being rather than of becoming; here, in a civilization of great antiquity, lay the cultural values to which the Romantics sought to convert the Europe of their own day. The need was for receptivity; the task was one of communication. 'It is to the East that we must look for the supreme ideals of Romanticism', wrote Friedrich Schlegel in his *Rede über die Mythologie*. 'If only the treasures of the Orient were as accessible to us as those of Classical Antiquity!'[2] And it is in the writings of Friedrich Schlegel, above all in the treatise *Über die Sprache und Weisheit der Indier*, that the Romantic view of the East, in both its philosophical and practical aspects, finds its most significant expression.

Friedrich Schlegel was a man of impulses, of sudden conversions

---

[1] *Fragmente*, vol. i, ed. E. Wasmuth, Heidelberg, 1957, p. 134.
[2] *Athenaeum*, iii (1800), p. 103.

to new ideas. As in his early career he had immersed himself in the study of Classical literature; had then, in the novel *Lucinde*, given unbridled expression to the Romantic demand for the liberation of human passion from the false restrictions of social convention; had, under the influence, and partly in emulation, of his elder brother August Wilhelm, half turned back to the Classics and then begun to formulate in the *Athenaeum* the new aesthetic doctrines of Romanticism; and was a few years later to become a convert to Roman Catholicism; so now, at the opening of the nineteenth century, he was gripped by the desire to experience directly, through the medium of the original language, those values of Indian culture which had hitherto been communicated in translation and paraphrase. In India, he wrote to Tieck, lay 'the real source of all tongues, of all thoughts and utterances of the human mind . . . everything—yes, everything without exception—has its origin in India'.[1] The religion of Buddha had spread from India to the remainder of Asia; China had become what he later called, in the language of Indian sources themselves, 'a colony of the Indian warrior caste', while Egypt had become 'a colony of the Indian priest caste'.[2] When he wrote 'Orient', he thought only of India.

The Germans, contended Friedrich Schlegel, were of all European peoples spiritually the closest to Asia, and therefore had not only a unique opportunity but also an unequivocal responsibility to understand and reveal the nature of the Asiatic world. His own course was clear. The European centre of Oriental studies was Paris, and in 1802 he joined Fauriel, Chézy, Langlès, and other scholars there. In the following year the group studied Sanskrit under the tutelage of the only man in Continental Europe at that time who was known to be able to teach it—the Englishman Alexander Hamilton, who had been captured by the French in India and brought to Paris as a prisoner of war.

For Schlegel, as for Herder before him, the discovery of the East held an immediate meaning, spiritual and practical, for the development of German literature and thought, a meaning which derived from the informing power of the mythology that was embedded in the heart of Indian life. In their quest for a science of

[1] *Ludwig Tieck und die Brüder Schlegel, Briefe*, ed. H. Ludeke, Frankfurt-am-Main, 1930, p. 140.
[2] *Friedrich Schlegel. Kritische Ausgabe seiner Werke*, 1958 ff., vol. xiv, p. 30.

life the Romantics asserted the equality of faith and knowledge, believing that from the supreme moments of spiritual and intellectual achievement a religion might be distilled, the purest formulation of human virtue, the quintessential expression of the meaning of nature. Philosophical support for the quest came from Schelling's assertion that the evolution of nature and the evolution of the human mind were one and the same. The need now was for a new mythology in which the truths of this religion could be clothed, in and through which its beauties could be symbolized. Ancient mythologies appeared as interpreted nature; the prescience and premonitions characteristic of the mythological imagination were seen as the oldest sources of knowledge. In the modern context myths became what Schleiermacher called 'abbreviatures of the universe', finite forms of an infinite Christianity.

Friedrich Schlegel's pursuit of the new Romantic mythology involved every aspect of the human mind and implied a synthesis of all intellectual activities. Science would join with art, philosophy with poetry; the world of the spirit would merge with the world of nature, the antithesis of real and ideal would melt away, and the rule of transcendental unity, of *Allheit*, would prevail. This unity he saw in the luxuriant mythology of Sanskrit literature. Here was the divine revelation of *Allheit*, the new religion, which, like all true religions, 'has as its sole aim the reunion of fallen man with the Divinity'.[1] The history of the human race emerges as a theodicy.

And as art and life are one, and as the world is an aesthetic phenomenon, it is above all to the artist that this revelation will be made. Philosophy at one with religion; poetry infused into human wisdom; the supernatural woven into the events of the everyday: from this vision of aesthetic perfection the Romantics evolved their mythical image of India, an image which could serve as a symbol of their aspirations and longings. In so doing, they passed over the ethical content of Indian mythology as Herder had passed over its aesthetic content, and their pronouncements on the East, as on other objects of their enthusiasm, have the unsubstantial quality of an idealization rather than the solid ring of comprehensive and considered knowledge.

There was also a political aspect to this activity. In 1803, while in Paris, Friedrich Schlegel founded and edited a short-lived

[1] *Kritische Ausgabe*, vol. xi, p. 9.

journal called *Europa*, devoted in the main to interpreting the achievements of French culture to the German public. On the basis of a Franco-German *rapprochement*, he believed, a unified Europe could be built, a Europe which was needed if the characteristic culture of the West was to be preserved in a condition worthy to exist alongside—indeed, eventually to merge with—the parent culture of India. To a nationally divided Germany and a politically divided Europe the apparent unity and contentment of the world portrayed in Hindu legend possessed the quality of an ideal: all activity in this ideal life, personal, social, and political, was directed from a single, central point by a single, central inspiration, fostering not only the purity and nobility of personal character but also the serenity and wisdom of the Hindus as a people.

Europe, wrote Novalis in his essay *Die Christenheit oder Europa*, seemed intent on destroying itself: 'Only religion can rouse Europe and protect the nations, openly raising Christendom to a renewed glory in its ancient role of peacemaker'.[1] Friedrich Schlegel, writing in the first number of his *Europa*, found the source of the disintegration of Europe in the atomization of its culture, the separation of the arts and the sciences, the growth of ever more, ever lesser autonomies: 'What grandeur and beauty there once was has been so utterly destroyed that I do not know how one can possibly claim that Europe still exists as an entity'.[2] And when followed to its roots in the individual consciousness, the decay, diagnosed by Schlegel in terms indistinguishable from those of Novalis, was seen to proceed from an 'incapacity for religion, the complete numbness of the higher organs. There are no lower depths to which man can sink.'[3]

The culmination of Friedrich Schlegel's Sanskrit studies came with the publication in 1808 of *Über die Sprache und Weisheit der Indier*. This consists of a technical investigation into the character of the Sanskrit language, its development and its historical relationship to other languages (he believed it to be the *fons et origo* of all tongues, European and Asian); an exegesis of Hindu philosophy, including such subjects as metempsychosis and astrology; and a sketch of the historical circumstances from which the language and philosophy of Sanskrit emerged, concluding with a group of

[1] *Schriften*, ed. J. Minor, Jena, 1907, vol. ii, p. 43.
[2] *Europa*, i (1803), p. 32.
[3] *Ibid.*, ii, p. 292.

observations on social and political institutions and on the nature of Oriental studies in general.

Two ironies attended the publication of this epoch-making book. Even before he had finished writing it, Schlegel was turning his eyes away from the East and towards the architecture and literature of medieval Europe, towards the writings of the Church fathers, towards—Roman Catholicism. One creed of universality began to yield to another, one mythology to be edged out by another, one set of symbolic meanings to be superseded by another. And in the same year that *Über die Sprache und Weisheit der Indier* appeared, he underwent the last of his conversions: in the company of his wife Dorothea, daughter of Moses Mendelssohn, the apostle of German Enlightenment, he entered the Roman Catholic Church. From this moment until his death twenty-one years later, the Orient was reduced to a mere historical concept, devoid of its one-time power to command enthusiasm, worship, and love.

The other irony lies in the nature of the influence which the book was to exert on German intellectual life. For Friedrich Schlegel himself the study of Sanskrit was a means to an aesthetico-philosophical end, a duty attendant upon the exposition of Indian culture; moreover, through his insistence on the organic nature of nationality and culture, of which purely physical factors such as climate and land-formations were an intrinsic part, he had thought to offer a model for the study of the history of civilization in relation to the ideals of Romanticism. But these ideals were fading. And in the records of history his work is accorded its chief significance in the realm of the comparative study of language, the dispassionate, analytical investigation of words, not as vehicles of thought but as units of sound—in short, it stands as an exercise in the establishment of cold historical 'facts'. Grammarians such as Jakob Grimm and Franz Bopp owed much to it; above all, his brother August Wilhelm, already established as an aesthetician and a critic of European literature, was stimulated to learn Sanskrit, becoming in 1818 the first professor of Indology in Germany and publishing the first critical editions of original Sanskrit texts.

In this growing activity Friedrich Schlegel took no part. He had left the world of Asia behind—if, indeed, for all his knowledge and apparent former passion, he had ever really been part of it. Here, perfectly expressed in the career of this one man, lies the crux of

O

the Romantics' relationship with the East. Novalis, in *Die Lehr-linge zu Sais*, might equate Sanskrit with Holy Writ;[1] the Oriental-ist Friedrich Majer, contributing to Tieck's *Poetisches Journal* of 1800, might enthuse over ancient Indian mythological poems as 'dreams from the dawn of the human race';[2] Friedrich Schlegel might proclaim, at the moment when the tide of Romantic theory was at its flood: 'It is to the East that we must look for the supreme ideals of Romanticism'.[3] In reality the Romantics were not seeking their ideal in the Orient. They were not seeking an external ideal at all. They were seeking themselves. Like the hero of Novalis' fragmentary novel *Die Lehrlinge zu Sais*, they set out on the quest for understanding, for knowledge; like him, they found no satis-faction in the sciences and philosophies of man, in the achieve-ments of history, in the ideals of society and nation, in the promises of religion; like him, they ended the search where they had begun it—in their own selves.

> In the temple at Sais, a man once lifted the veil of the goddess,
> And found—O wonder of wonders!—and found concealed there—
>   himself.[4]

So, in their individual ways and from individual motives, the Romantics left behind their ideal conception of the East as a fructifying power for the philosophy and art of their day. Specific motifs drawn from the Orient, whether poetic or philosophic in character, lingered on as colourful souvenirs, but the central spell was broken. Heine, who, as a student in Bonn, had heard lectures on Indian literature from August Wilhelm Schlegel, imported into his poetry a number of the decorative commonplaces of San-skrit literature and gave them symbolic status—the love of flowers and animals, the cult of lotus blossom, the sacred mystery of the Ganges. The character of the magician in Romantic tales— the agent of the supernatural and the miraculous—is also Eastern in inspiration. Similarly, certain Oriental poetic forms found their way into German verse as first-hand knowledge of the original languages spread. Friedrich Rückert and August Graf von Platen-Hallermünde, for example, following the lead given by Friedrich Schlegel, exploited the Persian *ghazal*—a highly stylized poetic form 'closely akin', in Friedrich Schlegel's description, 'to the

---

[1] Ed. cit., vol. iv, pp. 3–4.
[2] *Poetisches Journal*, ed. L. Tieck, Jena, 1800, p. 176.
[3] *Athenaeum*, iii, p. 103.   [4] Novalis, ed. cit., vol. i, p. 259.

gloss, the sestina and the sonnet'[1]—the former translating widely, not only from the Persian, but also from the Arabic and the Sanskrit.

There remains, finally, the influence of the moral philosophy embedded in Sanskrit literature, which from the days of the early translations by Wilkins and Jones had been shown to underlie the spiritual and intellectual history of the Indian peoples. Neither Kant nor Hegel knew anything of the Indian philosophers— although a parallel has been traced between Hegel's *Negativität* and the Buddhist concept of *sunyata*—but Fichte and, to a greater degree, Schelling, the two philosophers most closely linked with the German Romantic movement, both showed affinities with certain concepts of Hindu thought. The latter considered the Upanishads to be the oldest source of human wisdom, and accorded them a higher importance in his ethical canon than the Biblical writings.

But it is above all, perhaps, in Schopenhauer that the strictly religio-philosophical virtues of Indian civilization find a European echo. Already as a student he had come under the influence of the Romantic poets' enthusiasm for India. While maintaining that the seemingly Indian elements in *Die Welt als Wille und Vorstellung*— his pessimistic view of the world, derived from his postulate that the Will is ethically evil; his advocacy of asceticism; his statement of an ideal course for European civilization which, seen as a doctrine of salvation without God, is virtually that of the Buddhist *nirvana*—were the products of his own European thought-processes, he admitted at the same time to a sense of satisfaction at discovering their relatedness to such noble predecessors:

If I were to take the conclusions of my philosophy as the criteria of truth, I would have to accord Buddhism pride of place among religions. In any case I cannot but be gratified to find that my teaching agrees in such large measure with the religion which, of all world-religions, has the greatest number of adherents. This agreement is all the more gratifying since, in the course of my own philosophical activity, I was certainly not influenced by it.[2]

One should learn to see the world as a 'place of penance', as a 'penal colony':

[1] Letter to A. W. Schlegel, January 15, 1803.
[2] *Die Welt als Wille und Vorstellung* (*Grossherzog Wilhelm Ernst Ausgabe*), vol. ii, 888.

This view finds theoretical and objective justification, not only in my philosophy, but in the wisdom of all ages, in Brahmanism, in Buddhism, in Empedocles and Pythagoras . . . even in authentic Christianity our existence is clearly depicted as the consequence of Sin, of the Fall.[1]

And in his *Kritik der Kantischen Philosophie* he specifically acknowledges his debt to Hindu philosophy as, together with Kant and Plato, the main formative influence on his thought.[2]

Plato, Kant, India—much of the history of German Romanticism could be written from these three points.—Platonic idealism: utopian, metaphorical and allusive, introspective, Orphic-mystical.— Kant: the appeal to the heart, the challenge to the supremacy of reason, the opposition to utilitarianism. — And India? *Ex Oriente lux*. Friedrich Schlegel wrote:

The primary source of all ideas and all intellectual development—in a word, of the whole of human culture—is unquestionably to be found in the traditions of the East.[3]

The light of this knowledge, he believed, would reveal to man the essential unity of the human race and of its seemingly divergent, irreconcilable civilizations. And—to think with the Romantics— if man is to understand what unity means, and where the path of true progress, political as well as spiritual, lies, he must be guided by a vision of the ultimate fusion of East and West in the realization of this higher unity.

Let the final expression of the ideal be Friedrich Schlegel's:

As therefore Asiatics and Europeans form a single great family; as Asia and Europe together make up a single indivisible whole; so we should strive the more to see the literatures of all cultured peoples as one continuous development, as a single closely-knit structure, as a unique entity. In this light certain ignorant and prejudiced attitudes will automatically disappear; much will become intelligible for the first time in this universal context; and everything—everything—will take on a new meaning.[4]

---

[1] Ed. cit., vol. v, pp. 328–9.   [2] Ed. cit., vol. i, p. 543.
[3] *Vorlesungen über Universalgeschichte. Kritische Ausgabe*, vol. xiv, p. 167.
[4] *Über die Sprache und Weisheit der Indier. Sämtliche Werke*, Vienna, 1846, vol. viii, p. 381.

XIII. BRITISH ATTITUDES TO ASIA

George Bearce

The Earliest Attitudes

Up to the last quarter of the eighteenth century, the English response to Asia was made up of two main elements—a sense of wonder concerning this vast continent and an impulse to profit from Asian commerce. The earliest English contacts with Asia, starting at the end of the sixteenth and the beginning of the seventeenth centuries, did not result in very complex attitudes. Adventure, cupidity, and a thirst for knowledge impelled these few English travellers to experience the dangers and novelty of Asia, but the continent was too difficult, its people too different, and the travellers' time too brief for them to acquire any significant understanding of Asia. For Britain, up to the eighteenth century, Asia was still largely an unknown continent.

Up to the middle of the eighteenth century, moreover, there was not much real British imperialism in Asia. To be sure, in *Oceana*, James Harrington had in the seventeenth century urged the Puritan commonwealth to become an imperial power and spread the benefits of English civilization among less fortunate people in the world. This patriotic proposal, however, did not develop much before the time of Robert Clive and Warren Hastings. The East India Company, which possessed the incomparable monopoly of the Asian trade of Great Britain, merely reflected the prevailing commercial outlook of the British. The company's possessions were trading privileges, and the company and its officials cared for little more than the chance to get rich. In any case, this puny joint stock company could not have made much headway in the seventeenth and eighteenth centuries in carving an empire out of the vast territories ruled by the Mughals, the Manchus, and Nadir Shah. The company was in awe of these powers.

Something of the spirit of the Tudor and Stuart adventurers in Asia can be seen in their deeds and in their travel accounts, especially as Hakluyt recorded the facts that were reported to him. Booty was the initial motive of Sir James Lancaster's voyage in 1592 to India and South-east Asia. His subsequent voyages, however, were undertaken on behalf of the East India Company 'for the discovery of a trade in the East-India, to bring into this realm spices and other commodities'.[1] In their commercial affairs and in their earliest political relations with the princes of Asia, Lancaster and his associates stuck closely to their mission; but they returned with something more than spices. They also brought back what Mandeville had put into his mythical picture of Prester John, what Shakespeare conveyed in the magnificence of Cleopatra. They brought back the image of the Eastern prince, a Malayan ruler at 'Achen' surrounded with exotic riches and pomp—two hundred elephants in his procession, two hundred naked swords of pure gold carried before him, his horse with a covering of beaten gold, his servant with a betel box and a fan of pure gold, and the prince himself robed so richly that the scene was indescribable.[2] Such was the durable picture of the Eastern prince from the time of this Malayan chieftain up to the Kings of Oudh and the Nizams of Hyderabad. Asia was synonymous with pageantry, wealth, and ease.

This earliest response was reaffirmed by the travellers of the eighteenth century as well. Jonas Hanway, who acutely observed the Persia of Nadir Shah (in the 1740s), still exemplified the mercantile approach to Asia. The justification for his travels to Persia was that 'the glory and welfare of the British monarchy' depended 'on the acquisition and preservation of trade'.[3] He and his associates represented the English trading company in Russia, and they traversed the arduous regions of the Caspian Sea and Central Asia in order to open up trade in Persia. They also tried, not always with success, to understand something more than Persian commerce and to appreciate the people as well as the commodities of that ancient land. They found some of the Persians quite merry over their cups, but they could not appreciate the

[1] W. Foster, *The Voyages of Sir James Lancaster*, London, 1940, p. 75.
[2] W. Foster, *The Voyages of Thomas Best to the East Indies 1612–14*, London, 1934, pp. 168–71.
[3] Jonas Hanway, *An Historical Account of the British Trade over the Caspian Sea*, 4 vols., London, 1753, I, vol. i, p. vii.

'very untunable and shrill' music which they were obliged to endure. They liked some of the mountain scenery, but they found other parts of the land barren and unendurable.[1] Jonas Hanway exceeded his associates in his grasp of Persian society and politics, but his was a rare achievement. There was little incentive to attain to this level of understanding, and it was always difficult for men of one culture to confront and appreciate the features of another. The historian William Robertson sagely observed in 1791:

Men in every state of their career are so satisfied with the progress made by the community in which they are members, that it becomes a standard of perfection, and they are apt to regard people whose condition is not similar, with contempt and aversion. . . .[2]

These travellers to Persia were experiencing what soon became, despite all the difficulties, frustrations, and misunderstanding involved, a self-imposed obligation of the British. They had to come to grips with the society and culture of Asia, which in turn was obliged to discover the West.

The earliest English attitudes to Asia, the mercantile impulse and the sense of wonder, never wholly disappeared. Manchester merchants and cotton manufacturers in the nineteenth century approached India and China with little more than this bare commercial instinct. The sense of wonder about Asia found glorious expression in the Romantic in Coleridge, Shelley, Keats, Scott, and Thomas Moore. Indeed, this quality has never been lost. Lord Curzon, writing about Russian Central Asia in 1889, thought that this romantic picture of Asia, this 'era of the Thousand and One Nights, with all its strange mixture of savagery and splendour', would soon fade away in a scientific world. But even Curzon was something of a romantic, who could not avoid noticing the 'mingled gloom and grandeur' of Central Asia. This setting, the great boulders of the Oxus basin under a pale moon in cold solitude, made Curzon think of the debris of many civilizations scattered in this region.[3]

---

[1] J. Spilman, *A Journey Through Russia into Persia*, London, 1742, pp. 10, 17.

[2] G. D. Bearce, *British Attitudes Towards India 1784–1858*, London, 1961, p. 27.

[3] G. N. Curzon, *Russia in Central Asia in 1889*, London, 1889, pp. xii, 138–40.

The Emergence of Modern Attitudes to Asia

In the last quarter of the eighteenth century, when the East India Company was consolidating its recent conquests in Madras and Bengal, British attitudes to Asia were being transformed. The earlier simplicity was now complicated by new insight and fresh experience; a more varied, at times a more profound, understanding of Asia emerged. Several factors accounted for this transformation.

Between 1780 and 1840, Britain itself was being transformed. The country was developing a novel industrial system, together with new social institutions, reformed political practices, and even new cities. Its intellectual outlook was changing fast, for the country became an arena of contesting ideologies: the liberalism, democracy, and socialism which emerged from the Enlightenment and the French Revolution; the counter-revolutionary philosophy of Burke's conservatism; the literary response, romanticism; and a host of other religious, political, and humanitarian movements which sought to change first Britain, then the world. British attitudes to Asia were now shaped by these new ideologies and movements. Indeed, British attitudes to Asia were largely conditioned by the environment and intellectual outlook at home.

The time was gone for good when a few aristocrats could set the general attitudes and speak for the country. The individualism of the new age encouraged every man, great or small, to speak his thought about Asia, if he were so impelled. The emerging social freedom of the times meant the rise of new associations, anti-slavery societies, and chambers of commerce, capable also of self-expression. The extension of education and the increase in literacy developed a British public opinion, indeed a mass opinion, hitherto unknown in eighteenth-century society, capable of playing an important role in the formulation of cultural and political attitudes.

By the nineteenth century British attitudes to Asia were articulated in a complex framework. At the highest intellectual level were the individuals who provided philosophic originality and artistic insight to British attitudes towards Asia, the great men such as Edmund Burke, Sir William Jones, James Mill, Thackeray, John Stuart Mill, Kipling, and E. M. Forster. On a lower, ideological level were the spokesmen of special groups and the popularizers of various viewpoints. On this same level, there were also the various spokesmen of the governments in Britain and in British possessions in Asia, who contributed much information and many ideas, especially in regard to the policy and administration of British India. At the lowest level was the general public, whose attitudes emerged sometimes as isolated individual opinions, very personal in character, and sometimes as a fictitious mass opinion reported by journalists.

This lowest level of opinion was intellectually unimpressive, but not unimportant or uninteresting. In *The Newcomes*, for example, Thackeray vividly reported perhaps the only reaction which a maidservant could express towards India. Upon being told that Colonel Newcome had fifty servants in India (the normal staff of a zamindar or a high British official), the maidservant exclaimed: 'Lor, mum, what can he do with 'em, mum?'[1] Indeed, the response is not without significance. How difficult it was for a maidservant and for the mass of Englishmen to understand the way of life in India even on what appeared to be a simple level. The comment of an English silk worker at a House of Commons inquiry showed the same difficulty in visualizing Asian conditions:

I certainly pity the East India labourer, but . . . I think it is wrong to sacrifice the comforts of my own family for the sake of East India labourers, because his condition happens to be worse than mine.[2]

The silk worker was a man of feeling, but he had not seen India and had no conception of conditions there.

Such personal responses to Asia cannot easily be summarized or assessed. They range from the distaste which a British interloper in Mecca felt for its greasy food to the deep personal agony which Britons endured while living or travelling in Asia. For example, about 1800, a British officer in India, D. Ochterlony, had to decide whether to raise his daughter, the offspring of a mixed marriage, as an Indian or a European. He recognized the awful prejudice which his British countrymen felt towards Eurasians, and he knew that English society was no life for the girl, but he found the prospect of raising the child as a Muslim woman hidden in purdah equally distasteful.[3] From one end of Asia to the other, Britons endured many agonies, which came

---

[1] W. M. Thackeray, *The Newcomes*, London and New York, 1899, p. 51.
[2] *Parliamentary Papers*, 1840, vii (527), p. 451.
[3] London, C.R.O. India Library, Eur. MSS. D547, pp. 133–4.

when their accustomed comforts were missing or when their preconceptions about life were jolted. The oppressive heat, the dust
and bad water, the deadly malaria for which Java especially was
notorious, the poverty, the swarms of beggars, the filth of cities—
any of these things could bring intense agony. One wonders how
much they affected British attitudes generally. It might be interesting to speculate whether some sort of collective national
memory of agony, misfortune, and frustration made it easier
for the British to relinquish their empire in Asia. At any rate, the
personal responses of Britons to Asia reveal how costly this
empire was, how painful to soldiers and officials, wives, children,
and families at home, even to the exalted like Dalhousie and
Curzon.

British attitudes to Asia, after the time of Clive and Hastings,
were also significantly affected by the paramount place of India in
Britain's Asian interests. Of course, India did not dominate everything which the British thought or did regarding Asia—far from
it. But until British rule in India ended in the middle of the
twentieth century, India was Britain's major experience in Asia,
the experimental ground for British administration and policy,
the example which supposedly explained the rest of Asia, and the
country whose security required the subordination of all other
British interests in Asia.

British official attitudes viewed everything in Asia in terms of
India. Russian Central Asia was of interest because the Russians
might attack India through those territories. Persia was considered as a possible bulwark against Russian encroachment to
India and as an important consumer of Indian goods. China,
through most of the nineteenth century, was the main market for
Indian raw cotton and opium. South-east Asia, including Malaya,
Burma, Thailand, the Sarawak of the Brooke family, was generally
considered in reference to the security of India and the trade of
British India. The Dutch were allowed their control of Indonesia
because this was a simple way of having an innocuous power on
India's flank. Mesopotamia was officially significant to the British
because of steamboat and later railway communications through
it to India.

Private individuals could no doubt develop attitudes towards
other parts of Asia without considering India. A number of
British travellers visited the ancient civilizations of the Middle

East and even the forbidden shrines of Islam for their own sake.[1] But the problem of India intruded. For example, British missionaries to China could not escape the role of Indian opium in depressing Chinese society and making their labours more difficult.[2] Asia had largely come to mean India to the bulk of the British, for this was the brightest jewel in the imperial crown.

In the transformation of British attitudes from the late eighteenth century on, an increased knowledge of Asia, especially India, played an important part. The thinkers who laid the philosophical and ideological foundations for various British attitudes to India, such as Edmund Burke, James Mill, and J. S. Mill, were exceptional for their empirical knowledge of the politics and culture of that distant land. The leading imperial administrators of the period, Warren Hastings, Munro, Elphinstone, Bentinck, Dalhousie, Curzon, all sought to improve their knowledge of India and Asia and to base their administrative policies on such knowledge. Some of this knowledge of Asia was distorted and misleading by the time it was used, but an awareness of the facts of Asia—its history and monuments, its poverty, disease, and disorganization, its religions and customs—provided the basis often for intelligent attitudes and policies. Well-informed attitudes were not always advocated or followed, but they were always present in British society.

Conservatives, Reformers, Romantics, and Imperialists

The eighteenth-century British conservatives were the first to create a comprehensive and philosophic understanding of Asia, and it was a very favourable image. In view of the narrow mercantilism and naïve sense of wonder current in British attitudes, this conservative understanding of Asia was indeed extraordinary. It was, in part, the result of European admiration for 'Oriental' wisdom, especially of China, and through increased contacts with India, Persia, and China, the admiration for 'Oriental' society and culture was extended and elaborated. This favourable image was also the result of the aristocrat's respect for his own ancestors and

[1] J. S. Buckingham, *Travels in Assyria*, 2 vols., London, 1830, vol. i, pp. 476–505. J. E. Alexander, *Travels from India*, London, 1827, pp. 137–9.
[2] Rev. George Smith, *Consular Cities of China*, New York, 1847, pp. 439–41.

cultural traditions. Conservatives explained and defended old institutions and traditions wherever they found them, if such a defence was rationally possible.

In Britain itself the conservatives had risen to the defence of the British constitution. Edmund Burke, who provided the political philosophy necessary for this defence, thought that conservative principles were eternal. Every civilized state had its own time-tested institutions, and the enemies of culture, the tyrants and plunderers, were ever present to threaten all states. Burke had to defend the institutions, culture, and societies of Asia, North America, France, and Ireland, if with any consistency, he wished to defend the British constitution. It became a passion with Burke, as one sees in his prosecution of Warren Hastings, the governor-general of Bengal, to justify this conservative conception of society and culture, which were founded on natural law and were fulfilling God's will in history. He was willing, even anxious, to show Asian societies in a favourable light. Even Haider Ali, the usurper of Mysore, became for Burke a statesman of world stature; China was a supremely well-governed empire; and the Indian polity of village republics was incomparable in its role of preserving and transmitting the good features of traditional society.[1]

Having perceived the merit of Asian societies and governments, the British conservatives also felt that the Asian masses were happy. The eighteenth-century historian William Robertson referred to the Indians as 'a most happy race of men'. A historian of China wrote of the Celestial Empire:

With respect to happines, taking them as a general body, they possess as much as a numerous society can possibly enjoy.[2]

The art, letters, and learning of Asia, which were just being discovered in the West, met with lavish praise. Sir William Jones, the first great Orientalist scholar from Britain, exclaimed about his opportunity to live in India in the 1780s:

It gave me inexpressible pleasure to find myself in the midst of so noble an ampitheatre, almost encircled by the vast regions of *Asia*, which has ever been esteemed the nursery of sciences, the scene of glorious actions, fertile in the productions of human genius. . . .[3]

[1] *Annual Register*, 1783, pp. 88–90. London, C.R.O., India Library, Home Misc, 525. pp. 154–8.
[2] *A Complete View of the Chinese Empire*, London, 1798, p. lxiii.
[3] *Works*, 13 vols., London, 1807, vol. iii, p. 2.

In this spirit Sir William Jones and his associates began to reveal the greatness of India's ancient literary and philosophical culture. The Baptist missionaries near Calcutta, led by William Carey, sought to translate and publish great works from Chinese civilization as well as from India. These pioneering scholars collected manuscripts, formed into literary societies, and published their findings about the culture and history of Asia.[1] Even the culture of less advanced areas, of Cochin China for example, met with favour:

Though these people have hardly any scientific principles, yet in the culture of their lands, and in the few manufactures which they have, they equalled those nations among whom the sciences flourish. . . .[2]

The conservatives could not wholly approve of Asian religions, which they hesitantly tolerated. But some Britons in India came to admire Hinduism. Warren Hastings' agent, Scott-Waring, felt complimented upon being called a Hindu by a missionary critic. General Matthews prayed to a Hindu deity (at the suggestion of Brahmins) to cure him of stomach pains and gave liberally to the temple afterwards.[3] Oriental art was also not so easy to comprehend, because none of this painting was done according to Renaissance perspective, and it was not until modern painting overthrew the tyranny of Renaissance style that Oriental art could be fully appreciated. But the British were intensely interested in the ancient monuments of India and began to uncover the glorious work at Mahabalipuram, Ellora, and other places. The conservatives were determined not only to understand Oriental civilization but also to preserve it from its foreign and domestic enemies.[4]

This favourable outlook towards Asia flourished from about 1780 to 1815, and then began to wane in the wake of imperialist sentiments and reformist zeal. About the beginning of the nineteenth century various sorts of social critics and reformers began to appear in Britain, and though they were first concerned with their own country and its defects, they were not slow in bringing Asia also under their critical scrutiny. There emerged two main

[1] *Indian Historical Quarterly*, June, 1944, pp. 114–31.
[2] *A Complete View of the Chinese Empire*, p. 144.
[3] Eur. MSS. Mackenzie Collection: general, XXV, pp. 162–3.
[4] New Delhi, National Archives, Bengal, Home Dept., Public Proceedings, 1794, pp. 2540–49. Mackenzie collection: general, XXI, pp. 163–6. W. Hodges, *Travels in India*, London, 1794, pp. 150–1.

groups of reformers. There were the Evangelicals and religious reformers, who wished to transform the moral and spiritual life of Asians, whom they considered to be steeped in superstition and darkness, needing the light of Protestant Christianity. Then there were the reformers with a secular outlook, who emphasized liberty and representative government in politics, utility as the guiding principle in administration, and social improvement as the goal. Liberals, utilitarians, humanitarians, democrats, and socialists, these reformers were influenced by Jeremy Bentham and the philosophical radicals and became a decisive power in shaping British attitudes and policy to Asia. In general, almost all these reformers were bent on 'Westernizing' Asia, so that Western social habits, Western standards of living, Western thought and religion might replace the inadequate ideas and institutions of Asian countries. Asia could not remain as it was, they believed, unproductive, disorderly, diseased, and unenlightened.[1]

This reformist and critical attitude towards Asia was partly encouraged by new and extensive observation of that continent. No doubt, these observers could be prejudiced and misled, but they gathered considerable information about Asia. Physically, many parts of Asia seemed quite unpromising. An observer reported in 1813:

The town of Aden has at present a miserable appearance from the Sea, being nearly a heap of ruins out of which two minarets and a mosque rear their heads.[2]

These British travellers also came in contact with some primitive people, who interested them anthropologically, and they tended to characterize the civilized Asians as decadent in contrast to these primitives. In their contacts with Asians, whenever differences in culture prevented understanding, the British could become angry and critical. One British archaeologist described the Indians as 'jealous' when for religious reasons they would not let him examine their antique Buddhist sculptures. Other observers noted the 'indecency' of Indian sculpture and dance, and the sexual 'depravity' of the people, though this comment reflected almost as much on the observer as on the observed.[3] These British travellers to China and

[1] L. Stanhope, *The Press in British India*, London, 1823, pp. 61, 193–4.
[2] W. Milburn, *Oriental Commerce*, 2 vols., London, 1813, vol. i, p. 111.
[3] F. Buchanan, *An Account of the District of Shahabad in 1809–10*, Patna, 1934, pp. 57, 214.

India returned with descriptions not of a happy race of men but of a superstitious, poverty-stricken, despot-ridden people, who allowed infanticide, idolatry, and all sorts of reprehensible customs. Unfortunate in their social, commercial, and diplomatic relations, many Britons came to view Indians and other Asians as deceitful and dishonest racially.[1]

The outlook for the reformers also was essentially derived from the changing intellectual climate in Britain itself. James Mill, the influential historian of British India, first synthesized the main principles of this new outlook. He had never been to India, and he felt he did not need to visit Asia in order to condemn conservatism, wherever its stagnant laws and institutions, corrupt politics, and social privilege existed. James Mill would no more preserve India as it was than keep Britain as it was, with its unreformed Parliament and antiquated laws and administration.

The publication of James Mill's *History of British India* in 1817 was a turning-point in the formation of British attitudes to the East. Already many Britons—missionaries, freetraders, and Mill himself—had written pamphlets condemning the political, commercial, and religious system of India. Mill's history was an elaborate and painstaking defence of this new viewpoint. With copious illustrations, Mill wrote an extremely critical survey of Indian culture and examined the recent history of Indian and British rule. He found little, indeed nothing, to praise. What India needed, in his view, was a sweeping programme of reform: Western education, a free press, the encouragement of individual initiative, stimulation for the development of capital resources, light taxation, and the application of utilitarian principles in law and administration.

Mill's programme for the improvement of India was accompanied or followed by a variety of religious and secular projects designed for Asia. Sometimes, as in the case of some *laissez-faire* liberals, the projects were selfish at heart, designed, for example, to undersell Indian cotton manufactures and provide Manchester industries with cheap raw cotton. Often the projects of reform seemed to impose unwelcome alien changes on Asian peoples. In the main, however, the liberals and their democratic and socialist

[1] F. Shoberl (ed.), *China*, 2 vols., London, vol. i, pp. vii–x. J. F. Davis, *Sketches of China*, London, 2 vols., 1841, vol. i, pp. 1–4, 174–5.

successors suggested well-intentioned schemes, designed to produce modern, self-supporting Asian states.

Under the impact of the reformers, the appreciation of Asian culture waned until the present century. By the 1830s there was little interest in the traditional literature and learning of India, for science and technology now seemed to be superior branches of knowledge. Indian miniature painting, under a mistaken impulse to adopt Western perspective, went into permanent decline, and the Kangra and Basholi schools of miniature painting had no successors. For lack of interest, some of the major collections of Indian manuscripts were nearly lost. Still, as a residue of the earlier conservatism, something of the old interest in Indian and Asian antiquities persisted. Britons still visited Persepolis and the archaeological wonders of Mesopotamia. In 1862, the British established a director-general of archaeology to save some of the great Indian sites. By the beginning of the twentieth century, as exemplified in Curzon's broad interest in Asian archaeology, the British had helped to save many of the monuments of the past which otherwise might have been lost.

The Romanticism which was a strong element in British character in the nineteenth century undoubtedly helped to bridge the differences between the conservatives and the reformers in their attitudes to Asian societies and cultures. The British were never altogether happy with the way in which the reformers would transform both their country and the world. They yearned for a simpler existence, which they might find by travelling in Oriental countries.[1] They yearned for the past, which was so evident all over Asia. They sought rural life, deserts, and mountains, in their efforts to escape urban society. One traveller in India's mountainous region expressed this feeling simply:

I was almost sorry that I could not cast off ties of another world, as it were, and remain in these mountains for ever.[2]

These British travellers were truly delighted when they could discern the charm and beauty which Thomas Moore depicted in his vision of Oriental life in *Lalla Rookh*. The British still wanted some of the magic and pageantry of Asia, and they were not inclined to see it all condemned in the name of secular progress.

---

[1] Richard Burton, *Pilgrimage to El-Medinah and Meccah*. 3 vols., London, 1855, vol. i, p. 3.   [2] Bearce, op. cit., p. 113.

Another circumstance also tempered the worst effects of liberal and missionary zeal in India. In the early nineteenth century, a group of extremely able British officials in India, including Sir Thomas Munro, Mountstuart Elphinstone, and Sir Charles Metcalfe, synthesized the best features of conservatism and liberalism. They were interested, on the one hand, in governing in harmony with the feelings and interests of the Indian people and, on the other, in introducing as many improvements as Indian society would willingly accept. They did not want to force changes from above, but would have Indian society improve itself. They considered British rule in India as a solemn trust which in time would come to an end. As Elphinstone wrote about 1820:

There can be no doubt that when the natives get more extended notions they will expect first a share in their own Government and then the whole.[1]

Britain's task then was to prepare India—through the introduction of liberty, education, good government, and an improved economy —for eventual self-government. This conception of administration was a constant example to the British in Asia, though unfortunately it was not consistently or uniformly followed.

The spirit of imperialism, which arose at the same time as conservatism and liberalism, is fundamentally in opposition to those ideologies. The earliest imperialism, which was expounded when Lord Wellesley was governor-general of India (about 1800), was based on the feeling that it was glorious for a nation to achieve naval and military victories and acquire an empire. To this basic feeling in the course of time were added a number of other conceptions which would justify the preservation and expansion of the empire. The imperial spokesmen emphasized the idea that Britain owed a duty to the people whom it conquered. Further, some statesmen argued that the British had a humanitarian mission to extend the blessings of good government to the rest of Asia.

In the 1830s, Lord Ellenborough, the president of the Board of Control for India, emphasized the idea of establishing such mutual interests between Britain and India that they might remain for ever joined. He thought that if Britain were the manufacturing state and India were the producer of raw materials, this end might be

[1] Ibid., p. 140. Madras Record Office, Board of Revenue, 18045, Col. Munro's Proceedings, pp. 63–64, 265.

P

accomplished.[1] By the end of the century, the imperial statesmen of the time, such as Joseph Chamberlain and Lord Curzon, had prepared an elaborate justification for Britain's becoming 'the trustees for the East' and 'the rulers of the second largest dark-skinned population in the world'. Curzon had a full programme for Persia's salvation as a nation, and he was conscious of how all this would serve British interests and check Russian influence.[2] By this time the British public had become convinced of its racial 'superiority' and was prepared to take up the white man's burden in Asia. This was the apogee of British influence in Asia, but such a mistaken attitude was a most shaky foundation for British power.

The End of the British Empire in Asia

Ultimately, imperialism was not of the essence in determining British attitudes to Asia. At its simplest, imperialism represented an honest sense of achievement and a feeling of responsibility to Britain's Asian possessions. The conservatives and the liberals alike held such attitudes, but both were fundamentally prepared to recognize something more important. To the conservatives, every country had a distinctive culture and constitution which Britain should not disrupt, and the people of those countries ultimately had to shape their own progress. To the liberals, every country had the right of self-determination, and while it made sense for an Asian country to accept Britain's political tutelage for a while, the liberals could not expect permanent British rule in Asia. The other sentiments which Britons expressed, their romanticism about Asia and their personal agonies and frustrations in Asia, were in the long run equally opposed to permanent British rule in India and other parts of Asia. Imperialism thus could never be Britain's paramount contribution to Asia, and it is unfortunate that the imperialists resisted the dissolution of the empire in Asia. They opposed the Indian National Congress at its foundation with a hostility much greater than necessary.[3] They resisted, as much as possible, the growing demands for self-government. They left bitter memories behind in the suppression of political agitation.

But, on the whole, British attitudes to Asia were enlightened

[1] London, C.R.O., Board of Control to East India Company, VII, pp. 239–41, 349–51, 390, X, pp. 276–9.
[2] G. N. Curzon, *Persia and the Persian Question*, 2 vols., London, 1892, vol. i, pp. 4, 462–3. [3] *Indian Historical Quarterly*, xxxi (June 1955), pp. 134–52.

more often than not. Of course, greed existed; the plundering of Indian resources occurred; Asians and Britons were at war with each other many a time; differences in culture remained eternally troublesome. One instance of this misunderstanding and violence which occurred in Bihar in 1775, is quite symbolic of Britain's interaction with Asia. A distinguished Muslim gentleman was on his way to visit an important British official, bringing gifts also, when he was attacked and robbed by dacoits. The Muslim, however, would not give the necessary evidence against the dacoits in order to convict and punish them. The British official flew into a rage, frustrated as he was in dealing with dacoits, and he caned the Muslim, whose honour was so injured by this deed that he threatened to commit suicide. The British official knew he should not have committed this act and he repented it.[1] The whole of the difficult and frustrating interaction of two cultures emerges in this instance. The Indian did not grasp the British passion for law and order, and to the Briton, the Muslim's response was certainly an enigma. Two societies were in collision, one bent on reform, despite hypocrisy and error, and the other concerned with the traditional values of religion and honour which did not seem in 1775 to require such urgent change. This interaction persisted until the end of the British empire in Asia.

Of course, the main British attitudes to Asia were often irritating to Asians. When Macaulay told the House of Commons in 1833, in regard to India,

We are free, we are civilized, to little purpose, if we grudge to any portion of the human race an equal measure of freedom and civilization,[2]

he was hardly speaking to the civilized Brahmin or the courtly Mandarin or the aristocratic Persian with tact. Indeed, the speech seems to threaten what these persons would have considered true civility. On the other hand, the Brahmin, the Mandarin, and the Persian aristocrat seemed unaware of the burden of poverty and underprivilege in Asian society. British attitudes, in contrast, often represented the disruptive knowledge that the old order had to change and that improvements beneficial to the mass of society had to be introduced into Asia.

[1] Bihar, State Central Records Office, Bhagalpur Collectorate Records, Revenue, 165, Mohamed Ramzaum Cauzey to James Barton, September 27, 1775, Barton to W. Hastings, November 14, 1775.
[2] Great Britain, 3 Hansard XIX, pp. 523–36, July 10, 1833.

CLAIMS TO UNIQUENESS

Johnson: *Sir, the man who has vigour may walk to the east just as well as to the west, if he happens to turn his head that way.*

Boswell: *But, sir, 'tis like walking up and down a hill; one man will naturally do the one better than the other. A hare will run up a hill best, from her fore-legs being short; a dog, down.*

Johnson: *Nay, sir; that is from mechanical powers. If you make mind mechanical, you may argue in that manner.*

XIV. THE UNIQUENESS OF EUROPE

as seen by a European

Henri Brugmans

I

At the very outset three preliminary questions have to be answered so as to obviate certain misunderstandings. *First of all, is there such a thing as 'Europe'?* Can we define or describe a community so heterogeneous in time and space? Is there anything which characterizes Scandinavians as well as Sicilians, Portuguese as well as Poles, medieval knights, Renaissance artists, philosophers of the Enlightenment, as well as contemporary trade-unionists? Is there anything which makes them belong to one and the same human group, united though diversified? I think there is because all European nations and nationalities are bound together by a fundamental fourfold heritage—barbarian, Roman, Greek, Judaeo-Christian—and because their common past is a long series of experiences they have shared and lived through.

It is true enough that the focal point was not always to be found at the same spot. Royal France was the cradle of Gothic architecture, while Thuringhia saw the birth of the Lutheran Reformation, and the Midlands laid down the foundations of the first Industrial Revolution. But Gothicism has spread from Gallic 'Finisterra' to Wilno on the border of Lithuania, Lutheranism became a challenge to sixteenth-century Christians all over Europe, and the Industrial Revolution gained the Asturias as well as Lodz. No doubt, different regions reacted differently during the various crises which Europe underwent. For example, Sweden emerged from the wars of religion as a leading Protestant State, whereas Spain became the heart of Tridentine Baroque. None the less, both countries had struggled their way through the common drama of self-renewing and self-devouring Christianity. Again, all nations did not participate with the same intensity in new movements in Europe. Romanticism, for instance, was a state of mind (or a mental disease, if you like), typical for a certain period in European history. But Germany was well ahead of Poland in that respect, and the Netherlands around 1800 were too sleepy to make any valuable contribution at all. However, diversification did not exclude a basic unity.

Secondly, is 'European' civilization really unique? The answer is a qualified affirmative. The fundamentals of European society are, of course, not exclusive to that society alone. The feudal system, for example, which is so typical for Europe after the *Völkerwanderung*, can fairly well be compared to similar solutions found in similar situations which have occurred elsewhere. Cultures other than ours have lived through periods of 'Renaissance' when they rediscovered hidden sources of inspiration. Moreover, some of our most important inner transformations were caused by increased contact with the outside world. The great philosophical synthesis of Aquinas, for instance, was directly due to the influx of Moslem and Jewish thinking which, in their turn, had deeply absorbed the ideas of Aristotle. In general, closed civilizations are rare and any living society always wants to communicate with others, to give and to receive, to enrich and be enriched.

Despite these qualifications, the fact remains that the history of Europe is different from that of the score of the other units of civilization in which Professor Toynbee sees legitimate fields of study. Europe may be identified by reference to Christianity, which is no doubt universal in its very essence. In dying on the cross, Jesus did not think of one particular part of the world, of one race or one culture, but of mankind as a whole. But this does not detract from the unquestionable historic fact that during fourteen centuries the Christian message was preached nearly exclusively in Europe. Outside Europe, there were the Jacobite Christians of Malabar and there was the insular community of Monophysites in Ethiopia. But for a very long time, the overwhelming majority of the faithful lived in Europe and made Europe what it became: not a 'Christian' community to be sure, but a society deeply influenced by the Christian Church (or Churches, as was the case after the Reformation). This phenomenon is undeniably unique, regardless of how we wish to judge it.

My *third* question is—*don't we Europeans 'idealize' our civiliza-*

tion? Of course we value and even love it simply because it is ours. There are millions of mothers in the wide world but only one is our own. But do we have to idealize in order to remain attached? That is a different matter. In a way, a group is like an individual: it can only develop harmoniously in so far as it understands itself, knowing its origins and its calling, its qualities and its weaknesses. Moreover, we feel entitled to concentrate on the positive contribution Europe might be able to make to an increasingly unified world. Which positive forces in European culture can have a universal bearing? In trying to answer this question, we do not make any attempt to plead a cause as opposed to other causes. We only want others to understand us better.

This is so much the more essential as Europeans are known overseas in a social context which is alien to them. Up to a certain extent, the change of climate implies a change of mentality. The fact is—to give a concrete example—that a Republican Spaniard who fought Franco during the Civil War, more often than not, becomes a colonialist diehard as soon as he sets foot on colonial soil. In spite of Marxist theories about the fundamental solidarity of the proletariat, 'white' workers in colonized countries found themselves linked much more strongly to their richer compatriots than to their fellow-toilers. Consequently, the kind of 'Europe' which was known overseas was more racialist than universal, more oppressive than emancipating, more arrogant than humanist, and infinitely more self-centred than Christian.

Now that the era of colonialism is over, we still have to carry the burden of the past. We cannot possibly blame the newly emancipated nations if they interpret Europe and the Europeans according to the experiences they have had. They have encountered a dominant race, technically competent but hopelessly race-conscious. The colonial tradition has hidden the real Europe from the eyes of other communities, instead of making them more familiar with what we consider as essential in ourselves. We do not aim at acquittal and even less at oblivion. We simply want others to understand who and what we are.

II

Even our bitterest critics have admitted our technical skill. In our former colonies we have been blamed for many imperfections and even crimes; but never has it been said that our engineers built their roads, their bridges, their harbours, and factories incompetently. Here, at least, our success has never been seriously questioned. Europeans, all over the world, have been surprisingly active. They are a 'promethean' race. Let us ask ourselves why. In my view, the root is religion, which in Europe means Christianity. Christianity being deeply unfatalistic, has immensely stimulated our dynamic forces. It did so in various ways.

First of all, the Gospels (and indeed the Old Testament already) do insist on the decisive importance of life, lived on this earth. To the Christian mind, as there is no metempsychosis, everything depends on our activities, *hic et nunc*, here and now. Work is worship and idleness 'the devil's pillow'. No doubt, there is an old tradition of Christian monasticism which continues vigorously up to our own day. But even the most severe religious orders impose manual or intellectual work on their members: *ora et labora*, 'work and pray' is one of the lasting themes of Christian monastic life, the object of which is not to forget or overcome reality but to transform it to the glory of God. Has not the Creator given this earth to man, in order that he should cultivate it and dominate the forces of Nature? That is at least the message of Genesis, the first book of the Bible. Furthermore, the world should be dominated by an effort which had to be efficient and systematic. Again I turn to the monks, as St. Benedict organized them around the year 500. True enough, there were mystics among the Benedictine fathers and their founder was one himself—nevertheless, he gave his brothers an annual agenda and a daily time-table which are surprisingly practical and singularly precise. The Roman administrative tradition of punctuality and accuracy was thus brought to the realm of worship and prayer. Nobody can doubt the decisive importance of this emphasis on work if he has at all studied the influence of monasticism in the making of Europe.[1] That influence was not only religious and moral but economic and social as well. At a later stage, Puritanism achieved another synthesis of asceticism and activity.

[1] *The Making of Europe*, by Christopher Dawson, is a classic analysis of the 'dark ages', when our Continent achieved its own personality, after the collapse of the Christian Roman Empire, and gave birth to a new, specifically European civilization, characterized by Romanesque architecture. The influence of monasticism on medieval institutions has been studied by Professor Leo Moulin in various publications.

Secondly, the Christian tradition has always laid great emphasis on the rational formulation of the faith. Whoever speaks about theology, speaks Greek: the word itself is Greek, and so are 'heresy', 'orthodoxy', 'liturgy', and 'hagiography'. Thus the spirit of the Hellenes, their strict mode of reasoning, their passion for clarity pervaded the Church, which in turn pervaded Europe. Later, in the thirteenth century, a new influence came with the revival of Aristotle who, after heavy fighting among clerics, became integrated into Christian philosophy. The Greek spirit was one of relentless curiosity and the uncompromising will to push further. 'The Classics', which Europeans have cultivated for centuries, did not sterilize their intellectual efforts. On the contrary, we found in their writings a passion for anything new and startling. They did not provide us with a philosophical code to be adopted and revered rather than re-examined, such as was the case during certain periods of cultural decline. On the contrary, they stimulated original thinking and scientific research. It is not by chance that the 'classical' Renaissance brought about two parallel movements: a more intimate comprehension of fine art and a fresh enthusiasm for daring exploration in regard to Man and Nature.

Thirdly, the two traditions we have mentioned have lived together in uneasy competition. More often than not, they have struggled against each other. We have stated that the Church had its intellectual roots partly in Greek philosophy. But it is no less true that serious tensions arose between organized Christianity, on the one hand, and 'classical' free thinking, on the other. This was particularly obvious in the sixteenth and the eighteenth centuries. Although the Jesuits were both champions of the orthodox creed and the Greco-Roman heritage, Roman Catholicism in the Baroque age developed a natural tendency towards conservatism against which the intellectual vanguard of those days waved the banner of 'classical' logic and 'pagan' ethics.

Nor is this the only self-contradiction in European culture. In fact, our political traditions are partly due to the immense prestige of Roman law and partly to the primitive ideals of local government and popular freedom. In the fourth century, the Roman Empire was christianized, but in the fifth it fell, overpowered by the onslaught of Germanic tribes. In their turn, these barbarians were baptized and a new style of political organization developed, Christian but no longer imperial. Nostalgia for the old universal,

Christian state remained, but never again could a new Augustus reign over Europe. Rome upheld its splendour and its impact, even politically, but it had become the fountain-head of a society which was no longer centralized and authoritarian: it had become feudal, somewhat anarchic, but diversified and libertarian.

Europe is a society where new impulses have been given constantly, without any of them ever eliminating or emasculating the others. If the world needs an example of real 'co-existence', here it is. Political and social, religious and cultural forces, old and new, renewed or traditional, are living together without anyone ever suffering a final defeat or enjoying a definitive triumph. This was perhaps what a Greek thinker had in mind when he declared that 'war is the father of everything', a war without victors or vanquished, originating out of dialectical tensions and waged for renovation-in-tradition. In conclusion, Europe's dynamic temperament is due, not only to its stimulating climate or to its diversified geography, but at least as much to 'the different souls struggling in her breast'. The day when Europe will be satisfied and at peace with herself, she will be dead.

III

Europeans, in spite of their basic traditionalism, always try to change things. Wherever they settle down, they transform the surroundings. They destroy and renovate, they often corrupt and disrupt, but they never leave the situation as it was. Menaced by spleen, they seem to fear nothing more than weariness. Their periods of welfare, internal order, international peace and competent administration are hardly appreciated in their own historical mythology. Even in such a deeply conservative, petty-bourgeois country as France, the bold adventurer keeps all his prestige. Whereas the most French of kings, Louis-Philippe, is despised, Napoleon has his grave at the 'Invalides' and even his wicked, mischievous 'Hundred Days' are told in schools as an epic poem rather than as a national misfortune.

Europeans like to think of themselves as 'crusaders'. In the name of what are they crusading? For two reasons, this is a tricky question. First, because we will have to speak about ideals, and ideals, formulated in words, easily become platitudes. Secondly, there is a great danger of self-complacency and self-idealization.

None the less, we have to try and find out what lies at the bottom of the Europeans' heart and mind, when they become so appallingly active. The very general answer, it seems to me, is that Europeans want to make life better for themselves, individually, and for their fellow-men, in this generation or in the next. *The measure of man is man*: this humanistic confession is acceptable, even for the Christian mystic whose faith tells him that God Almighty, Creator of the Universe, did not disdain to adopt the flesh with all its weaknesses, and become 'Immanuel,' 'God with us'—that is: Man among men. Therefore, Europeans might crusade for the glory of God—they never forget that the Lord is served through the men He saved. The 'dignity of man' was formulated during the Renaissance, but in the opinion of Pico della Mirandola who first coined the phrase, the creed of Humanism is inseparable from the Christian dogma of Incarnation. Of course, in later generations and centuries, a process of emancipation set in and Humanism lost to some extent its original character of Christian piety. Today, however, the 'drama of atheistic Humanism' (as Father de Lubac called it) is again one of the main themes of discussion among philosophers.

Humanism, in some form, belongs to the constant data of European civilization. What did and does it mean in practice? First of all, a certain respect for the individual. We write these words with apprehension. No doubt, this ideal was hardly even applied fully in European history and our past is full of the 'sound of rumour', where the cry of individual suffering is lost in the exultation of collective cruelty and fanaticism. Nevertheless, the preoccupation remains and Christians particularly remember that their Saviour was crucified with the 'collectivist' argument that 'it is better for one man to die than that the whole people should perish'. In the eternal conflict between the weak and the mighty, the individual and the state, popular sympathy goes instinctively to the former. Admittedly, this sympathy was neither always wise nor always efficient, but it was constantly there. It became active in the gradual humanization of criminal justice, in such movements as the one in favour of Captain Dreyfus, which shook France to her very foundations around 1900. In our times it is voiced by men like Arthur Koestler, when he attacks the barbarous principle of capital punishment; it also caused his break with Communism, which consciously sacrificed entire generations 'like dung on the fields of the future'. No doubt, passionate ideologists as they are, Europeans can be seduced for a moment by a doctrine so consistent and so ruthless. But they can hardly silence their 'petty-bourgeois' interest in personal sorrow. In France, where Republicanism has become a kind of 'laymen's religion', the decapitation of the royal family in 1793 is always remembered with pity, and the monument of 'expiation' erected to the memory of Louis XVI and Marie-Antoinette has never been destroyed by any left-wing government. 'Poor people', the Parisians say, 'They paid a heavy price for Progress'.

A second point, closely connected with the previous one, is the respect, not only for individual life, but for individual conscience. True enough, we believe that majority rule has great advantages, that it is better 'to count heads than to cut them'. Still, experience shows that very small minorities, nay isolated individuals may be right, against the blindness of the many.

Here again, the Greek tradition goes hand in hand with the Christian faith. During the Nazi period, many Germans took comfort in the message of Sophocles' *Antigone*, where the conflict is shown between Authority, fully equipped with legitimacy and public consent, on the one hand, and the testimony of a girl, on the other, simply stating that there are 'laws unwritten', which should prevail against the regulations of any state. Is this different from St. Peter's affirmation that 'it is better to obey God rather then men'? Or, to take another parallel of the same nature, there is Socrates, suffering rather than doing wrong—and Jesus preaching 'what is the use to man of gaining the whole world if his soul is harmed?' I know of course that Europeans are not daily pondering over these examples. But any popular leader who quoted them is sure to ring a bell somewhere in the unconscious layers of the European soul.

Finally, European Humanism as it has developed is deeply democratic. It believes in the basic equality of men. This seems so much the more surprising as the Christian Church which, for so long, has spiritually ruled Europe—Roman Catholicism—is fundamentally hierarchic. But here again, contradicting principles do not exclude each other. The problem is not 'either—or', but 'and —and'. No doubt the Holy See stands at the top of an ecclesiastical monarchy. But that does not mean that the Pope should be sinless. An obscure priest hears his confession just as anybody else's.

During his reign he may meet with faithful who, without even being priests, might eclipse him in saintliness. Again, the hierarchy does not spring from a certain social group. The Middle Ages have seen many a son or a serf called upon to rule Christianity, and the late John XXIII sprang from a large, comparatively poor peasant family. Surely, there must be rulers and ruled. Even social inequalities are probably inevitable. But this does not preclude that in the eyes of God, all men are equal in dignity, as He created each man's individual soul, for the salvation of which His Son died on the cross. Millions of Europeans know that, even if they do not go to church, even if they pretend to be 'anti-clerical'.

Egalitarianism is even more pronounced in Protestantism, where ministers are elected, like bishops in the primitive Church, and where the whole principle of sacred hierarchy is superseded by representative government. The English Levellers were a Protestant community and so are the Quakers, those Christian Humanists in faith and life. Among them, the word 'responsibility' gains its full significance, as each individual has to 'respond' for his own deeds, and the group as a whole feels engaged in a common social calling. Consequently, Christianity in one form or another lies at the basis of European Humanism—or, as we prefer to call it in the manner of Emmanuel Mounier, 'Personalism'. Often as we have failed in practice, we find our real image here, both unique and universal in its bearing.

IV

So far, we have not mentioned freedom. The word is used constantly in the political struggles of today. It therefore has been devalued. I remember a local Nazi paper having the title of *Freiheitsbanner*, and a good many dictatorial states in our time want to be called 'popular democracies' although they fail to grant the basic right of opposition, which is the liberty of liberties. In spite of all this confusion—or rather because of it—we have to speak of freedom if we want to sketch a 'portrait of Europe'. What we shall try to give here is neither a logical definition nor a metaphysical justification, but rather a description of how liberty has functioned in the European context. We shall therefore start from the assumption that freedom has something to do with decentralized and representative government. Freedom, we think, whatever its philosophical foundations, is incompatible with uniformity and with uncontrolled, unrestricted rule.

We have to go to the Middle Ages to discover the roots of European liberties. This may seem strange to those who hold that liberty cannot exist apart from modern forms of democracy and that modern democracy started with the French Revolution. In my opinion, however, such a view is erroneous. Words like 'freedom' and 'parliament' are medieval words, even if they were not used then in the same sense as we do now. More important, those countries which did not break with those ancient values are today, not less, but much more, democratic than the others: traditionalist Britain has shown infinitely greater political skill and a keener sense of democratic order than has revolutionary France. Let us therefore go somewhat deeper into European history and see what ideas were held, what battles raged.

The first phenomenon that strikes us is the constant struggle between Church and State. It has taken different forms, such as the quarrel of the Investitures, opposing the Emperor to the Pope, or the conflict between Thomas Becket and his king Henry II. It has continued ever since and will continue, as long as men admit that political action is subject to moral judgement and that an institution such as the Christian Church has a right—nay, a duty—to 'interfere' with politics. During the nineteenth century, the old strife seemed to have come to an end, as religion, it seemed, had become a 'private matter' no longer to be taken seriously in public. But the rise of modern dictatorship has brought home to us that the problem is as important as ever. Hitler had to face the staunch opposition of the Protestant 'Confessional Church' as well as an encyclical letter 'Mit brennender Sorge'. In the Communist countries, Christianity is the only opponent which the regime takes seriously. In short, the principle of restricted government—of 'government under the law of God', as it was called in less secular times—remains at the centre of political theory and practice. It is not merely that priests may intervene at crucial moments, and remind rulers of eternal ethical commandments. The quarrel becomes institutional, as soon as matters like marriage and education come in. Whatever our personal opinion on such subjects, it remains true that any government in Europe has always had to deal with them and that their internal sovereignty has thereby been restricted. Constantly, people have sided with

Pope or Emperor, with Bishop or King, with Calvin's 'consistoire' or with the city's administration—and these discussions have been a permanent asset to public debate and public spirit.

A second trend in European history has been towards diversification within the State itself. Just as fiercely as our society rejected 'cesaro-papism', it opposed the centralization of powers. Montesquieu found himself in line with our best traditions when he formulated the law of 'trias politica', under which the executive, the legislative, and the judicial powers are no longer concentrated in one hand, but clearly distinguished from each other, although they cannot be separated altogether. It is true enough that political trials may be unavoidable, even in a free state—who does not think of Algeria? But in spite of pressure, the 'majesty of the law' (as the French revolutionaries called it) is different from the will of the monarch, as it is (or has to be) from the passions of the mob. Surely, Europeans have greatly sinned against this principle, as against so many others they have proclaimed and sometimes invented. But the principle remains, and every European knows it as the expression of his own ideal, as a criterion of real justice and human freedom, as a check to arbitrary rule.

Nor does institutional pluralism stop here. One of the basic features of European society is the growth of local self-government and more especially the rise of those autonomous towns and cities, to the history of which Henri Pirenne has devoted a great part of his energy. An urban centre, from the thirteenth century onwards, was not just a commercial agglomeration around a feudal castle or a cathedral, though it may have been that at the start. It was a community in its own right and, if it was not democratic in the contemporary sense of the word, it enjoyed a considerable amount of recognized sovereignty, and could take its destiny into its own hands. Here—like in the Benedictine abbeys, which, in that respect, served as a model—elections were held and decisions taken by majority vote. Social and political parties or factions clashed, more than once undermining the municipal state itself: families and their clients against rivals, handicraft corporations against patricians, 'small' people against the 'fat', as they were called in Italy. Of course, these bloody conflicts were far from commendable; none the less, they were another source of public participation in public affairs. The scene is similar in Siena as in Salamanca, in

Q

Bruges as in Augsburg, in Cracow as in Novgorod—but not in Moscow, where medieval engravings do not show us town-halls and belfries as in the West.

Finally, such a diversified society as Europe had to cope constantly with the problem of its inner cohesion. The dream of unity is a necessary counterpoint to the complexity of so many divergent factors. For that reason, the present drive towards Federal Union is of historic importance and has a more than continental, indeed a universal, bearing. For four or five centuries we have lived within the framework of independent nation-states, each of them trying to achieve the greatest possible amount of homogeneity, each of them refusing any kind of binding supranational law. It may be that this was a necessary phase of transition: in fact, feudal self-righteousness had lead to anarchy and the autonomous cities had developed an unbearable power of collective egoism. Nevertheless, nationalism in its twofold manifestation of centralism and absolute sovereignty ran counter to the fundamental traditions of European culture which, in essence, remained multiform and universalist. In spite of so many inter-state conflicts, the undercurrents in our civilization—even from the sixteenth century onwards—were common to East and West, North and South, to monarchies and republics, in peace and war. Nationalism itself, as a political theory and as an emotional faith, developed everywhere under the influence of the French Revolution and German Romanticism. A great liberal like Mazzini even dreamt of uniting 'patriots of all fatherlands', Poles and Italians, Germans and Hungarians, in one rebellious brotherhood, the 'giovane Europa', 'young Europe'.

Universalism never died out. Nor did pluralism, in spite of all the efforts made to 'assimilate' diversities. Even the over-centralized Jacobine French Republic failed to wipe out local languages, which often fell down to the level of dialects but did not altogether disappear. In Franco's Spain, so much akin to France in that respect, Catalan culture is persecuted but resists bravely. And even in the Russian-dominated U.S.S.R., the problem of nationalities has not been solved by Stalin's doctrine that they should be granted a culture 'socialist in its contents but national in its form'. The problem before us, to do justice both to universalism and to plurality, can be solved by federalism, which means diversification-against-uniformity and solidarity-against-separatism. The present European dream of restored unity is an effort to overcome nationalism. If it succeeds, it might contain a message for the whole world, as mankind today is groping towards its global union-in-diversity.

V

How shall we conclude? Is Europe 'guilty' or 'not guilty'? We stated in the beginning that we did not intend to make a plea. But while we cannot ask anybody to share our European patriotism and our faith in the resurrection of our part of the world, we want others to understand some of the reasons for our hopes and aspirations.

It may be true, indeed it is probable, that not one of the characteristics of European civilization that I cited remains a monopoly of Europe alone. But we are out for inspiration rather than for monopolies. At any rate, European history, which explains the present situation of our continent, is an original one, with its imperial dreams and its particularist rivalries, its crusades and its civil wars, its obstinacy in defending local liberties and its enthusiasm for a national dynasty, its reactionaries and its radical reformers, its popular revolutions and its aristocratic liberalism, its down-to-earth, mercantile capitalism, and its undying utopias. All in all, a strange community, in constant conflict with itself, both wise and foolish, saintly and wicked, criminal and unselfish at the same time. In fact, it is always more complicated than outside observers think it is.

Those who blame Europe for its hard-boiled 'business mentality' should not forget the numberless missionaries who gave their lives for what they thought was man's salvation; they may have made gross mistakes but at least they did not gain any personal profit. And those who blame us for uprooting more or less primitive societies, so as to gain new raw materials and new markets, should not forget the numerous scientists who were often more deeply interested in local cultures than the local inhabitants themselves. Those who only know Europe from the other side of a colour bar should find comfort in the thought that the real human relations between civilizations and continents can start only now that equality has been reached. And lastly, those non-Europeans whose contacts with Europe have been centred exclusively around one specific country—France or Britain, Portugal or the Netherlands —should not forget the riches of an entire continent, a 'community of communities'. In that respect, it might become, provided it achieves its federal unity, a source of fresh inspiration for the world. A European Federation would give evidence that integration does not mean assimilation, that solidarity is different from hegemony, and that diversity is not a force of disruption but a stimulus and an asset.

XV. THE UNIQUENESS OF EUROPE

as seen by an Asian

Wang Gungwu

Every culture is considered to be unique by the people who share it. In what way then can I, a Malaysian Chinese, portray the uniqueness of a culture which originated as far away as Europe? It is not easy to talk about a culture I have learnt about largely through books and through short periods of stay in the lands of its origin. It would certainly be impossible to do it justice if we take 'uniqueness' to mean the opposite of 'universality'. But I do not believe that a culture, just because it is regarded as unique, cannot contain individual factors of universal value or that the total culture cannot have universal significance. This is particularly true when what is essential to that culture is perhaps its propensity to change itself as well as those cultures which come into contact with it. If a culture is dynamic, it can decisively influence another and some of its features can even be grafted on to other cultures. When this happens, one can be expected to recognize the unique-ness of a culture even without belonging to it. And if one has been exposed to the culture of Europe both directly and indirectly, one has to some extent shared in it and may even be qualified to pronounce on what is unique to that culture.

It is much more difficult to discover what Europe is. What are the features that have combined to make Europe? On what foundations has Europe been built? It has been well demonstrated that Greece by itself is not Europe. Its people came from the East and its earliest civilization derived much from the older civiliza-tions of Egypt (Africa) and Babylonia (Asia). And if we accept the boundaries of the modern atlas, much of ancient Greece was in Asia. Also, the Alexandrian empire was largely outside Europe and Hellenism was as much part of Europe as part of Asia and North

Africa. Even Rome was not exclusively European and its inter-continental empire was compounded of much that was common to peoples who lived on the shores of the Mediterranean Sea. This is not to deny that the Greek and Roman civilizations were both unique, each in its own way. It is merely to say that neither could be wholly identified with Europe except retrospectively when the later Europeans prided themselves on being the bearers of Greco-Roman traditions.

It can, of course, be argued that modern Europe can be traced back several thousand years to the fringes of Asia, to Homer, even to Abraham and Moses, then forwards through the Greek city-states, the Roman Republic, and the early Christian communities. While our knowledge of this ancient lineage might help to explain the development of Europe, it does not mean that Europe found its identity as early as all that. It was perhaps an essential pre-condition of the development of Europe as we know it that it should have been at an early stage isolated from the ancient civilizations of Asia and Africa. What was definitely crucial was the fission of the Judaic tradition, especially the rise of fiery Islam which cut adrift the northern half of the ancient Mediterranean world. A defensive Christian culture developed which laid the foundations of a Europe that could be later recognized. Although Christian Europe itself divided into the Catholic and Byzantine halves and, later, Catholic Europe into Catholic and Protestant portions, the divisions were never deep enough to alter the course of a distinct growth. Later on, the Crusades were to give a special stamp to this Europe. Their failure, followed by the Tatar and then the Turkish invasions, led to a greater isolation and a greater need for Europe to seek its own particular genius.

I think it is important to see that that genius was not found in Christianity alone. The Christian Church led the early Europeans to a merry dance and it was not until they were able to stand aside from their intense faith that they were able to break through into a new world of thought. But Christianity did play a vital role in two different ways. First of all, it transmitted, although im-perfectly, the rudiments of the ancient learning of the Greeks and Romans. Secondly, it provided, along its long and tense frontier with Islam, a stimulating relationship with the inheritors of the ancient tradition which was eventually to result in the rediscovery of Greek science.

I come now to identify the Europe I recognize. This is the Europe of science and expansion. It began with the liberation of the mind and eventually led to the physical expansion of Europe itself. To trace the history of this expansion is not necessary here. The eventual victory of reason and the emergence of rationalism may be decried a little today, but no one can be unaware of its impact first on Europe and the Americas and then on Asia and Africa through different stages in the past four centuries. When Europe discovered its own identity and broke through its isolation, it released a creative energy that the world had never known before. Its freedom from dogma and from unyielding traditions marks the ultimate uniqueness of Europe. This Europe did not appear until it had acquired a particular faith in reason in the seventeenth century. Geographically, this occurred in Western Europe, especially in England, France, Italy, and Germany. Having identified this Europe, I have no wish to pursue here the question whether any civilization, in the last analysis, is ever entirely unique. Let me merely say that Europe was so to me and consider why it was so to someone brought up at one of the cultural crossroads of the world—the Malay peninsula.

The Malay peninsula lies between two other worlds, the Indian and the Chinese, and has from the earliest times served as one of the stopping-places in the relations between the two. The culture of this area was still not rigidly formed when it began to receive the more sophisticated faiths and ideas from both its west and its east. The peoples of the peninsula found from the first the ideas from India easier to digest and absorb and soon came under the influence of Buddhism and Hinduism. But the grafting of Hindu-Buddhist ideals was incomplete and rather superficial. When they were seriously challenged by the mono-theistic faith of Islam, an offshoot of the ancient world of which Europe was another, these ideals were quickly overthrown. By the nineteenth century, on the eve of Europe's physical expansion to South-east Asia, the dominant religion on the peninsula was Islam.

Europe arrived in Malaya largely in the holds of British ships, not the anti-Moslem crusading Europe of the Portuguese and Spaniards, but a Europe willing to trade with both infidel and heathen. Its only flag, it claimed, was that of reason, reasonable profit and advancement, progress, and enlightenment. Although it

was not a missionary flag, it flew at the masthead together with the
conviction that all that stood in its way were obstacles to progress
and deserved to be modified if possible and destroyed if necessary.
By this time, Europe was full-grown, completely transformed by
science, the 'experimental method' or 'the method of abstraction'.
The methods of science had successfully postulated a mechanistic
world which the frail human mind could grasp and analyse. They
had sustained generations of minor Fausts who felt their minds
were freed from the limits of Christian scholasticism. The liberation of the mind and the physical expansion of Europe were both
creative forces, each stimulated by the other. First had come the
revolution in the pursuit of wealth which streamlined the lines of
technological development. Accompanying this was the shift from
'status' to 'contract' as the basis of society, which was perceptively
described by Sir Henry Maine in 1861. And finally, there came the
codification of bourgeois politics which began so dramatically in
the French and the American revolutions.

By the time the impact of Europe was being felt in the Malay
peninsula, a microcosm of Asia, its uniqueness was manifest. The
world was presented with what was seen as a new juggernaut which
no other civilization could successfully defy. At first, Europe
appeared merely as made up of superior ships and guns, the
nuclear missiles of the nineteenth century. It was thought that all
that was necessary to counter this armed force was the reproduction of an equal force, a mere quantitative exercise not really
worthy of the great spiritual value Asia could boast of. The
uniqueness of Europe reduced in terms of tonnage and firing
power was impressive but worthless and contemptible. 'Western
materialism' was the scornful counter-slogan of the Asian who
cursed this barbarous Europe roundly in what the modern Chinese
novelist Lu Hsün has called 'the spirit of Ah Q', the indomitable
spirit of the traditionalist who spits on what he cannot understand
or control.

Only one Asian country responded rationally to the challenge
of reason. Japan, having more adaptable traditions of its own, saw
Europe as a source of power. Its leaders deliberately set out to
reproduce that power in Japan. Their success was measured, within
forty years, by their complete victory over a part of Europe itself
in the Russo-Japanese War of 1904–5. But it is doubtful if the
Japanese at the time saw what Europe really represented. Might

and victory were universal and easy to comprehend. To have won was to have proved this. Certainly the Asian leaders elsewhere who hailed the victory did not see any uniqueness in a power system which could be transplanted and copied. If anything, the Japanese experience confirmed their deepest conviction that, in that power, they too could have their revenge.

It would be churlish of me to mock the desire for revenge. There is in all of us the urge to take our revenge against bullying and aggression, which was all that was perceived in the expansion of Europe. Indeed, there was bullying and aggression which the Europeans tried hard to disguise as rational progress and innate superiority. But that was not the essence of Europe. Far more important was the release of creative energy which had cauterized the running sores of traditional thought and action. It was an adventuresome energy, often unhappy and self-conscious but never comfortable, always challenging and never self-satisfied. This was the Europe which was put before me when I grew up as a Chinese boy in a European-dominated Malaya.

It would hardly be true to say that I was aware of this Europe from the start. The Chinese immigrant family is no different from any other. It clings to its own traditions with little understanding but much rigidity. China's early response to Europe was still real to the Chinese who left China to seek a living in a European-dominated South-east Asia. Their civilization, they were as convinced as their compatriots at home, was ancient and rich beyond compare. Its survival against all its enemies could always be taken for granted. As for Europe, it was merely a matter of ships and guns and these China could easily produce if it wanted to. But some of the Chinese were wavering. By the 1930s, China's traditions had been badly mauled by its own young rebels, the embryonic 'Europeans'. Many had already opened a window to Europe. They were those who had had the elements of science and mathematics and had been thrilled by the revolt of the romantics. From Goethe to Darwin, Spencer, Shaw and from Bertrand Russell, they had learnt to peer into some of the inner chambers of the European spirit. But most Chinese still remained uncommitted to that spirit. They could not really believe that this Europe could be a substitute for China. All they were prepared to concede was that Europe could enrich the traditions of China.

This, however, was enough to set me on the rough road to

Europe. The rest was provided by the Europe which had taken Malaya and sent its representatives to fight mosquitoes, propel engines, install electricity, open schools, and rule over us. Their work was all around me and I was made keenly aware when I was still very young that there was 'Europe' and 'non-Europe'. 'Non-Europe' I saw mainly as morality, religion, and codes of behaviour peculiar to the Asians. As for 'Europe', it was science which first made sense to me as a kind of magic, a new, more effective magic which, unlike 'non-Europe', was dynamic and concrete.

The feeling that this science was magic would probably have rubbed off in time, naturally and gradually, as I began to master some of its basic concepts. But I was not given a chance to do so. The Second World War reached out to Asia and the Japanese Army drove out the British from Malaya and broke the spell. The all-powerful science was no longer exclusively European. In the hands of the Japanese, it was equally effective. There was power and there was control. There was even the creative energy I had thought was peculiar to Europe. It was a startling experience and I still regret that I was too young to record it as I made the discovery. I believe that the same experience befell many others in Asia at this time, both among those who endured the Japanese conquerors directly and among those who saw their Europe flaying its arms in agony. Perhaps that is the real reason why Asia could never be the same again after the war.

What became clear to me was that the creative power of Europe had not been produced by the European God, nor by the spiritual life of the Europeans. What was unique to Europe was not what it had done with an originally non-European Christianity nor what that Christianity had brought out in Europeans. It was their careful and calculated extension of ancient science into fresh paths that had led to freedom and independence for the mind, and the logic behind that power was distinct from their religious faith. It was, instead, a dangerous higher paganism which the rest of the world either had not wanted or had not thought it necessary to adopt.

The two World Wars, one so soon after the other, seemed to have undermined the European reliance on their supreme rationalism. But it appeared to me that Europe was not afraid and certainly not prepared to give it up. After the peace, the Europeans returned to Asia, to Malaya, ready to start again. I, too, resumed my study of Europe, perhaps unconsciously also hoping to learn from it as well as the Japanese had done. But it was no longer easy to learn from the Europeans. If Europe appeared still real and recoverable to me, this feeling certainly was not strengthened by the Europeans I met. The older generation of colonial officials were merely eager to get back to the glorious past. Even though they were far from their base of post-war reconstruction in Europe, they were unbelievably lacking in the creative element that had distinguished them before the War. As for the younger generation of officials and teachers, they had acquired a scepticism about what was peculiar to Europe which made them more relaxed and better companions but also shorn of the old magic. This was a generation who read Kafka and Mann, who were stunned by the cold bestiality of Hitler's Germans, who preferred Oakeshott to Laski. In school, I found that I was already absorbing some of the doubts of my young teachers, not about the content of the sciences but about the ultimate value of this old magic to the new world. Perhaps these doubts really marked the uniqueness of Europe. Were they not, after all, signs that Europe, as in the past, was ready to shed its old skin in order to emerge with a new one? Was this not part of the restless creative energy which had brought Europe round the world?

At this point, I finished school and went to a university in China and lost the chance to find the answers immediately. For in China, a different spirit prevailed. There was the confidence and discovery of an earlier Europe. Even in the middle of the Chinese civil war, my fellow-students spoke only of science, of science in natural phenomena and in every thought and action of man. I was reassured. This was the assertion of all that was so unique in Europe, not the romantic magic which had enriched my youth but a relentless and incontrovertible logic which was to direct all men for their own good. I was enthralled by signs of this power which would give man his ultimate freedom from fear. It was particularly fascinating to see the uniqueness of Europe so completely enshrined in a new determinism. Everyone I spoke to evoked the spirit of Europe. Every discussion ended in a plea for scientific thought. Obeisance to this plea was demanded and received. I was happy to see Europe acknowledged, even though not always in a recognizable form. If science was to conquer, I argued, it must conquer all.

It took me nearly two years to discover that what I had identified as Europe was not science but a new dogma wearing the clothes of science. The spirit of Europe as I understood it then was the power to destroy lies and illusions in order to bare truth. The new science, it seemed, represented the power to employ useful truths in order to control men's minds. It was amply justified in terms of China's poverty and the suffering of the masses and I was not unsympathetic. After all, to achieve true liberation, one must begin with the freedom from hunger and want. And what is science if not the power to relieve man from first his physical and then his mental burdens? But I had kept a naïve faith in the perfection of European science at the time, and concluded that the use of science to control men's minds was a serious distortion of the basis of that science.

Thus when I returned to Malaya to continue my studies, I was more cautious. I still had faith in the natural sciences. Only the social sciences roused my suspicions. Were these also convenient truths to control men's minds? This did not, however, move me from my belief that science characterized Europe. I had, by this time, become more aware that there was also a spiritual Europe and that this Europe, too, was outgoing and reached every corner of the world either ahead or in the wake of the secular. Religion played an important part in Europe's expansion, particularly in the propagation of its image in missionary schools. The work of the missionary penetrated deeply into the consciousness of 'non-Europe'. But although I knew that religion sustained the Europeans in their multifarious enterprises and gave some of them perhaps a special glow, it was the enterprises themselves which made Europe seem to be the incomparable source of energy that vitalized the world.

The post-war world changed too rapidly for me to keep my image of Europe whole. I was myself caught up in the Asian revenge against Europe. My bright mirror of Europe was clouded over by the memory of the exclusive ethos by which the colonial officials had dominated over us in Asia. The queue of men who waited for Europe to be humbled had become long and noisy. The old counter-slogan of 'Western materialism' was now replaced by another more concrete and appealing, 'colonialism-imperialism'. Europe was made out to be immoral. It had crushed our native genius savagely and was still trying to cling on to its superior ways. With great glee, we saw Europe divided like a cell at the point of reproduction. Its own dialectic seemed to be bringing about a qualitative change. The codified bourgeois world was being threatened by the revolt of the masses. Out of this division, there was a weakening, a ripeness that has been described as 'the highest stage of capitalism', 'the Indian summer of imperialism'. It was, in fact, not long before the world-wide framework of Europe appeared to collapse. Old empires disappeared and new nations emerged. Everywhere Europe seemed to have retreated and it was thought that there was only a smaller Europe left which was content to co-exist and hope for mutual respect.

It was certainly difficult to think clearly about Europe during those heady days of national independence. It is difficult even now while the dust of nationalism is still settling. But one thing seems clear enough to me. The science of Europe now belongs to the world. It is time to ask if Europe still exists. Of course, there is a Europe on the map, but is this Europe not merely the breeding-ground, the first laboratory of the new world?

The expansion of Europe had not only been an extension of territory but also an intellectual conquest. The two, however, were mutually dependent from the start. We read of the colonization of South and North America; the spread of European Russia into Central Asia and Siberia; the colonization of South Africa, Australia, and New Zealand. Into all these areas, Europe was transported either in part or in full, but always with the essentials of a rational state and economy, a 'contract' society and a scientific education. In all these areas, Europe itself underwent modifications, sometimes a broadening of the social base and a sharpening of institutional features, and sometimes a temporary relapse into barbarism or a preliminary fusion with other traditions. But wherever Europe came, there was a change and a slightly different course in development. Every new condition enriched the European heritage either by re-exporting to the Europe at home or by strengthening the colony itself.

In addition, there was the extension of Europe to the populous regions of the old world, especially to Southern and Eastern Asia. Here, Europe came much later as fully grown and much less ready to learn and to adapt. But it had a great deal to give if and when the older peoples were prepared to receive. And during the twentieth century, one after another, taking the lead of Japan, the older traditions opened their doors little by little until today no part of the world can be said to be completely free from Europe's extension. Apart from deep-rooted religion and the precepts of morality, modern society everywhere has followed the pattern of Europe. In secular education, in national identity, in economic goals, in transportation, in mass media and communications, no country can escape the need to use the range and scope of the scientific method. No one, in fact, can afford to ignore the universal features of unique Europe.

Thus while Asia and Africa have been engaged in the ejection of the Europeans, the peoples and their governments have tacitly accepted the material culture of Europe and the finished products of its civilization. This was not regarded as dangerous, since matter, it was thought, especially in the Islamic, Hindu, and Chinese worlds, could not really subvert the ancient ideals. But there is some doubt as to how long the traditional mind can hold out against the exacting reason of European science. For, in the final analysis, it is not a question of matter against mind, but of mind against mind, the mind that recognizes the importance of matter and attempts to control and harness it against the mind that is draped in dogma and absolute faith which cannot see matter for what it is. In Kemal Ataturk and Nasser, in Nehru and in the Chinese Communists, the European mind is already manifest. Its ultimate victory may only be a matter of time, for the European mind breeds its own demands and its own standards and these will in turn produce the institutions, the values, and the thinking which reflect it.

Having gone so far, it would be easy for me to conclude that the European mind will be the world mind and that the world will be a 'Greater Europe'. But this cannot be so. The very success in Europe's extension will lead to the submersion of the original Europe. I have noted earlier that Europe was produced in isolation, during the centuries of Islamic and Tatar pressure. A coherent civilization emerged from that pressure to fight back, to shake the enemies off its shoulders, and it succeeded splendidly. But the victories were won because Europe held its own secrets to power. Now these secrets are no longer Europe's to keep. In the new struggle for power and in the transmission and dissemination of scientific knowledge, two major changes have already taken place.

First of all, the 'non-Europe' which Europe had dominated is now more or less free. And although Europe, with its extensions throughout the world, is still able to encircle Asia and Africa, this Europe is divided between the 'Western' and Soviet blocs locked in a cold war while the secrets of European power are now available to Afro-Asia. And while it is true to say that the two halves of the extended Europe are, for the sake of their war, trying to woo the new nations of Asia and Africa, it is also true that Afro-Asia can hope to thrive on the war which has so exhausted their age-old enemies. In the new struggle, Europe, the original Europe which shook the world, can hardly expect to be dominant again.

Secondly, the science which had released men's minds from their dying traditions has been massively advanced to meet the needs of the new world struggle. Mankind has already been brought, and will continue to be brought, to the brink of total destruction. The greater the danger, the greater the need to organize men and the lesser the resistance to totalitarian control. I said earlier that when I was a student in China, I saw the beginnings of a new kind of science which aimed at employing useful truths in order to control men's minds. I had concluded then that this was a distortion of the spirit of Europe. It has taken me years to realize that this distortion was not peculiar to China, that it had taken place in Europe itself and is now specially notable in the Communist world but also apparent in other parts of 'Greater Europe'.

I mentioned earlier that, after the Second World War, even Europeans could no longer confirm the uniqueness of their Europe. Several visits to Europe and America during the past ten years have helped me understand why this was so. The spirit of Europe has played its role in history. New lands, new frontiers, new peoples have enlarged that spirit and changed it to suit the vastly different conditions. Europe will be denying its own spirit if it merely looked back to its traditions. The whole world has been touched by its magic and now an even more penetrating spirit may appear from the shadows of Europe's distortion. And if this new spirit should succeed in saving the world from itself, it might rightfully claim as its main heritage the uniqueness of Europe.

XVI. THE UNIQUENESS OF ASIA

as seen by an Asian

Hajime Nakamura

The 'uniqueness' of Asia, in the cultural sense of the term, has been taken for granted as something clear and obvious by many intellectuals, but it is really very problematic and questionable. Limiting the problem chiefly to the ways of thinking of Asians, we must see it from a comparative standpoint. Is it possible for us to identify the features of the ways of thinking common to the peoples of the East? In the East as well as in the West we often hear people asserting that a certain trait is 'Oriental'. What is commonly implied by this term?

First of all, Europeans have often contended that in the East man's individual existence is not fully realized, and the individual is subordinated to the universal. Hegel, for instance, asserted that God or the Absolute has in the East the feature of *das Allgemeine*.

The fundamental principles of the various religions of the East are that the single *Substanz per se* is *das Wahrhafte*, and an individual has no value within itself, nor is it capable of attaining any value so long as an individual holds itself, while standing against *das Anundfürsichseyende* which is absolute; that an individual is only capable of assuming true value by uniting itself with the *Substanz* when this individual, however, is no more a *Subjekt* but is dissolved into the unconscious.[1]

And as to the difference between Eastern and Western thought, he declared:

On the contrary, with Greek religion or Christianity *Subjekt* is aware of its freedom; and we ought to think in this manner.

In the philosophy of the East, however,

The negation of the finite is existent. But that negation is the One in the sense that an individual only attains its freedom in unity with what is substantial.

[1] Hegel, *Vorlesungen über die Geschichte der Philosophie*, herausgegeben von Michelet, S. 135–6.

Hegel had only a limited knowledge of the classics of the East, acquired through his reading of translations, but his views are shared by many people in the West even today. To what extent then are Hegel's statements to be considered accurate? It could be contended that in the East a blind subordination to authority in some form or another was conspicuous. But is it possible to hold seriously that in the West 'the self was free' and exempt from such subordination? The complete and blind faith in religious authority during the Middle Ages in the West and the subsequent destruction of heterogeneous culture has no real parallel in the East. Further, was the phenomenon of 'being united with the *Substanz*', as Hegel called it, not conspicuous at times in the West rather than in the East?

It is again often held that the peoples of the East are 'intuitive' and, accordingly, not systematical or orderly in grasping things; by contrast the Westerners are said to be 'inferential' or 'logical' and try to grasp things in an orderly and systematic manner. But even if the ways of thinking of the Chinese or the Japanese could be characterized as 'intuitive', in the case of the Indians this label is hard to apply. For example, the intricate and subtle arguments of the Abhidharma literature are extremely logical and can hardly be called 'intuitive'. There is no need to refer to the difficult literature of theology in order to point out how far removed from any intuitive simplicity is the complicated, fantastic and rich sentiment found in Indian painting and sculpture. Such art evokes in us a complicated association of ideas and leads the spectator into a strange romantic atmosphere.

Further, it is sometimes asserted that the ways of thinking of Eastern peoples are 'synthetic', while those of Westerners are 'analytic'. Chinese terms, for instance, give us the impression that they are 'synthetic', but they may well be placed on a stage prior to analysis. So long as they have yet to pass through the process of analysis, they could not properly be called 'synthetic'. On the other hand, it is generally recognized by scholars that the Indians showed a great skill in the analysis of linguistic as well as psychological phenomena. We cannot say that Westerners alone tend to be analytical. The Indian grammatical works were most advanced in the analysis of words and phrases, but very weak in their consideration of the synthetic construction of sentences. On the other hand, Greek grammarians have left excellent

R

achievements concerning syntax dealing with the synthetic field of words and phrases. Altogether, it makes for confusion rather than clarity to characterize the ways of thinking of Eastern peoples simply as being 'synthetic'.

Another contrast made is in relation to knowledge. Max Weber said:

The premise which is common in the last analysis to all philosophies and soteriologies in Asia is that knowledge—whether it be that of books or mystical gnosis—is the only absolute way of leading to the supreme bliss of this world as well as of the next world. A careful examination would reveal the fact that 'knowledge' does not mean to know the things of the world, nature, social life or laws regulating both of them. Rather, it is the philosophical knowledge of the 'meaning' of life and of the world. It is naturally understood that such a knowledge cannot be replaced by Western empirical learning, if we are to do justice to the purpose proper to the learning.[1]

It is true that knowledge as conceived by Eastern people seems to conform to the definition given above. But even in the history of Western thought we can find comparable notions of knowledge. The word *gnosis* itself is Greek, and a gnostic tendency may be seen in various religions in Western Asia, and is not peculiar to India and China alone. In the West, too, it explicitly revealed itself in Neo-Platonists such as Plotinus, and it has been traced back to Plato. It is generally presumed that such philosophical schools were influenced by Indian or Persian thought, but this relationship is yet to be clarified. Under the influence of Greek philosophy the Gnostics arose as a movement to elevate Christian belief to the status and certitude of knowledge. Likewise in the Middle Ages, a similar inclination is noticeable in some of the mystics who were termed heretics, such as Tauler and Eckhart.

There are some people who maintain that as all the major religions of mankind arose in Asia, we could therefore label the whole area (including Western Asia) of the East as 'religious', whereas Europe (and America) or the West may be regarded as 'non-religious'. Such a view was fairly dominant in Japan prior to the Pacific War, and it has never completely disappeared. However, while the Indians in particular are extremely religious, the disposition of the Japanese or the Chinese could not be regarded as particularly religious. On the contrary, there is some evidence

[1] Max Weber, *Aufsätze zur Religionssoziologie*, II, S. 364–5.

that the peoples of the West are more religious than the Japanese or Chinese in that they highly esteem the religious congregation.

In the same way, it has been repeatedly contended that Western civilization is 'materialistic', while Eastern civilization is 'spiritual'. This is erroneous. A non-religious people can hardly be called 'spiritual'. The ancient civilization of the West and especially its modern civilization, which restored the old, were markedly superior in their concern with the conquest of material nature, and consequently the West, with all its power, advanced towards the East. The Asian peoples, menaced by this invader, labelled the West 'materialistic', and characterized the less advanced East as 'spiritual'. The feeble capability to control material nature can be seen in the aborigines of Africa as well as of America, and is in no way peculiar to the peoples of Asia alone. It is also questionable whether we could characterize the peoples of the East as 'introvert' and 'subjective', and those of the West as 'extrovert' and 'objective'.

Again, it would be a very superficial observation to describe the East as being 'ethical', for some sort of ethics is a part of any and every society. Observing that the traditional ethics of the Japanese and Chinese are not practised in the modern West, some conservative Japanese, anxious to preserve the ethics of old, made this characterization. In connection with the above observation it is often held that Eastern thought is to be regarded as 'metaphysical' and that the basis of Eastern thought is the concept of 'nothingness'. This results in the frequent use of the phrase 'nothingness peculiar to the East'.[1] It goes without saying that the abstruse concept of 'nothingness' was propounded in the philosophies of Lao-tzu and Chuang-tzu. On the other hand, Indian philosophy generally inquires into the 'existent'. (The meaning of 'existent', however, is different from that in Greek philosophy.) In Indian philosophy, there is a dominant current of thought that the 'existent' can only be substantiated on the basis of 'what is existent'. In the case of Śaṅkara, the ultimate reality is the 'existent', and it is rather the phenomenal world which is void, so that his thought is diametrically opposed to that of Lao-tzu, at least as far as our literal understanding is concerned. In Buddhism, especially in Mahāyāna Buddhism, 'voidness' is expounded but this is different from 'nothingness', a fact often emphasized by

[1] Cf. Kumataro Kawada, *Mu no Keitoron teki Kenkyu.*

Indian Buddhists. These two ideas were either identified or confused when the method known as Ko-i (the evaluation and interpretation of Buddhism through the medium of Chinese doctrines
such as Confucianism and Taoism) was practised after the introduction of Buddhism into China. Chia-hsiang-tai-shih, however, repeatedly affirmed that Buddhist 'voidness' and the 'nothingness' of
Lao-tzu or Chung-tzu are not to be equated. Altogether, it is very
misleading to ascribe to the whole of Eastern thought the phrase
· 'nothingness peculiar to the East'. Moreover, it could not possibly
be argued that the East is 'metaphysical' and the West is not so,
especially as most of the Chinese and the Japanese in particular
have been much less 'metaphysical' than Europeans.

Again, it is often said that Westerners are 'rationalistic', while
Asians are not. Such characterizations seem to have acquired
general acceptance and usage in Japan especially after the Second
World War. It is particularly emphasized that the Japanese are not
'rationalistic'. It is true that the Japanese have in the past shown
little aptitude for formal logic. But when we consider this matter
more deeply, we find that in practice the Japanese generally tend
to follow a certain pattern—devotion to a particular ethical system
is a general tendency, upon which they base their criteria for the
evaluation of conduct. In this sense we can say that ethical
rationality did exist, if 'rational' is the correct term for the intelligent evaluation of conduct.

At first sight the Chinese give us the impression of being
essentially non-rational. The manner of expression in the Chinese
language is extremely ambiguous, and the historical fact that there
has never been a developed tradition of formal logic among the
Chinese seems to support this view. This does not, however,
necessarily mean that they are 'irrational'. It is widely known that
Chinese thought, due to its rationalistic character, exerted a great
influence upon the philosophy of the Enlightenment in modern
Europe. In this respect it is the Chinese rather than the Westerner
who is far more 'rationalistic'. And it is solely due to its 'rationalistic' character that Chinese thought inspired the thinkers of the
Enlightenment such as Voltaire and Wolff and came to serve as a
weapon against the shackles of medieval scholastic traditions.

Although the Indians did not achieve any spectacular developments in the natural sciences as the West did, they conducted far
more elaborate speculations than the Westerners of antiquity and

the Middle Ages in fields of inquiry such as the theory of numbers, the analysis of psychological phenomena and also that of linguistic structures. The Indians are highly 'rationalistic' in so far as their ideal is to discover, and adhere to, eternal laws in nature governing the past, present, and future. The thought represented by Tertullian's aphorism, *credo quia absurdum* ('I believe because it is absurd') had no chance to occur in India. The Indians are, at the same time, 'logical' since they generally have the tendency in their thinking to deduce the particular from the universal; they are at once 'logical' and 'rationalistic'. On the other hand, many religious beliefs of the West are 'irrational' and 'illogical'. This is acknowledged by some Westerners themselves. For example, Schweitzer, a pious and most devout Christian, says that compared with the 'logical' religions of East Asia, the gospel of Jesus is 'illogical'.[1] On this point, the East is, if anything, more 'rational', and the West is more 'illogical'. Again, a 'rationalistic' attitude is seen consistently in Dharmakirti's logic or in the natural philosophy of the Vaiśeṣika school in India. Consequently, we cannot imprudently adopt the classification that lumps together Eastern peoples and contrasts them with the 'rationalistic' West.

It may be noted here that there has also been an attempt to make a distinction between the 'rationalism' of the East and the West. For example, Max Weber says:

The practical rationalism of the West is extremely different in nature from that of the East, notwithstanding the outward or actual similarity of the two. The post-Renaissance rationalism was especially rationalistic in the sense that it abandoned the restrictions of tradition and believed in the power of reason existent in nature.

This statement appears to be well grounded. However, the intellectual tendency, which was bent on disregarding traditional authority and its restrictions, appeared as early as the turbulent days of the so-called 'Chu'un-ch'iu' up to the beginning of 'ch'in' in China, and in India it was conspicuous in urban society in the time of the Buddha, and even afterwards it was propagated by naturalistic philosophers and logicians. In modern Japan as well, even prior to the introduction of Western civilization, the germination of free thought may be perceived. It is a fact beyond doubt that disregard for conventional authority and restrictions was

---

[1] Albert Schweitzer, *Das Christentum und die Weltreligionen*, S. 52.

dominant in the modern West, and much less apparent in traditional Asia, but this is merely a difference of degree or extent; it is not a difference in essence. Even if this tendency is uppermost in the modern West, it was anything but that in the Middle Ages, and, therefore, it would be improper to distinguish sharply the East from the West on this score.

In this connection it may be noted that a 'nostalgic conservatism' was until recently very conspicuous among the Chinese, and can also be seen to a considerable degree among the Japanese, while in India it was at least once set aside decisively. In the case of the Moslem converts, who make up a fairly large part of the Indian populace, they seem, at any rate on the surface, to have disengaged themselves almost wholly from indigenous and long-established religious traditions. Therefore 'nostalgic conservatism' cannot be considered an endemic and ineradicable feature of Asian peoples. Although this 'nostalgic conservatism' is partly common to both the Indians and the Chinese, the former are prone to be concerned with universal law underlying the past, present, and future, while the latter are inclined to revere a specific previous example as a significant precedent. Thus the basis of this common tendency in India and in East Asia is connected with a considerable difference in outlook if not of thought.

Again, we might think that it is characteristic of all Asians to grasp transitory things 'passively'. This seems to be a conspicuous feature of the ways of thinking of the Chinese and the Indians. On the other hand, peoples elsewhere in Asia and the Japanese in particular are intensely sensitive to fleeting phenomena. Buddhist teaching and Confucian learning alike have been transformed into something dynamic in character since their introduction into Japan. It is, therefore, misleading to sum up the ways of thinking of East Asians in general as being merely 'passive'. And although the thinking of Westerners might indeed be called 'dynamic', the idea of material 'evolution' and of continual 'progress' in nature and history has manifested itself clearly only in modern times and could not possibly be said to have existed in the West since classical antiquity.

It is often pointed out that as India, China, and Japan are climatically situated in the monsoon zone, the thought-currents of these three zones are generally 'passive', submissive to objective nature, and lacking in the will to conquer it by means of rational and measured thinking. It is further argued that when the peoples of Asia make a move *en masse*, they are easily subordinated by a specific authority as they do not like to assert themselves positively. Accordingly, even when various ideas are found to be violently opposed to one another, Asians are likely to concede to all of them their *raison d'être* and to compromise and synthesize, rather than to adopt any one of them to the exclusion of the rest. It is, in fact, repeatedly contended that in contrast to Western thought, the spirit of tolerance and mutual concession is a salient feature of Eastern thought. The West, however, emphasizes the inescapable necessity of struggle, for the sake of religion, and even scripture is cited:

If any man come to me, and hate not his father, and mother, and wife, and children, and brethren, and sisters, yea, and his own life also, he cannot be my disciple.[1]

Throughout the religious world of India a comparatively tranquil and peaceful atmosphere has prevailed from time immemorial. It is significant that Gotama Buddha and Mahāvīra ended their lives in peace. Recognizing the fact that in China a remarkable freedom of faith had been allowed since ancient times, Voltaire, who was called 'the apostle of the freedom of faith', was genuinely fascinated by Chinese legal codes. In Japan, although the principle of the freedom of faith has not been fully realized, especially when political influence was exerted through state interference, hatred against the heretic has been mild among the people in general. Even the followers of the Jōdo Shin sect, the most clear-cut sect in its uncompromising attitude towards other sects, believed that in order to spread their faith it would be wiser to wait calmly for a suitable opportunity rather than to force the situation. More generally, among Asian peoples the self-consciousness of individuals and groups has, to a greater or lesser extent, been conditioned by the strong conviction that *all* men are one in essence.

The idea of tolerance and mutual concession is based on a standpoint which admits the compatibility of manifold philosophical views concerning the external world. The Indians are prone to tolerate the co-existence of various schools of philosophical thought from a metaphysical viewpoint; the Chinese are inclined to try to reconcile and harmonize them from a political

---

[1] *Luke*, xv, 26; xii, 49–53.

and practical viewpoint; and the Japanese tend to emphasize the historical and physiographical features of such diverse types of thought. Interference with religions on the part of the state was not very noticeable in India, but in China it occurred to a considerable extent, and in Japan it was occasionally extreme. Consequently, we hesitate to lump together these attitudes under the label 'Asiatic'. While in the modern West the spirit of tolerance and mutual concession was advocated especially by the thinkers of the Enlightenment or the Pietists, in the history of Asia and particularly of Iran, heretical views on religion have at times been relentlessly persecuted.

It is often emphasized by Westerners that Eastern thought has a tendency towards 'escapism' and that it is rather indifferent towards social and political action. We are told that Christianity preaches the importance of activity in this world whereas the dominant religions of Asia teach men to shun this world. Such sweeping criticisms seem to have become all too common in the West. It was Max Weber who asserted about Asian religions that, unlike the Protestant ethic, they inculcated indifference to the world,

be it in the form of external escapism, or be it expressed in actions indifferent to this world, although taking place in this world.[1]

On the other hand, the fundamental creed of Protestant ethics in the modern West is 'inner-worldly' asceticism.

It attempted to rationalize this world ethically by accepting the will of God positively, rather than to tend toward escapism as in the case of meditation. Daily conduct is elevated, through rationalization, to the level of a god-sent vocation, and this is also man's assurance of happiness.[2]

The ethics of Protestantism may indeed have been as described by Max Weber. But Western thought in and prior to the Middle Ages was not always characterized by an attitude of 'inner-worldly' rationalization. 'A herd of meditative, fanatic or insensitive devotees', as Max Weber called the religious men of Asia, have existed in the West as well as in the East. On the other hand, the fact that the religious men of the East were also conducting 'inner-worldly' activities can be noticed in various countries and periods. The religion that pervaded the various

[1] Max Weber, op. cit., II, S. 367.   [2] Ibid.

countries of East Asia was Mahāyāna Buddhism, which stresses such 'inner-worldly' activities. And we can also see in the religion of Iran a distinct tendency towards the worldly.

In this connection, it is often asserted that the Asian peoples follow nature and seek to realize the harmony of man and nature, whereas Westerners attempt to conquer nature. However, the attempt of man to assert himself and to conquer nature was not uncommon in Asia. In China and in India as well, the construction of canals, river banks, water tanks, and ramparts was regularly undertaken. On the other hand, the yearning for nature appeared also in the West, and there were periods when people sought to 'return to nature'. Accordingly, on this point also, it is very difficult for us to make a sharp distinction between the two hemispheres. Even at a philosophical level, the opposition of subject and object, for instance, was already taken up in ancient Indian philosophy. The reason why natural science has made remarkable progress in the West, especially in modern times, is interesting but it cannot be examined here. In any case, the attitudes towards nature in the West and the East are difficult to define or distinguish.

Max Weber states that during or prior to the Middle Ages, the ascetic life in the Christianity of the West had been tinged with a 'rational' character.[1] But then we must not overlook the fact that the workaday practices at Zen monasteries in Japan are extremely 'rationalistic', and the social work of Japanese priests even prior to the Middle Ages was very extensive. It is the writer's opinion that it is difficult to make a clear-cut distinction between the East and the West even on this particular point.

After having examined what have hitherto been designated as features peculiar to Eastern thought, we find ourselves in reality incapable of isolating a definite trait which can be singled out as a basis for contrast between East and West. It seems possible to recognize a few similarities common to the peoples of Asia, but it would be very misleading to regard them as general features that uniquely characterize the entire East and are wholly non-existent in the West. These features were regarded as 'Eastern' because they were conspicuous in certain countries in a certain period or among certain peoples. It is, therefore, hardly surprising that those features are not without some basis in fact. But we must

[1] Max Weber, *Die protestantische Ethik und der Geist des Kapitalismus*.

acknowledge the fact that there exists no single characteristic that is exclusively 'Eastern' or uniquely Asian. On the contrary, there have been diverse trends and ways of thinking in Asia, and none of them characterizes the whole of Asia.

This can be confirmed by a comparison between the cultures of the Asian peoples and by noting the fact that even Buddhism was received by various peoples of East Asia according to the character of the recipients. In other words, Buddhism, which is essentially universal in its message and transcends the distinctions between social classes and between nations, was adopted with certain modifications which were made according to the distinctive ways of thinking of each recipient people. No doubt there are basic similarities in the ways of thinking of Buddhists of various nations, since Buddhism is a world religion and it has especially exercised a profound influence over the spiritual and social life of the East Asian peoples. Buddhism, in so far as it is Buddhism, must be basically consistent wherever it may be found. But to say that there are similarities and parallelisms among the Buddhists of different Asian nations is obviously not tantamount to showing the parallelisms and similarities among the peoples of Asia as a whole.

We must necessarily conclude that there are no features of the ways of thinking exclusively shared by Asians as a whole. Furthermore, if the characteristic ways of thinking differ with each people, then the cultures of the peoples of Asia are indeed heterogeneous and cannot he lumped together even in contrast with European culture. A Japanese scholar recently remarked that the three nations, India, China, and Japan, have established respectively their own distinct cultures.[1] As far as the ways of thinking or folk-traits of each people are concerned, it seems proper for us to admit the truth of this remark. There is no single way of thinking generally applicable even to the East Asians. Why then are such phrases as 'Asian thought' or 'East Asian culture' used as if they were axiomatic concepts? Originally such concepts as 'East Asia', 'the East', or 'the Orient' were set up in opposition to 'the Occident'. In spite of their obscure connotation, these terms came to be used freely by the peoples of Asia when they were oppressed by the military and political superiority of Westerners. It was a natural attempt to preserve their respective cultural traditions. But

[1] Sokichi Tsuda, *Shina Shiso to Nippon.*

the famous slogan 'Asia is one' uttered by Kakuzo Okakura is not entirely accurate and does not accord with the reality of the history of Asian thought. The nations of East Asia, which have long cherished the desire to preserve and develop their respective cultures, inadvertently adopted Okakura's slogan because of the common feeling that they shared the same objective. This was simply a way of defending their respective cultures against the dominance of the West.

The desire on the part of various nations to preserve and develop their distinctive cultural traditions is indeed legitimate. We ought to respect this desire. But it behooves each nation to see to it that while being critical of foreign cultures, it remains critical of its own indigenous culture. With due modesty and self-awareness, a new culture should be formed through enlightened criticism. The neglect of self-criticism and the mere affirmation and preservation of the past would be tantamount to annihilating one's own culture. On the other hand, if we accept foreign cultures uncritically, this would be merely blind acceptance, and consequently, no positive contribution towards forming a common culture for mankind will have been made. Different cultures should develop in such a way as will be of universal significance for mankind in the future.

XVII. THE UNIQUENESS OF ASIA

as seen by a European

Hugh Tinker

The uniqueness which is here attributed to Asia is not envisaged as a quality which sharply differentiates Asia from the West. Rather, 'uniqueness' is interpreted to mean the special quality of Asia; that which gives Asian life and thought its meaning. This attempt to subsume the uniqueness of Asia is illustrated by three themes: man in harmony with time, man in harmony with nature, and man in harmony with man. These three prismatic aspects of harmony are specially vital to an understanding of Asia: but probably no Asian thinker (except the most debased and chauvinistic) would wish to claim any monopoly of virtue or insight in fostering these themes. After all, the Chinese, perhaps the most inward-looking of the great Asian cultures, tell us that 'In the Four Seas, all men are brothers'.

To the European, Asia will always be (geographically) the East. Where does Asia begin? Kipling said: East of Suez. And—though some specialists dislike the expression—'the Middle East' is a description that has symbolic truth. The narrow cleft in the barren hills which opens onto the antique city of Megiddo or Armageddon has a good claim to be regarded as the meeting point, and the flash-point, between North and South, East and West. Here, in 1948, Jews fought against Arabs; here, in 1918, Allenby's British and Australian troops fought against the Turks; here Franks fought against Saracens, Greeks fought Egyptians, and so back to the dawn-mists of man. If the Middle East has seen cultures in collision, it has also brooded over their birth. There is Ur of the Chaldees, the site of the Sumerian capital, with its great cumulus, *Ziggurat*, dating from before 2000 B.C. *Ziggurat*, 'Mountain of God', is connected with the cult of the sacred, royal mountain, Mount Meru, which was bequeathed by Hindu India to South-east Asia and the Far East. More than a thousand years after the raising of *Ziggurat*, in the little kingdom of King David, he who is called the Preacher proclaimed:

Vanity of vanities; all is vanity. What profit hath a man of all his labour which he taketh under the sun? . . . The thing that hath been, it is that which shall be; and that which is done is that which shall be done: and there is no new thing under the sun.[1]

Is not this Asia speaking? But is this not also the forerunner of Calvinist Protestantism?

The Semitic world and its religions evade our classification. Islam straddles Asia, Africa, and Europe (for there are indigenous Muslim communities in Hungary and Yugoslavia). Intellectually, this religion with its concepts of *halal* and *haram*, Lawful and Unlawful, stands apart from the Right and Wrong of Western Christianity and the *Dharma* of Hinduism. The Middle East, then, is middle ground between Europe and Asia; and here we will be mainly concerned with that Asia which stretches between Iran and China. This area (where dwell one-half of the human race) is still far wider than any scholar can comprehend. The writer does not pretend that this essay has any scholarly value: it is a personal statement, made by a man who has passed nearly a quarter of a century in an evolving relationship with Asia. During these years the writer was often well aware that he was seeing 'through a glass, darkly'. His emotional attitude towards Asia and Asians has registered excitement, wonder, bewilderment, frustration, bitterness, resignation, and finally—if such a claim is permissible—acceptance, with an affection infused, possibly, with some understanding.

The Harmony of Man with Time

> I saw Eternity the other night,
> Like a great ring of pure and endless light.

Henry Vaughan and William Blake, to go no further, remind us that Western man can know harmony with time. A cyclical sense of time, linking past and future, is common to most cultures. There is the sense of an ancient innocence, a Golden Age, and the sense

---

[1] Ecclesiastes, i, 2–9.

of promises to be accomplished: the Fullness of Days. Yet what mechanical view of time has come about in the West, partly through the Industrial Revolution! What do we say? 'Time waits for no man; time is money; on time; a waste of time.' We used to be aware of continuity: Edmund Burke wrote of the contract 'between the dead, the living, and those yet unborn', but increasingly Western man feels himself to be isolated from the past. First came 'the new woman', now we have 'the new men'. And in the nuclear age, the new men know that time for them is a kind of ledge upon which they stand poised over the abyss. 'Time is running out. . . . Living on borrowed time': these are the phrases of today. This divorce from time, this living in the fleeting moment, is demonstrated in everything: 'No time like the present', or just 'No time'. We live in a little compartment, the present. We are obsessed with our own importance: the characteristic religious phenomenon of our day is that of the Jehovah's Witnesses, insisting that Jesus Christ returned to this earth in 1914. No time to wait for the fullness of time! We want it here and now. Living in dread of The Bomb, people have ceased to have faith in tomorrow. Hence the popularity of 'deferred terms': 'Live now, pay later'. Perhaps you will never have to pay. Have a good time now. What is there to look forward to? Only annihilation.

Something of this Western neurosis was glimpsed by Rabindranath Tagore (though he never knew the present decline of the West). He supposes the West to put to Asia the proposition: 'You do not make any progress, there is no movement in you'. To which Tagore replies:

You have to judge progress according to its aim. A railway train makes its progress towards the terminus station—it is a movement. But a full-grown tree has no definite movement of that kind, its progress is the inward progress of life. It lives, with its aspiration towards light tingling in its leaves and creeping in its silent sap.

Tagore concludes:

Europe, while busily speeding to her engagements, disdainfully casts her glance from her carriage window at the reaper reaping his harvest in the field, and in her intoxication of speed cannot but think him as slow and ever receding backwards. But the speed comes to its end, the engagement loses its meaning and the hungry heart clamours for food, till at last she comes to the lowly reaper reaping his harvest in the sun.

The Asian sense of harmony with time is really a sense of time-lessness. The Malays have a saying, 'From the endless past to the endless future', and the Burmese say: 'Life is but a bubble on the ocean's surface'. It is interesting that this timelessness is illustrated by two great nations with entirely different views of history. It is not unreasonable to say that Indians had no consciousness of history, until their British mentors began to reconstruct the time-scale of India's long evolution.[1] Today, within a few miles of Delhi, one may listen to peasants telling stories about Prithvi Raj, the last Hindu ruler to resist the Muslims. Prithvi Raj lived before Robin Hood: but he is much more real and 'recent' to these village folk than Robin Hood ever was to English rustics. Such an absence of consideration for time could be expected of a people who, by and large, ignore history: but what of the Chinese, perhaps the most history-minded nation in the world? No other country has such a long and elaborate tradition of compiling official historical records: and of constantly referring to them. Yet, one element which the West regards as fundamental to a study of history is largely absent: a concern with social and political evolution. Nothing really changes in the Chinese historical view. Because the Chinese records state that 'tribute missions' were received from Tibet during the Ming dynasty, Tibet today is claimed as part of China, as of right. Confucius, who lived 2,500 years ago, is re-garded (or was, till yesterday) as the authority on contemporary social and political modes.

The sense of time as a continuum is perhaps most completely expressed in the concept of rebirth or transmigration, first elaborated in India, as recorded in the Upanishads. The spirit, or the essence of personality, does not belong to one person for one life: it is transmitted through an endless cycle of lives, carrying with it the burden of all the births that have gone before, fated to pass on to future existences this great legacy, together with the little more contributed during the present existence. The wheel, emblem of endless progression, always the same, is the symbol of life; and the wheel is placed at the centre of India's national flag. Gautama Buddha sought to liberate mankind from the endless wheel of life. His teaching denied the existence of the soul as an entity; denied

---

[1] The Muslims at once provide an exception. There is a considerable school of Indian (or Indianized) Muslim historians, and it is significant that the generic term for history, *Tarikh* (derived from Persian), means chronology or dates.

the very existence of an omnipotent God. Yet the doctrine of re-birth is as firmly embedded in Buddhism as in Hinduism. Indeed popular Buddhism places even greater emphasis on the trans-mission of the spiritual legacy from the past into the future: *karma*. Nirvana is a state of perfection to be reached only after aeons of progression. Men may acquire merit, but the burden of *karma* cannot lightly be dissolved. Relationships between individuals are made more complex because of the burden of causality which all carry.

The ritual of the festivals which mark the seasons of the year still yields a significance which has departed in the West. Whether Easter is conceived as a pagan festival of the spring, or as the Christian festival of the death and resurrection of Jesus Christ, it has ceased to be significant, except to a minority. To the mass, it is merely the first chance to take a trip to the sea, or otherwise relax. But in Asia, time and season still cannot be ignored. *Holi* in India and *Thingyan* in Burma both take the form of a Saturnalia; and both come when the hot weather is building up, and some relief of tension is needed. *Divali* in India and *Thadingyut* in Burma follow the rainy season. The crops are planted, and all is going well. The atmosphere is relaxed, sociable, thankful. In both these festivals a thousand little oil lamps glimmer in grateful illumination. Although these festivals serve to denote the passing of time, they also serve the deeper purpose of emphasizing eternity (as, indeed, the Christian festivals also do, to the believer). They serve to remind even the most impatient that no man, however ingenious, can advance the date of harvest or defer the onset of the hot weather. In the West, some may try to hoodwink time (one remembers the Earl, in Aldous Huxley's *After Many a Summer*) but in Asia time is not defied because time is timelessness. We may contrast our familiar English saying 'Hope deferred maketh the heart sick' with the Urdu *Dur ayd durust ayd*: 'That which comes slowly, comes well'. There is no virtue in hurry; neither is there any special virtue in punctuality. (This antithesis of the Anglo-American cult of hustle, of keeping to time, has been a cause of much misunderstanding.)

Because yesterday and today are one, the Asian attitude to the upkeep of old buildings and ancient things of beauty differs from the Western. The latter either shows contempt for the past—tear down the Guildhall to build the flyover—or else, reverently preserves the past as an interesting relic. Of course, there are ancient cathedrals, colleges, and other buildings still employed for their original purpose. But they are becoming the exception. The Asian way is to include the past within the present. This projection of the past into the present can be disconcerting to a Westerner. Ayudhia, the former capital of Siam, was sacked by Burmese invaders in 1767; the city is now largely a creeper-covered ruin, but to the Thai it is still a centre of their culture. Until a few years ago, a vast sitting Buddha contemplated the desolation from the picturesque remnants of an ancient, monumental shelter. Today, the Buddha, freshly painted with gold, is topped over by a brand-new scarlet and black pagoda. To Western tastes, a composition of ageing beauty has been gauded up like an effigy in a fun-fair. To Thai minds, a puissant symbol of the Noble Eightfold Path is renewed and restored, and Thai splendour re-established. And yet, as the Buddhist knows full well, neither past nor present are important for all this world is *Maya*, illusion. Let the last word come from Po Chü-i, a Chinese scholar-official, who lived A.D. 772–846.

> Can it be that when the mind travels backward
> The body also returns to its old state?
> And can it be, as between body and soul,
> That the body may languish, while the soul is still strong?
> Soul and body—both are vanities:
> Dreaming and waking—both alike unreal. [1]

Perhaps it is because the present, ourselves, is so important to Westerners that we have lost contact with past and future; whereas to the Asian the present is not entirely real, so past and future have an equal validity.

The Harmony of Man with Nature

Again there is really no 'confrontation' between the traditional attitude of the West and the traditional attitude of Asia. From Langland to Edward Thomas, poets have been nourished upon the English countryside; from Thoreau to Robert Frost, a similar symbiosis has inspired the poetry of New England. When we turn from art to life, this harmony still holds good. The vineyards of France; the rich, rolling farmland of southern Germany; the sheeplands of the Cotswolds: on all these man has bestowed his

[1] From Arthur Waley's translation, see *A Hundred and Seventy Chinese Poems*, Waley, London, 1923.

S

mark. For a thousand years he has cultivated, and fashioned the landscape with his tillage: but he has not abused his trust, and nature remains supreme.

With the Industrial Revolution, Western man renounced his ancient trusteeship and commenced, though with no system or purpose, to destroy nature. Let us take a short journey between Warrington and Wigan and view the refuse of the early Industrial Revolution. There are the spoil-heaps of the coal mines and other industrial waste; high, like hills, with no plant or other living thing upon them. There are the choked and stagnant canals. There are the rows of hutches in which the workers dwell. Even on a summer day the scene is dark, drab, unnatural. But it was not only the wrecking of the landscape which began with the Industrial Revolution; it was a new view of nature. The sailing-ship or the water-mill must respect nature; the engines of the Industrial Revolution gave man the illusion that he is master of nature. Nowhere is this carried to greater lengths than in North America. This is a continent where nature is mighty, and sometimes cruel. Man declared war on nature. First there was the extermination of wild life; the destruction of the buffalo, followed by the even more gruesome systematic massacre of the 'domesticated' bovine species in the stockyards of Chicago, the Belsen of the bulls. Then came war against the continent. What are the symbols of the American Way of Life? The great dams, which turn rivers around and despatch them, on man's business, in a direction contrary to that which they intend. The skyscrapers, pressing down on the earth. The super-highways—which do not, like the roads of man's natural fashioning, follow the contours of earth's breast, but gouge through hillside and stride over valley on concrete and steel. These are the symbols of man's conquest of nature. It is not surprising that nature fights back. With floods, avalanches, hurricanes, blizzards, nature takes revenge upon the insolence of man. Notwithstanding, Western man goes blindly on. Beyond the conquest of nature he plans its destruction. His ultimate aim is the reconstitution of nature itself, by the tearing apart of the basic unit of nature, the atom. Nuclear fission is man's highest bid to conquer nature; it is also his formula for destruction.

It is with relief that one returns to an Asia that lives in accord with nature. One need not pretend that this is inherent in primordial Asian cultures. Throughout a great arc of monsoon Asia,

the earliest form of agriculture is the shifting cultivation, sometimes called 'slash and burn'. The forest is roughly cleared, crops
are sown in the cleared ground for a number of years, and then,
when the fertility of the soil is exhausted, the cultivator moves on
to a fresh clearing. This type of agriculture—called *jhum* in India,
taungya in Burma, and *ladang* in the Malay-speaking world—is
still practised; and except where the rainfall is unusually high, the
effect is to upset the balance of nature. Throughout hundreds of
miles of South-east Asia, the traveller can see the evidence of
former shifting cultivation in a wretched wilderness.

Indeed, the life of primitive man in Asia was singularly out of
harmony with the universe. Among the simple tribes that live on
the Burma–China border, one still discovers a world of fear. The
jungle is supposed to be filled with evil spirits; the most simple
agricultural operation is fraught with hazards introduced by
hostile demons. The sense of harmony only enters with the rise
of the major civilizations of Asia. And even today, the Asian
peasant nurtures a sense of resignation, of acceptance of calamity,
which arises from folk-memories of the power of nature. The
Indian peasant who knows that he can never be certain that the
monsoon will come to bring his crops to bear and to feed his herds
and flocks; the Chinese peasant who recalls how the great rivers
have flooded and changed their courses, bringing destruction to
millions: these know that harmony with nature cannot be taken
for granted. It must be patiently cultivated, by carefully observing
the right rules, the right customs.

This cultivated harmony is aptly illustrated by the 'Royal
Ploughing' which was observed in China and South-east Asia. In
Burma and Siam, it was customary for the king to inaugurate the
season of ploughing by himself ceremonially ploughing the first
furrows of the royal fields, which lie beside the walls of the royal
palace. As he broke the earth, Brahmins, Buddhist monks, and
'spirit charmers' (*natsok*, in Burmese) would chant prayers and
ritual charms; and if all were properly performed, the country
would be ensured of a prosperous harvest. Today, in Thailand,
the ceremony is still performed; though the Minister of Agriculture
is now deemed the appropriate dignitary to carry out this function!
Propitiation of the spirits of stream, forest, and field is still carefully observed by most of the farmers of South-east Asia and China.

On a more practical plane, the harmony of man with nature is to be seen in the careful regulations which are applied in areas of irrigation. Karl Wittfogel wrote his *Oriental Despotism* to show that systems based upon irrigation (what he termed 'hydraulic society') were especially under the power of arbitrary human will: despotism. In reality, it appears that irrigation systems bring about the highest degree of social consultation and co-operation. In the irrigated areas of Burma and Ceylon, village societies developed their own codes of regulation whereby the precious water was utilized for the general good. Village tribunals (notably, the *gansabhawas* of Ceylon) ensured that the individual cultivator respected the needs of society.

Perhaps the most distinctive way in which man and nature are in harmony in Asia can be seen in the attitude of man to the animals. It is here, perhaps, that there is the sharpest contrast with Western, Christian attitudes. Despite Anglo-American sentimentality about dogs ('man's best friend') there is a clear difference between man and the animals, sometimes termed 'the lower creation'. Man has a soul, and the prospect of immortality. Animals are brutes, insensate; and their purpose is to serve the needs of man. It may be argued that neither Islam nor the culture of China have more than a neutral attitude towards animals: but in the Hindu and Buddhist view, the animals and man are all part of the divine process. Certain animals, it is true, are on a more elevated plane: these include the monkey, the snake, the elephant, and the cow. The cult of the snake, *naga*, as an emblem of royalty, spread through South-east Asia, and into the Far East. The cult of the cow has also been spread (though less widely) to the neighbours of India. The cult of the cow and the cult of the mother have a certain similarity. Many trees have a sacred quality. The pipal tree, known also as the *bo* tree, is revered in India and South-east Asia because it was beneath its branches that Lord Buddha attained enlightenment. Similarly, the banyan tree is sacred to Hindus, and many shrines will be found among the banyan roots; while disputes are often resolved under its branches, and solemn oaths ratified by the placing of hands upon the banyan tree. Among plants, the lotus has a symbolism which gives it a quality of sanctity. Rivers, also, may have divine qualities; everybody knows that the Ganges is considered sacred; but other Asian countries have what, for them, are equally sacred waters; for example, the *Chao Phaya Menam* of Thailand. Sacred mountains recur in the theology of many lands, and almost every Asian country has its Olympus. Ceylon has a mountain upon which the footprint of the Buddha is said to have been imprinted: this is known as Adam's Peak, because (according to the Arabs) it was here that Adam looked his last on the Garden of Eden. India has the Himalaya, regarded as the foothills to Mount Meru, the mythical centre of the world, the abode of the gods, described in the *Mahabharata*; Burma has Mount Popa (another Meru) and China has the Kwan-lun mountains, the abode of Hsi Wang Mu, the Queen Mother of the West. Japan has sacred Mount Fuji.

This awareness of the divine presence in nature leads to a different treatment by Asian man of animals and even plants and the terrain. Today, in India, most of the States enforce laws against cow slaughter, while in Burma strict control over slaughter-houses has the same purpose. This is the political expression of a social attitude. It cannot be argued that all Asian societies are concerned to preserve animal life. It might be said that the Chinese, for example, are quite indifferent about protecting animals, yet this would ignore such phenomena as the ritual importance assigned to the preserving and feeding of turtles in Chinese temples. There are many paradoxes in Asian attitudes: for example, the Burmese Buddhist, who abhors the taking of life of warm-blooded creatures, finds no evil in catching and eating fish or prawns. But underlying all, there is this awareness that the animal world is not separate, inferior, but that it has a living association with the world of man.[1] We have the well-known story from the youth of the Lord Buddha when, as Prince Siddhartha, he rescued the wild swan shot by his cousin Devadatta and, refusing to hand the bird over to its hunter, nursed it, until it was whole again.[2]

---

[1] Rudyard Kipling is so often dismissed as depicting the Sahib's India that it is worth recalling that he did intuitively understand this empathy between man and the animals. The *Jungle Books* in their entirety illustrate this understanding, but a special quality illuminates 'The Miracle of Puran Bhagat'. Because Kipling's books bore the sign of the swastika, critics suggested that he was a proto-Nazi; but the swastika (reversed in the Nazi version) is the ancient symbol of the mingling of the complementary forces of nature.

[2] A paradigm of this story of the Buddha is contained in 'The Drum of Justice' (see Htin Aung, *Burmese Law Tales*, O.U.P. 1962) where a crane is killed by a prince and the crane's widow seeks retribution from the king by sounding the drum of justice. She is promised the life of the prince, but by a clever twist of the story, she is assuaged, and the prince's life is saved. 'Remember that the aim of justice is to give satisfaction to all parties, so that the King's subjects may live in accord and harmony': so ends this legal parable.

The feeling of the identity of man with nature is symbolized in the constant reproduction of the macrocosm of the world in the microcosm of the locality. Many Asian cities were designed to reproduce the universe in their shape (circular or rectangular), with their own moat (the surrounding sea), their symbolic gates, representing the points of the compass, and at the centre an elevated tower or mount (Mount Meru). In China and Japan there is the cult of the miniature garden, which encompasses nature within a little space. The painting and other graphic art of Asia is primarily concerned with nature. This is specially true of Chinese art, with its scroll pictures of Chinese rivers, depicted from the source to the sea, and its incomparable studies of birds, horses, flowers, and foliage. Such a pinnacle of perfection is not attained, say, in the paintings of the Rajput school, or in the Ayudhya style of Thailand. But there is the same sense of nature constantly welling up in the life of man.

Perhaps this sentiment may appropriately be illustrated by a vignette drawn from Burmese village life. It does not attain the high artistic quality of many better-known Asian evocations of nature (for example, the delicious poem by T'ao Ch'ien translated by Arthur Waley as *Reading the Book of Hills and Seas*), but it has a simplicity which gives it power. The passage is taken from *Konmara Pya Zat*, a play by U Pok Ni (1879), and the translation is by Dr. Hla Pe, slightly adapted.

It is . . . the evening twilight and the sun's crystal beams are dim; the villagers, as is their usual practice, are hailing one another and . . . they have kindled the mosquito-fires among the feeding troughs, big and small. Everywhere darkness prevails. Fog and mist envelop the whole place. . . . According to the [common] saying, we have come to the time 'when brothers hardly recognise each other', 'the time when the unbroken cattle are driven into the pen'. . . . In our country village, with its threshing floor on the rising ground and the mists all round, there is no sweet-pealing time drum. Just like our fathers before us we are satisfied to take the crowing of the golden cock . . . as giving the correct time. The evening cockcrow denotes and heralds unmistakably 'the children's bed-time'. A little later it crows with a full voice: all the adults will be lying in their beds. It is termed 'the head on pillow cock'. Again, after that, it is rightly called 'bachelor's return'. After this is 'midnight cock'. Before the glassy colour has appeared on the sky; in the hour of half-dark and half-light, the cock crows and declares the time and it is known as 'cock of earliest dawn'. One crow after this the [glow of sunrise] emerges. Glassy colours spread out and boldly tread the eastern sky. This is usually the 'day-break crow'. . . . Noisily up to the third stage of night, for three several times, the cock flapping its wings has crowed.

Here, man's routine, the passage of time, and the ritual of nature are all blended and expressed through the common rustic terms for the different phases of night-time. Here, there is understanding: and communion. Of Japan, Rabindranath Tagore said: 'She does not boast of her mastery of nature, but to her she brings, with infinite care and joy, her offerings of love'.

The Harmony of Man with Man

Perfect harmony between man and man can never be in this world. Every great religion teaches brotherhood; but always man creates some flaw in the jewel. It is the peculiar failing of the West to have substituted for the ideal of harmony between man and man a series of intellectual justifications for disharmony, which have led to the growth of difference not merely due to ignorance or sin but actually promoted by ideologies and institutions.

The first great division arose from the exclusive nature of the Christian religion. Like Islam, it is a vigorously proselytizing faith, and like Islam it judges all those who are not true believers as infidels. Of course, Buddhism is also a missionary religion; while Hinduism is an exclusive system, regarding those beyond its boundaries as *mleccha*, unclean. Yet both these religions can make some claim to being tolerant. Buddhism can make such a claim with justice: the example of Mindon Min, King of Burma, who erected at his own expense at Mandalay an Anglican church, an American Baptist church, and a Roman Catholic church, has no counterpart in the West.[1] Christianity has been specially prone to that most hideous form of war, the war of religion. First there were the wars against the Muslims, the Crusades; then came internecine wars between Catholics and Protestants in Europe; and finally there are even battles among Protestants—as, for example, the bloody persecution of the Mormon pioneers in the United States.

[1] Ceylon, from 1956 onward, has demonstrated that Buddhism, debased for political purposes, can be as intolerant and vicious towards other faiths as any of the militant religions: but see the later argument that Asia is in danger of surrendering its uniqueness today.

If religion was the first major source of division in the West, the next great divider was nationalism. This has proved the cause of even more extensive wars. Based upon the principle that those who speak the same speech form one nation and one state, nationalism went on to brand all those outside this category as foreign, potentially hostile. E. M. Arndt in his poem *The German Fatherland* declaims: 'What is the fatherland of the German? Name me the great country! As far as the German tongue sounds. . . . That is the fatherland of the German—where anger roots out foreign presumption, where every Frenchman is called enemy, where every German is called friend.'

Allied to nationalism is the even more perverted fissile concept of racialism. It may be argued that the sentiment—'Here's a foreigner: let's throw a brick at him'—is characteristic of all times and places.[1] Again, it is the noxious distinction of the West to have elevated this atavism into a principle. At any rate, in its popular form, Darwinism, 'the survival of the fittest', appears to offer a scientific justification for the ancient wrong that the strong may domineer over the weak. In the nineteenth century, the West was supreme in economic and military strength; Asia and Africa were negligible. As they became the rulers of vast areas of Asia, the Europeans (perhaps not surprisingly) saw themselves as Olympians, and their wards as

> Your new-caught, sullen peoples
> Half-devil and half-child.

The Pandora's Box of racialism will continue to play havoc among mankind for many decades yet, The concept of class has, perhaps, passed its apogee. This insidious form of division acquired its most subtle quality in nineteenth-century Britain. Barriers of pretence have been evolved, which mean nothing, but are vital to those obsessed by class ritual. School, club, regiment, college, profession—even church or county: all these have their own code of U and non-U, recognized by the cognoscenti. All quite harmless? Outside observers do not think so.

Out of the concept of class have emerged the two dominant political philosophies of the West. It is very much in accordance with the general argument of this essay that the most potent

---

[1] For a more coherent analysis of the concept of racialism in Asia, see the present writer's 'Race, Nationalism and Communalism in Asia' in *Man, Race and Darwin*, ed. Philip Mason, O.U.P., 1960.

ideology to come out of nineteenth-century Europe, Marxism, postulates the existence of a state of conflict between the classes, based upon the exploitation of one class by another. The principal answer evolved to counter this thesis is that of 'private enterprise', the freedom of the individual to make his gain by the operation of the market; that is, the free-play of economic forces, without regard to social obligation. In neither of these political concepts does the community, or social harmony, have any place. The basic premise is that there is a struggle, in which success can only be achieved when an advantage has been gained; whether of one class over another, or of the individual over others.

Among the consequences of the acceptance of one or other of these ideologies, coupled with the rise of the nation-state, has been the disintegration of society. First, the community was destroyed by the Industrial Revolution, leaving men (in the phrase of the Indian social philosopher Jayaprakash Narayan) as a 'fortuitous concourse of atoms'. In the process, that social unit which has been the foundation of mankind since the dawn of time has broken up: the family. First the extended family of brothers and cousins disappeared from European thinking. Then, more tragically, came the disintegration of the closest relationships. No longer do sons accept an obligation to protect their parents in old age. Indeed, the elderly have now become a separate category, unwanted, and often rejected by society. Close behind the alienation of the old came the weakening of the ties of marriage. Inevitably, then came the alienation of the young; the diminution of the sense of parental responsibility, and the growth of the concept of the 'teenager' as a separate species, viewing parents and the adult world at large as unfriendly, even enemy territory.

This picture of disharmony in the West is, no doubt, drawn in darker tones than many would accept. The purpose is to illumine the profounder sense of social harmony which infuses Asia even to this day.

The whole social and political philosophy of traditional China was founded upon the concept of harmony. Within the family, a code of parental care and filial piety secured the amenities of family life by a pattern of courtesy and adjustment. Because the family owed its origins to the ancestors, an elaborate ritual of ancestral observances was evolved. The family was the microcosm of the empire, and the Emperor was the father of his people. He, too, governed under a divine system. The Mandate of Heaven was bestowed upon a dynasty, but if authority was abused or neglected, signs and portents, natural disasters, would indicate that the Mandate was exhausted. When the Mandate was withdrawn, the dynasty inevitably came to an end, and the Mandate of Heaven was bestowed upon a new ruler, distinguished by his virtue. For over two thousand years, the Middle Kingdom, empire and family, followed the tenets of Confucius. It would not be entirely fanciful to suggest that, in Chairman Mao, the Chinese people have again found a universal father-figure, and in Maoism a new harmony.

We may admit that Asia has had its full share of conflict: of wars, persecution, and other categories of 'man's inhumanity to man'. We have to accept the existence of paradoxes. For example, Buddhist teaching constantly emphasizes that to take human life is the worst of evils: yet two of the most devout Buddhist countries, Burma and Ceylon, have today the worst statistics for murder in the world. Often, the apparent paradox is resolved on closer examination. Many would say that the most extreme example of social fragmentation, the setting apart of one man from another by absolute social laws, is provided by caste in India. Yet caste is also a syncretism, to enable society to operate in harmony, with mutual recognition of functions. The concept of *jajmani* involves a complex nexus of relationships between patrons and clients which links high and low castes in a strange brotherhood. At the most intimate moments—birth, betrothal, and death—the high castes are ministered to by such low-caste folk as the barber and the sweeper. When the highest of all the Rajput princes, the Maharana of Udaipur, was installed upon the throne, he was anointed upon the forehead with the *tika* of sovereignty by a Bhil, an aboriginal, outside of caste. It was not altogether without justification that Rabindranath Tagore could say of the caste system that it represented

experiments in evolving a social unity within which all the different peoples could be held together while fully enjoying the freedom of maintaining their own differences ... [within] a social federation whose common name is Hinduism.

The aboriginal peoples or *adibasis* have, over the centuries, been accepted into Hinduism by a process which anthropologists now term 'Sanskritisation'. Moreover, caste is emphatically not class.

A Brahmin may be a scribe, or a soldier, or a cultivator; he may be rich or poor. Among the *biradari* or *bhaiband*, the fraternity of the caste, every level of wealth and poverty, education and illiteracy, is likely to be found.

Social harmony is founded in the family. From babyhood to oldest age, the family shields, protects (and, it must be admitted, often stifles). Seniority is strictly observed, and the young must show deference to their elders; but there is seldom any likeness to the reign of terror which occasionally gripped the Victorian English family. In English eyes, the Asian child (whether he or she be Indian, Chinese, Burmese, or Malay) is absurdly cosseted. A crying baby is almost unknown.[1] Throughout life, the individual is supported by the family. A colleague of the present writer, a senior Indian administrator, once confessed: 'I never make a decision without consulting my mother'. The family spreads out to take in cousins, nephews, and nieces. Somewhere among the relatives there will be one who has become successful or wealthy: he is under an obligation to provide a kind of family social security system. A Burmese proverb declares that: 'A good tree can lodge ten thousand birds'. One need not be sentimental about the Asian family welfare system: the orphaned cousin who is taken in will be often treated as an unpaid servant. But even at its worst, the system does ensure that, in Asia, there are very few aged grandparents living alone in garrets, and few fatherless children immured in orphanages.

Social manners in Asia express very clearly the importance of harmony. Under all circumstances, one should preserve the amenities, maintain a polite accord. The Malays, whose manners are (even by Asian standards) a model of courtesy, pride themselves on never showing upon their features any disturbance, on always preserving an urbane decorum. This difference has, presumably, led to the Western stereotype of 'the inscrutable Oriental' who never reveals his feelings. Yet behind the politeness there lies a wealth of human feeling; and once a friendship has been formed, the Asian delights to show his affection for his friend to an extent that the truly reserved Englishman finds embarrassing.

Beyond the family there is the association of the village. So much has been written about the 'village republics' of Asia, that it

[1] Kipling called Japan 'The land of little children, where the Babies are the Kings'.

is superfluous to enlarge upon the importance of village solidarity in the outlook of Asia. The Arabic-Persian word *watan* often is employed in southern and western Asia to denote 'home' in the wider sense: meaning one's native place, where one belongs. To many, village and *watan* are synonymous. The brotherhood of the village community is illustrated by proverbs; for example, the Burmese: 'When it is scarce, share it; when it is plentiful, take your fill', or the Malay: 'When the right leg is wounded, the left also feels the pain'. This village spirit is well exemplified in the Philippines, where the term for the mutual obligations of the village kinsfolk is called *lusong*. The Filipino villager often wishes to shift his bamboo house to a new site: he will then invoke the claims of village loyalty, and his kinsfolk will gather with stout branches and all will join in carrying the house to its new site. This operation, called *bayanihan*, is often cited to illustrate the sense of village co-operation.

Rabindranath Tagore was expressing an underlying truth when he wrote:

In India the production of commodities was brought under the law of social adjustments. Its basis was co-operation. . . . But in the West it is guided by the impulse of competition, whose end is the gain of wealth for individuals.

Tagore understood that the India of his day was moving away from an age-old community outlook towards the individualism of Western competition. Therefore, he devoted his later life to social reconstruction; while his great compeer, Gandhi, although involved much more in political strategy, was essentially a social reformer, urging voluntary service and co-operation. The *khaddar* movement of Gandhi, which to many Western observers seemed a cranky aberration, was vital to the Mahatma's purpose. By insisting that all his followers, including the most intellectual, the most urban, should spin and weave a quota of handloom cloth, they thereby became identified with the ordinary labour of ordinary Indians. In this, Gandhi was only the last of a line of Indian teachers, such as Kabir, Nanak, and Chaitanya, who have preached and practised dissolution of caste and the ultimate brotherhood of men.

After the first heady experiences of independence had abated, some of the more clear-sighted Asian leaders began to search for means to reassert the values of tolerance and harmony in the new and feverish atmosphere of party politics. Dissatisfaction with attempts to operate parliamentary and cabinet government, based upon a Western-type party system, led to a revulsion against what critics called 'Fifty-One Per Cent Democracy' and attempts to promote harmony through emphasizing consensus. This is a trend that could (though it need not) lead to authoritarianism.

Indonesia under President Sukarno has always placed great emphasis on consensus. Frequent reference is made to the traditional village sense of mutual help or *gotong rotong*; on the necessity to approach problems through consultation (*musjawarah*) and to reach decisions through the collective 'sense of the meeting' (*mufakat*). In announcing his *Pantja Sila* or Five Principles in 1945, Sukarno began with *Bhinneka Tunggal Ika* or 'Unity in Diversity'. Having experimented with parliamentary government, in 1957 Sukarno inaugurated Guided Democracy. Parliament was superseded by a National Council, broadly representative of functional groups, while the cabinet was made equally representative of the four main political movements. Similarly Nepal, after a chaotic parliamentary interregnum, has now embraced 'partyless panchayat democracy', based upon corporate village and functional representation.

Though India is still a parliamentary democracy, the major emphasis in contemporary political thinking is to discover a solution to the factionalism of party politics. The most complete solution is that of *Sarvodaya*, 'uplift for all', or philosophy of social harmony, based upon *dharma* or the moral law, and *satyagraha*, the soul-force of non-violence. This philosophy is closely linked with *Bhoodan*, the land-gift movement, and it attempts to further Gandhi's ideal of a decentralized federation of village republics, in which the true spirit of India will re-emerge, freed from the accretions of the West. The goal is a 'participating democracy', which the ordinary people would contribute towards their own governance by word and deed, and where particular interests and political factions would give way to the people: or what Jayaprakash Narayan calls 'the communitarian society'. Even such a Westernized thinker as Nehru was influenced by this approach. Nehru stated: 'All our schemes and planning, our ideas of education and of social and political organization, have at their back the search for unity and harmony'.

Without doubt, it was this 'search for unity and harmony' that was behind the attempt to promote international harmony in Asia: Peaceful Co-Existence. The final communiqué of the Asian-African Conference at Bandung in 1955 called upon the participating nations to be 'true to the age-old tradition of tolerance and universality' of their cultures, and to work for international co-operation. We may properly be cynical about some aspects of Neutralism. When President Sukarno says: 'Internationalism cannot flower if it is not rooted in the soil of nationalism; nationalism cannot flower if it does not grow in the garden of internationalism' —we are bound to evaluate this in terms of his peculiar form of internationalism in action. At its highest, though, Neutralism is an attempt to place international relations on a new plane. Here are words spoken by U Nu, formerly Premier of Burma, at Bandung:

It may have been permissible in the days of conventional weapons for nations to live in a perpetual atmosphere of suspicion and mistrust. But in the nuclear age, such a concept is obsolete. We cannot afford to live in mistrust of our neighbours. We have to learn to live in mutual trust and confidence, and where this happy state has not existed in the past, someone has to break the ice. For trust also begets trust, and confidence begets confidence.

Neutralism, the attempt to foster trust, foundered in the high Himalaya. It was never viewed with sympathy in the West. The alternative international concept of the 'Cold War' follows the line of conflict which has bitten so deep into Western attitudes.

How far is the conflict between India and China a reflection of traditional attitudes, how far a sign that Asia is absorbing so much of the spirit of the West that it will soon be impossible to speak of the uniqueness of Asia? On the Chinese side, it may be argued that there is a re-assertion of traditional sentiments about the Middle Kingdom and its relations with surrounding tributaries and the barbarians beyond. India's attitude, however, appears to derive entirely from Western concepts of boundaries and claims based upon 'national' rights. It is all too obvious that the Asian of today is still trying to attain an international equality of status by imitating the West; and in the process taking over many of the Western aberrants discussed in this essay. There is the general paradox that Asia is adopting the essentially material criteria of development which the West has evolved in economic growth.[1] In this process, Asia is losing its own values. By becoming committed to a series of Five Year Plans, for example, Indian leaders have accepted the shallow, compartmentalized view of time which has become general in the West. By accepting nationalism, with all its slavish restrictions, Asian leaders are in a fair way to outdoing nineteenth-century Europeans in contributing to divisions between man and man. Today, in Asia, it is the village people and the elderly who preserve the Asian spirit; the leaders and the new men still pay lip service, but not the service of their hearts.

This essay has not attempted to enter the sphere of Asian philosophy, of which the writer is quite unqualified to speak. Surely the spirit of harmony finds its highest expression here? Whether it is the *Tao* of China, or the complementary nature of *Yin* and *Yang*; whether it is the harmony with nature and harmony in society cultivated in the *Shinto* Canon of Japan, the *Dharma* of Hinduism, or the *Damma* of Theravada Buddhism: the essence is harmony. Even an outsider may taste of the essence. The writer has memories of three great centres of Buddhism. He has lived near Sarnath, the deer-park in which the Buddha attained enlightenment, where there is a green stillness and a brooding calm. He has penetrated to the central shrine, deep in the massive stupa of the Ananda pagoda at Pagan in central Burma; there to find the kneeling figures of King Kyanzittha, its founder, and his monk-minister Shin Arahan. For more than eight centuries they have knelt, gazing up at the massive figure of the Lord Buddha, standing, his hand raised in compassion. The serenity of the Ananda transcends the boundaries of religion. And then the writer has wandered amid the monuments of Anuradhapura, where green trees and scented air surround the great seated Buddha, 'with that deep hush subduing all'. From out of such experiences, the writer is 'richer by Asia'. He finds himself out of sorts with the petty class differences of his own country, the vulgar pursuit of affluence, the futile cultivation of the remnants of Imperial grandeur. He is appalled by the noise and hustle, sickened by the callous disregard of gentleness. He tries to find that harmony with nature, with time, and with mankind, which he sees as the main mark of the Asian genius.

---

[1] For an original view of this subject see E. F. Schumacher, *Roots of Economic Growth*, Gandhian Institute of Studies, Banaras, especially 'Economics in a Buddhist Country', and 'Non-violent Economics'.

To cultivate the Asian spirit, it is not necessary for the European to minimize his own intellectual inheritance. Western man is able to enjoy in widest measure the gift of individuality. Individual salvation is inherent in Hinduism and Buddhism; individual decision is emphasized by Zoroastrianism; yet the Western tradition—Christian and Humanist—was the seedbed for the intellectual renaissance, beginning in the sixteenth century, which developed the concept of individuality to its highest point in political and moral philosophy.

The present writer, while cherishing this concept of the free individual, as elaborated by the West, is much exercised by the dilemma of upholding freedom for the individual, while recognizing the need for the integration of the community and the need for social action and co-operation in the West.

It may be that the vision of Asia can open the door. Both the Man of Galilee and Gautama the Buddha have taught that the individual can only find liberation through subsuming his spirit in a wider union.

> Seeking nothing, he gains all;
> Foregoing self, the Universe grows 'I'.

This is the message of Asia: will the Asia of today and tomorrow listen?

TOWARDS CO-EXISTENCE

The 'East-West' division is a myth, but it is no less dangerous for that; indeed it is, perhaps, for that very reason, the more dangerous. The younger Tolstoy relates in his Reminiscences that his father used to tell a story of a man who thought he was made of glass and begged his friends not to jostle him. By way of a joke, one of them did; and the poor fellow cried 'ping' and died.

What to do with such myths? To judge from the experience of Jewry there are many ways, all of them useful up to a point, none of them perfect or complete. One (cf. the Irishman who found himself in a field of bulls) is to look them firmly in the face and pass on. A second is to create other and more powerful myths to fight them. A third is to spread more accurate knowledge of the facts. This last method, though appealing to the academic intelligence, is the least practical. Parva est veritas; it is the received 'image' (myth!) which prevails. Yet even in our day truth is of some small significance. It can at least be advanced as a basis for argument, and when argument is allowed there is hope. Unfortunately, recent history seems to rest on the assumption that argument is not allowed.

LEON ROTH

T

XVIII. THE DIALOGUE BETWEEN
ASIA AND EUROPE[1]

Joseph Needham

For three thousand years a dialogue has been going on between the two ends of the Old World. Greatly have they influenced each other, and very different are the cultures they have produced. We have now good reason to think that the problems of the world will never be solved so long as they are considered only from a European point of view. It is necessary to see Europe from the outside, to see European history, and European failure no less than European achievement, through the eyes of that larger part of humanity, the peoples of Asia (and indeed also of Africa).

Pride and Prejudice

Many people in Western Europe and European America suffer from what may be called spiritual pride. They are firmly convinced that their own form of civilization is the only universal form. In deep ignorance of the intellectual and social conceptions and traditions of other peoples, they think it quite natural to impose upon them their own ideas and customary practices, whether of law, of democratic society, or of political institutions. Yet they propagate a culture which is somewhat self-contradictory, for Europe has never fully succeeded in reconciling the material and the spiritual, the rational and the romantic. And their way of life tends to corrode and destroy those of neighbouring cultures, some of which may embody saner values.

Now the rise of modern science and technology in Western Europe, bringing in its train powers over nature previously unimaginable, has given Americans and Europeans an almost

[1] Adapted from the Presidential Address to the Britain-China Friendship Association, 1955.

unconscious psychology of dominance. This mentality has been confirmed by the annexations, wars of conquest, and 'punitive expeditions' of the period of colonial expansion, so that today European-American values are offered, as it were, at the point of a Bren gun, with the atomic mushroom looming in the background. Christian civilization shows no better Christian humility today than it did at the time of the Crusades, when yet the civilization of Islam was on the whole a higher one than that of Europe. But a self-esteem then merely absurd is today a grave menace to all human beings.

Universality and Superiority

It is sometimes said that European culture has a universal vocation, a superior creative dynamic activity, distinguishing it from all others. Its expansion is held to be the natural consequence of this 'superiority'. And Western European culture seems still to be spreading through the whole world, while other cultures remain local, and hard put to it to defend their territories.

Universality and superiority are comforting conclusions for Westerners to reach about themselves. Yet there is a fallacy in it. That the civilization of Europe did indeed produce the modern unified world entity of the aerofoil and the radio wave is a historical fact. But this was done not by lawyers, by theologians, by politicians, by writers; it was done by engineers and scientists. What must be asked, therefore, is which parts of modern 'European' world civilization are universal, and which parts are locally and parochially European? Once the question is rightly stated the answer is obvious. The real universal factors are modern science and modern technology, together with the philosophies which made them possible. And it should be clearly understood that Europe did not give rise to 'European' or 'Western' science, but to universally valid world science.[1]

[1] It is extremely interesting that this distinction was appreciated by the Chinese from the very beginning of the introduction of modern science from Europe by the Jesuits. About 1640 there was discussion in Peking as to whether the new sciences were primarily 'Western' or primarily 'New'. The Jesuit missionaries wanted the accent to be on the Western origin because the religion which they propagated was Western in Chinese eyes, and their aim was to support and commend it by the prestige of the science which accompanied it. But the Chinese objected to the word 'Western' used by the Jesuits in the titles of the scientific books which they wrote and translated; and in 1669 the Khang-Hsi emperor finally insisted that it should be dropped in favour of 'New'.

Now scientists and engineers of all races and peoples well understand each other whenever and wherever they meet; they speak the same language, they know the same truth. For Nature is no respecter of persons. All human beings, irrespective of race as of sex, given the training and the adequate qualification, are equal in the presence of the natural fact. And science is essentially a social undertaking. Observers of Nature form a world community. If I descend into the depths my brother is there also; if I fly up into the heavens, my pilot can be a Chinese, my co-pilot an Indian; my navigator an African. He that despiseth man despiseth not Man, but—Nature. This kind of mistake is not made with impunity.

The basic fallacy of Europocentrism is therefore the tacit assumption that because modern science and technology, which grew up indeed in post-Renaissance Europe, are universal, everything else European is universal also.[1] Roman law is 'obviously' the greatest achievement of the human mind in jurisprudence, Greek philosophy (it goes without saying) the nearest approach to metaphysical truth ever attained by humanity, our own religion (with all its most minor accidents of time, place, and theory) revealed truth incumbent upon all men everywhere to believe. European painting and sculpture is 'absolute' painting and sculpture; that which artists of all other cultures must have been trying unsuccessfully to attain. European music is music; all other music is anthropology. And what is good enough (in cinema, reading-matter, or way of life) for the European (or American) man in the street, must be good enough for everybody.

Drastic revision of these unspoken assumptions is urgently

[1] Some eminent European scholars say that modern science and technology, in their victorious spread throughout the world, have been accompanied by a mutilated secularized form of European civilization. And they note with distress that the European religious values have been decisively rejected by all Asian and African movements of national independence. For these scholars regard the civilization of Christendom as formally inseparable from the modern scientific view of the world; the necessary concomitant of the latter. From this it might be but a step to the preaching of a new crusade to impose fuller forms of European religion upon the rest of the world. Crosses might figure on its banners, but needless to say, capitalism and imperialism would carry them. Exactly what philosophy is the necessary accompaniment of modern science and technology has never yet been adequately formulated, though the problem has been in the minds of all the great Chinese reformers and revolutionaries for the past hundred years. Chinese scholars of the present day would certainly point to dialectical materialism as the answer. The Far West has not so far offered any serious alternative.

necessary. The view often put forward that Western European civilization alone has produced a true historical sense is quite inadmissible. If any civilization were to be chosen for this honour it should be that of the Chinese, whose twenty-four dynastic histories, from 90 B.C. onwards, constitute a state-supported (but largely independent) corpus of historical writing unapproached elsewhere in the world. This is to say nothing of the lesser, though still very great, compilations such as the *Tzu Chih Thung Chien* (eleventh cent. A.D.) and the *Wên Hsien Thung Khao* (fourteenth cent. A.D.). Even if the term 'historical sense' be taken to mean 'philosophy of history', the European contributions were not the earliest. Ibn Khaldun lived some three centuries before Vico. Again, in philosophy, the ideas that in Chinese thought 'celestial immobility' was the supreme value, and that this corresponded with a 'static' quality of Chinese civilization, are both quite indefensible. The 'unmoved mover' was an essentially Greek idea; the Chinese conception of the Tao implied constant and unceasing activity, as in the apparent diurnal revolution of the stars. Of course instances of both kinds of valuation of rest and motion can be found in both civilizations. There was never anything static about Chinese civilization, except that (a) it proved capable of having a longer continuous history of recognizable identity as to language and culture than any other has been able to show (with the possible parallel of Israel), and (b) it did not produce any social phenomenon comparable to that of the European Renaissance with all its concomitant and following changes. There were in China periods of rapid advance and periods of relative quiescence, as in all other cultures.

Europeans must realize today that they should share with their brothers of Asia the fruits of all those incalculable benefits which modern science confers (actually or potentially) upon the world. No longer can they insist that Asians should at the same time adopt conceptions of thought and life which are alien to the styles of their own great civilizations. Meanwhile the newly awakening peoples of Africa should have full opportunity to borrow from non-European sources in their social and national development. Europeans must follow the lead of doctors like Albert Schweitzer, of teaching engineers like Rewi Alley, surgeons like Norman Bethune, sociologists like Verrier Elwin. They must cease to appear to the great majority of humanity in the guise of the inventors of the 'know-how' of napalm, of saturation bombing, of the atomic bomb itself.

Science is something which can only be shared in fullest freedom among all the world's peoples. Most of these, indeed, and not only Europeans, cut and laid its very foundation-stones. And each people should freely develop the intrinsic consequences of their own centuries of thought, being in no way bound to adopt the thought-forms which developed in Europe; still less their current vulgarizations. European culture should take its place in an equal brotherhood of cultures; 'neither afore nor after other; without any difference or inequality'.

It is not to be denied that Europeans are called upon to make a certain moral effort in accepting this view of the situation. It is common to hear Westerners say that Asia has merely copied the intellectual and technical achievements of Europe. Europeans, it is implied, bore the burden and heat of the day in forging the instruments of all the modern sciences, and now Asians enter into the enjoyment of the hard ground-work previously done. But this historical perspective is wrong in many ways. To learn to use modern techniques is never mere copying, because it implies that people learn to understand their theory, and since the knowledge of nature is never static and never complete, many inevitably go on to extend its frontiers. Moreover, to suppose that pure and applied science sprang fully formed from the body of the European Renaissance is entirely false; there had been a long preparation of centuries which had seen the absorption by all Europe of Arabic learning, Indian thought, and Chinese technology.

The physico-mathematical hypotheses of Galileo can hardly be visualized without Indian numeral notation. The arsenal in which he set the scene of one of his world-changing dialogues could not have accomplished much without mastery of the characteristic Chinese technique of iron-casting. And again, the early phases of science in Europe were not so laborious and difficult as some would like to think; on the contrary, there were periods when great discoveries could be made at every scratch of a scalpel—once the basic technique of discovery had been discovered. It is impossible as well as absurd, therefore, for Europeans to think of science as their private property. It is not something which they can use to impose their own traditions and way of life on the rest of the world. It is not something for which they can take out an everlasting patent.[1] Always it has belonged to the world community.

Ignorance and History

Since pride is often accompanied by ignorance it is not surprising to find that even well-educated Europeans generally show gross lack of knowledge, and even lack of interest, in the history and thought of the Asian peoples. Chinese, Indian, and Arabic studies are even now the Cinderellas of Western European universities, and often treated, even when pursued, as the investigation of dead things irrelevant to the modern world. British speakers have been heard to maintain that since we alone understand true democracy it is our duty to impose our conceptions even by force upon the non-European inhabitants at least of colonial territories—yet they admitted, upon being asked, that they had never heard of the *panchayat*, or the *asabiyah* of Ibn Khaldun; of Mencian authority for tyrannicide, the civil service examinations of the T'ang dynasty, or the *Yü Shih Pu* (the 'Censorate').[2] In ignorance of the most elementary facts of Chinese, Indian, or Arab history, Europeans or Americans within the framework of the United Nations

[1] At one point during the Persian oil dispute of 1951, my eye was caught by a headline in one of the British newspapers which referred to the 'Oil Grab Men'. On looking more closely, I found, to my surprise, that the persons in question were not the foreigners who had until then been in control of Persian oil, but the Persian prime minister, Dr. Mossadeq, and his colleagues who were nationalising it. Such a reversal of the terms which might otherwise have seemed appropriate was at first startling. But I reflected that the apologists for foreign exploitation of the oil would undoubtedly argue that if it had not been for occidental technology and occidental enterprise the oil would in all probability have been lying unused in the earth's bosom still. No doubt this is historically true, but what non-Europeans will never admit is that henceforward Europeans are still justified by their high technical level in exploiting the natural resources of other people's countries for their own advantage.

[2] The *panchayat* was of course the council of five elders spontaneously elected by the ancient and medieval Indian village. The *asabiyah* was the mystical sense of brotherhood and vocation, which, according to Ibn Khaldun (fourteenth century), the father of social history, inspired the early Islamic states. Mêng Tzu (Mencius), in the fourth century B.C., distinguished between assassination of a tyrant, which might be a righteous deed, and regicide, the wicked murder of a good prince. It is now generally admitted that the civil service examination system, which in China goes back to the first century B.C., was in fact the model for the examinations introduced in Europe and America after the French Revolution. The *Yü Shih Pu* was a Chinese governmental organization which despatched 'Censors' throughout the country, having independent authority as imperial representatives to report on the justness and uprightness of provincial administrators. That they often did so at the peril of their lives was the theme of much literature and drama.

(so lamentably situated) think nothing of trying to impose their own concepts, the fruit of absolutely different historical developments, upon the representatives of countries which seem (to the unseeing eye) miserable and inferior because as yet they lack the full force of modern industrial power.

Take again the question of languages. One of the worst features of the situation in Malaya was that for the past half-century only the smallest minority of civil servants saw fit to learn any Chinese. How many French officials in Indo-China really knew the languages of those countries? How many Arabists were there among them in North Africa? Few foreign business men in the Chinese treaty-ports before the war ever bothered to acquire the Chinese language sufficiently to entertain a conversation with an educated group. Recently the editor of a famous scientific abstract journal in England, though desirous of receiving current Chinese periodicals, declined to have the papers in them abstracted unless they were already summarized in English, French, or German. And this although Chinese has long been an official language of the United Nations.

The same applies to the world's literatures. A non-European, unable to read any European language, who should stand in the great dome of the British Museum reading-room, and wonder what all this vast mass of books really amounted to, would be thought a laughable barbarian. Yet there are other literatures of comparable scope, the Chinese for example, of which most Europeans can decipher not one word. They themselves are in this respect barbarians. It is true that there have been notable translations of the Chinese classics and of Chinese poetry, but in extent and variety of genre and subject-matter they are still totally insufficient.

Occidental ignorance extends not only to political and philosophical history but also to the history of science and technology. Most people regard this as a highly academic subject. Yet if science has been the true unifier of our world, its history acquires unexpected importance. For example, a writer in *The Times*, no less than the Keeper of the Oriental Books and MSS. in the British Museum itself, stated in 1952, with regard to the Tunhuang MSS., that while block-printing was known and used in eighth-century China, it was left to Europeans to devise printing with movable types. This is of course nonsense; the second invention is due to Pi Shêng (*fl. ca.* A.D. 1070), who used porcelain or earthenware, while the Koreans were doing a good deal of printing with copper or bronze founts at the end of the fourteenth century, i.e. well before the time of Gutenberg. Yet the Museum of Printing at Mainz contains no reference to the Chinese inventions, and organizers of commemorative exhibitions in our own country have generally been loth to acknowledge them.

It is often not realized that European superiority in technique is a very recent phenomenon. Marco Polo (about A.D. 1280) found Hangchow a paradise compared with anything that he knew in Europe. As late as 1675 the Russian Tsar asked for the services of a group of Chinese bridge engineers. As late as the early nineteenth century the Chinese wanted practically nothing of what Europe produced, and Europe was sending missions of investigation down to the middle of the century to search out the secrets of traditional Chinese industries (ceramics, textiles, dyeing, tea, lacquer, etc.).

Much depends, for our world outlook, upon the estimate which we place upon the rise of modern science and technology in Renaissance Europe. If Galileo and Vesalius, Newton and Leibniz, Vieta and Harvey, were essentially a racial, a genetic, phenomenon, then we are the people and wisdom was born with us. But perhaps second thoughts would suggest that the structure of European society might have had something to do with the matter. It certainly differed deeply from the bureaucratic feudalism of Asia. If other civilizations perhaps lacked the social conditions which proved the essential fostering soil of this plant, must we now refuse to share its fruits with them? Pushing even further back, perhaps differing social conditions may have owed something to different geographical environments. In any case, nothing suggests that the men and women of the other civilizations do not make as good scientists and engineers as anyone born in Europe.

That the Greeks owed an incalculable debt to the Babylonians and ancient Egyptians is now generally accepted. But there is also a mass of evidence not as yet fully appreciated by Europeans, which shows that during the first fourteen centuries of the Christian era, Europe accepted from Asia a host of fundamental inventions and discoveries, often not knowing very clearly where they had come from. In the time of Robert of Chester and Abelard of Bath Europeans had to learn Arabic in order to acquire the best that was to be had in science and learning, and from the Arabs and the steppe peoples they received not a few techniques which took their places in the foundations on which the Renaissance built. How many people realize that the system of star co-ordinates universally used by astronomers today is essentially Chinese and not Greek? How many people appreciate that the technique of those deep bore-holes which bring to the modern world the universal fuel, petroleum, can demonstrably be traced back to the engineers of ancient China? Europe boasts of the exploratory voyages of Columbus and other navigators. Europe does not so readily inquire into the inventions which made them possible—the magnetic compass and the stern-post rudder from China, the multiple masts from India and Indonesia, the mizen lateen sail from the mariners of Islam.[1]

But it will be said that the foundations of science were laid by the ancient Greeks.[2] These estimable people (though they produced many men incontestably great) are still receiving more than their fair share of credit. According to a recent formulation, it was the Greeks who first attempted to determine the conditions requisite for the establishment of general truth, and to distinguish science from opinion. Yet this entirely overlooks the work of the Mohists, and the Confucian doctrine of the rectification of names. The Greeks, it is said, were the first to think about the respective contribution to knowledge of experience and reason. Yet this was precisely the substance of the argument between the Taoists and the Naturalists.

Abstraction and Law

That the Greeks were the first to conceive of the Euclidean ideal of a body of natural knowledge logically deduced from a limited number of axioms may indeed be granted. But has this devotion to the abstract always been a beneficent ideal in Europe? Roman

---

[1] Europeans generally speak as if the whole world had been discovered by Europe. This is a very limited conception, not true at all before the Renaissance. The Greeks in Bactria did not discover China; on the contrary, it was the Chinese (in the person of Chang Chhien) who discovered them. No Roman, so far as we know, ever got as far east as would have corresponded to the coming of Kan Ying and other Chinese to the Persian Gulf. By the middle of the Ming dynasty the Chinese flag was seen all over the Pacific from Zanzibar through Borneo to Kamchatka.

[2] Most biologists talk as if Europeans had been the only people ever to *classify* fauna and flora, for example. But Europeans must cease to be indifferent to the achievements of other peoples. Over the centuries the Chinese developed immense systems of classification of plants, animals, and diseases; not of course with the systematic accuracy of a post-Renaissance Linnean world, but very remarkable nevertheless. In certain respects, indeed, the ideographic language was particularly favourable for this work, as was appreciated in fourteenth-century Persia.

law, though a great intellectual achievement, could lead to paradoxical injustices impossible in Chinese jurisprudence.[1] Medieval
scholastic philosophy, spinning its webs between the stems of
uncriticized premises, turned before long into the abominable
dogmatism of the Inquisition.[2] Many Western economists in the
nineteenth century encouraged the idea of labouring men as so
many 'hands', and of the national homes of colonial peoples as
just so much 'territory'. Though modern statisticians have achieved
much of value, flesh-and-blood individuals tend to vanish in their
world, and it is characteristic of the condition of the European
mind that religion should be the only means of bringing them back
again. Whatever may be said of Asian failure to develop modern
natural science,[3] it does not seem that Chinese or Arabic social
philosophy, at any rate, ever lost sight of the concreteness of
humanity.[4] The world of today would do well to approach Asian
humanism in a more receptive spirit.

Constantly it is said that man's (i.e. Western man's) over-

[1] It is of much significance that (as Hudson and Boxer have pointed out)
nearly all the early Portuguese travellers in China in the sixteenth century, who
had ample opportunity of seeing the working of the law from beneath, reported
in glowing terms upon the care which was taken by the Chinese magistrates to
see that justice was done. The Portuguese were not surprised at the medieval
barbarities of the prisons, which were about on a par with those of Europe, but
they were convinced of the superiority of Chinese juristic methods and found
that life was counted less cheap than it was in their experience of Europe. In
this they confirmed earlier impressions of which they never knew, notably that
of a Timurid embassy of the fifteenth century.

[2] It is relevant and significant that Chinese history contains nothing really
comparable with the European Inquisition. There is doubt about the historicity
of the 'Burning of the Books' by the first emperor Chhin Shih Huang Ti, and
although in later ages there were many attacks on the Buddhists, in which
thousands of monks and nuns were secularized, they were not put to death for
their religion. Of course there was political persecution through the ages as now
one party was dominant, now another, and the so-called 'literary inquisition'
in the Chhing dynasty, directed to rooting out books written by supporters of
the Ming, was of this kind; it was an inquisition without *autos-da-fé*. India too
showed through the centuries remarkable examples of religious toleration.

[3] In spite of the start of several centuries which Europe has had in science
and technology, many world views are still to be found there which are more
parochial and more backward than some which were produced in Asia long
before the era of modern science.

[4] My aim is not to idealize Asian social philosophy, but to redress the balance.
Asia has suffered just as terribly as other parts of the world from wars, social
oppression, and natural calamities such as floods and droughts. The lot of the
masses of the people varied greatly; in China, for instance, it was much better
during stable dynasties than at times of dynastic collapse. Certain problems,
such as the control of the great rivers, were probably formally insoluble until
the coming of modern technology, though the history of hydraulic engineering
in China is long and heroic.

whelming control of natural processes in the atomic age has out-stripped his own moral strength and psychological development. Before it is too late, let him take one at least of the essential steps towards self-knowledge, that is to say, knowledge of others. Let him study the words of their saints and sages as well as those of his own. Let him experience his own humanity in the image of theirs.

An outstanding instance of European spiritual pride concerns law and jurisprudence. The highly abstract character of Roman law (so congruent with Euclidean geometry) has been praised for centuries. The Code of Justinian is rightly regarded as a great monument of European culture, and Anglo-Saxons are proud of their structure of case-law and precedent accumulated over the centuries. But in self-satisfied aloofness, European jurists have produced few scholars who were prepared to study the achieve-ments of other peoples in this important field. Early British administration in India did, it is true, lead to a certain interest in Indian customary law, but it was neither sympathetic nor long-lived. The name of but one scholar in all Europe today is re-nowned for his work on Chinese law. Yet the Chinese had had an immense and remarkable legal tradition, and it was based on principles quite different from those which prevailed in Europe. While the West has a penchant for legal fictions, Asians are less deceived by professional sophistry.[1] There was throughout Chinese history a resistance to codification, a determination to judge every case on its own merits, a passion for compromise and harmony. As Arthur Waley has well said, no Chinese magistrate, having de-livered what he knew to be an unjust judgement, would ever have congratulated himself on having applied with precision the laws of the land. There was hardly any rift which put society asunder which Chinese jurisconsults could not join together. Ancient and medieval China knew the rule of law, but consciously preferred the rule of equity.

Then in our own time came the League of Nations, followed by the United Nations. Agreements among sovereign states dedicated to the Rule of Law. But whose law? European law, of course; who could take seriously any other? No voice of dissent, of course, from

---

[1] Historians, looking back upon our own times, will probably select as an example of a legal fiction outstanding in scope and ramifying results the inter-pretation by the UN-controlling powers of 'China' as meaning a small minority of refugees from that country.

internationally prominent Asian lawyers all trained at occidental universities; and therefore knowing little or nothing about the history of law in their own countries. Indeed, one of the evil influences of the West (seen in countries like the Philippines) is the emergence of a group of lawyer-politicians. Then comes crisis, and the interpretation of terms such as 'collective security' by the best (Western) legal minds.[1] The Western attitude is that one should always take advantage of a point if the letter of the law is on one's side. One should act 'according to the rules of the game' assuming that in course of time one's adversaries would take advantage of an equal number of like opportunities. Thus the principle of 'collective security' having been erected into a logical and abstract theoretical structure, one should go ahead and apply it no matter what the concrete circumstances might be. But Asian systems of jurisprudence have not been so prepared to sacrifice the spirit to the letter.

Of course, law has always had the function of 'acting as a brake upon inevitable social change' (Eggleston). Chinese jurists were often no less reactionary than those of the Temple in London whose papers the rebels went first to burn upon reaching the capital in A.D. 1381. But the genius of a people may moderate even social factors which are similar everywhere, and Europeans should cease to think that they have nothing to learn from the legal systems of Asia.

Democracy and Bureaucracy

The Occident is torn today between rival conceptions of democracy. Christian conviction and centuries of theology (an inheritance which the Eastern European countries share equally with the Western) have induced a profound belief in the value of the individual, and his or her right, from childhood upwards, to the fullest possible development of innate capacities. But the con-

---

[1] C. P. Fitzgerald, in his excellent *Revolution in China* (Cresset, London, 1952), has given three outstanding examples of Western legalistic thinking which China could not appreciate. First, the shooting down of students demonstrating in Shanghai (30.5.25) against arrest of strikers in a Japanese mill, (pp. 53 ff.). Second, the arguments (1927–37) concerning the status of the international settlements (p. 203). Third, the 1945 American airlift of Kuomintang troops to North China and Manchuria, though these areas were effectively communist-controlled (p. 86).

ception of democracy varies enormously in different parts of the Occident. Most Englishmen cannot conceive of any system of democracy other than that of parliamentary representation, with its special virtues such as the security of the person. An American cannot think any system democratic which does not hold before each log-cabin child the prize of White-House achievement. The Russians cannot imagine any truly democratic system without free educational opportunities for every individual, and the guarantee of full employment. The Yugoslavs value participation in day-to-day industrial administration.

Perhaps the oppositions of some of these points of view would seem less irreconcilable if anyone ever looked outside Europe and asked whether China, India, and Arabia had anything to teach on these subjects. Reference has already been made to some of their contributions. Was not the *carrière ouverte aux talents* a Chinese invention made nearly two thousand years before Europe heard of it? Did not the 'divine right of kings' persist in Europe for at least a similar length of time after the rulers of China had accepted the theory of the Mandate of Heaven? And as to Heaven was it not said, 'Heaven hears as the people hear, Heaven sees as the people see'? And were not those rulers admonished to 'love what the people love, and hate what the people hate'? Was spontaneous local government unknown in ancient India? Who put brotherly love and respect more firmly into practice (irrespective of colour) than the followers of the Commander of the Faithful? Who stated the principle of the 'right of rebellion against unchristian princes' twenty centuries before Bishop Ponnet?[1]

Particularly relevant to our present anxieties is the Chinese experience of bureaucratism. The humanization of bureaucracy is probably the greatest problem of modern civilization, and it presents itself as absolutely vital on both sides in the 'cold war'. A high degree of bureaucratic government seems quite inevitable given the technological complexities of modern society, but modern science has provided a thousand aids and adjuncts which could make it work well. These are as yet very imperfectly used. Telephones, portable radio communications, automatic card-filing and sorting systems, calculating machines, photographic

---

[1] A sixteenth-century English churchman who stated with particular clarity this old patristic doctrine in the interests of Protestantism. One of the first things the Parliament did during the Civil War was to reprint him.

documentary reproduction—all these and many more are available. Nothing is lacking except goodwill. Goodwill is the commitment to treating ordinary people with sympathy and understanding, and the realization that no expenditure on equipment is wasted which sets forward this aim. This is the promised peace on earth, and whoever puts first the real needs of real people will inherit it. Let us hope that the bureaucracies of the future will function with as much true humanism as a good *hsien*-city government under the dynasties of Thang or Sung. That was the time when poets like Su Tung-Pho and Pai Chu-I, scholars like Shen Kua, were officials. If this was not changing philosophers into kings, it was certainly making poets bureaucrats, and if we for our part had given a man such as William Blake such a charge, we might face the Asian tradition with a better countenance. Here the Chinese may have a great task to perform in the teaching of the rest of the world, for their bureaucracy has an experience of two millennia. There may yet be virtue in Confucian traditions, as there was in the eighteenth century when the Latin translations of the classics revealed to an astonished world the existence of a morality without supernaturalism, and of a great continuing culture which had emphatically not been based upon the pessimistic doctrine of original sin.

Many other aspects of this question might stand out in a Confucian light. Looming upon the world is a great unanswered question: what is science really for?[1] Perhaps several centuries hence, the chief meaning of democracy will be seen to lie in the question whether or not science is used primarily *for people*. 'Science for science's sake' seems only too often to cloak the conceptions of 'Science for the sake of big profits', and 'Science for the sake of defence' (i.e. the piling up of armaments). At any rate the supporters of the first notion rarely seem to criticize the second or the third. It is true that science will never flourish in a stifling atmo-

[1] We are living through a terrible period of misuse of applied science. The Japanese were the first to experience the loathsome effects of an atomic conflagration. Korean women and children have been tortured by the indiscriminate use of the liquid fire known as napalm. Scientific ingenuity created, during the Second World War, an astonishing array of engines of war against fascism— the proximity fuse, shaped plastic explosives, the radar detector, phosphorus bombs, rockets or pilotless planes with devastating warheads, etc., etc. Are these now to be used to impose upon the world a new fascism, carrying the banner of democracy but without a trace of its true spirit, and designed to perpetuate the material supremacy of the white race?

sphere of government control, but under private corporate enterprise its utilization primarily for the benefit of the people as
a whole seems often far from obvious. Calculating machines—
supersonic rockets—cybernetic devices—servo-mechanisms—sub-
stances injurious to plants and animals—new drugs—cloud-
seeding—atomic power—for what, for what, for what? If the
Western world has thrown religious sanctions out of the window,
can we afford to kick even ethics downstairs? Perhaps the whole
world as well as China needs Confucius, Mo Ti, and Lao Tzu
more desperately than ever.

Unity and Contradiction

Many Western Europeans and Americans feel themselves the
representatives of a civilization with a mission to unify the world.
The civilization of the Occident alone, they think, is universal.
This is because it is itself united, itself a unity, itself the One
capable of subsuming all the others, the Many. Such pretensions
are baseless.

From the beginning of their thought-history, Europeans have
passed continually from one extreme world-outlook to another,
rarely finding any synthesis. On the one hand there was God, or
the gods, with accompanying supernatural assemblies of angels,
spirits, demiurges, entelechies, and the like; on the other there
were atoms and the void. Theological spiritualism and mechanical
materialism maintained perpetual war. The former component
arose, no doubt, from Israel and the ancient civilizations of Egypt
and Babylonia, the latter was mostly a product of bold Greek
thought. Not until the time of Leibniz and after were any serious
attempts made to reconcile this divergence, and no great success
was attained until our own time.

It ought therefore to be more widely recognized that Chinese
civilization never participated in this disjunction of thought.
Organic naturalism was the *philosophia perennis* of China. Fundamentally neither the Confucians nor the Taoists had any use for
the supernatural whatever its form—but the mechanical interplay
of atoms was not appreciated either. Though atomic theories were
always being introduced from India and elsewhere, they never
gained any permanent acceptance. When Chinese thought found
its greatest expression in the Neo-Confucianism of the twelfth

U

century A.D., it appeared in a shape remarkably akin to the general world-outlook of modern science. Nothing more was necessary for the construction of the universe than matter-energy on the one hand, and organization (at numerous levels of complexity) on the other. The single act of creation was not felt to be a necessary notion. Nor is it possible to accept the contention that Europe has been the centre from which radiated the idea of making the human race one single society. 'Within the four seas all men are brothers' is a Confucian statement belonging to the sixth century B.C. and never subsequently forgotten. In India, Kabir was only one of many poets and prophets of human solidarity. Even in its most enlightened moments, Europe is liable to make unwarranted pretensions.

Europeans, therefore, should devote much greater attention than they have so far been willing to do to the philosophies of Asia. And they should so devote it with intellectual humility, not the closed mind of *a priori* superiority. Much may be learnt which will moderate the common Western European belief that not only science and technology, but also philosophical truth, must necessarily radiate from that peninsular continent to illumine the heathen.

We have noted the historical fact that modern science and technology grew up in Europe and its extension in the Americas. Everyone in these countries accepts this fact as a matter of course. It is probably the main half-conscious self-justification for those feelings of superiority which many of them still entertain towards other peoples. How little real ground there is for this attitude has already been indicated. But what is often not so clearly recognized is that the psychology of dominance which has for some centuries past characterized the peoples dwelling round the Atlantic seaboard has been the direct result of that vast power over nature which the scientific movement of the Renaissance brought forth. Today this psychology has become a menace to the world.

Naturally it began in a small way, and of course with war techniques. Chinese and Arab fire-lances and barrel-guns of primitive kinds (tenth to thirteenth centuries) were quickly developed in fourteenth-century Europe to form the artillery which battered down not only feudal castles but also (in the seventeenth and eighteenth centuries) the forts of Indian princes. Cortes had armour, weapons, and horses which in the sixteenth century overcame without much difficulty the obsidian clubs of Aztecs and Mayas. The boisterous merchant captains disliked by coastal Chinese mandarins in the seventeenth century reappeared before long in the guise of nineteenth-century admirals of the fleet to force opium through the inadequate defences of Commissioner Lin Tsê-Hsü. In the later nineteenth century the pace quickened in all continents. And now no longer is there talk of annexation or 'protection', for empire-building has gone out of fashion. It looks much better, no doubt, to have small sovereign states sitting in the United Nations, with strings which can be pulled from behind the scenes. This in itself might be considered a concession to modern sensibilities. But we still face the imposition of characteristically West European ideas upon other peoples under threat of destruction by the most up-to-date weapons; with Korea as the object-lesson of what will remain of a country after it has been 'liberated' by modern means. Truly there is no solution save an understanding of the worth of the cultures of other peoples, and a realization that the West European or American 'way of life' cannot and must not be forced upon them.

Towards World Commonwealth

Knowledge of Nature is no one's private property. The world is like a holy vessel, says the *Tao Tê Ching*. Whoever grabs at it will lose it irretrievably. How can anyone hope to keep secret for ever the information that precisely two milligrams of vitamin B_I are necessary each day for the health of one human individual? The impact of modern Western civilization on China and other Asian countries has inevitably induced in their people a determination that they too must share in the higher standards of life which modern science and technology have placed at the disposal of modern man. They insist upon moving forward to a point at which all can satisfy what we now know to be the minimal needs of civilized human beings. And in some cases they have decided (as in China) that they would do this by a mighty leap, short-circuiting long periods comparable with those of the 'dark Satanic mills' of nineteenth-century Europe, the miseries of the 'Industrial Revolution'. This whole movement is one of primary historical significance, and the more Occidental peoples oppose it, the worse will the judgement of world history be on them.

How then should Europeans and Americans react to these events? By a policy which denies United Nations representation to six hundred million people? By maintaining pirate strongholds off the China coast? By prohibiting the export of sulpha-drugs and antibiotics which the Asian masses so greatly need? Somehow or other the West must understand that to the average Asian man or woman the whole current mobilization of the self-styled 'free world' seems directed, not so much towards the 'containment of communism' as against the rising upsurge of political consciousness, the national independence movements, and the struggle for industrialization and the raising of living standards of all Asian and African peoples.

Perhaps the whole question reduces to the active practice of humility and brotherly love. We need a real conviction that all racialism, all self-satisfied beliefs of cultural superiority, are a denial of the world community. We need a list of diabolical clichés, e.g. that Asian people 'cannot be understood'. We need to free ourselves from what Claude Roy has so well called 'the iron curtain of false enigmas'. Europe and America must stand ready not only to share with all Asians and Africans those treasures of understanding and use of Nature which modern science and technology have brought forth, but also to learn from them many things concerning individual life and society which they are more than competent to teach. If this is not done, the achievements of Europe (and America) will in any case become the common property of mankind, but our civilization will go down to history as distorted and evil, unwilling to practise what it preached, and worthy of the condemnation of ten thousand generations.

XIX. LIVING RELIGIONS AND
WORLD COMMUNITY

Robert Lawson Slater

I

Any adequate discussion of human differences such as that pursued in this present symposium means, in the long run, a reference to the role of religion in regard to such differences. Both Dr. Toynbee and Dr. Iyer, in their very interesting dialogue, attribute to religion a very fundamental role. Both also see it as a dual role. Religion brings people together and makes for community. At the same time, religion is seen to disturb and break community or to result in rival communities.

It is also apparent from the dialogue that discussion of the subject today must be in the perspective named by Dr. Iyer when he concludes that we must 'get to the standpoint of the Stoic who saw the whole world as a single city'. We may begin by thinking in terms of East and West, or, more particularly, in terms of Asia and Europe, but the kind of outlook suggested by such terms is today giving place to a new outlook, a world outlook, as the kind of history to which they belong, parochial history, is giving place to a new kind of history, global history.[1] More and more leaders of opinion see the whole world as a single city. If they look to the past, it is from the standpoint of a new concern: a concern for world community.

Even if we continue to think in terms of East and West, with a glass curtain 'of a psychological sort' between them, there is need for the wider world perspective. For the growing sense of world community means that we have to consider a new East and a new

[1] Cf. Hans Kohn, *The Age of Nationalism: the first era of global history.* (World Perspectives, vol. 28, Harper & Brothers, New York, 1962.) Foreword, p. xv: 'All preceding history has been parochial history. In the middle of the twentieth century mankind has entered the first stage of global history.'

West, each affected by the change of outlook which has come with new prospects of a world community. It is not, indeed, a change of outlook shared by all. There are still a good many whose outlook is narrowly parochial and this is one of the factors of the situation to be kept in mind. Nevertheless, world community is not just a dream of tomorrow. It already exists in embryo. Over against the great majority whose outlook is still parochial, there is a significant minority of travelled men and women who, by the very nature of their professional interest, have come to share a world experience and a world outlook. Besides the statesmen and the diplomats, there are the journalists, the scientists, the traders, and a good many others, including some religious leaders, who must, so to speak, see the world every day. Among them are some who realize that much that has to be done in the world today, even with reference to particular and local situations, can only be done by action on a world scale organized by world bodies.[1] It cannot be done by the local leaders alone.

A case in point is Dr. de Vries' recent analysis of the processes of rapid social change in Asia, Africa, and South America.[2] A social scientist who was formerly a member of the staff of the World Bank, Dr. de Vries emphasizes a growing recognition of the fact that a great many local issues, economic and social as well as political, cannot be decided by local action alone. 'Within a decade the idea of international co-operation . . . has spread and been accepted throughout almost the whole world. . . . There is an increasing feeling of world solidarity.'[3] And, it might be added, there is something more than feeling. There is existing international 'machinery', however inadequate. There is action in accord with this feeling of world solidarity with men like Dr. Vries as agents of such action. They are already enrolled, as it were, as citizens of the world.

Dr. Vries' analysis also emphasizes the possible role of religion in this making of world civilization, for he has written at the instance of the World Council of Churches. It is further significant that in a companion volume, reflecting the same study initiated by

[1] Cf. Woodrow Wilson in his Second Inaugural Address: 'The greatest things that remain to be done must be done with the whole world for stage and in co-operation with the wide and universal forces of mankind'.
[2] Egbert de Vries, *Man in Rapid Social Change*, published for the World Council of Churches by Doubleday and Company, New York, 1961.
[3] de Vries, op. cit., ch. xiv, pp. 202–3.

the World Council, Dr. Paul Albrecht deals with the subject of what Christians may do in regard to this world-wide social change. He also observes that anything that they may do must be done 'in close relationship to the non-Christian religions and cultures'.[1] At the same time he is alive to the issue presented by religious differences in regard to such co-operation.

I begin with this reference to a body of men and women who have special experience of world conditions because their interest and concern sharpen our question of what may be expected from the 'forces of religion'. Observing as they do the possible role of religion in contributing to world community they are not likely to let the question rest. They also point to the wider implications of the question. For they have in mind something more than the issue of world peace which is the issue most generally emphasized when the subject of religious differences and world community is discussed. They are thinking also in terms of world health. Even if there were no threat to world peace, they see the welfare of mankind at this stage in our history as dependent as never before on the growing sense of world community.

The issue of world peace certainly makes our question more urgent. At the same time it tends to obscure the fact that the demand made of the forces of religion is a twofold demand. Besides the frequent demand that religious people should 'forget their differences and come together' in the interests of world peace, there is also a further demand for that dynamism which is associated with religious conviction. It is a demand suggested by the very phrase, 'forces of religion'. When what is conceived is not only world peace, but a better peace, as it were, a peace which means world civilization, this demand becomes explicit. Professor Hocking, for example, argues that religion is politically essential. He points to the modern secular states in which attempts have been made to do without religion. Such attempts, he says, have failed. They have failed particularly in the fields of law and order, education and social care. 'The state depends for its vitality upon a motivation which it cannot by itself command.'[2] And the coming world civilization will depend upon such motivation, that is, upon religious motivation.

[1] Paul Albrecht, *The Churches and Rapid Social Change*, Doubleday and Company, New York, 1961, ch. xiv, p. 205.

[2] W. E. Hocking, *The Coming World Civilization*, Harper & Brothers, New York, 1956, ch. l, pp. 4 ff.

We have, then, *first* a demand for religious co-operation and *secondly* a demand for religious conviction. But whereas the demand for co-operation is often taken to mean a 'forgetting of religious differences', the demand for religious conviction might be said to require the very opposite since it is frequently observed that where there is strong conviction it is often in regard to what is 'different' rather than in regard to what is held in common with others. The question therefore arises whether we can indeed have it both ways. To ask this question, however, is to raise a prior question: to what do we refer when we speak of 'religion' in relation to world community?

II

Much of the confusion which clouds the discussion of our subject is due to the failure to recognize that there may be more than one reference when the term 'religion' is used in this context. The general reference, it might be said, is clear enough: it is to religious motivation. But the reference to religious motivation is in itself a multiple reference. When, for example, it is argued that people will only be good world citizens if they are religious, the reference may be to religious beliefs which encourage respect for law and order or regard for one's neighbours. But when it is observed that religion also keeps people apart the reference may be not only to separative beliefs but to attitudes, dogmatic or otherwise, towards these beliefs. Professor Zaehner, for instance, portrays what we might call a glass curtain between East and West in terms, not only of divergent beliefs, Hindu or Christian as the case may be, but also in terms of attitudes to what is believed. In the West, he says, ideas have been taken with 'desperate seriousness' and beliefs have been held with a 'passion' which is alien to the Eastern mind.[1]

Or suppose we take the term, 'forces of religion'. Here again, there may be reference to the strength of religious motivation. But when appeal is made to the forces of religion to 'forget their differences' the reference appears to be to what is called 'organized religion', or to the various 'religious bodies' or communities and the rivalry between them. And here indeed the reference may be confused and confusing. The fact is often overlooked, for example,

[1] R. C. Zaehner, *The Concise Encyclopaedia of Living Faiths*, Hawthorn Books, New York, 1959, Introduction, p. 16.

that the same John Churchman to whom appeal is made to promote the cause of world community may be the John Citizen who is concerned about world community. What may be meant in such a case is that this John Churchman should see to it that his religious differences do not stand in the way of his interests as John Citizen. But it might also be said that what is really in view here is the fact that organized religion involves separate leadership. Over against the princes and prime ministers who rule the nations there are the priests and prophets who may disturb or assist that rule. Political leaders and religious leaders may issue contrary directions in regard to the same issues and it is conceivable that on certain issues and in certain quarters the word of an Archbishop of Canterbury may be more effective than the word of a British Prime Minister.

The intent of the question, What are the forces of religion going to do about world community?, may therefore be, What are religious leaders going to do about it? In asking what religious leaders may do about it, however, we may find ourselves asking what they may think about it and how they feel about it. There is also a possible inquiry, if we want to estimate the extent of their influence, as to what their followers may think and feel about it. We are back again in the realm of motivation. At the same time our reference is still to organized religion.

In brief, there is a tanglewood of references. While the attempt to avoid confusion leads us to distinguish one reference from another, respect for the reality of what is most evidently a complex situation leads us to observe how some of these references are related. To observe this relationship may point us to the conclusion that *the term 'religion', whatever else it may do, refers us to people*, a fact which is too often obscured by our abstractions, distinctions, and classifications.

There is particular need to observe this reference to people when we come to consider the contemporary resurgence of religion; for the significance of this resurgence is sometimes minimized on the ground that the motives behind it are anything but pure, an argument which ignores the fact that human motives are generally mixed. In passing it may be observed that the resurgence of religion is not confined to the East. There is a good deal more evidence of religious revival in the West than is sometimes recognized. It is true that it is no longer proper to identify the Western world, and Europe in particular, with Christendom, but it is no less evident that religion in the West cannot be dismissed as a spent force. The Western world is still the scene of persistent, widespread, and influential Christian activity, and there are significant signs of revived religious interest, especially perhaps in the universities. 'Thirty years ago,' observes Rabbi Gittelsohn with reference to America, 'those few of us who were deeply concerned with religion as undergraduates found sparse and infrequent company. . . . Today the picture has changed almost beyond belief.' He refers to an inquiry which concludes that 80 per cent of American students are interested in religion and cites the increase in church membership in the United States from 20 per cent of the population a century ago to 63 per cent today.[1]

But it is what is happening in the East rather than what is happening in the West that is generally in view when the resurgence of religion is discussed. It is also with reference to the East that the purity of the religious motivation is questioned. For whether we turn to the new pride in Hindu culture which is manifest in India or to the quickened zeal for Buddhist culture in countries such as Ceylon and Burma, the resurgent religious interest is obviously associated with resurgent Asian nationalism. In Burma, for example, where there has been a remarkable movement which has produced some two hundred new retreat centres for the laity, some of the laymen have said that by taking part in such retreats they hope to be better citizens of the new Burma as well as better Buddhists. Immediately the whole movement is dismissed by some Western observers as just another case of religion being exploited by astute politicians. In reply to such criticism it may be held that to see the situation in this light is to attribute Western ideas of the separation of Church and State which are foreign to the East. But it is perhaps a more fundamental reply, and one that applies to both East and West, to say that even when religious motives are mixed with others they may nevertheless play a large part in determining human conduct and attitudes.

The consequences of religious motivation are also mixed. This is a consideration which is frequently ignored by those who can only view the present resurgence with dismay as they recall how often in the past the entry of religion has proved divisive, with thought, maybe, of the Constantines and Muhammeds who have

---

[1] Roland B. Gittelsohn, *Man's Best Hope*, Random House, New York, 1961, ch. i, pp. 3, 4.

waged holy war. It is also a consideration which is ignored by those who can only see the resurgence of religion as all to the good from the standpoint of world community as they make a different selection from the pages of history and emphasize, maybe, the example of Constantine of Nicea or of Muhammad of Medina bringing men together in the name of religion. A more comprehensive view of past history, however, will avoid such either/or judgements and expectations. As it allows for the ambiguous role of religion in the past, now divisive, now unifying, so it may better allow for a resurgent religion today which operates in both directions. If resurgence is associated with divisive nationalism, it is also associated with new movements of religious life and thought which spell community. All the great religions today, for example, announce a sense of world mission, and Hinduism can no longer be regarded as an exception in this respect.[1] As for Buddhists, there were notable expressions of this sense of world mission at the Sixth Great Buddhist Council held in Rangoon a few years ago. There are also the movements of our day designed to promote religious unity. Besides the Christian ecumenical movements, there is the pan-Buddhist movement which seeks to bring the two halves of the Buddhist world, Thēravada and Mahayana, more closely together. Granted that the unity here conceived is a unity within the walls of a particular tradition, it is still a new expression of that spirit of toleration which is required to transcend our 'glass curtains', if not to remove them. It is an exercise which may point the way to that further enterprise in religious co-operation which will be required if there is to be any effective coming together of believers the world over in the interests of world community.

III

Whatever else these various movements betide (and others of similar import might be named) they point to the fact that the religion which we have to take into consideration is living religion.

[1] Some writers have distinguished Hinduism and Judaism from 'universal religions' such as Christianity, Buddhism, and Islam, exhibiting world outlooks. But this classification is open to question now that we have such developments as the overseas outposts of the Ramakrishna Mission and such statements as the following: 'The Hindus will soon be recognized by all . . . as a force leading humanity to its goal'. D. S. Sarma, 'The Nature and History of Hinduism' in *The Religion of the Hindus*, ed. by Kenneth W. Morgan, The Ronald Press, New York, 1953, ch. i, p. 47.

All too often the issue of what may be expected of religion in regard to world community is presented in a way which implies that what we have to deal with is static religion or the religion of yesterday. Everything else in the changing world of today is seen to be on the move except the realm of religion. Sufficiently full account is taken of new conditions which mean new pressures on the realm of religion but not nearly sufficient account is taken of changes within the realm of religion itself, changes which may mean a very different response to these pressures than might be the case if we only had the religion of yesterday.

One approach to our subject which is open to qualification in this respect is the historical approach. As we have observed, judgements of what may be expected today are often formed on the basis of a glance at past history. The pages of past history are turned and certain pages are selected, whilst others are ignored, to support the view that the entry of religion can only mean division or the contrary view that such entry will do more than anything else to bring the nations of the world together.

There is indeed room and need for historical reference. To say the least, there are legacies from the past which may affect the present situation. For example, defensive attitudes formed against Islam at a time when the Muslim invasions threatened the whole of Christendom may still be reflected in Christian attitudes, not only to Islam itself, but to other religions. But to judge the whole present situation in the sole light of past history amounts to allowing the past a strangle-hold on the present which reference to the past in itself forbids. For to turn these same pages of history is to observe how again and again the forces of religion have taken new directions in response to changing conditions.

Even more misleading, perhaps, and more subject to qualification, is the approach which in effect pins down a particular religion to some 'classic' formulation of belief and fails to allow for later and present developments. The Hindu religion, for example, is frequently treated in this way. It is presented as a system of thought dominated by what is described as the 'monistic' interpretation of Hindu scriptures promoted by Śaṅkara and his followers. It is then concluded that between Hindus thus persuaded and Jews, Christians, and Muslims whose whole outlook is dominated by belief in a personal, living God there is indeed a thick glass curtain which can never be transcended. Now apart

from the question whether Śaṅkara's interpretation is properly
described as 'monistic', there is the question of whether all Hindus
are so fully persuaded by the Śaṅkara interpretation as this view of
the situation suggests. What of the strong, persistent Hindu
bhakti tradition of theism? According to some observers, an
increasing number of Hindus are expressing their faith in these
definitely theistic terms so that their outlook more nearly approaches
that of Christians and other believers in a personal God than might
be supposed.[1]

It is a development which may in part be attributed to Western
invasion and influence. But it is more than a mere borrowing of
Western ideas. Besides claiming that what is thus being developed
is very much their own theistic tradition, Hindus might say that
it is a change stimulated by new conditions, world conditions, and
consequent movements of thought which are neither Western nor
Eastern but due to the coming together of East and West. They
might also say that if this has meant a somewhat closer approach
by Hindus to the Western outlook it is not an approach to the
Western outlook of yesterday; it is better described as an approach
to an understanding of the theistic position which is developing in
the West itself today. Some might add that Hindus themselves
have contributed to this understanding. If there has been borrowing or influence it has not been all on one side. On any showing we
have here significant changes in the realm of religious ideas or
belief for which there may be failure to make due allowance unless
it is recognized that religion which confronts us is living religion.

Equally probable, however, and perhaps even more important
from the standpoint of what may promote or hinder world community are changes in religious attitudes. According to Professor
Will Herberg a very clear case in point is what is happening to
Jews today in North America. No understanding of Jewish life, he
says, is possible, in terms of what he calls perennial 'Jewish'
factors alone. Account must also be taken of the non-Jewish
environment or the situation in which Jews find themselves in any
particular place and time. In the United States there has been a
remarkable change in the Jewish situation which in turn is due to a
change in the North American religious situation in general. Thirty
years ago Protestantism could be described as America's 'national

[1] Cf. A. L. Basham, 'Hinduism' in *The Concise Encyclopaedia of Living
Faiths*, Hawthorn Books, New York, 1959, p. 239.

religion'. Today North America is more properly described as a 'three religion country'. 'The normal religious implication of being an American today is that one is either a Protestant, a Catholic or a Jew.'[1] Thus the Jew in America need no longer regard himself as excluded from any effective say in the life of the nation because he is a Jew. On the contrary, he has his place and say in the national life not in spite of his religion but because of it. In America today it is religion more than anything else which signifies community, with Judaism accepted as one of the 'three great faiths' of the American Way. Hence an increasing number of younger Jews are renouncing the secularism of their elders who were disposed to desert a Judaism which in former days isolated them from the American Way. A change in the situation has also meant new attitudes to their religion on the part of Christians, both Protestant and Catholic.

As far as the Jews are concerned, Professor Herberg sees both promise and peril in this change—promise if their return to religion means real religious commitment, peril if it means commitment to the American Way rather than to God. In other words, what is here emphasized is a change in attitudes as the result of new conditions rather than a change in ideas or beliefs. It is an emphasis which may lead us to consider more closely the importance of religious attitudes in relation to world community.

IV

Among the various religious attitudes, none perhaps are of greater consequence when it comes to prospects of religious co-operation in the interests of world community than the different attitudes which may be taken towards statements of belief. As we have observed, it has been suggested that one of the grounds of tension between East and West, and between Hindu India and the Christian West in particular, is a profound difference of attitudes

---

[1] Will Herberg, *The Integration of the Jew Into America's Three-Religion Society*, a paper read at the Seventeenth Annual Conference of the American Council for Judaism, 1961. A similar observation, it may be added, has recently been made by a Catholic writer, Father John Courtney Murray, S.J. Using the term conspiracy in its Latin sense of a breathing together, Father Murray names four 'conspiracies' or major groups which may and should conspire together in the national interest, Protestant, Catholic, Jewish, and secular. James Courtney Murray, S.J., *We Hold These Truths: Catholic Reflections on the American Proposition*, Sheed and Ward, New York, 1960, Introduction, pp. 22 ff.

in this respect. On the one hand there is the extreme rigidity of the attitude associated with what is generally described as dogmatism. On the other hand there is the extreme flexibility of relativism.

Hindu India is sometimes portrayed as the very home of relativism. Hindus may disagree on many things, but the one thing on which most of them are agreed is that statements of belief, their own or those made by others, should not be pressed too far. For none of these statements, they hold, can be regarded as exhausting all the truth. All of them at most are only relatively true, relative to the glimpse, no more, of the Reality which they strive to express, relative to the particular experience they reflect. A favourite analogy is that of the many rivers leading to the one ocean. In keeping with this allowance for many streams of religious experience and truth there is liberal tolerance of the various schools of thought and life within the one Hindu household of faith. There is little or no thought of excluding any believer from this household because his beliefs differ from other believers or because he does not toe the line of some one clear-cut formulation of dogma accepted by all. There is indeed no such line for him to toe. On the other hand, there is often a very vigorous criticism of anyone who prescribes such a line or makes exclusive claims for statements of belief to which he himself subscribes. Hence there is strong criticism of much that is observed in the West.

For if Hindu India may be described as the home of religious relativism, Western Christendom may be described as the home of exclusive dogmatism, dogmatism not in the sense that Christianity presents particular dogmas or tenets held in special respect, for all religions do that, but dogmatism with respect to the way in which some of these dogmas are valued. They are valued either in the light of specific Divine revelation or in the light of reason, or in both lights, as true and sufficient beyond question. The consequent attitude is described as exclusive because of the way in which such dogmas are used. They are used as criteria of religious community. Those who deny these dogmas are regarded as excluded from the fellowship of believers who accept them. Thus one prevalent form of religious community in the Christian West has been the confessional church, so described because the members are expected to subscribe to the particular confession or statement of their faith authorized by their church.

It is the tension between these two attitudes, dogmatic and

relativist, which accounts for the glass curtain between East and West as much as any difference in what is believed. For Buddhists and others in the East, no less than Hindus, are also sharply critical of Western dogmatism. Western believers, on the other hand, have often been as critical of Hindu and Buddhist relativism, which they dismiss as obscurantist to a degree which vitiates any decisive or effective action.

One of the things which is happening today, however, is a remarkable growth of the relativist attitude in the West itself. It is not, indeed, a relativism which is in all respects similar to Hindu relativism, for it is a relativism which is very much of the West's own making. Nor is Western relativism all of a piece. While in some of its aspects it may be stimulated by Western interest in Oriental religion, Western relativism cannot be attributed to this interest alone. There is, for example, the relativism which may be attributed to the growth of the scientific outlook in so far as this outlook betokens a readiness to re-examine all traditional statements, a readiness which is certainly averse to any rigid dogmatism. But when this aversion is also associated with the growth of Western scepticism we have a relativism which proposes something more than a review of religious dogmas. It amounts to the view that none of them should be taken seriously since all religious opinions are, at best, no more than guesses in the dark or expressions of human hopes and fears. This is very far from what the Hindu relativist intends.

But there is another expression of relativism in the West today, very differently rooted and often disregarded, which is more significant from our present standpoint. This is the relativism which arises when a distinction is drawn between the poetic symbols of religious faith and the rational, systematic presentation of religious belief. In some cases this has meant distinguishing between the form and content of the Biblical message and what theologians have done with this message. And here, indeed, it may be considered, we have something more akin to the intention of Hindu relativism. For in this religious or Biblical relativism, as it may be called, there is certainly no contempt of religious dogma. At the same time in the appeal to the Biblical message which is seen as a source of constant correction of all theological statements, there is an implicit rejection of dogmatic rigidity. It might be argued, however, that this Western Biblical relativism is nevertheless different from what is found in the East in one important respect. The Hindu is free to roam where he will. His relativism knows no restraint. But not so the Christian. He may refuse to be bound by this or that particular interpretation of the Christian symbols. But he is still restrained by these symbols themselves; his relativism has to do with these symbols; it remains within the limits of the Christian faith. A further glance at Eastern religion, however, may raise the question whether Oriental attitudes, all told, are quite so free from restraint or so different from Christian attitudes as might at first appear.

V

More particularly our question has to do with what may be called 'confessional religion', or with religious community gathered around some one distinctive symbol, or group of symbols, acknowledged or confessed by those who belong to such a community. As the attitude of the Biblical relativists leads us to distinguish between an outlook of this kind and that which is labelled dogmatic, so we may ask whether in the East there is not, after all, a near approach, if not to Western dogmatism, at least to Western confessionalism. In other words, are there, in the East no less than in the West, certain beliefs taken so seriously that here, too, there are limits to religious toleration? And beyond these questions there is a further issue: is there, in the East, something which has to be distinguished not only from the rigidly dogmatic attitude but also from the attitude which is usually associated with relativism, something which comes in between these two extremes, something which we may now describe as 'confessional relativism'? If so, we may reach a conclusion of considerable consequence in regard to what may be expected from the forces of religion.

To begin with, it may be held that even in the case of Hinduism the confessional element is not so entirely absent as might at first appear. For while it is true that many and various schools of thought are embraced in the Hindu household of faith, it is also true that most if not all Hindus share certain fundamental assumptions. They believe in transmigration, or the passage of sentient life from one form of existence to another. They believe that this passage is subject to the operation of the law of *karma*, so that as a man sows so shall he reap, if not in this present existence then in

X

some future existence. And they conceive the goal of life as union with Absolute Brahman. It is proper, then, to speak not only of Hindu views of life but of *the* Hindu view of life.

Next there is the consideration that the relativist attitude and the consequent criticism of Western dogmatism is not confined to Hindus. It is shared by Buddhists. Now, as we have observed, one of the things that is happening in the Buddhist world today is a pan-Buddhist movement similar to Christian ecumenical movements, a movement which seeks to bring the two main Buddhist traditions, Hinayana and Mahayana, more together. If we ask what it is that will most serve to bring them together, it may be answered that all Buddhists aspire to a way of life which is in character with what has been manifested by all the Bodhisattvas and Buddhas. In the Hinayana or Theravada tradition there is a central reference to the teaching and the example of the founder Gotama Buddha. He is named *the* Light of the World. In the Mahayana tradition there is reference to other Buddhas besides Gotama. But all manifest the same character of life. As, then, it is sometimes said that Christianity is Christ, may it not be said that Buddhism, Buddhist religion, is Buddha?[1] And have we not also here a community of believers gathered around and confessing a central, unifying Symbol? And hence, too, a central reference which qualifies Buddhist attitudes to all religious statements, including their own? Knowing their own distance from the enlightenment experienced by the Buddha they may be tolerant of other believers whose condition may be regarded as similar. But it can scarcely be a tolerance which extends to anything others may have to say in contradiction to what has been received from the Buddha. As followers of the Buddha they are restrained in this respect, like the followers of Christ, by a confessional allegiance.

Even if we confine our observation to Buddhists and Christians (or to some Christians) we may conclude, then, that we have, the world over, both East and West, a considerable body of believers whose attitude to differences of belief is comparable. And Hindus are not so far from sharing this same attitude as might at first be supposed. Scrutiny of other positions, if space is allowed, might also show that Jews and Muslims, too, come within this category.

It remains to consider what the prevalence of this attitude be-

[1] See *A Survey of Buddhism* by Bhikshu Sangharakshita, Indian Institute of World Culture, Bangalore, 1956.

tokens in regard to prospects of world community. We observed earlier that there is a twofold demand of the forces of religion. There is first the more general demand, often impatient, that religious believers should 'forget their differences and come together'. But there is also a second demand for the dynamic of religious motivation in the interests of world community, a dynamic which may mean anything but a forgetting of differences. The question was therefore raised whether it is possible to have it both ways. The one demand would seem to cancel the other. Now if the attitude betokened by confessional relativism is, as here suggested, the more prevalent attitude, it might indeed be possible, with some qualification, to have it both ways. For it means that, East and West, we can look for believers who approach the issue with all the dynamic associated with the allegiance to some particular confession of faith. At the same time the relativism associated with a confessionalism of this kind avoids that dismissal of other believers which follows from dogmatic presumption and rigidity.

On such a view there may be no forgetting of differences but rather an acceptance of differences, or perhaps, more precisely, the acceptance of those who maintain such differences; acceptance not of other beliefs, but of other *believers*. Some may hope for more than this. But the question we have been considering is what, on a realistic appraisal of the situation, may be expected. Our conclusion perhaps amounts to this: there is at least ground for anticipating a sufficient degree of tolerance on the part of a sufficient number of religious believers to allow for co-operation in the interests of world community without loss of conviction and dynamic faith.

XX. CONFLICT AND CO-EXISTENCE

Raghavan Iyer

The main, if modest, purpose of this symposium is to offer a provisional framework for a frank dialogue between Asians and Europeans on the Glass Curtain that seems to separate them. In as much as the Glass Curtain is a reality in the minds of men, there is no gain in merely wishing it were otherwise or in predicting its automatic disappearance, let alone in giving dogmatic answers to difficult questions. Actual tensions cannot be resolved by abstract panaceas. If there is indeed an intractable psychological barrier to mutual understanding between Asians and Europeans, every attempt to transcend inherited myths and misconceptions will itself be conditioned by them to a greater degree than we would care to admit. It is a sign of the persistence of the Glass Curtain that both Asians and Europeans have at times claimed that the problems raised by it are less acute in their own part of the world or that they are uniquely able to show the way out of the common predicament. Some Europeans have held that East-West understanding can be achieved through the 'Europeanization' of Asia, or the spread of Christianity or of truths exclusively taught by it. Similarly, Asians have exhorted Europeans to learn from their exemplary tolerance, from Confucius or the *Sanatana Dharma*, and it has also been asserted that the problems of the West will find a 'higher solution' in the East, with its timeless wisdom and traditional eclecticism. Further, those who talk of combining European technology with Asian spirituality or 'Eastern wisdom' with 'Western love' are simply begging too many questions. Mutual understanding can hardly be secured through such barter between rival claimants.

The crucial first step towards greater comprehension may well be a willing recognition of the nature and magnitude of a long legacy of misunderstanding, neither exaggerating nor minimizing its importance. The active acceptance of the need for co-existence has often resulted only after a protracted and profitless conflict. Historians like Romein have even held that the mutual hostility between Asians and Europeans was necessary before the possibility of co-operation could be grasped, that 'only in anticipation of a better future can one put up with a tragic past'. On the other hand, the very concern with an East-West dichotomy has been seen by some Asians as a mere device to confirm European superiority, while its rejection has been regarded by a European scholar as essentially a camouflage for Asian claims to superiority. In any case, it has meant different things to different people. Even if it is now out of date, its past reiteration has cast a dark shadow that cannot be overlooked. The verbal celebration of human brotherhood is too often a mere compensation for the painful awareness of the immediacy of inward bitterness, a pious hope rather than a binding pledge. We may deplore the common human craving for walls, but we dare not take human solidarity too much for granted.

Max Scheler spoke in prophetic terms of the approach of 'the hour that harbours in its breast the future of humanity, the hour when Asia and Europe will enter upon a discussion of the principles of their religions and metaphysical life'. But any such dialogue cannot wholly ignore the historical encounter between the peoples of Asia and Europe, unless we take the gloomy Hegelian view that the only lesson taught by history is that men learn nothing from it. It is easy but evasive to say 'let bygones be bygones', to urge Asians and Europeans alike to start with a clean slate, but many of them know only too well the truth of the maxim—'history is what we remember'. We cannot just sweep away the painful memories of the recent encounter between Asia and Europe.

In the first three parts of this symposium there have been overt and indirect references to the disturbing historical memories that have shaped the attitudes of diverse peoples in Asia and Europe; the tensions and paradoxes connected with the search for national identity; the ways in which the awareness of cultural differences can lead to condescension and resentment as a result of the changing balance of political power and material advantage; the extent to which colonialism represents a state of mind as well as a system; the degree to which nationalism is a search for parity of esteem as well as an assertion of independence; the mixture of aggressive and defensive emotions displayed both by Asians and by Europeans; the manner in which the idealization and denigration of alien peoples are equally bound up with the internal needs of societies at different times; the periods of isolation and superficial intercourse as well as of enforced and painful contacts in the long encounter between the peoples of Asia and Europe; the good and the harm done by religious evangelism and by Orientalist studies; the complex interaction between the sources of tradition and the forces of social change.

While Mr. Venkatachar points to the consequences of the different attitudes of Asian societies and European states to the transmission and assimilation of cultures, Mr. Hudson stresses the crucial role of mercantile capitalism in differentiating Europe from Asia. Mr. Campbell and Mr. Sherrard refer to Greece's spiritual and cultural links with the East, the contrast between Greek and Latin Christianity, the Greek contribution to the European Renaissance and the impact of European nationalism on modern Greece. Mr. Utechin points out that Russians have seen Russia as the synthesis but also as the antithesis of both Europe and Asia, and the emergence of attitudes to the Chinese similar to those shown by the West to Russians. Mr. Luard chooses to sharpen the contrast between Chinese and Western thought and culture, and he also emphasizes the connection between the traditional ethnocentricity and the contemporary messianism of China.[1] Mr. Storry portrays the ambivalent emotions of the Japanese towards Europeans, the derogation of Chinese status implicit in their admiration for European modes of thought and conduct, the contrast they continue to make between Eastern ethics and Western science, their view of the West as glamorous and inscrutable. Mr. Somjee considers how far the earlier Indian indifference to Europe has given way in recent history to the adoption of the European concept of secular progress, combined with the rejection of European claims to a monopoly of religious truth and cultural greatness. Mr. Parker discusses the adoption by the Arabs of

---

[1] It is ironical that Marx, who was hardly free from the European prejudices of his time against the East, spoke slightingly not only about Russia but even more so about 'China's barbarous hermetic isolation from the civilized world'. A much-needed corrective to such glib characterizations is Geoffrey Hudson's *Europe and China*, Needham's monumental work, and J. R. Levenson's perceptive writings, especially his essay in *Studies in Chinese Thought*, ed. by Arthur F. Wright (Chicago, 1953).

'Westernism' as an escape from irksome Ottomanism and their subsequent disillusionment and bitterness, while Mr. Lewis explains how the end of Ottomanism led to the wholesale and inevitably incomplete 'Westernization' of the Turks as a policy amounting to dogma. The part played by Jesuit accounts of China, ironically enough, in shaping the thought and tactics of the anti-clerical French *philosophes* is shown by Mr. Shackleton.[1] The German idealization of India, depicted by Mr. Taylor, was also an attempt to meet an internal need (unlike the generous praise in classical times of the Indian Gymnosophists by Greeks like Megasthenes). Altogether, the horizons of Western scholarship were widened by the French Enlightenment and the German Romantics only at the cost of creating new myths about the 'enlightened despotism' and the 'mystical pessimism' of the East. The complex British attitudes to Asia, as Mr. Bearce points out, were more directly related to personal experience, but they too reflected diverse currents of thought at home and also represented the collision of divergent societies which were changing at a different pace.

Every attempt to consider aspects of the historical encounter that shaped the changing attitudes of Asians and Europeans is involved with complex issues which are bound to be controversial, and not only when it is European scholars who portray Asian attitudes. These are all worthy themes for a dialogue that could develop fruitfully if it were conducted in a climate of tolerance and civility. But it is far more difficult to confront rival claims to 'uniqueness' in a manner that avoids a *dialogue des sourds*. There cannot even be any Asian or European consensus, let alone common agreement, regarding any specific claim to cultural 'uniqueness' that may be advanced. Yet such claims cannot be ignored as long as the need to make them is widely felt. It is useful to bring into the open typical points of basic disagreement so long as the aim is not to secure a hasty or cheap refutation of the opposite viewpoint but really to understand. If individuals do, in fact, seek to identify themselves or others as Asians or Europeans, 'Orientals' or

[1] For a fascinating account of the francophilia of (and the belated impact of the French Enlightenment on) the 'Chinese *philosophes*' early in the twentieth century, see C. Brandt's 'The French-Returned Elite in the Chinese Communist Party' in *Economic and Social Problems of the Far East*, Hong Kong University Press, 1962.

'Westerners', the confronting of rival claims to uniqueness may help to put them in a perspective in which they lose their rigidity even if they do not shrink into insignificance. The desire for recognition is a potent force in history, and the temptation to generalize about 'alien' peoples and cultures is difficult to resist.

Many Europeans would perhaps concur with Mr. Brugman's attempt to base the 'uniqueness' of Europe upon an essentially Christian foundation[1] and the dynamism of Europeans as 'a promethean race'. Equally, most Asians would agree with Mr. Gungwu in esteeming Europe for the Enlightenment rather than for its Christianity, in connecting the creative power of modern Europe with the scientific outlook rather than the religious heritage of Europeans. On all such matters, there is room for endless debate but no hope of certitude. Again, whereas Mr. Nakamura understandably distrusts every claim to Asian 'uniqueness' that overlooks Asian diversity or European parallels, Mr. Tinker is truly concerned that contemporary Asia should not entirely discard its traditional emphasis on social solidarity, harmony with nature, and a sense of timelessness. Here too we have material for further reflection and for discussion.

The importance of all claims to uniqueness lies in the fact that their psychological potency is independent of their intellectual validity or measure of acceptance. The difficulty with all such claims is that we are faced with a familiar dilemma: if they are too general and abstract, they do not differentiate sharply enough and may even obscure concrete if subtle divergences; if they are too specific and precise, they may often be true only in a tautological or trivial sense. Also, strong claims look like arbitrary assertions to those whom they exclude, while the admission of enough qualifications renders them too weak to evoke enthusiasm among those needing self-assurance. In either case, the same phenomena could be explained very differently and all too often subjective preferences masquerade as objective truths. It is not uncommon for the clash between claims and counter-claims to degenerate into mere

[1] Asians have usually thought otherwise. Vivekananda held that Europe had, as it were, conformed to the activism of the *Gita* while Asia had, to its cost, stressed the 'Christian' virtues of meekness and non-retaliation. Hwuy-Ung argued that Europe would not have been a 'power' if it had practised Christianity. Baron Tsuzuki asked over fifty years ago how Western missionaries could expect Asians to show blind acceptance of the 'miracles' of Christ, while Western professors 'teach us the supremacy of reason, the necessity of scrutiny, and disbelief of anything supernatural'.

shadow-boxing. The same terms are used in different senses—words like 'freedom', 'democracy', 'progress', 'happiness', even 'individual worth'—and there are many shifts of meaning in a developing dialogue. Mutual misunderstanding results not so much from conflicting values as from the tendency to appropriate universal values in making claims to uniqueness.[1]

Whereas the thinkers of the French Enlightenment sought to ground ethical and political conceptions like 'freedom' in human nature itself, and this is no less true of the values proclaimed by the greatest saints and sages in all religious traditions, we find that the clever apologetics which feed religious, political, and cultural propaganda are concerned with labels like 'Christian love' or 'Buddhist compassion', 'Western freedom' or 'Eastern tolerance'. Perhaps the chief obstacle to effective communication between peoples is the common habit of comparing the best (or worst) in one's own culture or religion or tradition with the worst (or best) features of other cultures or religions or traditions.[2] It is also tempting to see the vices of Europe (or Asia) merely as aberrations that cannot tarnish its resplendent virtues and to plead that what Europeans (or Asians) ought to get rid of can be easily separated from what they ought, by all means, to preserve. But only the most naïve would go so far as to view Asia (or Europe) as the nursery of every imaginable virtue and Europe (or Asia) as the home of every conceivable vice.

It would be futile to hope that in any honest dialogue between Asians and Europeans about their cultural and religious traditions they could readily concede each other's claims to uniqueness. It would be merely an escape from the realities of the Glass Curtain if they were expected—to use a phrase of Mill—to 'recognise each other's reciprocal superiorities'.[3] The basis for East-West under-

---

[1] A preposterous claim of this sort is cited by the noted Sinologist E. R. Hughes in his preface to *The Individual in East and West*. And yet, even the doctrine of universal brotherhood has been repeatedly regarded as a Christian or Confucian, European or Asian, invention.

[2] See G. F. Hudson's trenchant comments (at the close of *Europe and China*) on such comparisons based on conveniently selected evidence, often not wilful. See also O. Rasmussen's *The Reconquest of Asia*. Similar examples of inept or unfair comparisons can be found in plenty in the writings of Asians.

[3] In a note to the author, a Western savant and life-long student of Eastern philosophies made the following statement: '*The question of authentic differences between East and West, and the justice or usefulness of comparisons drawn between*

standing has often been sought in some simple formula concerning the 'complementarity' of Eastern and Western thought, values, or cultures. The search for such a formula was a persisting element in the intellectual history of modern China, but it did little more than reflect the perplexities of Chinese intellectuals and nationalists. The *t'i-yung* formula in which Chinese values were to serve as *t'i*—substance—and the approved Western accretion as *yung*—use—was needed to justify the acceptance of European guns and ships and railways, while the superiority of Confucian values remained inviolable. The *chin-wen* formula sought to sanction cultural borrowing by appealing to the Chinese classics, without separating *t'i* from *yung*. The subsequent plea for syncretism in Yüan-p'ei's formula—'select the best in East and West'—chiefly expressed the wish to see the East as an equal and authentic partner, the desire for a genuine reciprocity in the meeting of minds. All such efforts have their parallel in other Asian cultures in recent history as well as in European attitudes to cultural borrowing from the East.

The concern for a real dialogue on equal terms is indeed more significant than the anxiety to reach agreement or to find specific solutions. In so far as the Glass Curtain signifies an inner reluctance to carry understanding beyond a safe limit, an inability to see other people as moved by aspirations that are largely comprehensible, the desire for dialogue on equal terms is itself a vital step forwards. It might at least mitigate the sense of total estrangement that distorts any actual disagreement with an extraneous element of bitterness or despair. Sometimes, however, the need for a new psychological climate for fruitful encounter is over-stated. For example, the Lebanese Christian, Charles Malik, has contended that 'East and West can come together in peace only if they repent together under transcendent judgment'. It is more im-

---

them, depend, finally, upon the normative values which frame the investigation. What paradigm of the Good—good man, good society—is the criterion? Without clear and explicit attention to this question, comparisons of East and West too easily become exercises in cultural egotism, even when pursued with manifest goodwill and an air of impartiality. Quite possibly, until a body of thought concerned with this paradigm is available, the study of "differences" should avoid value judgements and be limited to thoughtful and accurate description. Until this becomes the habit in scholarship, exploration and identification of differences may have the effect of concealing the actual riches in diversity, making them appear as barriers, built-in enmities, and sources of legitimate conflict. In other words, evaluation of the differences ought to depend upon comparison with a paradigm—an over-arching ideal—which does not really exist as yet for modern man.'

portant to see the psychological and contingent connection between authentic commitment and cultural receptivity, spiritual frustration and cultural aggression, between real strength and humility. Those who do least credit to their cultures often tend to boast most about it. The more a man is committed to truth and the more deeply he is rooted in a rich culture, the more likely he is to be non-coercive in his relations and dialogue with those of different backgrounds. He is perhaps less prone to regard his fundamental beliefs as citadels to be guarded against an outside enemy. If a meaningful dialogue and real understanding are to be achieved between Asians and Europeans, we need to seek out those who are deeply committed to traditional as well as emerging values in their own cultures, who are capable of combining integrity with sensitivity, tolerance with civility, who have the imagination needed to see the world through the eyes of others. Even if people of this sort are few and far between today, there are at least many more now who would find incredible Montesquieu's question 'How can one be Persian?'

Asians and Europeans alike would do well to pay closer attention to the cultural interactions that took place between Asia and Europe at different times. Professor Zelinski of Petersburg pointed out over fifty years ago that every cultivated man is a member of two cities, his own and that of antiquity. If we widen the concept of classical antiquity instead of confining it today to any single area of the world, more and more Asians and Europeans may cease to think in continental or national categories, gradually replacing these by a global perspective, a far-ranging vision of human excellence in art and in science as well as of human frailties and strivings in religious and political life. An acute sense of the cultural borrowings of mature peoples may be potent as a purifier of the imagination. Mr. Needham, in his essay, pleads for this wider vision especially in regard to science and he also points to Europe's technological debts to Asia.[1] Similarly, Mr. Slater draws attention to the constructive ways in which the great religions have affected each other in recent times. Some people would argue

[1] Professor Blackett has argued that Europe should give technical assistance to Asia as a way of paying off its scientific and technological debts in an earlier period (*The Listener*, September 5, 1957). A variant of this view is Harold Gould's article on 'The West's Real Debt to the East'—the Industrial Revolution—in *Quest*, Winter issue, 1961–2.

that while technology may herd us together, it cannot make us appreciate diverse cultures and traditions. But it could equally be contended that religions in practice more often promote human conflicts than transcend them.[1] It is not easy for religious or secular ideologists to renounce their claims on the souls or societies of those who firmly reject their doctrines. In general, a greater recognition of the cultural debts of all civilizations is indeed to be welcomed, though it is notoriously true that in the past peoples have rarely been willing to acknowledge openly their debts (even where these debts are easy to establish). Until Asians and Europeans appreciate the extent of their important debts to each other, they will not merely be inclined to keep old wounds open but will also fail to profit from the achievements and blunders, the deeper as well as the superficial aspects, of cultures other than their own.

The real problem raised by the Glass Curtain is not just to achieve greater understanding and sympathy between the intelligentsia of Asia and Europe, but how to bring these to bear upon the pervasive myths and misconceptions that breed prejudice and suspicion. Persisting misrepresentations, whether arising from ignorance or perversity, do impinge even if indirectly upon the policies of governments and the negative emotions stirred up by political and religious propagandists. This larger problem does not admit of any easy solution. It is possible to argue that while some people will always be slaves of slogans and be seduced by clever falsehoods, maturer minds must simply learn to put up with the myths of hostile propagandists and refuse to be affected by them. At the same time educationists cannot abdicate from their responsibility in regard to the revision of school textbooks and university syllabuses, the correction of gross misrepresentations and a deliberate broadening of horizons. This challenge has been taken up by R. H. Dance in his forthright volume *History the Betrayer*. Although he is chiefly concerned with European parochialism and prejudice in the teaching of history and the treatment of non-Christian religions, his book has a practical message for Asian as well as European propagandists. Indeed, no one who

---

[1] The ineffectiveness of religions in promoting world solidarity is discussed by H. W. Schneider in 'International Relations and World Religions', *Bulletin of the Blaisdell Institute*, Claremont, March 1963.

is seriously concerned about the Glass Curtain can afford to ignore this pioneering little volume.

Now that mutual toleration, if not mutual comprehension, is a condition of survival, civilized men cannot afford to overlook the 'civilities' in societies other than their own. The pursuit of such understanding is more exacting and rarer than is usually realized. In his excellent study *Islam and the West*, Norman Daniel shows the tenacity of a distorted image of Islam and how the distortions corresponded with what was once believed to be a Christian need. He put his finger on a basic problem, which is immensely important in the context of the Glass Curtain.

A body of firmly held opinions may be compatible with the capacity to imagine an attitude which is totally unlike them, and more or less contrary. Yet the association of the two is rare, not only among the ill-educated, as might be expected, but perhaps equally among the trained academic. Historical discipline requires this imaginative capacity, but even among historians it is often confined within professional limits. Historical discipline of any kind is of comparatively recent growth; the imaginative reconstruction of strange and remote societies is even more so; and a sympathetic exploration of their beliefs, with 'suspension of unbelief', is still rarely met. It is even less frequent that societies which are contemporary achieve knowledge and understanding of each other.

The imaginative shortcomings of historians harm the cause of human understanding, but today this is no less true of social scientists and especially of studies of comparative religion, though we may be losing the naïve sense of the absoluteness of our own cultures or religions.

The task of securing greater understanding between Asians and Europeans cannot be delegated to scholars alone if we are to make rapid and significant progress. We might get more effective communication if educated men generally could adopt a new etiquette that replaces self-glorification by self-examination, which requires them to look for the best in other cultures and to be aware of the worst in their own. Today this is not merely a moral or intellectual virtue, or a sign of maturity, but also sheer common sense. Propaganda and intellectual imperialism are peculiarly self-defeating in our own day. The more exaggerated the claims made for any particular political system or religious or cultural tradition, the more easily the gap between claims and reality strikes the intelligent traveller and observer who is the victim of ideological propaganda. Fukuzawa urged Asians and Europeans to teach each other and 'neither be ashamed nor boastful'. This is easier said than done, but we must make the attempt. At the least, we must avoid the 'heads I win, tails you lose' approach which is all too common in cultural dialogue.

It is paradoxical that Asians and Europeans alike are seeking for a deeper sense of world community at the very time that we see a declining sense of community in both Asian and European societies. The problems of status, adjustment, and moral direction have assumed a new and transcending importance in both developed and developing communities. We see before us today the spectacle of masses of individuals adrift, alienated intellectuals and elites in all parts of the world. The need for commitment is bound up with the problems of co-existence. The distortions in dialogue introduced by the Cold War and the Glass Curtain express as well as enhance the feeling of insecurity. However, the mood of eclecticism and the quest for distinctiveness in most Asian states and also in parts of Europe will increasingly dissolve simple ideological divisions and give a new meaning to the problem of co-existence between different systems. Further, neither Massis's plea in the twenties to preserve Europe from 'pernicious' Oriental influences nor Madame Louis-Barthoud's wish in the thirties for a Chinese wall to prevent the Occident from 'poisoning' the Orient have any real relevance to our time.

Today, more than ever before, it is dubious for any set of people to claim a privileged access, by virtue of racial identity or national status or geographical contiguity, to the legacy of classical Greece or China, of Christianity or Buddhism, of science or art. The hereditary principle which the French Revolution rejected no longer applies even in the realm of values and skills. It now makes little sense to assume that there is the same kind of cultural identity for all those who live within the frontiers of a nation-state, let alone an entire continent, even if it was plausible to do so in the past. It is possible to argue that in the fast-changing world of today, the Glass Curtain may not vanish overnight but merely become more and more irrelevant to more and more people. A few may find it neither unpleasant nor far-fetched to pin their faith in K'ang Yu-Wei's prediction at the close of the last century:

There will be a day when everything throughout the earth, large or small, far or near, will be like one. There will be no longer any nations, no more racial distinctions, and customs will be everywhere the same. With this uniformity will come the Age of Great Peace. Confucius knew all this in advance.

It is perhaps more likely that the condescension towards foreigners may co-exist with a growing recognition of the fundamental equality of humanity, as in the days of Isocrates and Eratosthenes. The former recognized that the influence of education—'the great leveller'—is greater than that of geography, and the latter is reported to have said that men should not be classified as Greeks or barbarians but rather as good or bad. As contemporary differences in *nomos* ('convention') become less significant owing to the rapid pace of change, the recognition of human equality on the basis of a common *physis* ('nature') may receive much wider dissemination than in the past. We may now be readier to incarnate the ideals of Stoicism, the noblest product of the classical encounter of Asia and Europe, than ever before. More and more people in East and West may come to see themselves, whatever their ancestral culture or religion, as equally citizens of the world (*cosmopolitai*). Even the belief of Aristides, the Greek orator from Smyrna, that in the Roman republic 'Asians are treated exactly the same as Europeans' may apply more aptly to the world forums of the future.

This cheerful prospect of transcending the Glass Curtain has been well expressed by Geoffrey Hudson:

. . . the new generalized cosmopolitan culture of this age has at least put us at a new point of vantage for apprehension of all the great cultural systems of the past, since all these, including our own, have lost their exclusive hold, while the whole cultural heritage of humanity, of whatever civilization, is more available and accessible to the ordinary educated man, if he wishes to explore it, than it has ever been before. The arrogant cultural self-sufficiency of 19th century Europe, judging Eastern philosophy, literature and art by its own standards and conventions, is giving place, under conditions in which there is no longer any European world supremacy, to a much greater freedom of approach to all cultural phenomena, a more comprehensive and eclectic taste. In spite of the current excesses of political nationalism a genuine citizenship of the world has become more of a practical possibility in the cultural sphere than at any time in the past history of man.[1]

[1] *Oxford Opinion*, October 1958.

An ancient dream may have now become a practical possibility, but what is the actual probability of realizing it to a reasonable degree in the world as it is today? Our assessment of the future relevance of the Glass Curtain will depend upon our answer to this difficult question. Looking back at the 'gigantic Asian movements of the past', Hyndman wrote in 1919 that a new Mohammed is quite as likely to make his appearance as a new Buddha, a reborn Confucius, or a modern Christ. But if we shun speculation about ancient and future events and confine our gaze to the present day, we notice that Asians and Europeans have certain assets and handicaps in realizing the possibility of 'a genuine citizenship of the world'.

One of the odd consequences of European dominance in recent centuries is that the Asian today is in a position to know more about European civilization than the European does about Asian cultures. The European may be well in advance of most Asian peoples in technical and scientific attainments, but he perhaps suffers from a cultural handicap in his effort to become a man of universal culture. On the other hand, the Asian intellectual seems increasingly to be alienated from his spiritual and cultural past at a time when the European is consciously seeking to discover his roots. But again, the Asian may have yet another advantage. Whereas under European rule he was obsessed with making claims for his culture, he has now won a new confidence and a sense of excitement in current world developments. By contrast, many Europeans appear to have been so wounded by the loss of their recent ascendancy that they now seem anxious to compensate by aggressive cultural self-assertion.[1] But the European too may have a second advantage over the Asian. While the Asian is entering a phase of intense nationalism—a 'powerful anaesthetic', as Tagore called it—the European is today more willing to look beyond nation-states to a wider plane of concerted action in a larger community.

Both Europeans and Asians must now recognize their assets and handicaps in becoming *cosmopolitai*, in seeking a feasible ideal of human fraternity that can rise above the clash of cultures and may even make nonsense of the Glass Curtain. The challenge to both

---

[1] Bertrand de Jouvenel has suggested a criterion of 'European decadence'—'Europeans now fear History instead of making it', *The Guardian Weekly*, April 1, 1954.

in the dangerous world in which we live may be put in the broadest terms, with their own concrete implications. Who speaks for man, for human needs and humane values, in the councils of the world? Who will excel in learning the lessons of history, of past cultural and political encounters? Who will be the first to show at least a partial transcendence of partisanship and say about his *soi-disant* rivals:

> He drew a circle that shut me out—
> Heretic, rebel, a thing to flout.
> But Love and I had the wit to win:
> We drew a larger circle and took him in!

Y

A DIALOGUE ON THE
GLASS CURTAIN

A DIALOGUE ON THE
GLASS CURTAIN[1]

Arnold Toynbee and Raghavan Iyer

I

LAWSON: The Unesco Project for understanding between the Orient and the Occident, and I suggest that henceforth in this discussion we refer to it, if at all, as the East-West Project, presupposes that there is an urgent need for greater understanding between the two parts of the world. Is there, in fact, a division between Asia and the West? Dr. Toynbee, do you see some kind of curtain existing between them?

TOYNBEE: We know there is an iron curtain, of a political sort, between Russia and America, or the Communist world and the Western world, but I see a much more subtle and ancient curtain between the West and what I would prefer to call 'the non-West' rather than 'the East', not of a political or military kind, but of a psychological sort.

LAWSON: Could you, Dr. Iyer, give any particular name to that type of curtain?

IYER: I think that it could be called a glass curtain, which by its very nature is not as obvious as the iron curtain. There are many people who would deny that there is any curtain at all between Asia and Europe or that 'East' and 'West' are easily manageable terms, but I think there is some sort of invisible yet impenetrable curtain, and when I say this I really don't want to invent it. We don't need to invent another kind of curtain standing for incompatible interests or irreconcilable ideologies, but I think there does exist this subtler curtain, which although it may be

---

[1] This is a slightly revised but complete version of an unscripted one-hour discussion, recorded for the Radio Division of Unesco in April 1959, with Terence Lawson as Chairman.

transparent, seems to be ever-present. We may replace old glass panes with new, but there are no chinks in this curtain.

TOYNBEE: Of course, with the iron curtain, you know it is iron and you can't get through; with a glass curtain you mistake and think there's nothing there, and then as soon as you try to get through you find that there is. It is a more awkward thing to manage, isn't it?

IYER: And it is not incompatible even with genuine goodwill, or of course, with apathy. It is in fact the problem of seeing through a glass darkly, a condition similar to that of the schizophrenic who felt that between him and the rest of humanity there was some kind of hard glass pane through which he couldn't make real contact with the other side.

TOYNBEE: Yes, but I think it's connected with a feeling of uneasiness on both sides. As one looks at the other man through the curtain, one feels doubtful about one's own position psychologically.

LAWSON: Could you produce some actual examples of this distorted vision?

IYER: Well, for instance, I would think that whereas in the case of the iron curtain people don't claim on both sides to have the same values, in the case of the glass curtain they do. Universal values are made the basis of unique claims. For example, there is the feeling on each side that it possesses a unique respect for individual worth and dignity, that it has a wholly unique concept of freedom or charity or love; one could multiply examples.

TOYNBEE: That's a sure sign of lack of self-confidence, I think, when one makes these universal claims just for oneself as opposed to the other man. I think this is mutual and although there may be many differences of political power which vary at different times between people on both sides of the glass curtain, it is this psychological uncertainty on either side that is the permanent thing about it, which makes it so hard to get through.

LAWSON: But isn't there something inevitable about this? Aren't all human societies parochial and prejudiced, don't they all have somewhat distorted views of the other?

IYER: I think this is so, but the trouble, of course, with this particular curtain is that we are dealing with two enormous categories, vague amorphous concepts into which we could put whatever we like. 'East' and 'West' become in fact baskets into which we put whatever we like, in the case of our own part of the world, and whatever we don't like in the case of the other, and we go on doing this all over again at different levels. We may talk of 'Oriental despotism' or 'Oriental cunning' or 'Oriental stagnation', or, on the other side, we may talk of 'Western materialism', 'Western hypocrisy', 'Western decadence', and so on. I could again multiply examples: 'Oriental passivity', 'Oriental glamour', 'Oriental extravagance', or 'Western aggressiveness', 'Western vulgarity', 'mechanistic West', and so on, and above all the idea that the East is something vague, mysterious, and mushy, and the idea on the other side that the West is hard, harsh, dogmatic.

TOYNBEE: I think it all comes out historically from the recent ascendancy of the West which is now passing away. I think 'the East' or 'the Orient' is a Western invention; I think the West quite lately has set itself apart from the rest of the world and lumped the whole of the rest of the world together as 'the East'. Now this is probably a rather controversial view on which Dr. Iyer has a different opinion.

IYER: No, I do agree with you that 'the East' for many Westerners simply means: 'not West'.

TOYNBEE: It is true, of course, that all the non-Western peoples have had the same experience in modern times; they've all come up against the West and had rather an upsetting experience. That's true of Arabs, other Moslems, that's true of Indians, Chinese, Japanese, Russians; I would include even some Latin Americans. Common experience creates a sense of unity.

IYER: I agree with you there, but isn't there a little more to it than that? Isn't it the case that certain notions lying around are suddenly taken up for their propagandist uses, that there may be only a small core of truth underlying these categories, but in fact this gets heavily overlaid with myth that itself in time becomes a part of reality? 'The East' is essentially supposed to refer to the Chinese and Indian civilizations, to Taoism, Hinduism, and Buddhism, just as 'the West' is seen usually in terms of the Judaeo-Christian tradition and the Greco-Roman heritage?

TOYNBEE: Yes, that raises rather an interesting question, because if we divide by Christianity and Judaism, we can't stop there.

Islam comes on the Western side, whereas Taoism, Hinduism, and Buddhism are the other half.

IYER: Under such a rigid division, Islam would be one of those intermediate categories which isn't entirely Western or Eastern. But isn't that really true of so much else? If we push these two categories too far and lump everything in the world under either category, surely we are going to do injustice to all the intermediate states or overlapping civilizations. After all, even Greece is historically and ethnically both European and Asian, although it has been appropriated entirely to Europe. In fact, the farther in time we push back this division, the more what we call 'West' merges into the 'East' and the nearer we get to our own time, the more what we term 'East' comes closer to the 'West'.

TOYNBEE: The West has been separate even in our own time and then the East has reacted by trying to get even with the West, I think.

IYER: But don't you think that in reality this curtain, if it exists, emerged originally in the West, as a sort of Western, if not as an early Greek, invention?

TOYNBEE: Anyway, as a modern Western invention. I think it is connected with the rise of modern Western science and technology which gave the West its temporary overwhelming power until the rest of the world began to take it over and get even with the West in that way.

IYER: I agree that modern industrialism and science have given this curtain a new and compelling context, but surely the curtain is rather ancient, if it does exist at all.

TOYNBEE: It has existed on and off at different times, I think.

IYER: But perhaps the large differences within the East or the West have not appeared to be so important whenever Asia and Europe have significantly encountered each other?

TOYNBEE: Well, I think of the Middle Ages, when Christianity and Islam at the Western end of the world confronted each other, they faced each other on terms of equality at that time, I think. Each thought the other wrong, but they didn't feel this psychological distress, neither of them, in the presence of the other, in case the other might after all be right.

IYER: This point about the power balance and the sense of equality is indeed very important. It seems to me that there is a great danger now that the power balance between Asia and Europe has been altered to the detriment of the West, that some people may attempt to identify the iron curtain with the older glass curtain and in this way the glass curtain may itself end up by becoming something like an iron curtain.

TOYNBEE: This would be the very sad result of getting back to equality. The point of that and its purpose must be to get unity and a real human universal relation between all parts of the human race.

IYER: It would be nice to think that the glass curtain would automatically disappear with this increasing equality, but I fear we cannot afford to be so sanguine because on both sides there is a gap between the ancient and the modern world which I think is the real gap, a gap in time rather than in space, a gap in thought.

TOYNBEE: Don't I feel that! After all, I had a classical education, like my Chinese or Hindu contemporaries, and then I can't drive a car. Well now, when I go to Turkey, say, I meet far out on the road a Turkish lorry driver who can service his car and repair it and so on, as well as drive it. He doesn't know anything about the Persian and Arabic classics, so I feel he is the modern man and I am the ancient man. And I feel a kind of inferiority in front of him; I am sure he feels superior to me. It cuts across all these geographical divisions.

IYER: Unfortunately, when the Turkish intelligentsia becomes Westernized, it also gets uprooted from its own traditional culture. In other words, part of what we mean by this glass curtain is that neither side can fully respond to the other side without being in danger of becoming deracinated.

TOYNBEE: Very often the Westernized Turk can't even read the inscriptions over his own public monuments of a century or so ago. He is entirely cut off from his past.

IYER: We can see that some people in the West, when they think of the East, have an idealized concept of the traditional Orient that bears less and less resemblance to the modern Westernized East. Also, as a result of this East-West division, we find that a new class of persons emerges, people who claim to be on both sides at the same time, whether it be in Belgrade or Ankara or Cairo or Jerusalem, or even in Cyprus.

TOYNBEE: Intelligentsia, as the Russians call them.

IYER: I am referring also to people who actually trade on the

East-West distinction and say that they are on both sides and that they could uniquely synthesize.

TOYNBEE: They are interpreters and very important but they are an unhappy class.

II

LAWSON: It has been said that the 450 years which began with the arrival of the Portuguese in India in 1498 and ended with the withdrawal of the British forces from India in 1947, constitute a clearly-marked epoch of Asian history. What do you regard as the significance of this period in relation to the division and lack of understanding between Asia and the West, Dr. Toynbee?

TOYNBEE: It was obviously a most important period for the East and West as well as in the history of the world, but just because it matters to all of us living now so much, there is the danger that we may read back into the past the same East-West division that exists today. I think there have been many cases of this kind in the past, but I don't think all through history we get the same rigid division.

IYER: On the other hand, wouldn't you agree that if there is an iron curtain today between the Soviet Union and Western Europe, it is partly because it has its cultural roots in the tensions and dialogues of the nineteenth century, and that similarly here too, even if we cannot trace a constant curtain, there has been every now and again a consciousness of cultural tension between Asia and Europe?

TOYNBEE: Well, I think Russia is in the same position as Asia in relation to the West in modern times. We are talking about the nineteenth century, a very recent time. But looking further back, I think there was a similar case between the ancient Greeks and their Asian neighbours, but although the glass curtain may have been the same, the actors were different. The interesting thing about the ancient Greek case is that there we know the whole story, we know how it ended. Now we are in the middle of our story, we have no idea how it is going to end. We have our guesses, but we don't really know. But we can look back over about a thousand years of relations between the Greeks and their Asian neighbours and see how it ended. I think that's interesting and illuminating for us.

IYER: But isn't the beginning also of that process interesting because, when we push it back far enough, can we really say 'this is the East' and 'that is the West'? When we consider Crete and all the early formative influences on ancient Greece, we can't really make the same sorts of sharp distinctions that appeared later on, as when the Greeks encountered the Persians.

TOYNBEE: Yes, I think at that early stage there were just a number of different civilizations, shall we say, but we can't say that one is particularly Eastern or the other is particularly Western. They were distinctive—different from each other. But when we come to the Greeks and their neighbours, we know more because we have their literature. I think it begins rather as between the modern West and the Orientals with admiration and awe from the younger people towards the older. Then they get military victories and they become rather arrogant, and then they meet the Orientals that they conquer rather intimately and then further changes occur.

LAWSON: Well, in this lightning survey, what do you see as the next stage which is significant?

TOYNBEE: Looking back at the later chapters of the Greek encounter with the East, what happened in the end after the Thousand Years was that the East made a come-back on the religious plane. The Greeks conquered the East by force of arms, the East converted the Greeks first to Christianity and then they built their own forms of Christianity and drove out the Greek forms, and then Islam came and produced a distinctively Eastern religion which more or less ended Greek influence in the East. That wasn't the last word, because the Moslems then adopted Greek philosophy and science.

IYER: The fusion of thought that took place, for example, in Alexandria between Indian, Jewish, and Greek elements and Christianity, was in the end resisted not so much by the Greeks as by the Roman church.

TOYNBEE: Though, if you analyse Christianity of any form, you find the fusion in it, I think you find both the Greek and the Jewish and other Oriental and Indian ideas too.

IYER: This is what I find fascinating, that even where empires expanded, unifying and then dividing peoples as a result of new psychological barriers, almost all the major religions were initially and essentially syncretistic, bringing people closer together, perhaps more than they realized at the time.

TOYNBEE: Well, the same thing happened between India and China, didn't it, where there wasn't any military conquest by India, but the Chinese did adopt an Indian religion—Buddhism.

IYER: Yes, I think that is a very good case. Also it appears that the Japanese, the first impact on whom of Chinese or Indian influence was on a non-material plane, did not resent it and to this day they seem proud of being imitators more than inventors.

LAWSON: I think that we should now move on to the period of intense impact, the period of Western dominance.

IYER: Before we do that, shouldn't we say just a word about travellers' tales during the long period of comparative isolation and apparent self-sufficiency of East and West? These travellers' tales, the reports of missionaries and traders, were often both arrogant and ignorant and helped to keep alive facile epithets and categories, even though it is true that the intensity of ill-feeling only emerges in the modern imperialist era.

TOYNBEE: Yes, when there was a sudden violent contact, rather like the time after Alexander the Great.

IYER: What differences do you find between ancient and modern imperialism? Do you find that the same cycle is repeated, as you stated earlier?

TOYNBEE: In some ways. The Greeks in Egypt had this sense of political superiority and they were rather exploiters economically too. But they were always conscious, I think, that though intellectually and practically they might temporarily have been in a stronger position, in all matters of religion they were rather children. They always kept that feeling. And in the end, Eastern religion conquered them.

IYER: What I find interesting about this more recent phase is that although politically it represented intense conflict and frustration and to that extent was responsible for the curtain as we now know it, culturally and spiritually it gave birth to several unexpected, unintended movements of real significance. To take just one example, the British made possible the resurgence of traditional systems of thought in India, and the new Indian Renaissance which resulted, like the Italian Renaissance, from the rediscovery of the classics, in turn stimulated the Romantic Movement that has remained a continuous cultural undercurrent in Europe.

TOYNBEE: I think that's something new, I would say. I don't think the ancient Greeks would have thought of taking seriously the intellectual past of contemporary Oriental peoples.

IYER: But on the other hand, we find that in this period the East also becomes for the first time a category or a symbol that is invoked in the context of internal dialogues and disagreements within Europe itself. We have, for example, Voltaire's attitude to China. Again, the attitude to India of the German Romantics was surely part of their own self-exploration and their own difficulties with other Europeans.

TOYNBEE: Yes, I think so. The East became a symbol in a Western debate, really.

IYER: I think that in this latest phase, which we have now entered, of anti-colonialism and nationalism, with the deep sense of resentment both of the new 'haves' who didn't hold for so long any real power and also of the 'ex-haves' who seem to resent sharply their loss of former status, we are perhaps facing the worst kind of consequence and expression of the curtain.

TOYNBEE: Worst in one way, in the sense that feelings are rather high at present, but I think time will help to cure that. And I do think that psychological equality, rather than just political and economic equality, is the only way towards the unity of the human race, and we are at any rate getting closer to equality.

IYER: I am glad to hear you say that because so often today Asian nationalism is derided just because it is Asian, whereas in the West nationalism is considered to have had in the past a progressive function. We now seem to have reached a point where because of the loss of its former status and power Europe is really resenting the feeling that it has apparently lost both ways, —culturally it seems to have lost, though it really hasn't, and politically it has definitely lost its past dominance.

TOYNBEE: I think that will be temporary and we shall see very rapid changes now both on the Western side and on the Eastern side. Asian nationalism is bound to change very rapidly because it came into existence in recent times to put an end to Western domination. When that is achieved, it has to find new goals, and new problems will arise for it, and so it will certainly change very fast.

IYER: Yes, I think as time goes on, the apparent lack of gratitude of Asians at present for the great contributions of the West will, in fact, disappear. People everywhere don't normally like to acknowledge their debts, but they none the less have these debts and know them, and I think this is the hopeful thing about the new confidence in the East. We need more careful attention to all cultural debts, but no one can any more set himself up as a sort of expert on the whole of the East or even on every aspect of any one civilization in the East. Don't you think Orientalism is itself a product of the older phase of Western arrogance?

TOYNBEE: I don't like the word Orientalism—this is a kind of museum idea that the Orient is a funny old place which you have great specialists studying. My idea is that Eastern history —if you can call it Eastern—is just part of history and one should study all peoples of the world in the same sort of ways out of common interest in humanity, because we all contribute to the common treasures, to the common stock.

LAWSON: May I come in at this stage with a question to you, Dr. Iyer? Some people in the West, seeing the newly independent countries of Asia starting off with all the trappings of democracy and then seeing them develop into a highly nationalist phase with autocratic or military rule, feel this is a retrogression. Do you necessarily agree with that?

IYER: Of course, I think all autocracy is a bad thing. On the other hand, it was a great mistake, in fact an expression of this curtain of which we are talking, that people did assume too glibly in the West that democratic institutions of the Western kind and especially of the English kind, which are very peculiar to a small society with a homogeneous, insular culture and a unique political history, would work in the large and diverse nations of the East. It was also a mistake to ignore the fact that the East has had long experience of local democracy and very different sorts of political and social institutions, some of which may now have to be revived and remodelled into new forms.

TOYNBEE: Well now, when people start making wine in America or Australia, they make Australian hock, American burgundy, and so on. Now why burgundy and hock—this isn't France or Germany, why not make your own wine? Now that's what I think is going to happen in the East; they'll be democratic no doubt, but not according to a conventional, traditional Western pattern. They'll work out their own way.

IYER: Provided the East doesn't get heady with the wine of Western ideas and institutions.

III

LAWSON: The period of imperialism in ancient history and the Western dominance of Asia with its action and reaction resulting in anti-colonialism and nationalism, have contributed enormously to the division, the glass curtain, between Asia and the West. But is there more behind this division than merely the accidents and incidents of history? Are there wide gaps between the cultures of Asia and the West because of social and economic differences? Dr. Iyer, what relative importance do you ascribe to these?

IYER: Well, I think that even more important than the historical context in which this curtain emerged, and even more important than the conflicts of economic and social interest today which provide the new context of the curtain, the main problem connected with the curtain is religious, or more broadly, ideological. The competition and rivalry between different parts of the world, purely arising out of economic and commercial interests, does not by itself constitute a curtain. It may be very unpleasant, it can clearly assume various forms of bitterness and intensity, but I don't think it produces that persistent invisible barrier, the glass curtain, of which we speak. I doubt whether without this long-standing curtain, the various economic and political conflicts of today would be subsumed under a broad East-West division. On the other hand, I do think that the religious and ideological contribution to the so-called barrier between East and West is extremely important.

TOYNBEE: Well, I agree with you on that. I am thinking of, for instance, the bargaining and re-bargaining about oil between Arab and European countries, which is not so different from any other business transactions. In fact one party of Arabs and one party of Europeans do not really come in. It is just part of the ordinary business wrangle of the world. So I agree it is the ideological and religious issue that is the crucial one.

IYER: Of course, certain people in the East are trying to make use of the enormous disparities in economic and social standards between the East and the West to emphasize the existence of the curtain, and vice versa. But in the end, if we ascribe the curtain simply to some simple social or economic or physical factor, we are led to something like the crude determinism, the absurd position of saying, as with Hippocrates or even with Buckle in the nineteenth century, that climate is the cause of the curtain, that Europe is blessed with a cool and temperate climate and Asia is not. Similarly, some people assert that Asia has been spoilt by the abundance of its natural resources, whereas Europe has ingeniously overcome its material limitations.

TOYNBEE: Well, supposing we could air-condition the whole world so that we all lived in the same climate, and supposing we could equalize out all individual incomes, East and West, I don't think that would get rid of this glass curtain. I think we should still have this ideological barrier there just the same.

IYER: I agree, and I think this barrier is not because of a necessary incompatibility between alternative religious 'systems'. After all, 'Hinduism', 'Buddhism', 'Christianity', and the like are just as much logical constructions or mental abstractions as the terms 'East' and 'West'. On the other hand, I do think that religious ideology or religious propaganda has a lot to do with this curtain today, not any acute cleavage between the original teachings of the various religions, but the continual clash between the special claims made by competing apologists on behalf of these various religions.

TOYNBEE: Yes, and there are, as I see it, two main religious attitudes which go quite a long way back. There is, what I might call, the Hindu/Buddhist attitude which is rather the 'live and let live' attitude—there are more roads than one to the top of the mountain, there are alternative ways of approaching the truth. On the other side there is, what I might call, the Jewish/Christian/Moslem attitude, which says—right or wrong, yes or no, black or white, you must scrap the other and take this wholly—a more uncompromising attitude. Now we are living in an age when we come close up to each other with atom bombs in our hand, and it seems to me that the people belonging to, what shall we call it, the Jewish/Christian/Moslem group of religions, who have always thought it rather poor-spirited not to be uncompromising had better reconsider, in the light of the very dangerous world we live in, whether there isn't a lot to be said for the Hindu/Buddhist attitude in present circumstances anyway.

IYER: I am bound to say I agree with you on this, because I think that the identification of Christianity with the highest or the total truth, as well as the identification of Christianity with Europe, have both certainly detracted from Christianity and from Europe. They have not detracted from truth and indeed, it seems, many people in the East prize the secular virtues and the secular rationalist tradition of the West even more than its religious tradition. But what people in the East are apt to overlook is that some of the things they prize in the West originally arose out of the finer elements in Christianity. Also, despite the tradition of tolerance and the genuine attitude of religious relativity and humility in the East to this day, there are Asians, of course, who can be extremely condescending and they almost make a unique claim out of their very tolerance, and this makes them enormously self-righteous, oblivious even to recent outbreaks of religious or ideological bigotry in Asia.

TOYNBEE: Yes, of course we none of us live up to our ideals. All the same, the little I know of missionary movements of Buddhism say in Eastern Asia, China, Japan, Korea, and the rest, as compared with the missionary movement of Christianity or Islam, does make me think that Buddhism did not claim this complete monopoly. It was prepared to live and let live with other religions and ideologies and, therefore, the reactions that they produced—though it did produce a certain reaction among Confucians, for instance, in China—they were never so extreme. The violence of religious warfare that you get in the Western end of the old world you don't find in the Eastern end to the same degree anyway.

IYER: Buddhism has been missionary but not messianic, and Hinduism has often been messianic but not missionary. But I do think that when we get both messianic and missionary tendencies in any religion, very violent reactions are evoked. For example, it is usually possible for a European to become a Buddhist without feeling that he has lost all his cultural links with Europe, whereas it is not so easy, even to this day, for a Christian in the East to feel that he has retained any authentic roots in his own culture and not become largely 'Westernized', or pseudo-Westernized, I should say.

TOYNBEE: That is very absurd really, isn't it, considering that Christianity came out of Asia and there are still to this day

Z

Asian-Christian communities, and African-Christian communities, like the Abyssinians, the Armenians, the Southern Indian Christians, who date from centuries before the West came in.

IYER: I think it is a hopeful feature of our time that people can and will increasingly see various religions, including Christianity, as neither exclusively Eastern nor Western. But I doubt if the problem would end there because we will still find people judging any particular religion by the dominant culture with which it is most associated. It was quite common until not so long ago for people in the West to argue that Asians had no morals and that the other Eastern religions had no ethics as exalted as that of Christianity. Of course, people who seriously study these Eastern religions know that this claim was naïve. On the other hand, I am sorry to say that Asians also have too hastily assumed that Westerners are inherently incapable of attaining the heights of authentic religions or mystical experience, and that Christianity merely provided the ideological basis of the aggressive ambitions of peoples steeped in gross materialism.

TOYNBEE: Still a big change is taking place. One result of this much more intimate contact between the people of the world is, I think, that we are all becoming slightly uncertain about our own traditions, including our religious traditions. We are becoming uprooted for good as well as evil. It is very uncomfortable to become uprooted, but it may enable us to move on anyway. And it seems to me that what is happening as between Catholic and Protestant Christians, may happen in the world as a whole. Today in the Christian world people are much more able to choose between one Christian sect and another in grown-up life. They don't automatically, for the whole of their lives, have to follow the particular sect that their parents brought them up in. That may begin to be true about religions in general. People in grown-up life will choose to become a Moslem, or Hindu, or Buddhist or a Christian, according to their personal affinities.

IYER: I do agree there is much less religious intolerance everywhere. At least we have moved quite a distance from the days of the destruction of the Alexandrian library, or the closing of the schools at Athens, the Inquisition, and especially from the Hegelian idea that any one religion, Christianity or any other, could be called 'perfect'. But on the other hand, I am inclined to feel that since the late nineteenth century there has perhaps been a lowering in the tone of comparative studies of religions. Christian scholars, for example, seem to have lost their self-confidence, and many today are less just than some of their predecessors towards the other Eastern religions. On the other side, I find that Christian missionaries have also brought out the very worst in some of the followers of Eastern religions, who are now, unlike in earlier times, mainly anxious to make unique claims out of their religions. For example, the idea that Krishna is the only *Purna Avatar* or total incarnation of God as man, was not in the past regarded as the most important teaching in Hinduism, but now there are some Hindus who are inclined to emphasize it above everything else.

TOYNBEE: I hope this exclusive attitude is not going to last. There is one hopeful feature in the Christian world as a whole, I think, and that is that all the originally Western Christian churches that they founded, missionary churches in Asia or Africa, are now tending to put the governments of those churches into the hands of the Africans and Asians, so that we are going to get Christian churches growing up which are not particularly connected with the West or with Europe or America. And that may improve the situation perhaps.

IYER: Yes, I do think the situation is in a way improving, as you say, through the very fact that people have lost their roots. Individuals everywhere can now really draw from various religious traditions without feeling that they are wholly involved in the psychology of the glass curtain. But I think there is still the danger—I am sorry to appear pessimistic on this point but religion has brought out the worst and the best in man—that people will say that any one religion is uniquely fitted to transcend the curtain. Some Christians now want to stress that Christianity is the only universal religion, and, of course, the same claim is made for Hinduism or Buddhism. But surely while all these tributes to universality are very welcome, no one religion can exclusively and uniquely help us to transcend the curtain.

TOYNBEE: No one religion can include all points of view or all approaches to God or ultimate reality, whichever is the word we use. I think the traditional religions and the future modifications of them, are part of the common treasure of mankind, and we need them all, and I don't think humanity can dispense with any of them.

IYER: I wish more people would take that standpoint. I think certain important differences in outlook, arising from divergent concepts of space and time, will persist. But if only more religious believers could adopt the attitude of Eckhart that God is 'the denial of denials', that seekers after religious truth must be willing to go beyond mere verbal affirmations and strive to reach the core of mystical experience, which is the only firm basis for believing in any religious truth.

LAWSON: Well, very briefly may I say that we have decided that social and economic differences are not fundamental to this question of the glass curtain, this division between East and West, even though some people use them as an argument to perpetuate the division. We have also agreed that on the whole secular thought has had a bigger influence on the East than Western religious thought and tradition. But we have also seen some helpful signs in that Easterners and Westerners are drawing inspiration from both sides in religious matters in a personal manner. And we have emphasized that no one religion can help us to transcend this glass curtain, this division between East and West, to which religion has contributed significantly.

IV

LAWSON: It would be pleasant to believe that the problems of understanding between Asia and the West could be solved once we have succeeded in narrowing the economic gap between the established countries of Europe and the emergent countries of Asia, when we have reduced the enormous disparities in wealth, prosperity, and standards of living. Because then we could see the problems as purely material to which science and technology held the answers. We could shatter the glass curtain with one blow. But do you, Dr. Iyer, think it is quite as simple as that?

YER: I am afraid I don't. I am reminded of those Chartists who thought that it would be simple if only with one blow they could solve the whole problem of rich and poor. In the same way some people today like to think that with one bold economic assault or possibly a military blow, this curtain could be destroyed. I really think that if there is anything in this curtain, it is the fact that it is persisting and that it is connected with our sentiments and traditions and all that people on both sides regard as precious, even though in a rather possessive, aggressive, and delusive way. Even major political movements can't be detached entirely from their cultural context. I don't think that Pan-Arabism, for instance, can be explained in entirely political let alone economic terms. I think it has roots in something much deeper.

TOYNBEE: I would say so, partly as you mentioned, very old memories and traditions and in a sense of recent insecurity, which I think is very well justified. When you read a conventional Western history of Europe in the nineteenth century, it is taken as a glorious thing that the Italians and the Germans each obtained their unity, although a good deal of trouble followed from that actually, afterwards. But when today the question of Arab unity comes up, people in Europe draw back and they say 'well, we shall not be able to have a free hand in the Arab world if these people unite. What business have they uniting, changing the status quo?' What I am getting at is that there is still a difference of standard in Western minds, I fear, as to the natural rights of non-Westerners and of Westerners. That means the glass curtain is still there.

IYER: I do so agree and also I think that history is for most people what they can remember, to take the definition given in that popular parody *1066 and All That*. No doubt, we must make people forget these ancient antagonisms which are partly real and partly exaggerated, but we can't make them forget these simply by denying that they are deep-rooted, can we? But do you think that the assertion, often in an aggressive manner, by Asian peoples of their own rights, do you think that this is entirely an importation from the West?

TOYNBEE: No, not entirely. I suppose because human nature is like that, unfortunately. But it is mainly, I would say, a reaction to Western dominance and therefore I think it is going to diminish and abate. It's rather an awkward stage of the world's history, but I think we shall get through it.

IYER: People sometimes tend to argue that even the concept of universal human rights was entirely invented by the West. I think this is a very misleading way of looking at fundamental human rights. They may not have been articulated in that particular form in the East, because in Eastern languages you don't get a separate word for 'rights' and a separate word for 'duty'. On the other hand I do think that with the rise of the masses in more recent decades, it has for the first time become possible both in the West and in the East for reformers and for idealists to apply in a practical manner their ancient universalist notions.

TOYNBEE: I think that. Say in the eighteenth century, it wasn't in the West any more than in the East a practical question to give the amenities of civilization to everybody. There just weren't the economic means and I think the whole world has been faced with a new possibility by the industrial revolution coming out of modern science. Now that it is possible, not only the West but everyone all over the world feels that it is wrong that it shouldn't be realized.

IYER: In more general terms, I wonder whether at this point in world history we should stress the unique or the universal elements in the East and in the West, or somehow get beyond East and West in regard to all these matters.

TOYNBEE: I am very much against the unique. I don't believe that in human affairs anything is unique. And when I think of the East, meaning the Indian East, as opposed to the Christian-Jewish-Muslim East, what I value there is this sense that you seem to have in the Hindu and Buddhist view of life, a kind of non-uniqueness.

IYER: Personally, I do think that the Western, or perhaps I should say, the popular Christian and Jewish concept of time and history—the idea that every event is unique and irreproducible —has led to messianism and done a lot of harm. I think that the Greek, or Gnostic, or the Eastern view of time and of history and of cyclical movements in history is much more helpful to us to draw rough parallels between different periods so that we come to the point where we recognize, like that rare German historian Ranke, that all periods are in one sense equal in the sight of the great historian.

TOYNBEE: Now that is very interesting. I had an old-fashioned Greek and Latin education, the old-fashioned education of the West, and I found in travelling to India and in Japan, that because I was in many ways as familiar with the Greek and Roman religions say, as with the Christian religion, I felt quite at home in a Hindu temple, or in a Buddhist Shinto shrine in Japan, because I knew these from my education in Greek and Roman terms. This pre-Christian religion of the West was the same, I think, in attitude as that of the rest of the world.

IYER: That, of course, I can well believe. But it would be a great mistake for people to think that everyone could be another Toynbee and that simply by travelling round the world they would be able to find their universal perspective enriched and strengthened. Because I think for most people travel only confirms their deepest and sometimes their worst prejudices. Certainly Asian students who have come to Europe or the European business men who have gone to the East have often returned confirming rather than confuting the traditional East-West categories. I think travel is useful only when people are also prepared to destroy in their mental attitudes certain prevailing myths. Here I should like to know your view as to how we can go about destroying these various myths that have grown up—'Oriental despotism', 'Western materialism', and so on.

TOYNBEE: I always, from a very early age, mistrusted those myths and came, long before I ever set eyes on any country outside my own, to value enormously what other peoples stood for, in my mind and imagination. Persia—for fifty years I longed to see Persia, I longed to see the Persian people and the monuments of Persian art and architecture. I think travel gives us again what we bring to it. If we bring love, it gives us understanding and appreciation and enriches us. If we bring prejudice, as you say, it deepens our prejudice.

IYER: Well, you, of course, had a scholarly and sympathetic standpoint from the very beginning, perhaps even when at school you read popularized history where, of course, these myths are engendered and maintained. But what do you think about most people? Even though several scholars, for example, have pointed out that a book like the recent tome on *Oriental Despotism* is very muddled and misleading, still a number of people go on believing in this kind of thing at a more popular level. How do we tackle that?

TOYNBEE: Well, being a scholar myself, I know very well that scholars do not move the world, that they may move other people who may move the world. But I think that we have got to tackle it at a much more popular level and at an earlier level than children's education. I think it's these ideas you form in the first years of your conscious life that are really effective, so that's I think where we must tackle it.

IYER: But isn't there also a problem at the level of scholarship? How should we study cultures, religions, and societies other than our own? Often does not scientific and scholarly objectivity in fact conceal a great deal of subtle intolerance that persists, simply because even the best minds may put into their subject-matter what they believe is there already. Don't you think that danger remains a real one?

TOYNBEE: Yes, I do. This problem of objectivity in dealing with human affairs is a most awfully difficult one, of course.

IYER: It is, of course, tempting to think that historians or scientists or artists or philosophers when they come together will always reach beyond East-West categories, but I really wonder how easy this is. I don't think from my experience that people are able to do this very readily.

TOYNBEE: There are some very rare animals, like tip-top mathematicians, or tip-top physicists.

IYER: I quite agree, but another widely prevalent illusion today is that somehow through a study of art and literature, we can automatically destroy the curtain. I think there is no substitute in the end for understanding religious and philosophical conceptions in the East and the West and the basic beliefs and values with which art forms are tied up.

TOYNBEE: You can't cut out art or literature from their spiritual background. I think they become unreal.

IYER: Indeed. I think this is illustrated in the present Western approach to Eastern art. It has suffered from such compartmentalization.

TOYNBEE: People think that they can appreciate the art without having to get deeper than that into the religion and the philosophy and that is a great mistake, I am sure.

IYER: In general, I think, we can't spread relativistic and tolerant attitudes unless we are really moved by an ardent love of truth and we have a mature confidence born of insight into our own tradition, but most people wrongly think that depth and breadth, honesty and humility are in fact incompatible. I think that this is a very dangerous notion, isn't it, that you can't really believe in something unless you create myths about those who cannot share that belief.

TOYNBEE: I am sure that our attitude to belief should be 'this is what is true and good as far as I can see it here and now at this moment with my life, but I know that I am a very limited creature and that there is a vast amount that any human being can't know'.

IYER: It seems to me that the real enemy in both East and West is a common enemy, the crafty enemy of subtle egotism which, when it takes collective forms, is not often seen for what it is. This enormous lack of love that prevails is fostered in the name of truth and in turn falsehoods and half-truths promote contempt and even hatred. I think we must get to the standpoint of the Stoic poet who saw the whole world as a single city. There is a basis both in East and West for a new humanism. The very word 'foreigner' doesn't exist in several Eastern languages.

TOYNBEE: Let us abolish it in all languages.

BIBLIOGRAPHY

(The following list of authors, arranged in alphabetical order, is a suggestive rather than exhaustive guide to further reading on the various topics treated in this book. R. N. I.)

Abegg, Lily. *The Mind of East Asia*. Thames & Hudson, 1952.

Ahmad, Jamal M. *The Intellectual Origins of Egyptian Nationalism*. O.U.P., 1960.

Aronson, Alex. *Europe Looks at India*. Hind Kitabs, Bombay, 1946.

Asian Relations. Asian Relations Organization, New Delhi, 1948.

Bannerjee, G. N. *Hellenism in Ancient India*. Munshi Ram Manohar Lal, Delhi, 1961.

Barnett, A. Doak. *Communist China and Asia*. Vintage Books, Random House, 1960.

Barraclough, Geoffrey. *History in a Changing World*. Basil Blackwell, 1955.

Bary, Wm. Theodore de and others. *Sources of Indian Tradition*. Columbia University Press, 1958.

—— *Sources of Japanese Tradition*. Columbia University Press, 1958.

—— *Sources of Chinese Tradition*. Columbia University Press, 1960.

Bearce, George. *British Attitudes Towards India, 1784–1858*. O.U.P., 1961.

Beloff, Max. *Europe and the Europeans*. Chatto & Windus, 1957.

Benedict, Ruth. *The Chrysanthemum and the Sword*. Houghton Mifflin, 1946.

Blacker, Carmen. *The Japanese Enlightenment*. Cambridge University Press, 1964.

Bozeman, Adda B. *Politics and Culture in International History*. Princeton University Press, 1960.

Burns, A. R. *Persia and the Greeks*. Edward Arnold, 1962.

Carpenter, J. Estlin. *Buddhism and Christianity*. Hodder & Stoughton, 1923.

Chaudhuri, Nirad. *A Passage to England*. Macmillan, 1959.

Chisholm, A. R. *Towards Herodiade*. A Literary Genealogy. O.U.P., 1934.

Christy, A. E. (ed.). *The Asian Legacy and American Life*. John Day, 1942.

Cook, J. M. *The Greeks in Ionia and the East*. Thames & Hudson, 1962.

Corral, Luiz del. *The Rape of Europe*. Allen & Unwin, 1959.

Dance, E. H. *History the Betrayer*. Hutchinson, 1960.

Daniel, Norman. *Islam and the West*. Edinburgh University Press, 1960.

Dhingra, Baldhoon. *Asia Through Asian Eyes*. Thames & Hudson, 1959.

Douglas, Norman. *How About Europe?* Some Footnotes on East & West. Chatto & Windus, 1941.

The East and West Must Meet. A Symposium. Angus & Robertson, 1959.

Eudin, Xenia & Robert C. North. *Soviet Russia and the East, 1920–7*. Stanford University Press, 1957.

Fairbank, John K. (ed.) *Chinese Thought and Institutions*. Chicago University Press, 1957.

Fradier, Georges. *East-West—Towards Mutual Understanding*. Unesco, 1959.

Gibb, H. A. R. & H. Bowen. *Islamic Society and the West*. 2 volumes. O.U.P., 1950, 1957.

Gokalp, Ziya. *Turkish Nationalism and Western Civilization*. Allen & Unwin, 1959.

Grousset, René. *Bilan de l'histoire*. Paris, 1946.

Guenon, René. *East and West*. Luzac, 1941.

Haas, William S. *The Destiny of the Mind: East and West*. Faber & Faber, 1956.

Hadas, Moses. *Hellenism—fusion and diffusion*. Columbia University Press, 1959.

Haim, Sylvia. (ed.) *Arab Nationalism*. University of California Press, 1962.

Halecki, Oscar. *The Limits and Divisions of European History*. Sheed & Ward, 1950.

Hammond, N. G. L. *History of Greece*. O.U.P., 1959.

Harris, Norman Dwight. *Europe and the East*. Allen & Unwin, 1926.

Hay, Denys. *Europe—the Emergence of an Idea*. Edinburgh University Press, 1957.

Hegel, G. W. F. *The Philosophy of History* (trans. by Sibree). Dover Publications, 1956.

Herodotus of Halicarnassus. Translated by Harry Carter. O.U.P., 1962.

Hourani, Albert. *Arabic Thought in the Liberal Age* (1798–1939). O.U.P., 1962.

Hrozny, Bedrich. *Ancient History of Western Asia, India and Crete*. Artia, Prague, 1951.

Hudson, G. F. *Europe and China*. Edward Arnold, 1931. Paperback, Beacon Press, 1961.

Hughes, E. R. (ed.) *The Individual in East and West*. O.U.P., 1937.

—— *The Invasion of China by the Western World*. A. & C. Black, 1957.

Hu Shih. 'The Indianization of China', *Independence, Convergence and Borrowing in Institutions, Thought and Art*. Harvard University Press, 1937.

Hwuy-Ung. *A Chinaman's Opinion of Us*. Chatto & Windus, 1927.

Hyndman, H. W. *The Awakening of Asia*. Cassell, 1919.

Jaspers, Karl. *The Origin and Goal of History.* Routledge & Kegan Paul, 1953.

Keene, Donald. *The Japanese Discovery of Europe.* Routledge & Kegan Paul, 1952.

Kohn, Hans. *Orient and Occident.* John Day, 1934.

Komroff, Manuel. (ed.) *Contemporaries of Marco Polo.* Jonathan Cape, 1928.

Levenson, Joseph. *Confucian China and its Modern Fate.* Routledge & Kegan Paul, 1958.

Levonian, Lootfy. *Christianity and Islam.* Allen & Unwin, 1940.

Lewis, Bernard. *The Arabs in History.* Hutchinson, 1950.

—— *The Emergence of Modern Turkey.* O.U.P., 1961.

Lewis, G. L. *Turkey.* Benn, 1955.

Lowes Dickinson, G. *An Essay on the Civilizations of India, China and Japan.* Dent, 1913.

McNeill, William. *The Rise of the West.* University of Chicago Press, 1963.

Maine, Sir Henry. *Village Communities in the East and West, and Other Lectures,* 1880.

Mallik, Manmath C. *Orient and Ocicdent.* T. Fisher Unwin, 1913.

Maraini, Fosco. *Meeting with Japan.* Hutchinson, 1959.

Marvin, F. S. (ed.) *Western Races and the World.* O.U.P., 1922.

Massis, Henri. *The Defence of the West.* Faber & Gwyer, 1925.

Mikes, George. *East is East.* Andre Deutsch, 1958.

Moore, Edward Caldwell. *West and East.* Duckworth, 1920.

Mukerjee, Radhakamal. *Democracies of the East.* P. S. King, 1923.

Nakamura, Hajime. *The Ways of Thinking of Eastern Peoples.* Tokyo, 1960.

Narain, A. K. *The Indo-Greeks.* O.U.P., 1957.

Needham, Joseph. *Science and Civilization in China.* Cambridge University Press, 1954.

Nehru, Jawaharlal. *Glimpses into World History.* Luzac, 1936.

Northrop, F. S. C. *The Meeting of East and West.* Macmillan, 1947.

Nusibeh, Hazem Zaki. *The Ideas of Arab Nationalism.* Cornell University Press, 1956.

Okakura, Kakasu. *The Ideals of the East.* John Murray, 1903.

Olschki, Leonardo. *Marco Polo's Asia.* University of California Press, 1960.

O'Malley, L. S. S. (ed.) *Modern India and the West.* O.U.P., 1941.

Otto, Rudolf. *Mysticism—East and West.* Macmillan, 1932.

Panikkar, K. M. *Asia and Western Dominance.* Allen & Unwin, 1953.

Parkinson, C. Northcote. *East and West.* Houghton Mifflin, 1963.

Penrose, Boies. *Travel and Discovery in the Renaissance, 1420-1620.* Harvard University Press, 1952.

Price, H. H. 'The Present Relations between Eastern & Western Philosophy', *Hibbert Journal,* April 1955.

Price, Maurice T. *Christian Missions and Oriental Civilizations.* Shanghai, 1924.

Radhakrishnan, S. *Eastern Religions and Western Thought.* O.U.P., 1939.
—— *East and West.* Allen & Unwin, 1954.

Rasmussen, O. D. *The Reconquest of Asia.* Hamish Hamilton, 1934.

Rawlinson, H. G. *Intercourse between India and the Western World.* Cambridge University Press, 1926.

Regamey, Constantin. *East and West.—Some Aspects of Historic Evolution.* Transaction 6, Indian Institute of World Culture, Bangalore, 1951.

Remy, Arthur F. J. *The Influence of India and Persia on the Poetry of Germany.* 1901.

Riencourt, Amaury de. *The Soul of China.* Jonathan Cape, 1958.
—— *The Soul of India.* Jonathan Cape, 1961.

Romein, Jan & Jan Erik. *The Asian Century.* Allen & Unwin, 1962.

Ross, Floyd H. *The Meaning of Life in Hinduism and Buddhism and Buddhism.* Routledge & Kegan Paul, 1952.

Runciman, Sir Steven. *A History of the Crusades.* 3 volumes. Cambridge University Press, 1952–3.

Saletore, B. N. *India's Diplomatic Relations with the West.* Popular Book Depot, 1955.
—— *India's Diplomatic Relations with the East.* Popular Book Depot, 1960.

Sansom, Sir George. *The Western World and Japan.* Cresset Press, 1950.

Schwab, Raymond. *La Renaissance orientale.* Paris, 1950.

Sherrard, Philip. *The Greek East and the Latin West.* O.U.P., 1959.

Sigerist, Henry E. *A History of Medicine.* O.U.P., 1961.

Singer, Charles. *A Short History of Science.* O.U.P., 1951.

Sinor, Denis. *Orientalism and History.* Heffers, 1954.

Slater, Robert Lawson. *World Religions and World Community.* Columbia University Press, 1963.

Smart, Ninian. *Reasons and Faiths.* Routledge & Kegan Paul, 1958.

Smith, W. Cantwell. *Islam in Modern History.* O.U.P., 1957.

Spear, Percival. *The Nabobs.* O.U.P., 1932. Paperback, 1963.

Spengler, Oswald. *The Decline of the West* (trans. by Atkinson). New York, 1932.

Storry, G. R. *A Short History of Modern Japan.* Penguin Books, 1961.

Tagore, Rabindranath. *Towards Universal Man.* Asia Publishing House, 1961.

Taylor, Edmond. *Richer by Asia.* Houghton Mifflin, 1947.

Teng, Ssu-yü & J. K. Fairbank. *China's Response to the West.* Harvard University Press, 1954.

Townsend, Meredith. *Asia and Europe.* Archibald Constable, 1905.

Toynbee-Jerrold Controversy. *Counsels of Hope.* Times Publishing Co., 1954.

Toynbee, Arnold. *A Study of History.* Volume 8. O.U.P., 1954.

Toynbee, Arnold. *The World and the West*. O.U.P., 1952.

—— *A Historian's Approach to Religion*. O.U.P., 1956.

Trevor-Roper, H. R. 'The Rise of Christian Europe', *The Listener*, 1963-4.

Unesco. *Humanism and Education in East and West*. Paris, 1953.

Utechin, S. V. *Russian Political Thought*. Praeger, 1964.

Vaughan, Dorothy. *Europe and the Turk*. Liverpool University Press, 1954.

Venturi, F. 'Despotisme orientale', *Rivista Storica Italiana*, 1960.

Vernadsky, George. *A History of Russia*. Yale University Press, 1954.

Vivekananda, Swami. *The East and the West*. Prabuddha Bharata Office, Almora, 1919.

Waley, Arthur. *The Opium War Through Chinese Eyes*. Allen & Unwin, 1958.

Ward, Barbara. *The Interplay of East and West*. Allen & Unwin, 1957.

—— *India and the West*. Hamish Hamilton, 1961.

Wint, Guy. *The British in Asia*. Faber & Faber, 1947.

Winter, H. J. J. *Eastern Science*. John Murray, 1952.

NOTES ON CONTRIBUTORS

DR. GEORGE BEARCE is Associate Professor of Modern History, Bowdoin College, Brunswick, and was Visiting Professor at the University of Osmania, Hyderabad. Publications include *British Attitudes Towards India 1784–1858*.

DR. HENRI BRUGMANS is Rector, College of Europe, Bruges. Publications include several works on federalism and two volumes of an *Histoire de l'Europe*.

DR. J. K. CAMPBELL is Fellow of St. Antony's College, Oxford, and was formerly Director of the Social Sciences Centre, Athens. Publications include *Honour, Family and Patronage*.

DR. WANG GUNGWU is Professor of History, University of Malaysia, Kuala Lumpur. Publications include *The Nanhai Trade, The Structure of Power in North China during the Five Dynasties*, and *Malaysia—A Survey*.

G. F. HUDSON is Fellow and Director of Far Eastern Studies, St. Antony's College, Oxford. Publications include *Europe and China, The Far East in Modern Politics*, and *Questions of East and West*.

DR. RAGHAVAN N. IYER, formerly Fellow of St. Antony's College, Oxford, and Visiting Professor at the Universities of Oslo, Chicago, and Ghana, is at present associated with the Center for the Study of Democratic Institutions, Santa Barbara. Publications include *South Asian Affairs* and a forthcoming volume on *The Social & Political Thought of Mahatma Gandhi*.

DR. G. L. LEWIS is Fellow of St. Antony's College and Senior Lecturer in Turkish at Oxford, and Visiting Professor at Robert College, Istanbul. Publications include *Turkey*.

D. E. T. LUARD is Fellow of St. Antony's College, Oxford, and was formerly a member of the British Embassy in Peking. Publications include *The Economic Development of Communist China, Britain and China, Peace and Opinion*, and *Nationality and Wealth*.

DR. HAJIME NAKAMURA is Professor of Oriental Philosophy and Dean of the Faculty of Letters, University of Tokyo. Publications include *Ways of Thinking of Eastern Peoples*.

DR. JOSEPH NEEDHAM, F.R.S., is Fellow and President of Gonville and Caius College, Cambridge. Publications include *Chemical Embryology, Biochemistry and Morphogenesis*, and *Science and Civilization in China*.

J. S. F. PARKER, formerly Fellow of St. Antony's College, Oxford, is Lecturer in Middle Eastern History at the University of Khartoum.

ROBERT SHACKLETON is Fellow and Tutor in Modern Languages, Brasenose College, and University Lecturer, Oxford. Publications include *Montesquieu—A Critical Biography*.

DR. PHILIP SHERRARD was formerly Fellow of St. Antony's College, Oxford, and then Assistant Director, The British School of Archaeology, Athens. Publications include *The Greek East and the Latin West*, *Mount Athos*, and *The Pursuit of Greece*.

ROBERT LAWSON SLATER is Professor of World Religions, Emeritus, at the University of Harvard, where he was formerly Director of the Center for the Study of World Religions. Publications include *Paradox and Nirvana* and *World Religions and World Community*.

DR. A. H. SOMJEE is Professor of Political Science at the University of Baroda and Visiting Professor at the University of Durham. Publications include *Voting Behaviour in an Indian Village* and a forthcoming book on *Democracy and Political Change in Village India*.

RICHARD STORRY is Fellow of St. Antony's College, Oxford. Publications include *The Double Patriots* and *A History of Modern Japan*.

RONALD TAYLOR is Senior Lecturer in German, University College of Swansea, and was Visiting Professor at Northwestern University and at the University of Chicago. Publications include *E. T. A. Hoffmann, Die weltlichen Lieder des Mittelalters*, and a translation of Hoffmann's *The Devil's Elixirs*.

HUGH TINKER is Professor of Government and Politics, University of London, and was Visiting Professor at the University of Rangoon. Publications include *Foundations of Local Self-Government in India, Pakistan and Burma*, *The Union of Burma*, and *India and Pakistan—A Short Political Guide*.

DR. ARNOLD TOYNBEE was formerly Director of Studies, Royal Institute of International Affairs. Publications include *A Study of History*, *The World and the West*, *A Historian's Approach to Religion*, and *East to West*.

DR. S. V. UTECHIN is Fellow of St. Antony's College, Oxford. Publications include *A Soviet Encyclopaedia* and *Russian Political Thought*.

C. S. VENKATACHAR, C.I.E., O.B.E., I.C.S. (Retd.), was Agent to the Governor-General of India in Malaya, Secretary to the President of India, and High Commissioner for India to Canada.